# Sustainable Development in Economic Growth Theory

Yoshihiro Hamaguchi

# Sustainable Development in Economic Growth Theory

Springer

Yoshihiro Hamaguchi
Faculty of Economics
Hannan University
Osaka, Japan

ISBN 978-981-96-7638-5 ISBN 978-981-96-7639-2 (eBook)
https://doi.org/10.1007/978-981-96-7639-2



This Springer imprint is published by the registered company Springer Nature Singapore Pte Ltd.
The registered company address is: 152 Beach Road, #21-01/04 Gateway East, Singapore 189721, Singapore

*Dedicated to my late supervisor, grandfather and devoted grandmother.*

# Preface

From climate change and climate crisis to the present era of global boiling, global warming is worsening. Increasingly severe natural disasters are causing irreversible damage to the ecosystem and the social economy. Although the traditional North-South problem was to be solved through the Millennium Development Goals (MDGs), environmental sustainability was only one of the items. However, it has been recognised that global warming is closely linked to the global environment, poverty, education, health, gender and other issues in developing countries. As a result of the integration of the North-South issue with global warming, Sustainable Development Goals (SDGs) were established.

Globally, there is a growing momentum to increase the planet's sustainability, with the participation of citizens, governments and businesses. Nonetheless, the implementation of internationally coordinated environmental policies is progressing slowly due to the heavy economic burden, energy economy trends and geopolitical issues. Planet boundaries have been exceeded in several areas while others are deteriorating rapidly. There is no time to spare for implementing environmental policies to improve sustainability. Development and growth, which have been dichotomous in the North-South issue, were sublimated into sustainable development in the Brundtland Commission's 'Our Common Futures'. In addition to intergenerational equity between the current and future generations, it aimed for harmony between the natural environment and economic growth. Hence, the main research topics in environmental economics and economic growth theory became—what are the socioeconomic mechanisms related to sustainable development and, if such mechanisms exist, what kind of environmental policies will promote sustainable development.

As economic globalisation progressed since the collapse of the Soviet Union, new environmental problems emerged, such as pollution exports by companies in developed countries and tourism pollution caused by the global tourism boom. As a result, there is a debate about whether trade liberalisation will worsen the environment or improve it. In addition, with the increasing importance of sustainable finance, attention is being paid to finance as a means of encouraging companies to decarbonise. However, there is a concern that the effectiveness of environmental policies is undermined by the increasing number of companies that are actively engaging in tax evasion and lobbying to escape environmental regulations.

Nonetheless, it is difficult to say that the research results on this topic are widely shared among researchers, policy makers, practitioners and citizens. The findings of endogenous growth theory, which significantly developed in the 1990s, have been applied to the analysis of sustainable development, with several books and survey papers published on the subject. However, since the analysis of applying the research and development (R&D)-based growth model, which regards innovation as the source of economic growth, to sustainable development has become active since 2000, there are very few books or survey papers on the subject. In particular, this R&D-based growth model has been applied to firm location, industrial structure, tourism, policy processes, international economics and financial economics since the early 2000s and has continued to develop further. However, its application to sustainable development is recent. As expectations for corporate innovation grow in the fight to halt global warming, there are limited opportunities to learn how environmental policies affect pollution emissions and economic growth through innovation. Furthermore, it is difficult to know how sustainable development through innovation is related to international economics, financial economics, tourism and tax evasion.

This book aims to disseminate the mechanisms of sustainable development through innovation. This knowledge sharing will provide a theoretical basis for SDG civil activities and support dialogue and implementation. It introduces applied analysis related to finance, tourism, politics and trade and applies to several SDG items. Furthermore, the content is based on various papers that the authors have published in peer-reviewed international academic journals, except for some parts, hence, the academic quality is guaranteed. Specific policy proposals based on such theoretical results are explained, therefore, useful information is provided to policy makers.

Young theoretical researchers may aspire to analyse sustainable development using R&D-based growth models. For them, this book provides clues for future research, as it explains the settings and assumptions that affect sustainable development mechanisms and the methods for deriving models and analysing policy effects. As the importance of environmental issues increased, international environment journals were published since 2000. Empirical research on sustainable development increased dramatically, coupled with the development of environmental data and statistical software. If the statistical hypothesis to be verified has a theoretical background, the analysis and results will be robust. This book provides empirical researchers with useful knowledge for constructing statistical hypotheses related to sustainable development and understanding their mechanisms. As author, I would be happy if the knowledge in this book is useful for researchers of the current and future generations.

This book was born out of the author's interactions with the people he met through his educational and research activities to date. At Shizuoka University, Professor Emeritus Ichiro Asari provided guidance on going to graduate school and questioned the author's resolve. Despite the author's limited knowledge, he watched over the author, who was brimming with cheekiness. At Osaka University, Professor Emeritus

Koichi Futagami trained the author from scratch in the basics of economic growth theory and dramatically improved the author's research capabilities. At times, I found his guidance harsh, as I was academically inexperienced, however, without his guidance and the hardships he put me through, I would not have been able to continually produce research results of an international standard. I am deeply sorry that I was unable to dedicate this book to my supervisor before he passed away.

During this time as a graduate student, the author's awareness of issues was sharpened through heated discussions with fellow graduate students and this led to the research topics. Communication with fellow graduate students provided a respite for the author, who was exhausted from his research activities. Osaka Seikei University, Kyoto College of Economics, Kyoto University of Advanced Science and Hannan University employed the author as a full-time lecturer and provided him with a place to carry out educational and research activities. In addition, as a young researcher, I was able to receive consideration regarding internal university affairs, resulting in smooth research activities and research grants. Through lectures on macroeconomics and environmental economics, I was able to sublimate my research results into educational activities. The impressions and comments of the students improved my teaching and research abilities and helped me improve my communication techniques in an easy-to-understand manner. Furthermore, in various settings, I was able to heal the fatigue of my daily research activities and nurture my spirit for future research. I am deeply grateful to all those involved.

When starting out as an independent researcher, I did not know how to publish papers in peer-reviewed international journals, hence, I was impatient and anxious. At the time, anonymous peer reviewers guided me about the process. While I was leaving my supervisor's guidance, my research ability was trained by peer reviewers worldwide. Furthermore, I serve as a peer reviewer and am happy if I can contribute to the development of international academia. I have received useful comments from participants at various international conferences and the Japan Economic Association, which have led to publications in peer-reviewed international journals. Through these academic activities, I have had the opportunity to contribute to joint research and co-author books, leading to interdisciplinary research activities. I express my deep gratitude to the global academic community.

Finally, I express my gratitude to Springer, who allowed this young researcher to publish this book. Although I have published several papers, due to my inexperience as a researcher and university duties, they contained misleading expressions and typos, the analysis was not always thorough and some places needed minor corrections. In writing this book, I was able to improve the robustness of the research results and build systematic knowledge on this research topic by re-checking such points and revising the entire book. I hope that this book will be read worldwide and the knowledge will be shared, contributing to the realisation of a sustainable society through various actors.

Osaka, Japan Yoshihiro Hamaguchi

**Acknowledgements** The author expresses his deep gratitude to the Japan Society for the Promotion of Science (JSPS), which funded the writing of this book through JP22K13409.

**Competing Interests** The author has no competing financial interests or personal relationships that could have influenced the work reported in this book.

# About This Book

This book is made up of five parts and 17 chapters. In each part, the basic R&D-based growth model is explained and the basic model is expanded by incorporating pollution emissions and environmental policy. In all the chapters, the overall picture of the economic model is presented in diagrams and environmental taxes or emissions trading are considered as environmental policy. As readers move from Parts I–V, the scope of the analysis will expand from a closed economy to an open economy, accounting for finance, tourism, corruption and other similar factors.

Part I presents the book's issues and research agenda based on a concise survey of research trends. The variety expansion model and the mechanism of sustainable development through labour migration from the goods sector to the R&D sector via environmental policy are explained. Since this economic model is simple, it can be applied to international economics, such as the location of firms and industrial structure. Furthermore, financial policy is introduced into this basic model and the mechanism of sustainable development through interest rate manipulation is analysed. This theoretical analysis provides insights because there are a limited number of analyses at present.

Part II shows that the growth-promoting effect of environmental policy in a variety expansion model with physical capital is influenced by household preferences, including leisure and social status preferences. Since social status preferences are an example of other-referenced behaviour in behavioural economics, the mechanism of sustainable development from the behavioural economics perspective is explained. Furthermore, when considering non-homothetic preferences, the effects of pollution reduction and economic growth through environmental taxes disappear.

In Part III, after the R&D-based location model is explained, pollution emissions and emissions trading are introduced and the mechanisms of the pollution haven hypothesis through direct regulation and industrial agglomeration are explained. Furthermore, the tourism sector reveals the mechanisms of sustainable tourism in international tourism. Part IV highlights that, under the overlapping double regulation, environmental taxes inhibit the pollution reduction effect of emissions trading, while the additional burden of double regulation provides an incentive to evade taxes. After clarifying the impact of environmental tax evasion in double regulation on the mechanism of sustainable development, the relationship with the pollution haven hypothesis is analysed.

In Part V, the R&D-based model with heterogeneous firms is explained concerning endogenous changes in industrial structure through the entry and exit of firms. Environmental policies affect industrial structure under a discriminatory environmental tax rate for local and export firms and the Porter hypothesis mechanism is explained. Furthermore, the impact of environmental tax evasion on industrial structure and economic growth is explained by applying the analysis of the previous chapters. The relationship between the Porter hypothesis and the pollution haven hypothesis is clarified. In Parts III–V, the impact of trade and environmental policies on sustainable development is explained.

In the conclusion, the main results of this book are outlined. In addition to the empirical implications and policy recommendations, the limitations of this book and future directions are discussed. Chapters 1–4, 8, 9 and 14 are based on peer-reviewed book chapters and conference reports. All the other chapters are based on papers published in peer-reviewed international journals, therefore, this book maintains an academic standard. Finally, this book contains the content of various papers and book chapters that the author has published in the past and it has been revised to correct typos and misleading expressions and make the explanations, formulas and methods more refined.

# Contents

# About the Author

**Yoshihiro Hamaguchi** received his PhD from Osaka University in March 2020 and currently serves as Professor of Macroeconomics at Hannan University, Osaka, Japan. His research aims to identify the mechanisms of sustainable development, utilising macroeconomic theories of economic growth and analytical methods from international and political economics. His research to date has elucidated how environmental policies can lead to pollution reduction and economic growth through innovation and he has applied his findings to the pollution haven hypothesis, sustainable tourism and sustainable finance. He has received several research grants from the Japan Society for the Promotion of Science (JSPS), reported his research at numerous peer-reviewed international conferences and published in the *Journal of Macroeconomics, Tourism Economics, Transport Policy, Frontiers in Marine Science, China & World Economy, Environment, Development and Sustainability, Journal of Environmental Management*, among others. Some of these papers were commended for obtaining the highest number of citations in a year. The organisation responds to peer-review requests from various international journals based on these results. He was a member of the Future Design Research Centre (FDRC) within KUAS, where he was involved in policy recommendations based on his research results and in social contribution.

# Abbreviations

| | |
|---|---|
| $a_t$ | A number of shares/varieties in North |
| $a_{L,t}$, $a_{E,t}$ | Number of varieties in local and export markets |
| $\overline{A}, \overline{\overline{A}}$ | Exogenous productivity parameter of final good firms |
| $A_t$ | A number of shares/varieties |
| $\dot{A}_t$ | A net increase of shares/varieties |
| $b$ | Allowance allocation rent per population |
| $B_1, B_2, B_3, B_4$ | Set of parameters |
| $B_t$ | Borrowing from household |
| $c_t$ | Consumption per capita |
| $C_t$ | Consumption |
| $\overline{C}_t$ | Average consumption in the economy |
| $d_t$ | Pollution emissions per firm |
| $D_t$ | Agricultural goods |
| $e_t$ | Extent of externalities caused by pollution emissions received by bureaucrats |
| $E_t$ | Expenditure |
| $\dot{E}_t$ | A net increase of expenditures |
| $\bar{E}_t$ | Expenditure per capita |
| $f_1, f_2, f_3, f_4, f_5\, f_6$ | Set of parameters |
| $F$ | Exogenous fixed costs in the R&D sector |
| $F_L$, $F_E$ | Exogenous fixed costs in the R&D sector for local and exporting firms |
| $F_{EL}$ | Relative exogenous fixed costs between firms |
| $F_I$ | Total fixed costs in the R&D sector |
| $F_t$ | Endogenous fixed costs in the R&D sector |
| $\bar{F}_t$ | Ex-ante fixed expected cost of developing varieties |
| $g_t$ | Economic growth rate |
| $\tilde{g}(\psi)$ | Probability density function |
| $G(\psi)$ | The corresponding cumulative distribution function |
| $h_t$ | Corruption per bureaucrats |

| | |
|---|---|
| $\hat{h}_t$ | Aggregate corruption |
| $H_t$ | Lump-sum transfer of seigniorage revenue |
| $\mathcal{H}_t$ | Total income |
| $i_t$ | Nominal interest rate |
| $\hat{i}$ | Threshold of welfare effect of nominal interest rate |
| $I_t$ | Investment |
| $\bar{k}$ | Set of parameters |
| $k_t$ | Number of firms owned by households in the North |
| $K_t$ | Physical capital |
| $\dot{K}_t$ | A net increase of physical capital |
| $K_t^P$ | Public capital |
| $l_t \in (0, 1)$ | Leisure |
| $l_{L,j,t}^X, l_{E,j,t}^X$ | Labour inputted by local and exporting firm with a variety $j$ |
| $L_t$ | Total population |
| $L_{A,t}$ | Labour inputted by firms in R&D sector |
| $L_{D,t}$ | Labour inputted by firms in agricultural sector |
| $\dot{L}_{M,t}, \dot{L}_{M,t}^*$ | A net increase in the number of tourists travelling from the home country to the partner country |
| $L_{M,t}, L_{M,t}^*$ | Number of tourists travelling from their home country to the destination country |
| $L_{T,t}$ | Labour inputted by firms in tourism sector |
| $L_{X,t}$ | Labour inputted by good firms |
| $L_{j,t}^X$ | Labour inputted by good firm with a variety $j$ |
| $L_{Y,t}$ | Labour inputted by firms in final good sector |
| $m_t$ | Real money supply |
| $m_0$ | Initial value of real money supply |
| $M_t$ | Nominal money supply |
| $\dot{M}_t$ | A net increase of nominal money supply |
| $n$ | Population growth rate |
| $\bar{N}$ | Prices related to tourism |
| $\hat{N}$ | Environmental carrying capacity |
| $N_t$ | Environmental quality |
| $\dot{N}_t$ | A net increase of environmental quality |
| $o_t$ | Pollution intensity |
| $p_t^e$ | Emission allowance price |
| $p_{j,t}$ | The $j$th intermediate good price/the good price with a variety $j$ |
| $\bar{P}$ | Emission allowance |
| $\hat{P}$ | Threshold of welfare effect of emissions allowance |
| $\check{P}$ | Threshold of credit effect of emissions allowance |
| $\tilde{P}$ | Parameter conditions on emission allowances |
| $P_1, P_2, P_3$ | Set of parameters |
| $P_t$ | Total pollution emissions |
| $\tilde{P}_t$ | Total pollution emissions in efficiency units |
| $P_t^e$ | Effective unit of total pollution emission |
| $P_{A,t}$ | Stock price |

| | |
|---|---|
| $\dot{P}_{A,t}$ | A net increase of share price |
| $P_{D,t}$ | Price of agricultural goods |
| $P_{M,t}$ | Price index of differentiated goods |
| $P_{N,t}$ | Price of tourism goods |
| $q_t$ | Production of goods per firm |
| $q_{j,t}$ | Production of goods per firm with a variety $j$ |
| $Q_t$ | Total production of goods |
| $r_t$ | Real interest rate |
| $r_1, r_2, r_3, r_4$ | Set of parameters |
| $R_t$ | Cumulated instantaneous real interest rate |
| $s_t, \bar{s}$ | Emission allowances per firm |
| $S_t$ | Saving |
| $t$ | transport costs |
| $\bar{t}$ | Parameter conditions on airfare |
| $\hat{t}$ | airfare with alien tax |
| $T_t$ | Lump-sum subsidy |
| $u_t$ | Utility of bureaucrats |
| $U_t$ | Lifetime utility |
| $V_t$ | Social status function |
| $w_t$ | Wage rate |
| $W_t$ | Household's asset |
| $\bar{W}_t$ | Average asset in the economy |
| $\dot{W}_t$ | A net increase of asset |
| $x_{j,t}$ | The $j$th intermediate good |
| $\hat{x}_t$ | Consumption of differentiated goods |
| $X_t$ | Technology level |
| $y_t \equiv Y_t/K_t$ | Final goods per capital |
| $Y_t$ | Tourism goods |
| $z_t \equiv C_t/K_t$ | Consumption per capital |
| $Z_t$ | Pollution abatement good |
| $\alpha \in (0, 1)$ | Labour share |
| $1 - \alpha$ | Capital share/Inverse price elasticity of demand |
| $\hat{\alpha}$ | Set of parameters |
| $\beta$ | Relative weight of consumption in utility |
| $1 - \beta$ | Relative weight of leisure in utility |
| $\gamma_t$ | Number of firms located in the North as a percentage of the number of firms in the world |
| $\Gamma$ | Shape parameter of the distribution |
| $\delta$ | Firm productivity parameters in the R&D sector |
| $\hat{\delta}$ | Set of parameters |
| $\Delta_t$ | Weighted average of the firms' productivity |
| $\varepsilon_t$ | Expenditure per wage rate |
| $\dot{\varepsilon}_t$ | A net increase of expenditure per wage rate |
| $\epsilon \in (0, 1)$ | Contamination distribution ratio |
| $\zeta_t$ | Rate of change in utility due to consumption |

| | |
|---|---|
| $Z_t$ | Mark-up rate in direct explicitly additive preferences |
| $\eta_P$ | Relative weight of pollution on utility |
| $\hat{\eta}_P$ | Set of parameters |
| $\eta_N$ | Relative weight of environmental quality on utility |
| $\eta_W$ | Relative weight of social status preference on utility |
| $\hat{\eta}$ | Set of parameters |
| $\theta_1, \theta_2$ | Set of parameters |
| $\theta$ | Pollution abatement productivity parameters |
| $\theta_C$ | A degree of social status preference for consumption |
| $\theta_W$ | A degree of social status preference for wealth |
| $\Theta_t$ | Effects of the competing firms in good market |
| $\iota_t$ | Knowledge spillover effect on manufacturing firms |
| $\iota$ | Firm productivity parameters in the manufacturing sector |
| $\hat{\kappa}$ | Elasticity parameter of pollution emissions |
| $\kappa$ | Set of parameter conditions |
| $\lambda_t$ | Co-state variable |
| $\dot{\lambda}_t$ | A net increase of co-state variable |
| $\Lambda_t$ | Relative R&D difficulty |
| $\mu$ | Constant growth rate of nominal money supply |
| $\nu_0, \nu_1$ | Set of parameter conditions |
| $\nu$ | Relative weight of differentiated goods in utility |
| $1 - \nu$ | Relative weight of agricultural goods in utility |
| $\xi_t \in (0, 1)$ | Probability of arresting corrupt bureaucrats |
| $\Xi_t$ | The endogenous time preference rate |
| $o_A \in (0, 1)$ | Share of R&D expenditure in CIA constraint |
| $o_H \in (0, 1)$ | Share of consumption expenditure in CIA constraint |
| $\pi_t$ | Dividend/Monopoly profit |
| $\pi_{j,t}$ | Monopoly profit by good firm with a variety *j* |
| $\pi_t^A$ | Profit of R&D firm |
| $\Pi_t$ | Inflation rate |
| $\varpi_t \in (0, 1)$ | Penalty rate |
| $\rho$ | Subjective discount rate |
| $\varrho \in (0, 1)$ | Bureaucrat's bargaining surplus weight |
| $\sigma$ | Elasticity of substitution between any varieties |
| $\bar{\sigma}$ | Intertemporal substitution elasticity |
| $\hat{\sigma}$ | Set of parameters |
| $\varsigma$ | Degree of knowledge spillover |
| $\tau,\ \tau_t^P$ | Environmental tax rate |
| $\hat{\tau}$ | Threshold of welfare effect of environmental tax rate |
| $\bar{\tau}$ | Efficient tax rate with tax evasion |
| $\tilde{\tau}$ | Tax evasion rate |
| $\bar{\bar{\tau}}$ | Tax rate disparity between North and South |
| $\tilde{\tau}_L$ | Threshold of environmental tax rate on firms' average productivity |
| $\upsilon$ | Productivity of the R&D sector in the lab-equipment model |

| | |
|---|---|
| $\varphi$ | Extent of trade liberalisation |
| $\hat{\varphi}, \bar{\varphi}$ | Threshold for FDI direction |
| $\bar{\chi}$ | Aggregate of preference parameters |
| $\chi_N, \chi_S$ | The relative weight of tourism consumption in the North and South in terms of utility |
| $\psi$ | Unit input requirement associated with production |
| $\bar{\psi}$ | Scale parameter of the distribution |
| $\omega_t \equiv K_t/A_t$ | Average capital |
| $\hat{\Psi}$ | Set of parameters |
| $\Psi(P_t)$ | Mortality depending pollution |
| $\Omega$ | Degree of trade liberalisation |
| $\bar{\Omega}$ | Degree of trade liberalisation with environmental tax |
| $\bar{\bar{\Omega}}$ | Degree of trade liberalisation with tax evasion |
| $\hat{\Omega}$ | Threshold for the welfare effect of trade liberalisation |

# List of Figures

# Part I
# Sustainable Economic Growth Theory

# Chapter 1
# Introduction

**Abstract** In this chapter, the outline of this book is explained based on a survey of previous research. Sustainable development (SD) is assumed to be the coexistence of pollution reduction and economic growth. In the externality effect, improving environmental quality leads to economic growth by increasing total factor productivity. Via the distaste effect, SD is affected by the elasticity of intertemporal Substitution. Via the generation turnover effect, the transition from the older to the younger generations leads to SD through savings. Via the profitability effect, the price pass-through of environmental taxes enhances innovation and SD. The outline of this book is as follows. In Part I, the basic mechanisms of sustainable development and sustainable finance are discussed based on the variety expansion model. In Part II, households' preferences such as leisure, social status and non-homothetic preferences determine the growth-enhancing effects. In Part III, the mechanism of pollution haven hypothesis and sustainable tourism are discussed. In Part IV, the impact of corruption and tax evasion on the growth-enhancing effect is explained. In Part V, Porter hypothesis and the impact of environmental policies on SD through industrial structure is discussed. In the conclusion, a summary of the book and future prospects are discussed.

## 1.1 Environmental Issues and Economic Growth Theory[1]

The concept of sustainable development, which aims to achieve pollution reduction and economic growth, is widely shared, however, its path has not been smooth. After World War II, developed countries aimed for post-war reconstruction and newly independent developing countries sought economic development through industrialisation. The emergence of a mass consumption society was accompanied by resources waste, environmental destruction and health damage caused by pollution. In 1972, the Club of Rome sounded the alarm in 'The Limits to Growth' that, if this situation continued, global economic growth would reach its limit. However, at the United Nations Conference on the Human Environment (hereafter, Stockholm Conference),

[1] This section is based in part on Hamaguchi (2023a).



Y. Hamaguchi, *Sustainable Development in Economic Growth Theory*,
https://doi.org/10.1007/978-981-96-7639-2_1

the developed countries' arguments for environmental conservation were opposed by developing countries aiming to industrialise. This is because of a strong belief that today's environmental pollution is due to the industrialisation of the developed countries during the colonial era. This belief has been carried over to the current climate crisis.

As the North–South problem expanded to environmental issues, the Brundtland Commission published 'Our Common Future' in 1987, defining sustainable development as development that meets the needs of the present without compromising the ability of future generations to meet their needs. At the 1992 Earth Summit, as global warming was recognised as a new environmental issue, Agenda 21, an action plan for sustainable development, was established and basic principles were stated in the Rio Declaration. After the conclusion of the United Nations Framework Convention on Climate Change, the Kyoto Protocol, which was adopted at COP3 in 1997, was published in 2005, specific reduction targets and methods for greenhouse gases and the obligation to reduce these gases were imposed on the ratifying countries. During this time, the Millennium Development Goals (MDGs) were used to address the North–South divide, however, environmental sustainability was only one of the goals. As global warming worsened, it became recognised that the natural environment and climate change, combined with various socioeconomic factors, would impact the economic development of developing countries.

As it became increasingly difficult to deal with the intensification of natural disasters caused by climate change through government policies and corporate efforts, the MDGs were elevated to the Sustainable Development Goals (SDGs), with a growing international momentum towards solving these issues in cooperation with citizens. However, there has been strong opposition to strict environmental regulations, which increase companies' costs, pressure their management and hinder economic development by reducing employment. In the 1970s, environmental policies were seen as contributing to poverty reduction and improving workers' welfare in industrial areas, therefore, in line with environmental justice. However, as the structural shift from secondary to tertiary industries progressed, strict environmental policies faced severe opposition as they were seen as taking away jobs from low-paid workers in carbon-intensive industries. As a result, there have been moves against decarbonisation and decontamination policies, such as the US withdrawing from the Paris Agreement.

In this context, the application of the economic growth theory to the elucidation of sustainable development mechanisms is recognised as an important research topic. Its findings can be used to persuade environmental policy opponents. The measures and policies implemented for sustainable development based on past empirical rules may lead to increased pollution emissions and economic stagnation. The findings of the theoretical analysis inform us of the conditions necessary for environmental policies to achieve sustainable development and prevent unexpected results. Hence, it is important to understand what the economic growth theory experts revealed about sustainable development mechanisms.

## 1.2 Literature Review of Sustainable Development

### 1.2.1 Externality Effect

Research up to the early 2000s was surveyed by Ricci (2007). Research trends since then were supplemented by Hamaguchi (2024c). Early research focused on the externalities of the environment and pollution on households and firms. The externality effect refers to the way in which environmental policies promote economic growth through the externalities of pollution reduction. The utility function of households is expressed as follows:

$$U_t = \int_0^\infty \left(\frac{C_t}{P_t^{\eta_P}}\right)^{1-\frac{1}{\sigma}} e^{-\rho t} dt, \tag{1.1}$$

where $C_t$ is consumption, $P_t$ is the pollution level, $\sigma > 1$ is the constant elasticity of substitution, $\rho > 0$ is the time preference rate and $\eta_P > 0$ is the relative weight of pollution on utility. The budget constraint of a household is $\dot{W}_t = r_t W_t + w_t L_t - C_t$, where $W_t$ is the asset, $L_t$ is population, $r_t$ is the real interest rate and $w_t$ is the wage rate. From the dynamic utility maximisation problem, the Euler equation of consumption is derived as follows:

$$\frac{\dot{C}_t}{C_t} = \sigma(r_t - \rho) - \eta_P(\sigma - 1)\frac{\dot{P}_t}{P_t}. \tag{1.2}$$

The pollution emission function defined by Gradus and Smulders (1993) is defined as $P_t = (K_t/Z_t)^{\widehat{\kappa}}$, where $K_t$ is capital stock and $Z_t$ is pollution abatement good. To simplify the analysis, the elasticity parameter of pollution emission $\widehat{\kappa}$ is normalised to 1. Pollution abatement goods are produced from the final goods. As explained later in Chaps. 4 and 6, the government allocates $\overline{P}$ emission allowances to firms, which are bought and sold at the emission allowance price $p_t^e$. From the market clearing condition, $P_t = \overline{P}$ holds.

The production function of a firm is defined by the Cobb–Douglas technology as follows:

$$Y_t = X_t K_t^{\alpha} L_t^{1-\alpha}, \tag{1.3}$$

where $Y_t$ is output, $X_t$ is technology level, $\alpha \in (0,1)$ is the capital share and $1 - \alpha$ is the labour share. Following the learning by doing model in Romer (1986), $X_t = \overline{A}(K_t/L_t)^{1-\alpha}$ is assumed, where $\overline{A} > 0$ is the exogenous productivity parameter. The profit function of a representative firm is expressed as follows:

$$\Pi_t = Y_t - w_t L - r_t K_t - Z_t - p_t^e\left(P_t - \overline{P}\right), \tag{1.4}$$

where the final good is numeraire. The first-order condition for profit maximisation yields the following:

$$r_t = \alpha X_t \left(\frac{L_t}{K_t}\right)^{1-\alpha} - \frac{p_t^e}{Z_t} = \alpha \overline{A} - \frac{1}{\overline{P}}, \tag{1.5}$$

$$1 = \frac{p_t^e}{Z_t} \cdot \frac{K_t}{Z_t} \Leftrightarrow \frac{p_t^e}{Z_t} = \frac{1}{\overline{P}}, \tag{1.6}$$

where $P_t = \overline{P}$ is used to derive (1.5) and (1.6).

By substituting (1.5) into (1.6), we have $g \equiv \dot{C}_t / C_t$ as follows:

$$g = \sigma \left(\alpha \overline{A} - \tfrac{1}{\overline{P}}\right) - \sigma \rho, \tag{1.7}$$

where $\dot{P}_t / P_t = 0$ holds due to the flow variable of emissions allowance. Reducing the total emissions allowance reduces pollution emissions; however, it reduces economic growth as well. Reducing the total emissions allowance increases the marginal capital cost and reduces the capital demand; hence, decreasing production. Due to this, the real interest rate falls, therefore, household savings fall, capital accumulation stagnates and economic growth due to capital accumulation decreases.

Here, the assumption $\overline{A} = \overline{\overline{A}} / \overline{P}$ implies that pollution reduction due to the reduction in the total emissions allowance improves the firms' productivity. Hence, (1.7) can be rewritten as follows:

$$g = \tfrac{\sigma}{\overline{P}} \left(\alpha \overline{\overline{A}} - \tfrac{1}{\overline{P}}\right) - \sigma \rho, \tag{1.8}$$

where a reduction in the total emissions allowance increases the capital demand due to improved productivity of firms, which, in turn, increases the real interest rate, expands household savings and promotes economic growth. This growth-enhancing effect is called the 'externality effect'. When $Q_t$ is the quality of the environment, Smulders (1995), Bovenberg and Smulders (1995) and Smulders and Gradus (1996) discovered this effect from $X_t = Q_t(P_t)(K_t/L_t)^{1-\alpha}$ and $dQ_t(P_t)/d\overline{P} < 0$. The analysis of human capital was conducted by Gradus and Smulders (1993).

The negative externalities of pollution affect household saving behaviour in (2) and, therefore, affect the economic growth rate. Assuming $Z_t = 1$ and considering the amount of pollution emissions as a flow variable, we have $\dot{P}_t / P_t > 0$. In (2), under $\sigma > 1$ ($\sigma < 1$), consumption and pollution are substitutive (complementary), that is, reducing pollution increases (decreases) household savings and raises (lowers) the economic growth rate. This effect, discovered by Mohtadi (1996), was called the 'distaste effect' by Michel and Rotillon (1995). As Hamaguchi (2021b) pointed out, this distaste effect disappeared when assuming emission allowances as $P_t = \overline{P}$. Furthermore, according to Kozluk and Zipperer (2015), the impact of the externality effect on productivity growth is not robust at the plant level and is almost always negative in empirical studies. Therefore, environmental policies that are theoretically robust and have a positive growth effect have been pursued.

### 1.2.2 Public Goods

In response to the externality effect, the growth-enhancing effects of environmental policies that do not rely on pollution or environmental externalities are sought. Environmental policies are a channel for economic growth through the promotion of the accumulation of physical and human capital, which are the sources of economic growth. The first is the growth effect through public capital (goods), as described by Greiner (2005). The pollution emission per unit of efficiency is $\tilde{P}_t = \theta Y_t$ and $\theta > 0$ is the pollution abatement productivity parameter. As in Byrne (1997), the negative externality of pollution suffered by households is assumed as $P_t = (\theta Y_t)/Z_t$ and $Z_t = \tau P_t$ is the public pollution abatement good. The production function is $Y_t = \overline{A} K_t^{\alpha} \left(K_t^P L_t\right)^{1-\alpha}$, where $K_t^P$ is public capital.

By substituting the marginal productivity of capital obtained from the first-order condition for profit maximisation in (2) with $\sigma = 1$, the following is derived:

$$g = \alpha \overline{A}(1 - \tau\theta)\left(\frac{K_t^P}{K_t}\right)^{1-\alpha} - \rho,$$

where environmental taxes have an inverted U-shaped growth effect. As explained in (7), through $\tau\theta$, an increase in the environmental tax rate leads to a decline in the economic growth rate as it stagnates capital accumulation. However, through $\left(K_t^P/K_t\right)^{1-\alpha}$, environmental tax revenue promotes the accumulation of public capital, which improves the marginal productivity of capital and encourages household savings, thereby promoting economic growth. Fodha and Seegmuller (2012, 2014) showed that environmental poverty traps occurred by considering the relationship between public pollution abatement goods and government debt.

In general, income tax and capital tax hinder efficient resource allocation. When environmental tax revenue is used to correct taxation inefficiency, it leads to efficient resource allocation and pollution reduction. This theoretical result is called the double dividend hypothesis of environmental tax and is supported by empirical analysis (Bosquet, 2000). The dual dividend hypothesis of environmental taxes is valid when environmental taxes promote economic growth (Bovenberg & de Mooij, 1994, 1997; Goulder, 1995; Nakada, 2010).

### 1.2.3 Human Capital

The second channel is the growth effect through human capital. Hettich (1998) focused on the substitutability of education time and leisure time. When $\beta$ is the relative weight of consumption in utility, $1 - \beta$ is the relative weight of leisure in utility and $l_t \in (0,1)$ is leisure in (1) with $\sigma = 1$, the marginal rate of substitution for consumption and leisure can be obtained as follows from the dynamic utility maximisation problem:

$$\frac{1-\beta}{l_t} = w_t\left(\frac{\beta}{C_t}\right), \tag{1.9}$$

where the detailed derivation process is explained in Chap. 7 in the variety expansion model. An increase in environmental taxes encourages final goods firms to invest in pollution abatement goods, which increases final goods demand. Final goods firms try to increase production by substituting pollution-intensive physical capital with human capital. An increase in labour demand increases the wage rate. As shown in (1.9), the opportunity cost of leisure time increases as the wage rate rises. Therefore, households replace leisure time with education time, which encourages the accumulation of human capital and economic growth. In addition, pollution per unit of capital decreases.

Gradus and Smulders (1993) considered that the accumulation of human capital stagnated because pollution damaged the health of households and increased mortality through the externality effect. Pautrel (2009) assumed that in a continuous overlapping generation model, $\Psi(P_t) > 0$ and $d\Psi(P_t)/dP_t > 0$ assume that pollution emissions increase the household mortality rate $\Psi(P_t)$. By replacing the environmental tax in Pautrel (2009) with emissions trading at $P_t = \overline{P}$, the Euler equation is expressed as follows:

$$g = \sigma\left[\left(\overline{A} - \frac{1}{\overline{P}}\right) - \rho\right] - \Psi\left(\overline{P}\right)\widehat{\Psi}\left(\overline{P}\right)\frac{K_t}{C_t}, \tag{1.10}$$

for

$$\widehat{\Psi}\left(\overline{P}\right) \equiv \left(\sigma\rho + \Psi\left(\overline{P}\right)\right) - (\sigma - 1)\left(\alpha\overline{A} - \frac{1}{\overline{P}}\right),$$

where $\widehat{\Psi}\left(\overline{P}\right)$ is the efficient time preference rate. The second term on the right-hand side (RHS) of (1.10) implies the generation turnover effect, where $K_t = C_t - C_{t,t}$ is the relative difference between the average social consumption level and newborns' consumption level. Young people, who have no assets at birth, try to increase their future consumption by saving labour income. When the generation turnover progresses from the old to the young generation due to an increase in mortality, the economy grows because savings increase.

As the marginal productivity of capital decreases due to the reduction in the emission allowance, final goods firms reduce their physical capital input. Hence, the decline in the real interest rate reduces household savings, causing the economic growth rate to fall. However, the decline in physical capital input narrows the gap between average social consumption and newborns' consumption. In addition, pollution reduction and the resulting mortality decline extend the lifespan of the younger generation. The younger generation saves more to equalise their consumption levels over their lifetime. When the 'generation turnover effect' is greater than the negative growth effect, the economy grows due to the increase in household savings. The growth-enhancing effect of Pautrel (2009) depended on the externality effect on mortality and $\sigma > 1$, however, applying it to the Uzawa-Lucas model showed the growth-enhancing effect of an environmental tax without relying on the externality effect under $\sigma = 1$.

### 1.2.4 Application of Behavioural Economics

Since the 2000s, the findings of behavioural economics have been applied to the economic growth theory. As surveyed by Gsottbauer and Van den Bergh (2011), behavioural economics is being applied in environmental economics. The status effect in Howarth (2006) is explained in Chap. 7 and applied to the growth-promoting effects of environmental policy. Borissov and Shakhnov (2011) analysed the case where the time preference rate for consumption and pollution differed, using Stokey's (1998) model. Chiroleu-Assouline and Fodha (2014) applied the different time preference rates between these goods to environmental tax reform. The relationship between growth and environment in hyperbolic discounting was analysed by Cabo et al. (2020a, 2020b; Strulik, 2021).

According to Chu et al. (2016), endogenous time preference can have a growth-enhancing effect on environmental policy. The time preference rate is assumed to depend on environmental quality in the past and present and the intertemporal utility function is expressed as follows:

$$U_t = \int_0^{\infty} \left(\frac{C_t}{P_t^{\eta P}}\right)^{1-\frac{1}{\sigma}} \exp[-\Xi_t]dt, \tag{1.11}$$

for $\Xi_t \equiv \int_0^t \widehat{\Psi}(P_s)ds$, $t$ in $\dot{\Xi}_t = \widehat{\Psi}(P_t)$. Here, $\Xi_t$ is the endogenous time preference rate. Hence, $\Psi'(P_t) \gtreqless 0$ holds. In Le Kama and Schubert (2007), $\Psi'(P_t) < 0$ implied that the deterioration of environmental quality due to pollution strengthened the patience of households. However, $\Psi'(P_t) > 0$ in Yanase (2011) and Valla et al. (2015) implied that the deterioration of environmental quality due to pollution weakened the patience of households. The economic growth rate in (7) is rewritten as follows:

$$g = \sigma\left[\left(\alpha\overline{A} - \frac{1}{\overline{P}}\right) - \widehat{\Psi}(\overline{P})\right],$$

where a reduction in the total emissions allowance lowers the economic growth rate when $\Psi'(P_t) < 0$, because pollution reduction weakens households' patience and decreases households' savings. However, a reduction in the total emissions allowance raises the economic growth rate when $\Psi'(P_t) > 0$, because pollution reduction strengthens households' patience and increases households' savings.

### 1.2.5 The Importance of Innovation

Similar to public capital and human capital, capital accumulation is not the only source of economic growth. Another important source is innovation. However, in early research, it was believed that environmental policy, even with innovation, would result in a trade-off between growth and pollution. In Stokey (1998), pollution intensity of $o_t \in (0,1)$ is introduced into the AK-type production technology as $Y_t = o_t\overline{A}K_t$. Aghion and Howitt (1998, Chap. 5) applied this production function to a Schumpeterian model, however, did not specify an environmental policy that would achieve a socially optimal solution. Grimaud (1999) first applied a variety expansion model when analysing sustainable development mechanisms. In this, the production function and pollution emission function are assumed to be $Y_t = o_t \sum_{j=1}^{A_t} x_{j,t}^{\alpha} L_{X,t}^{\alpha}$ and $P_t = o_t^{\widehat{\kappa}} Y_t$, respectively, where $A_t \in \left[0, j\right]$ is the number of varieties. In this case, an increase in environmental taxes reduces the economic growth rate and there is a trade-off between environmental quality and economic growth.

Grimaud and Tournemaine (2007) showed that pollution reduction and economic growth can be achieved simultaneously through environmental taxes by replacing physical capital with human capital in a variety expansion model. In this growth model, households gain positive utility from an increase in the human capital level. The pollution emission function is $P_t = Y_t/Z_t^{\widehat{\kappa}}$ and in-house R&D-based variety expansion reduces pollution by increasing pollution abatement goods through the production of final goods. An environmental tax reduces pollution by shifting labour from the goods sector to the R&D sector and by expanding variety. Since final goods firms pass on the environmental tax in the form of higher prices, the opportunity cost of education decreases compared to the consumption of differentiated goods. Hence, households replace their working hours with education hours, human capital is accumulated and the economy grows.

As explained in Chap. 4, in the variety expansion model, labour mobility between industries due to environmental policies leads to economic growth. In addition, as explained in Chap. 6, the reduction in the opportunity cost of leisure time due to environmental policies leads to economic growth as leisure time is substituted by working hours in the R&D sector. However, compared to these settings, Grimaud and Tournemaine (2007) assumed an unusual setting. With more general settings, Nakada (2004) shows the growth-enhancing effect of environmental policy in the variety expansion model without capitals. An environmental tax is passed on to the price of intermediate goods. This price increase expands the monopoly profit of intermediate goods firms. This increase in profits stimulates R&D activities and, as a result, the economy grows through a general equilibrium effect. This growth effect is called a 'profitability effect'. However, in this growth model, the environmental tax rate per wage rate is defined and the environmental tax rate is time-dependent. This implies that the environmental tax rate diverges to infinity when an infinite period is considered (explained in Chap. 6). Therefore, when a furthermore general setting is assumed in the variety expansion model, the question of whether environmental policies can bring about pollution reduction and economic growth through innovation remains a concern.

## 1.3 Overview of This Book

### *1.3.1 Contribution of This Book*

In the 1990s, when the international community became increasingly aware of the importance of sustainable development, the endogenous economic growth theory underwent rapid development, triggered by Romer's (1986) learning-by-doing model. Economic growth through human capital was presented in Lucas's (1988) Uzawa-Lucas model and Barro (1990) and Futagami et al. (1993) presented economic growth through public services and public capital. Alongside economic growth through capital accumulation, economic growth through R&D activities has been identified. In R&D-based growth models, innovation in the R&D sector improves productivity endogenously, increasing the economic growth rate. Based on the premise that an increase in the number of varieties increases the gross domestic product (GDP), Romer (1990) developed the variety expansion model, which was analysed by Aghion and Howitt (1992). However, based on the premise that an improvement in the quality of existing varieties increases GDP, Grosman and Helpman (1991) developed the quality ladder model.

In response to the development of the endogenous growth theory, the possibility of reconciling pollution reduction and economic growth was studied. However, it was only in the 2010s that R&D-based growth models were applied in earnest to sustainable development. During this period, empirical analysis confirmed the link between sustainable development and socioeconomic factors. For example, Erdogan (2014), Cherniwchan et al. (2017) and Dechezleprêtre and Sato (2017) examined the relationship between globalisation and international trade, while Oates and Portney (2003), Aidt (2011) and Hu et al. (2021) studied the relationship between corruption and political economy. Brekke and Howarth (2002), Gsottbauer and Van den Bergh (2011) and Shogren and Taylor (2008) examined behavioural economics. These studies proposed new hypotheses related to the topic, yet their statistical significance is an ongoing debate.

However, as the central analytical approach of environmental economics shifted from theoretical analysis to empirical analysis, the analysis of these empirical issues using the endogenous growth theory gradually declined in popularity. This book fills this gap by applying theoretical analysis related to the R&D-based growth model developed in recent years. In this book, sustainable development is defined as the mechanism by which innovation through environmental policy leads to pollution reduction and economic growth. Hettich (2000) conducted an extended application analysis of the Uzawa-Lucas model and examined the robustness of the growth-promoting effect of environmental taxes. The empirical relationship between economic growth and the environment was systematically summarised in De Bruyn (2000). This book complements such specialist books. However, there are important issues that are beyond the scope of this book.

This book is based on qualitative analysis using a deterministic continuous model and does not consider the quantitative analysis using the stochastic discrete model in Cuaresma et al. (2009), where auctions and lobbying activities in emissions trading are considered. Furthermore, since Nordhaus developed a dynamic integrated model of climate and economy, climate change models have been analysed in the endogenous growth theory. Bretschger (2023) is a pioneering study in this field. All these books discuss renewable and non-renewable resources. In particular, in Grimaud and Rouge (2008), strict environmental policies slow down the resource extraction rate and move labour in the R&D sector from dirty goods to clean goods, resulting in economic growth.

### *1.3.2 Parts I and II*

Based on a brief survey of previous research, Part I discusses the basic mechanisms of sustainable development. In Chap. 2, Romer's (1990) variety expansion model is explained and, in Chap. 3, it is extended to include a case involving a preference for variety, following Grossman and Helpman (1991, Chap. 3). In Chap. 4, pollution emissions and environmental policies are introduced into the R&D model of Chap. 3 and it is shown that both environmental taxes and emission quotas improve welfare and reduce pollution and economic growth. In Chap. 5, monetary policy and financial economics are introduced into this R&D model with pollution and it is shown that reducing the nominal interest rate leads to sustainable development. Chap. 5 is based on Hamaguchi (2024a).

In Part II, it is shown that the growth-enhancing effect of environmental policy in a variety expansion model depends on household preferences and the production technology of the R&D sector. The marginal rate of substitution between consumption and leisure in Hettich (1998) is applied in Chap. 6 to explain how emission allowances can promote economic growth through the opportunity cost of leisure. In Chap. 7, the social status preference in Brekke and Howarth (2002) is applied to explain that the marginal rate of substitution between consumption and assets determines the growth-enhancing effect of environmental policy. In both cases, the growth effect of environmental policy disappears when the production technology of the R&D sector is a case of goods rather than labour or when it does not include leisure time or social status preference. Chap. 6 is based on Hamaguchi (2021b) and Hamaguchi et al. (2022) and Chap. 7 is based on Hamaguchi (2019). Chapter 8 shows that the growth-enhancing effect of environmental policy in Chap. 4 disappears under certain non-homothetic preferences.

### 1.3.3 Parts III and IV

In Part III, the closed economy is expanded to an open economy and the relationship between the international economy and sustainable development is discussed. In Chap. 9, the R&D-based location model of Martin and Ottaviano (1999), which applies the variety expansion model of Grossman and Helpman (1991, Chap. 3) to the location of firms, is explained. In Chap. 10, the location model in Chap. 9 is extended to include emissions trading from Chap. 4 and the relationship between trade environment policy and the pollution haven hypothesis is clarified. In doing so, the degree of spillover in the R&D sector and the effect of pollution abatement productivity parameters on the results are discussed. In Chap. 11, the location model with pollution in Chap. 10 is extended to include the tourism sector and tourism mobility and the relationship between tourism environmental policy and sustainable tourism is discussed. Chapter 10 is based on Hamaguchi (2021c, 2023b) and Chap. 11 is based on Hamaguchi (2020b).

In Part IV, the political economy of environmental policy is examined and the impact of corruption and tax evasion is discussed. Chapter 12 explains that the additional regulatory costs of the overlapped double regulation introduced into the R&D model in Chap. 4 provide polluting firms with an incentive to evade taxes. Contrary to intuition, environmental tax evasion with bribery can promote sustainable development. In Chap. 13, environmental tax evasion in Chap. 12 is applied to the location model in Chap. 10 and it is shown that environmental tax evasion in developed countries leads to the pollution haven hypothesis. Chapter 12 is based on Hamaguchi (2020a), and Chap. 13 is based on Hamaguchi (2022). In Parts III and IV, it is shown that strict environmental policies lead to an increase in pollution emissions and a decline in the price of emission allowances. Furthermore, the mechanisms that inhibit the pollution reduction effects of environmental policies are explained.

### 1.3.4 Part V

In Part V, the impact of environmental policies on industrial structure changes through the entry and exit of firms is considered. To this end, in Chap. 14, the R&D-based growth model with heterogeneous firms by Gustafsson and Segerstrom (2010) is explained and extended to a full endogenous growth model. In Chap. 15, a discriminatory environmental tax is introduced into the heterogeneous firm model in Chap. 14 and it is clarified that the tax rate disparity affects the productivity of the industry through entry and exit. In Chap. 16, environmental tax evasion in Chap. 12 is applied and it is explained that political and economic factors lead to the Porter hypothesis and the pollution haven hypothesis. In the conclusion, the main results of this book are summarised, along with its contributions, limitations and future issues. In doing so, the robustness of the results regarding the effects of trade environment policies due to scale effects is explained by comparing the results of Chaps. 15 and 16. Chapter 15 is based on Hamaguchi (2024b) and Chap. 16 is based on Hamaguchi (2023c).

## References

Aghion, P., & Howitt, P. (1992). A model of growth through creative destruction. *Econometrica*, 60(2), 323–351. https://doi.org/10.2307/2951599

Aghion, P & Howitt, P. (1998). Endogenous growth theory, Cambridge: MIT Press.

Aidt, T. S. (2011). "Chapter 1: Corruption and Sustainable Development". In International Handbook on the Economics of Corruption, Volume Two. Cheltenham, UK: Edward Elgar Publishing. https://doi.org/10.4337/9780857936523.00007

Barro, R. J. (1990). Government spending in a simple model of endogeneous growth. *Journal of Political Economy*, 98(5, Part 2), S103-S125. https://doi.org/10.1086/261726

Bretschger, L. (2023). Economics of Sustainable Development, Zurich: CER-ETH Press.

Bosquet, B., (2000). Environmental tax reform: does it work? A survey of the empirical evidence. *Ecological Economics*, 34, 19-32. https://doi.org/10.1016/S0921-8009(00)00173-7

Brekke, K. A., & Howarth, R. B. (2002). Status, Growth and the Environment. Edward Elgar Publishing.

Borissov, K., & Shakhnov, K. (2011). Sustainable growth in a model with dual-rate discounting. *Economic Modelling*, 28(4), 2071-2074. https://doi.org/10.1016/j.econmod.2011.04.004

Bovenberg, A. L., & de Mooij, R. A. (1994). Environmental levies and distortionary taxation. *The American Economic Review*, 84(4), 1085–1089. https://www.jstor.org/stable/2118046

Bovenberg, A.L., & de Mooij, R.A. (1997). Environmental tax reform and endogenous growth. *Journal of Public Economics*, 63, 207–237. https://doi.org/10.1016/S0047-2727(96)01596-4

Bovenberg, A. L., & Smulders, S. (1995). Environmental quality and pollution-augmenting technological change in a two-sector endogenous growth model. *Journal of Public Economics*, 57(3), 369-391. https://doi.org/10.1016/0047-2727(95)80002-Q

Byrne, M. (1997). Is growth a dirty word? Pollution, abatement and endogenous growth. *Journal of Development Economics*, 54, 261-284. https://doi.org/10.1016/S0304-3878(97)00043-6

Cabo, F., Martín-Herrán, G., & Martínez-García, M. P. (2020a). Non-constant discounting, social welfare and endogenous growth with pollution externalities. *Environmental and Resource Economics*, 76(2), 369-403. https://doi.org/10.1007/s10640-020-00430-3

Cabo, F., Martin-Herran, G., & Martínez-García, M. P. (2020b). Present bias and the inefficiency of the centralized economy: The role of the elasticity of intertemporal substitution. *Economic Modelling*, 93, 702-716. https://doi.org/10.1016/j.econmod.2020.01.019

Cherniwchan, J., Copeland, B. R., & Taylor, M. S. (2017). Trade and the environment: New methods, measurements, and results. *Annual Review of Economics*, 9(1), 59–85. https://doi.org/10.1146/annurev-economics-063016-103756

Chiroleu-Assouline, M., & Fodha, M. (2014). From regressive pollution taxes to progressive environmental tax reforms. *European Economic Review*, 69, 126-142. https://doi.org/10.1016/j.euroecorev.2013.12.006

Chu, H., Lai, C. C., & Liao, C. H. (2016). A note on environment-dependent time preferences. *Macroeconomic Dynamics*, 20(6), 1652-1667. https://doi.org/10.1017/S1365100514000960

Cuaresma, J. C., Palokangas, T., & Tarasyev, A. (Eds.). (2009). Dynamic systems, economic growth, and the environment (Vol. 12). Springer Science & Business Media. https://doi.org/10.1007/978-3-642-02132-9

Dechezleprêtre, A., & Sato, M. (2017). The impacts of environmental regulations on competitiveness. *Review of Environmental Economics and Policy*, 11(2), 183-206. https://doi.org/10.1093/reep/rex013

De Bruyn, S. M. (2000). Economic growth and the environment: An empirical analysis (Vol. 18). Springer Science & Business Media. https://doi.org/10.1007/978-94-011-4068-3

Erdogan, A. M. (2014). Foreign direct investment and environmental regulations: a survey. *Journal of Economic Surveys*, 28(5), 943-955. https://doi.org/10.1111/joes.12047

Fodha, M., & Seegmuller, T. (2012). A note on environmental policy and public debt stabilization. *Macroeconomic Dynamics*, 16(3), 477-492. https://doi.org/10.1017/S1365100510000672

Fodha, M., & Seegmuller, T. (2014). Environmental quality, public debt and economic development. *Environmental and Resource Economics*, 57(4), 487-504. https://doi.org/10.1007/s10640-013-9639-x

Futagami, K., Morita, Y., & Shibata, A. (1993). Dynamic analysis of an endogenous growth model with public capital. *The Scandinavian Journal of Economics*, 607–625. https://www.jstor.org/stable/3440914

Futagami, K. (2012). Dynamic macroeconomic theory (Dougaku Makuro Keizaigaku : Seichou Riron No Haxtuten). Nihon Hyouron Sya, *In Japanese.*

Goulder, L. H. (1995). Environmental taxation and the double dividend: A reader's guide. *International Tax and Public Finance*, 2(2), 157–183. https://doi.org/10.1007/BF00877495

Gradus, R., & Smulders, S. (1993). The trade-off between environmental care and long-term growth—pollution in three prototype growth models. *Journal of Economics*, 58(1), 25-51. https://doi.org/10.1007/BF01234800

Greiner, A. (2005). Fiscal policy in an endogenous growth model with public capital and pollution. *The Japanese Economic Review*, 56(1), 67-84. https://doi.org/10.1111/j.1468-5876.2005.00299.x

Grimaud, A. (1999). Pollution permits and sustainable growth in a Schumpeterian model. *Journal of Environmental Economics and Management*, 38(3), 249-266. https://doi.org/10.1006/jeem.1999.1088

Grimaud, A., & Tournemaine, F. (2007). Why can an environmental policy tax promote growth through the channel of education?. *Ecological Economics*, 62(1), 27-36. https://doi.org/10.1016/j.ecolecon.2006.11.006

Grimaud, A., & Rouge, L. (2008). Environment, directed technical change and economic policy. *Environmental and Resource Economics*, 41(4), 439-463. https://doi.org/10.1007/s10640-008-9201-4

Grossman, G. M., & Helpman, E. (1991). Innovation and growth in the global economy. MIT press.

Grossman, G. M., & Helpman, E. (1991). Quality ladders in the theory of growth. *The Review of Economic Studies*, 58(1), 43–61. https://doi.org/10.2307/2298044

Gsottbauer, E., & Van den Bergh, J. C. (2011). Environmental policy theory given bounded rationality and other–regarding preferences. *Environmental and Resource Economics*, 49(2), 263–304. https://doi.org/10.1007/s10640-010-9433-y

Gsottbauer, E., & van den Bergh, J. C. (2014). Environmental policy when pollutive consumption is sensitive to advertising: Norms versus status. *Ecological Economics*, 107, 39-50. https://doi.org/10.1016/j.ecolecon.2014.07.001

Gustafsson, P., & Segerstrom, P. (2010). Trade liberalization and productivity growth. *Review of International Economics*, 18(2), 207-228. https://doi.org/10.1111/j.1467-9396.2010.00878.x

Hamaguchi, Y. (2019). Positive effect of pollution permits in a variety expansion model with social status preference. The Manchester School, 87(4), 591-606. https://doi.org/10.1111/manc.12270

Hamaguchi, Y. (2020a). Dynamic analysis of bribery firms' environmental tax evasion in an emissions trading market. *Journal of Macroeconomics*, 63, 103169. https://doi.org/10.1016/j.jmacro.2019.103169

Hamaguchi, Y. (2020b). Do pollution havens restrict tourism-led growth? Achieving sustainable tourism via a mix of environmental and tourism policies. *Tourism Economics*, 26(7), 1175-1196. https://doi.org/10.1177/1354816619868086

Hamaguchi, Y. (2021a). Environmental policy and social status preference for education in an Uzawa–Lucas model. *Bulletin of Economic Research*, 73(3), 456-468. https://doi.org/10.1111/boer.12259
Hamaguchi, Y. (2021b). Environmental policy effects: an R&D-based economic growth model with endogenous labour supply. *Journal of Economic Policy Reform*, 24(2), 236-252. https://doi.org/10.1080/17487870.2019.1631598
Hamaguchi, Y. (2021c). Polluting firms' location choices and pollution havens in an R&D-based growth model for an international emissions trading market. *The Journal of International Trade & Economic Development*, 30(4), 625-642. https://doi.org/10.1080/09638199.2021.1889644
Hamaguchi, Y. (2022). Effect of environmental tax evasion on pollution havens within the EU's dual regulation system. *SN Business & Economics*, 2(12), 194. https://doi.org/10.1007/s43546-022-00368-2
Hamaguchi, Y. (2023a). How to achieve the SDGs and sustainable development? -A review of recent research from the perspective of economic growth theory- In book: Towards sustainable societies, Kyoto: KoyoShobo. https://www.researchgate.net/publication/369332489
Hamaguchi, Y. (2023b). Pollution havens and agglomeration: The effect of globalization and technological spillover. Applied Economics, 56(19), 2223-2240. https://doi.org/10.1080/00036846.2023.2186361
Hamaguchi, Y. (2023c). Environmental tax evasion as a determinant of the Porter and pollution haven hypotheses in a corrupt political system. *Economic Analysis and Policy*, 79, 610-633. https://doi.org/10.1016/j.eap.2023.06.032
Hamaguchi, Y. (2024a). Comparative study of environmental and monetary policies in an R&D-based growth model. *Journal of Environmental Management*, 360, 121199. https://doi.org/10.1016/j.jenvman.2024.121199
Hamaguchi, Y. (2024b). Effects of a policy mix of uniform or unilateral environmental tax and trade liberalization on economic welfare. *Journal of Applied Economics*, 27(1), 2375913. https://doi.org/10.1080/15140326.2024.2375913
Hamaguchi, Y. (2024c). "Chapter 6: A survey of sustainable development in economic growth theory: achievements and future directions". In Handbook on Energy and Economic Growth. Cheltenham, UK: Edward Elgar Publishing. https://doi.org/10.4337/9781802204803.00013
Hamaguchi, Y., Bhuiyan, M. A., & Rahman, M. K. (2022). Analytical method to derive environmental policy effects in an endogenous growth model with leisure. *MethodsX*, 9, 101840. https://doi.org/10.1016/j.mex.2022.101840
Hettich, F. (1998). Growth effects of a revenue-neutral environmental tax reform. *Journal of Economics*, 67, 287-316. https://doi.org/10.1007/BF01234647
Hettich, F. (2000). Economic growth and environmental policy: A theoretical approach. Edward Elgar Publishing.
Howarth, R. B. (2006). Optimal environmental taxes under relative consumption effects. *Ecological Economics*, 58(1), 209–219. https://doi.org/10.1016/j.ecolecon.2005.07.007
Hu, H., Chen, D., Chang, C. P., & Chu, Y. (2021). The political economy of environmental consequences: A review of the empirical literature. *Journal of Economic Surveys*, 35(1), 250-306. https://doi.org/10.1111/joes.12396
Kozluk, T., & Zipperer, V. (2015). Environmental policies and productivity growth: a critical review of empirical findings. OECD Journal: *Economic Studies*, 2014(1), 155–185. https://doi.org/10.1787/eco_studies-v2014-1-en
Le Kama, A. A., & Schubert, K. (2007). A note on the consequences of an endogenous discounting depending on the environmental quality. *Macroeconomic Dynamics*, 11(2), 272-289. https://doi.org/10.1017/S1365100507060063
Lucas Jr, R. E. (1988). On the mechanics of economic development. *Journal of Monetary Economics*, 22(1), 3-42. https://doi.org/10.1016/0304-3932(88)90168-7

Martin, P., & Ottaviano, G. I. (1999). Growing locations: Industry location in a model of endogenous growth. *European Economic Review*, 43(2), 281-302. https://doi.org/10.1016/S0014-2921(98)00031-2

Michel, P., & Rotillon, G. (1995). Disutility of pollution and endogenous growth. *Environmental and resource Economics*, 6(3), 279–300. https://doi.org/10.1007/BF00705982

Mohtadi, H. (1996). Environment, growth, and optimal policy design. *Journal of Public Economics*, 63(1), 119–140. https://doi.org/10.1016/0047-2727(95)01562-0

Nakada, M. (2004). Does environmental policy necessarily discourage growth?. *Journal of Economics*, 81, 249-275. https://doi.org/10.1007/s00712-002-0609-y

Nakada, M. (2010). Environmental tax reform and growth: Income tax cuts or profits tax reduction. *Environmental and Resource Economics*, 47(4), 549-565. https://doi.org/10.1007/s10640-010-9392-3

Oates, W. E., & Portney, P. R. (2003). The political economy of environmental policy. In Handbook of environmental economics (Vol. 1, pp. 325–354). Elsevier.

Pautrel, X. (2009). Pollution and life expectancy: How environmental policy can promote growth. *Ecological Economics*, 68(4), 1040–1051. https://doi.org/10.1016/j.ecolecon.2008.07.011

Ricci, F. (2007). Channels of transmission of environmental policy to economic growth: A survey of the theory. *Ecological Economics*, 60(4), 688-699. https://doi.org/10.1016/j.ecolecon.2006.11.014

Romer, P. M. (1986). Increasing returns and long-run growth. *Journal of Political Economy, 94*(5), 1002–1037. https://doi.org/10.1086/261420

Romer, P. M. (1990). Endogenous technological change. *Journal of Political Economy*, 98(5, Part 2), S71-S102. https://doi.org/10.1086/261725

Shogren, J. F., & Taylor, L. O. (2008). On behavioral-environmental economics. *Review of Environmental Economics and Policy*, 2(1), 26-44. https://doi.org/10.1093/reep/rem027

Smulders, S. (1995). Environmental policy and sustainable economic growth. *De Economist*, 143(2), 163-195. https://doi.org/10.1007/BF01384534

Smulders, S., & Gradus, R. (1996). Pollution abatement and long-term growth. *European Journal of Political Economy*, 12(3), 505-532. https://doi.org/10.1016/S0176-2680(96)00013-4

Stokey (1998) Stokey, N. L. (1998). Are there limits to growth?. *International Economic Review*, 1-31. https://doi.org/10.2307/2527228

Strulik, H. (2021). Hyperbolic discounting and the time-consistent solution of three canonical environmental problems. *Journal of Public Economic Theory*, 23(3), 462-486. https://doi.org/10.1111/jpet.12497

Vella, E., Dioikitopoulos, E. V., & Kalyvitis, S. (2015). Green spending reforms, growth, and welfare with endogenous subjective discounting. *Macroeconomic Dynamics*, 19(6), 1240-1260. https://doi.org/10.1017/S1365100513000813

Yanase, A. (2011). Impatience, pollution, and indeterminacy. *Journal of Economic Dynamics and Control*, 35(10), 1789-1799. https://doi.org/10.1016/j.jedc.2011.06.010

# Chapter 2
# Endogenous Technological Change I

**Abstract** The R&D-based growth model, with innovation as the source of growth, began with Romer (1990) variety expansion model, for which he was awarded the Nobel Prize for Economic Achievement in 2020. This chapter explains the basic structure of this economic model. The economy consists of consumers, the final goods sector, the intermediate goods sector and the R&D sector. By purchasing the variety developed by R&D firms, entrepreneurs apply for patents and enter the intermediate goods market as monopolists. The monopoly profit is distributed as dividends to households that provide the R&D funds. As the variety increases, labour productivity improves and GDP rises. By introducing stocks in the market, total factor productivity is internalised and economic growth is generated through innovation. Through the scale effect, the increase in R&D workers, accompanying population growth, promotes economic growth. In the lab-equipment model, where R&D firms develop variety through goods rather than labour, the stock price remains constant, hence, the three-dimensional dynamic system becomes one-dimensional and the model analysis becomes simpler.

## 2.1 Structure of Variety Expansion Model

The economy has certain economic agents—households, final goods firms, intermediate goods firms and R&D firms. Final goods firms produce final goods and sell them to households through the input of labour by households and intermediate goods by intermediate goods firms. Intermediate goods firms produce intermediate goods by investing physical capital borrowed from households. These firms are monopolies because they have patent rights over the products. Therefore, it earns monopoly profits through mark-up prices. Entrepreneurs enter the intermediate goods market to gain a positive profit. Hence, they need a blueprint for a new intermediate goods variety. By investing household labour, R&D firms develop this blueprint. Entrepreneurs raise R&D funds by selling shares of their firm to households, who purchase this blueprint from the R&D firm. Based on this blueprint, the entrepreneur applies for patent rights and enters the intermediate goods market as a monopolist. The monopoly

 
Y. Hamaguchi, *Sustainable Development in Economic Growth Theory*,
https://doi.org/10.1007/978-981-96-7639-2_2

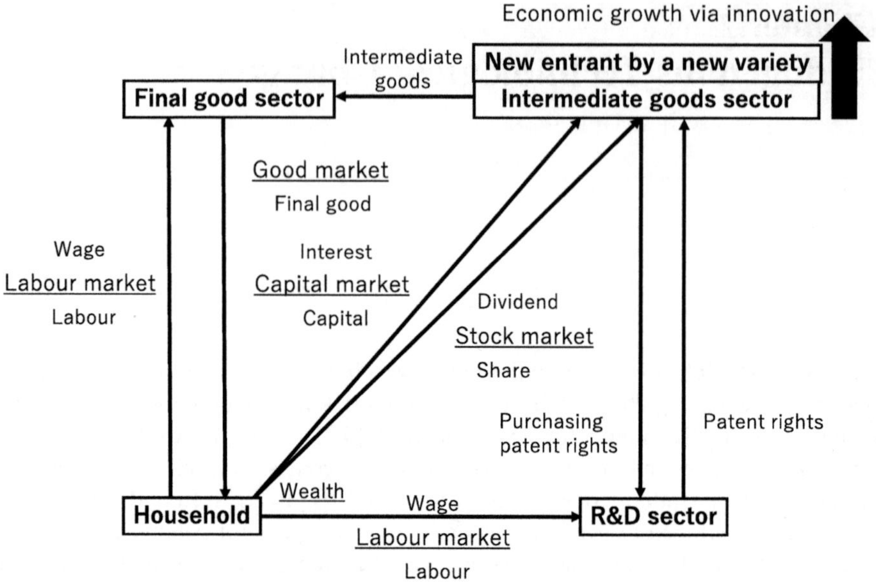


**Fig. 2.1** Structure of variety expansion model

profits are distributed to households as dividends. Households use the dividend and rental income from the intermediate goods firms, along with wages from their respective firms, to consume the final goods purchased. In this economy, the output of final goods increases as the variety of goods increases due to R&D activities. This rate of increase is regarded as the economic growth rate. The above economic structure is shown in Fig. 2.1.[1]

## 2.2 The Model

### 2.2.1 Household

Households derive satisfaction, called 'utility', from final goods consumption. Households in this economy are assumed to be representative individuals. A dynasty is an altruistic individual and the current generation sees the utility of its future generations as its own utility. When this individual household values the future generation's utility in terms of its present value, it is discounted at a subjective discount rate $\rho > 0$. The individual in period $t$ aims to maximise the sum of the discounted

[1] To the best of the author's knowledge, this graphical representation of the structure of macroeconomic models is credited to Futagami (2012), who, since the late 1990s, has used this graphical economic model in his lectures to understand and promote economic growth theory.

present values of the individual's utility in each period. Hence, the dynasty to which this individual belongs is called the 'household that lives for an infinite period' and the members of this household are the 'representative individuals'. This economy consists only of these households and its population is $L$. However, the population growth rate is assumed to be zero. From the above, the utility function of a household (representative individual) that lives for an infinite period of time is as follows:

$$U_t = \int_0^\infty \log C_t e^{-\rho t} dt, \tag{2.1}$$

where a logarithmic utility function is assumed for simplicity of analysis, hence, the income effect vanishes. Note that $U_t$ is lifetime utility and $C_t$ is consumption.

Households use labour, rental and dividend income to consume final goods, accumulate savings and buy stocks. Households' savings ($S_t$) become a net increase in physical capital ($\dot{K}_t$) in the capital market through firms' capital investment ($I_t$). Assuming a zero rate of capital depletion, $S_t = I_t = \dot{K}_t$. Let $W_t = K_t + P_{A,t}A_t$ be the household's assets. Hence, $K_t$ is physical capital, $A_t$ is the number of shares and $P_{A,t}$ is the share price. Hence, the household's budget constraint is as follows:

$$\dot{K}_t + P_{A,t}\dot{A}_t = r_t K_t + A_t \pi_t + w_t L - C_t, \tag{2.2}$$

where $\dot{A}_t$ is the net increase in share, $\dot{P}_{A,t}$ is the net increase in stock prices, $\pi_t$ is dividends (monopoly profits of intermediate goods firms), $r_t$ is the real interest rate (capital rental price) and $w_t$ is the wage rate. The left-hand side (LHS) of (2.2) implies a net increase in assets through savings accumulation and stock purchases. The right-hand side (RHS) of (2.2) implies rental and labour income from physical capital, respectively. In the labour market, the labour demand of firms in the final goods and R&D sectors maintain equilibrium with household labour supply through the equilibrium wage rate $w_t$.

Using $W_t = K_t + P_{A,t}A_t$ as in Appendix A.1 and rewriting (2.2), we obtain

$$\dot{W}_t = r_t W_t + w_t L - C_t, \tag{2.3}$$

which is derived by using the following non-arbitrage condition:

$$\frac{\pi_t + \dot{P}_{A,t}}{P_{A,t}} = r_t, \tag{2.4}$$

which implies that price adjustment mechanisms in the stock and capital markets make the rates of return on savings and shares equal. When $(\pi_t + \dot{P}_{A,t})/P_{A,t} > r_t$, households can increase their assets by investing in shares rather than saving, leading to a stock price rise and a drop in the real rate of interest. However, when $(\pi_t + \dot{P}_{A,t})/P_{A,t} < r_t$, the real interest rate rises and the stock price falls because households can increase their assets by investing in savings rather than shares. Due to the above arbitrage behaviour, (2.4) maintains equilibrium.

The households' utility maximisation problem across different time points can be formulated as follows:

$$\max_{C_t} \int_0^{\infty} \log C_t e^{-\rho t} dt, \text{ s.t. } \dot{W}_t = r_t W_t + w_t L - C_t.$$

When $\lambda_t$ is a costate variable, the first-order conditions for utility maximisation between different times yield the following[2]

$$\tfrac{1}{C_t} = \lambda_t, \tag{2.5}$$

$$-\dot{\lambda}_t + \rho \lambda_t = r_t \lambda_t, \tag{2.6}$$

$$\lim_{T \to \infty} \lambda_T W_T e^{-\rho T} = 0, \tag{2.7}$$

where (2.5) is the first-order condition on consumption, (2.6) is the shadow price of assets and (2.7) is the transversality condition. Substituting time-differentiated (2.5) into (2.6) and rearranging it, we derive the following Euler equation:

$$\tfrac{\dot{C}_t}{C_t} = r_t - \rho > 0, \tag{2.8}$$

which implies that an increase in savings due to an increase in the real interest rate expands future consumption, while a decrease in savings reduces future consumption when an increase in the time preference rate emphasises the consumption of the current generation.

### 2.2.2 *Final Good Sector*

The production technology of firms in the final goods sector assumes a Cobb–Douglas-type production function as follows:

$$Y_t = L_{Y,t}^{1-\alpha} \int_0^{A_t} x_{j,t}^{\alpha} dj, \tag{2.9}$$

where $L_{Y,t}$ is the labour input in the final goods sector, $x_{j,t}$ is the $j$ th intermediate good, $\alpha \in (0,1)$ is the capital share and $1 - \alpha$ is the labour share. This production technology has constant returns to scale. Here, $\int_0^{A_t} x_{j,t} dj$ implies that as the variety of intermediate goods increases due to R&D activities, the output of final goods and their value-added expand because the total amount of input intermediate goods increases.

[2] For details on dynamic optimisation problems and transversality conditions, see Chiang (1992).

This firm employs workers at $w_t$ and purchases each intermediate good at $p_{j,t}$ to produce the final good. Hence, the profit function of this firm is formulated as follows:

$$\Pi_t = Y_t - w_t L - p_{j,t} x_{j,t}, \tag{2.10}$$

where the final good is a numeraire, thus, its price is 1. The first-order condition of profit maximisation yields the following:

$$(1-\alpha)\left(\frac{\int_0^{A_t} x_{j,t} dj}{L_{Y,t}}\right)^{\alpha} = w_t, \tag{2.11}$$

$$\alpha\left(\frac{L_{Y,t}}{x_{j,t}}\right)^{1-\alpha} = p_{j,t}, \tag{2.12}$$

where the marginal costs of labour and intermediate goods are input to a point where it equals their respective marginal benefits in the following manner: $\alpha\left(L_{Y,t}/x_{j,t}\right)^{1-\alpha} > p_{j,t}$, when the net increase in sales from inputting a unit of production factor is higher than the intermediate good price, the law of diminishing returns allows firms to increase profits by inputting intermediate goods. Due to the law of diminishing returns, the marginal benefit of intermediate goods decreases with input. However, $\alpha\left(L_{Y,t}/x_{j,t}\right)^{1-\alpha} < p_{j,t}$, when the price of intermediate goods is higher than the net increase in sales from the input of a unit of production factor, hence, firms can increase profits by reducing intermediate goods inputs. Here, the law of diminishing returns dictates that the marginal benefit increases. From the above, (2.12) holds when firms maximise their profits.

### 2.2.3 *Intermediate Good Sector*

Each intermediate goods firm in the sector obtained patent rights based on its intermediate goods blueprints, protecting its right to produce its products in perpetuity. Therefore, intermediate goods firms are monopolies. These firms borrow a unit of capital from households, invest it to produce a unit of intermediate goods and sell the goods to firms in the final goods sector at a monopoly price.

The profit function of the $j$ th intermediate goods firm is defined as follows:

$$\pi_{j,t} = p_{j,t} x_{j,t} - r_t x_{j,t}, \text{ s.t. } p_{j,t} = \alpha\left(\frac{L_{Y,t}}{x_{j,t}}\right)^{1-\alpha}, \tag{2.13}$$

for $j = 1,2,\cdots, A_t$ and $r_t$ is the rental price of capital (real interest rate). Here, the constraint is an inverse demand function implying the demand behaviour of firms in the final goods sector. In a monopoly, profits increase as the production of intermediate goods expands, while profits decrease if sales fall due to a fall in the price of the intermediate goods. Therefore, the $j$ th intermediate goods firm determines the capital amount that maximises profit, given (2.12).

The first-order condition for profit maximisation yields

$$\alpha^2\left(\frac{L_{Y,t}}{x_{j,t}}\right)^{1-\alpha} = r_t \Leftrightarrow p_t = \left(\tfrac{1}{\alpha}\right)r_t, \tag{2.14}$$

where intermediate goods firms borrow capital from households to input until marginal revenue equals marginal cost. Here, $1-\alpha$ implies the inverse of the price elasticity of demand. See Appendix A.2 for the derivation of this inverse. Substituting (2.14) into (2.13), we obtain the monopoly profit of the intermediate goods firm as follows:

$$\pi_t = \left(\tfrac{1-\alpha}{\alpha}\right)r_t x_t, \tag{2.15}$$

Replacing this first-order condition in (2.14) with (2.12), the intermediate goods price is the rental cost of capital ($r_t$) multiplied by the mark-up rate of $(1/\alpha)$. This rental cost and mark-up rate are symmetric because they are common across intermediate goods firms. Henceforth, the subscript $j$ is omitted unless necessary. The result obtained by substituting (2.14) into (2.12) and rearranging $x_t = \left(\alpha^2/r_t\right)^{\frac{1}{1-\alpha}} L_{Y,t}$ implies that the output of each intermediate good is the same across firms.

### 2.2.4 R&D Sector

Firms in the R&D sector develop blueprints on new varieties by employing workers. Their production technologies include:

$$\dot{A}_t = \delta L_{A,t} A_t, \tag{2.16}$$

where $L_{A,t}$ is the labour input in the R&D sector and $\delta > 0$ is the productivity parameter of the R&D firm. Here, $A_t$ is a positive spillover effect in R&D, called the shoulder of giant effect, where the greater the amount of knowledge present, the easier it is to develop new knowledge.

This sector is in a perfectly competitive market, where firms are free to enter and exit R&D activities—an R&D firm employing workers at $w_t$ sells the blueprint of the new variety that it has developed at $P_{A,t}$, hence, its profit function can be formulated as follows:

$$\pi_t^A = P_{A,t}\dot{A}_t - w_t L_{A,t},$$

and the zero-utility condition of profit maximisation yields:

$$P_{A,t}\delta A_t = w_t, \tag{2.17}$$

where R&D firms employ workers up to the point where the marginal cost equals the marginal benefit, as follows: when $P_{A,t}\delta A_t > w_t$, the selling price of the blueprint is higher than the wage rate, therefore, the R&D firm can earn a positive profit by employing workers to develop the blueprint. At this time, there is a series of new entries into the market. As employment increases, the wage rate increases and prices fall due to the increased blueprints supply. However, when $P_{A,t}\delta A_t < w_t$, the wage rate is higher than the blueprints' selling price, hence, the R&D firm can reduce its negative profit by laying off workers and stopping development. As firms exit the market, the wage rate falls due to employment reduction and its price rises due to the reduced blueprints supply. Therefore, in equilibrium, (2.17) holds and the profits of the R&D firms are zero, hence, there is no entry into or exit from the market. Therefore, (2.17) is called the free entry condition.

### 2.2.5 *Market*

In this economy, there are capital markets, stock markets, labour markets and goods markets. In the capital market, the capital demand of intermediate goods firms is satisfied by capital supply by households, hence, the following holds: $\int_0^{A_t} x_{j,t}dj = A_t x_t = K_t$. By transforming this equation, we obtain $x_t = K_t/A_t$, which implies that the demand for capital is average capital. Substituting this average capital into $x_t$ in (2.9) and rearranging, we obtain $Y_t = K_t^{\alpha}\left(A_t L_{Y,t}\right)^{1-\alpha}$. This production function implies that an increase in the variety of intermediate goods due to profit-motivated R&D activities improves workers' productivity and final goods output. Hence, the variety expansion model succeeds in endogenizing the exogenous level of technology in the Solow model.[3]

In the stock market, entrepreneurs raise money to purchase blueprints for new varieties by selling their shares to households. They use the R&D funds to purchase the blueprints. Hence, the share price of the intermediate goods firm matches the price of the purchased blueprints. Households compare the rate of return on their savings with the rate of return on the stock and decide on investment. Hence, in equilibrium, the no-arbitrage condition in (2.4) holds, which determines the share price. This share price is equal to the sum of the discounted present value of profits from period $t$ onwards, $P_{A,t} = \int_t^{\infty} e^{-[r(\iota)-r(t)]}\pi_\iota d\iota$. By time differentiating this $P_{A,t}$, (2.4) can be derived. Alternatively, by integrating (2.4), this $P_{A,t}$ can be derived.

The quantity of labour supplied by households equals the demand of the final goods and the R&D sectors through the wage rate. If the wage rate in the final goods sector is higher than that in the R&D sector, labour migration occurs from the R&D sector to the final goods sector. Hence, the wage rate in the final goods sector falls while that in the R&D sector rises. However, if the wage rate in the R&D sector is higher than that in the final goods sector, labour migration occurs from the final goods sector to the R&D sector, causing the wage rate in the R&D sector to decrease

[3] On the significance of this endogenization for the economic growth theory, see Jones (2019).

and that in the final goods sector to increase. Hence, in equilibrium, the wage rates are equal in the two sectors. Hence, the market clearing conditions for the labour market are as follows:

$$L_{Y,t} + L_{A,t} = L, \tag{2.18}$$

where the amount of labour supplied by households is diachronically constant.

As in Appendix A.3, substituting (2.4), (2.9), (2.11), (2.12) and (2.14) into (2.2) and rearranging, we obtain the market clearing conditions for the goods market as follows:

$$Y_t = C_t + \dot{K}_t, \tag{2.19}$$

where the final goods produced by the final goods sector are distributed for consumption by households and investment by intermediate goods firms.

## 2.3 Equilibrium

In this section, we construct a dynamic system in this economy with final goods per capital as $y_t \equiv Y_t/K_t$, consumption per capital as $z_t \equiv C_t/K_t$ and average capital as $\omega_t \equiv K_t/A_t$. Next, we derive its steady state. Note that $y_t$ and $z_t$ are jump variables (non-pre-determined variables), as $L_{Y,t}$ and $C_t$ contained in them can be chosen at any level. In addition, $\omega_t$ is a state variable (predetermined variable) because the $K_t$ and $A_t$ contained in it are stock variables based on past accumulation and cannot be selected at any level.

### 2.3.1 Dynamic System

In Appendix A.4, the above results are used to construct a three-dimensional dynamic system as follows[4]:

$$\frac{\dot{y}_t}{y_t} = \frac{1-\alpha}{\alpha}\left(\alpha\delta y_t^{\frac{1}{1-\alpha}}\omega_t - \alpha^2 y_t\right), \tag{2.20}$$

$$\frac{\dot{z}_t}{z_t} = z_t - \left(1-\alpha^2\right)y_t - \rho, \tag{2.21}$$

$$\frac{\dot{\omega}_t}{\omega_t} = y_t - z_t - \delta\left(L - y_t^{\frac{1}{1-\alpha}}\omega_t\right). \tag{2.22}$$

[4] This publication does not provide an account of the mathematical properties of dynamic systems. For a detailed explanation, see the appendix to Barro and Sala-i-Martin (2004).

Under static equilibrium, in every period, the optimising behaviour of economic agents is adjusted for supply and demand in their respective markets. Under dynamic equilibrium, the net increase in consumption, capital, variety and output is determined from the current period to the next period. Here, $\omega_t \equiv K_t/A_t$ is the state variable and the number of physical capital and varieties at present is predetermined. Hence, this economy starts from an initial point in time at $t = 0$ in a balanced growth path (BGP) equilibrium, $g = \dot{C}_t/C_t = \dot{K}_t/K_t = \dot{A}_t/A_t = \dot{Y}_t/Y_t$ is established, hence, $\dot{y}_t = \dot{z}_t = \dot{\omega}_t = 0$. A state in which the jump and state variables constituting the dynamic system remain constant and unchanged over time is called a 'steady state' and the variables are marked with an asterisk. From (2.20)–(2.22), the steady state can be derived as follows:

$$y^* = \frac{\rho+\delta L}{\alpha(1+\alpha)},\; z^* = \left(1-\alpha^2\right)y^* + \rho,\; \omega^* = \frac{\alpha}{\delta}\left(\frac{1}{y^*}\right)^{\frac{\alpha}{1-\alpha}}, \tag{2.23}$$

where the steady-state value depends on the preference parameter in $\rho$, the technology parameters in $\alpha$ and $\delta$ and the population parameter in $L$.

Using this steady-state value, we can derive the variables in the equilibrium. From $L_{Y,t} = y_t^{\frac{1}{1-\alpha}}\omega_t$ and (2.18), the amount of labour in equilibrium is as follows:

$$L_Y^* = \frac{\rho+\delta L}{\delta(1+\alpha)},\; L_A^* = L - \frac{\rho+\delta L}{\delta(1+\alpha)}, \tag{2.24}$$

which are used to derive the following economic growth:

$$g^* = \frac{\alpha\delta L-\rho}{(1+\alpha)}, \tag{2.25}$$

for $\alpha\delta L > \rho$. Unlike the Solow model, the variety expansion model depends on parameters related to preferences, technology and population. Hence, policy parameters influence the economic growth rate. Here, $dg^*/d\rho = -1/(1+\alpha) < 0$ implies that a reduction in the subjective discount rate leads to economic growth through capital accumulation, as households become more willing to save as they are more concerned about consumption by future generations, leading to growth. Furthermore, $dg^*/dL = \alpha\delta/(1+\alpha) > 0$ implies that the economic growth rate increases as the number of workers employed in the R&D sector increases due to population growth. This effect is called the 'scale effect'.[5]

In addition, from $r_t = \alpha^2 y_t$ and $w_t/K_t = (1-\alpha)\left(y_t/L_{Y,t}\right)$, the real interest rate and wage rate per capital in equilibrium are obtained:

$$r^* = \frac{\alpha(\rho+\delta L)}{1+\alpha},\; \left(\frac{w}{K}\right)^* = \frac{\delta(1-\alpha)}{\alpha}, \tag{2.26}$$

---

[5] Jones (1995) argued that the scale effect is not supported empirically. Hence, an endogenous growth model was developed that did not include scale effects. This model is called the 'semi-endogenous growth model' and representative early studies include Dinopoulos and Thompson (1998), Peretto (1998), Young (1998) and Howitt (1999). Kruse-Andersen (2023) showed that scale effects were still not empirically supported. See Herzer (2022) for research trends on scale effects.

which are used to derive the following profit and intermediate good price in a steady state:

$$p^* = \frac{\rho+\delta}{1+\alpha}, \; \pi^* = \frac{\rho+\delta L}{\delta(1+\alpha)}. \tag{2.27}$$

By solving the dynamic system in (2.20)–(2.23) directly concerning the steady-state values, (2.23)–(2.27) can be derived. Another approach is to derive the consumption growth rate in (2.8) and the variety growth rate in (2.16), with the real interest rate as a variable. From the two growth rates, the interest rate and growth rate at steady state can be derived. As in Appendix A.5, the consumption and variety growth rates are derived, respectively, as follows:

$$g_C \equiv \frac{\dot{C}_t}{C_t} = r_t - \rho, \; g_A \equiv \frac{\dot{A}_t}{A_t} = \delta L - \frac{r_t}{\alpha},$$

where solving for the interest rate as $g^* = g_C^* = g_A^*$ yields (2.26) and substituting the interest rate into this growth rate yields (2.25). The derivation of equilibrium and the comparative statics analysis of environmental policy in Chap. 6 is proved along this approach.

Equation (2.23)–(2.27) assume that the economy has reached a steady state. However, there is no guarantee that an economy starting from an initial point in time will reach a steady state. To confirm this, it is necessary to analyse the stability of the dynamic system locally in the vicinity of the steady state. When the dynamic system in (2.20)–(2.22) has one stable root and two unstable roots, the initial value of this dynamic system is uniquely determined as determinacy. The stability analysis by Arnold (2000) showed that the equilibrium in the dynamic system in (2.20)–(2.22) was uniquely determined and the system converged from the initial point to a steady state.

## 2.4 Lab-Equipment Model

Although the variety expansion model is an excellent economic model, its analysis is complex because it is a three-dimensional dynamic system. Hence, River-Batiz and Romer (1991) developed a simplified R&D-based growth model. Two main changes were made. First, intermediate goods were produced from final goods rather than capital. Second, blueprints for new varieties were produced from final goods rather than labour. This economic model is called the 'lab-equipment model', as automated laboratories, rather than researchers, develop new varieties. Figure 2.2 illustrates the economic structure of this economic model.

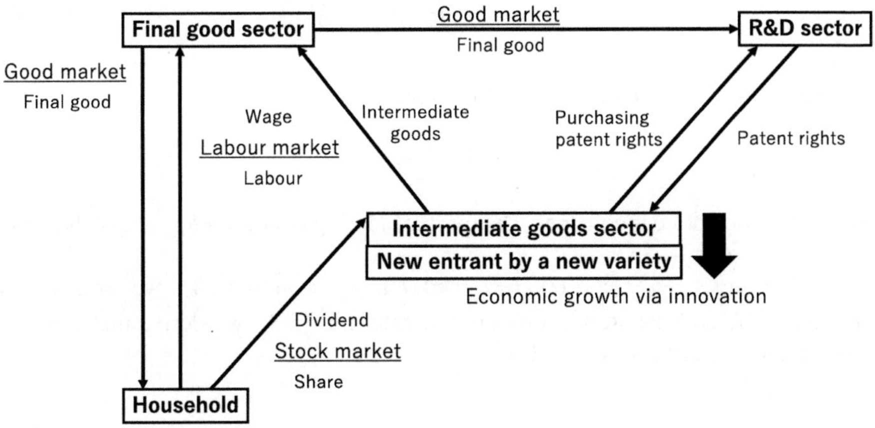


**Fig. 2.2** Structure of lab-equipment model

### 2.4.1 Intermediate Good Sector

Intermediate goods firms produce one unit of intermediate goods by inputting one unit of final goods. Since the final good is numeraier, its price is standardised to 1. Therefore, the profit maximisation problem for this intermediate goods firm is as follows:

$$\pi_{j,t} = p_{j,t}x_{j,t} - x_{j,t}, \text{ s.t. } p_{j,t} = \alpha\left(\frac{L_{Y,t}}{x_{j,t}}\right)^{1-\alpha}, \tag{2.28}$$

for $j = 1,2, \cdots, A_t$. Since the R&D sector does not employ workers, the market clearing condition for the labour market is $L_{Y,t} = L$. The first-order condition for profit maximisation yields as follows:

$$p = \tfrac{1}{\alpha}, \tag{2.29}$$

where the intermediate goods price is independent of the real interest rate and takes a constant value. Substituting (2.12) for (2.29) and $L_{Y,t} = L$, we obtain $x = \alpha^{\frac{2}{1-\alpha}}L$. Substituting this intermediate goods output into the $\pi_t$ in (2.28), we obtain $\pi = (1-\alpha)\alpha^{\frac{1+\alpha}{1-\alpha}}L$.

### 2.4.2 R&D Sector

The R&D firm develops a blueprint for a new variety of a unit of final good by inputting a $\upsilon$ unit of final good. The profit function of an R&D firm is as follows:

$$\max_{\dot{A}_t} \pi_t^A = P_{A,t}\dot{A}_t - \upsilon \dot{A}_t,$$

and the zero-utility condition of profit maximisation yields:

$$P_A = \upsilon,$$

where the stock price is constant. The market clearing condition for the goods market is $Y_t = C_t + A_t x_t + \upsilon \dot{A}_t$.

Substituting $\pi = (1-\alpha)\alpha^{\frac{1+\alpha}{1-\alpha}} L$ and $P_A = \upsilon$ into (2.4), we obtain $r = (1-\alpha)\alpha^{\frac{1+\alpha}{1-\alpha}} L/\upsilon$. Substituting this interest rate into (2.8), we derive the economic growth rate in equilibrium as follows:

$$g = \frac{(1-\alpha)\alpha^{\frac{1+\alpha}{1-\alpha}} L}{\upsilon} - \rho, \tag{2.30}$$

where, in the R&D-based growth model with pollution emissions, the environmental policy's impact on the economic growth rate differs between the variety expansion model and the lab-equipment model. This is discussed in Chap. 6.

## References


Arnold, L. G. (2000). Stability of the market equilibrium in Romer's model of endogenous technological change: A complete characterization. *Journal of Macroeconomics*, 22(1), 69-84. https://doi.org/10.1016/S0164-0704(00)00123-3

Barro, R., & Sala-i-Martin, X. (2004). Economic growth second edition. Massachusetts Institute of Technology.

Chiang, A. C. (1992). Elements of dynamic optimization. McGraw-Hill.

Dinopoulos, E., & Thompson, P. (1998). Schumpeterian growth without scale effects. *Journal of Economic Growth*, 3(4), 313-335. https://doi.org/10.1023/A:1009711822294

Futagami, K. (2012). Dynamic macroeconomic theory (Dougaku Makuro Keizaigaku : Seichou Riron No Haxtuten). Nihon Hyouron Sya, *In Japanese.*

Herzer, D. (2022). Semi-endogenous versus Schumpeterian growth models: a critical review of the literature and new evidence. *Review of Economics*, 73(1), 1-55. https://doi.org/10.1515/roe-2021-0023

Howitt, P. (1999). Steady endogenous growth with population and R. & D. inputs growing. *Journal of Political Economy*, 107(4), 715–730. https://doi.org/10.1086/250076

Jones, C. I. (1995). R & D-based models of economic growth. *Journal of Political Economy*, 103(4), 759-784. https://doi.org/10.1086/262002

Jones, C. I. (2019). Paul Romer: Ideas, nonrivalry, and endogenous growth. *The Scandinavian Journal of Economics*, 121(3), 859-883. https://doi.org/10.1111/sjoe.12370

Kruse-Andersen, P. K. (2023). Testing R&D-Based Endogenous Growth Models. *Oxford Bulletin of Economics and Statistics*, 85(5), 1083-1110. https://doi.org/10.1111/obes.12552

Peretto, P. F. (1998). Technological change, market rivalry, and the evolution of the capitalist engine of growth. *Journal of Economic Growth*, 3(1), 53-80. https://doi.org/10.1023/A:1009722031825

Rivera-Batiz, L. A., & Romer, P. M. (1991). Economic integration and endogenous growth. *The Quarterly Journal of Economics*, 106(2), 531-555. https://doi.org/10.2307/2937946

Romer, P. M. (1990). Endogenous technological change. *Journal of Political Economy*, 98(5, Part 2), S71-S102. https://doi.org/10.1086/261725
Young, A. (1998). Growth without scale effects. *Journal of Political Economy*, 106(1), 41-63. https://doi.org/10.1086/250002

# Chapter 3
# Endogenous Technological Change II

**Abstract** The variety expansion model is complex to analyse because it includes physical capital. Grossman and Helpman (1991, Chap. 3) showed that economic growth can be achieved by expanding variety and introducing preferences for a variety of goods instead of omitting physical capital. The economy consists of households, the goods sector and the R&D sector. New varieties developed by R&D firms are purchased by entrepreneurs to enter the goods market. The monopoly profit is distributed to households that provide R&D funds as dividends. The increase in production associated with the expansion of varieties leads to economic growth. Households have a preference for variety, however, the elasticity between varieties is constant. Under a fixed expenditure, in each period, the consumption quantity that maximises utility is selected and the demand function is derived. Under intertemporal budget constraints, the expenditure that maximises lifetime utility is selected and the Euler equation is derived. In addition to the scale effect, the degree of product differentiation decreases due to a decrease in the elasticity of substitution, hence, the economy grows.

## 3.1 Structure of Variety Expansion Model with Preferences for a Variety

The variety expansion model developed by Romer (1990) includes physical capital, which makes the dynamic system three-dimensional. When this R&D-based growth model is applied to international and political economies, the analysis becomes complex and it is difficult to obtain clear results. However, the R&D-based growth model developed by Grossman and Helpman (1991, Chap. 3) was improved as, instead of discarding physical capital, households preferred a variety of goods. The dynamic system in this model is one-dimensional, which makes it easier to analyse and simpler to prove the mechanisms through which environmental taxes and emission allowances reduce pollution and generate economic growth. Therefore, results can be obtained for international and political economies. This chapter describes the basic mechanisms based on this economic model.

 
Y. Hamaguchi, *Sustainable Development in Economic Growth Theory*,
https://doi.org/10.1007/978-981-96-7639-2_3

## 3.2 The Model

In this economy, there are households, goods firms and R&D firms. Goods firms produce goods by investing labour and sell them to households. Goods firms, in a state of monopolistic competition, hold perpetual patents for their varieties, hence, they earn monopoly profits through mark-ups. With this profit, the entrepreneur raises funds for R&D by selling shares to the household and buys the blueprints for the new variety from the R&D firm. The R&D firm develops the blueprints for the new variety by investing labour. The entrepreneur applies for a patent and enters the goods market under monopolistic competition, earning a positive profit. This profit is distributed to the household as dividends. By using labour and dividend incomes, the household consumes goods and perceives positive utility. This household obtains positive utility from the amount of consumption of each good and the increase in the number of varieties. The increase rate in the number of varieties is the economic growth rate. This economic structure is presented in Fig. 3.1. The model description in this chapter is based on Latzer et al. (2019).

### *3.2.1 Household*

The household utility function has the following intertemporal utility function:

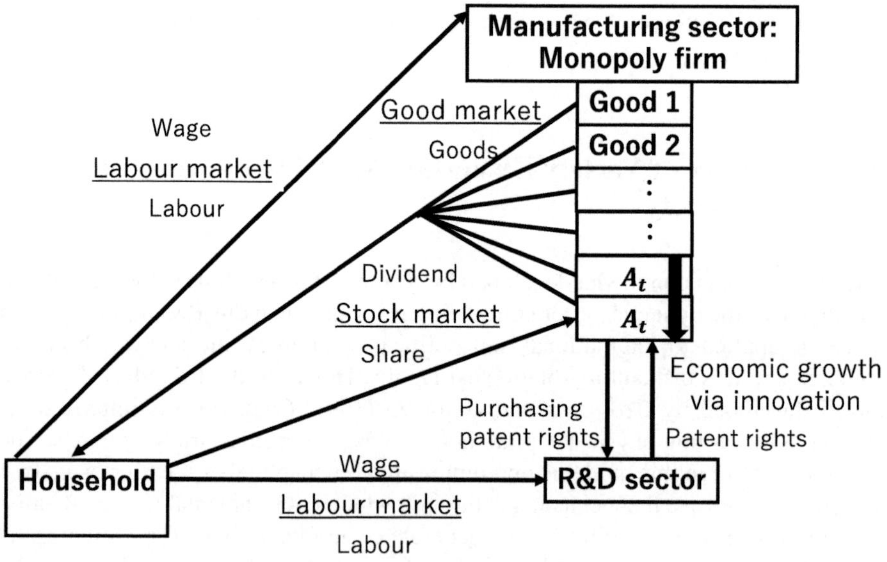


**Fig. 3.1** Structure of the variety expansion model with preferences for variety

$$U_t = \int_0^\infty \log Q_t e^{-\rho t} dt, \tag{3.1}$$

where a logarithmic utility function is assumed for the simplicity of the analysis. Following Dixit and Stiglitz (1977), the composition of differentiated goods in $Q_t$ is expressed as a CES-type function as follows:

$$Q_t = \left( \int_0^{A_t} x_{j,t}^{\frac{\sigma-1}{\sigma}} dj \right)^{\frac{\sigma}{\sigma-1}}, \tag{3.2}$$

where the number of any variety is $j \in [0, A_t]$ and $\sigma > 1$ is the elasticity of substitution between any two varieties. Assuming symmetry between goods firms, under $x_t = x_{j,t}$, , (3.2) can be rewritten as $Q_t = A_t^{\frac{\sigma}{\sigma-1}} x_t$. Households derive more utility from variety than from goods consumption (Love of variety). Following Latzer et al. (2019), instead of (2), we express the composition of differentiated goods as follows:

$$Q_t = \int_0^{A_t} x_{j,t}^{\frac{\sigma-1}{\sigma}} dj, \tag{3.3}$$

which is further rewritten under $x_t = x_{j,t}$ as $Q_t = A_t x_t^{\frac{\sigma-1}{\sigma}}$. Households feel more utility from the amount of goods consumed than from the increase in variety. Whether the preference for differentiated goods is expressed as (3.2) or (3.3) affects the welfare level and the welfare effects of economic policy.

Suppose $Q_t$ in (3.2) is consumer goods produced by the input of $x_{j,t}$ elements. However, under the condition that $x_t = x_{j,t}$, the amount of labour input into the production of the final good is $L_{X,t} = A_t x_t$. Hence, the consumption good per unit of production factor becomes $Q_t / L_{X,t} = A_t^{\frac{1}{\sigma-1}}$ and the expansion of variety improves total factor productivity. Ethier (1982) called this benefit from increasing the degree of specialisation the 'return to specialisation'.

The household's expenditure is $E_t = \int_0^{A_t} p_{j,t} x_{j,t} dj$ and its assets are $W_t = P_{A,t} A_t$. From (2.3), the budget constraint of the household is $\dot{W}_t = r_t W_t + w_t L - E_t$. When the household has a preference for variety, the dynamic utility maximisation problem is solved in two stages. Please refer to Appendix B for the derivation process. In the static utility maximisation, given the expenditure, the household decides how much of each good to purchase and the following demand function is obtained:

$$x_{j,t} = \frac{p_{j,t}^{-\sigma}}{P_{M,t}^{1-\sigma}} E_t, \tag{3.4}$$

where the price index for differentiated goods is defined as follows:

$$P_{M,t} \equiv \left( \int_0^{A_t} p_{j,t}^{1-\sigma} dj \right)^{\frac{1}{1-\sigma}}. \tag{3.5}$$

By incorporating (3.2) into (3.1), with (3.4) substituted, we obtain the indirect utility function $Q_t = E_t/P_{M,t}$. With the household choosing the expenditure that maximises this indirect utility, under the budget constraint, the following Euler equation is obtained:

$$\frac{\dot{E}_t}{E_t} = r_t - \rho, \tag{3.6}$$

where $r_t = \rho$ holds when this expenditure is used as the numeraire. Alternatively, the wage rate can be used as the numeraire. In this case, if we consider an agricultural firm that is in perfect competition and produces agricultural goods by inputting labour, it obtains a certain amount of expenditure from the price of agricultural goods, which is equal to the wage rate. In this case, $r_t = \rho$ holds. For more information on this point, please refer to Chap. 9.

### 3.2.2 Manufacturing Sector

Firms in this sector are in a monopolistic competition. When imitation is ruled out under an infinite patent period, each differentiated good is produced exclusively by its firm. Firms produce their differentiated goods using labour as the only production factor. The production technology is symmetric across firms and the production function is $q_{j,t} = L^X_{j,t}$. A firm that produces differentiated goods of variety $j$ determines the price that maximises its profit, given the demand for the good in (3.4), as follows:

$$\max_{p_{j,t}} \pi_{j,t} \equiv \left(p_{j,t} - w_t\right) q_{j,t}, \tag{3.7}$$

and the first-order condition for profit maximisation yields the following:

$$p_{j,t} = \frac{\sigma}{\sigma - 1} w_t, \tag{3.8}$$

where $\sigma/(\sigma - 1)$ is mark-up. The firm's pricing decision affects the demand for goods in (3.4) through the effect of the firm's price on $P_{M,t}$ in (3.5). However, when the market structure is of monopolistic competition, the effect of the firm's price can be ignored and the good's price in (3.8) is obtained. The RHS of (3.8) is common to all firms, hence, all firms are symmetric in equilibrium. Henceforth, the subscript $j$ is omitted unless necessary. Due to this symmetry, $q_{j,t} = q_t = x_t = x_{j,t}$, and $\pi_{j,t} = \pi_t$.

### 3.2.3 R&D Sector

A share is the right to receive the profits of a firm for an unlimited period. The profits are distributed to shareholders as dividends. If $P_{A,t}$ is the share price, it can be considered as the price of the patent for the good. This is because entrepreneurs use the profits from the sale of shares to purchase patents for new varieties.

The earnings received by shareholders are the dividends of $\pi_t$ and the capital gains of $\dot{P}_{A,t}$, while the earnings of the safe asset are $r_t$. Households decide where to invest by comparing the earnings of the risky asset (stock) and the safe asset. As explained in Chap. 2, the equilibrium condition of the capital market is as follows, based on the non-arbitrage condition:

$$\pi_t + \dot{P}_{A,t} = r_t P_{A,t}, \tag{3.9}$$

and share price is equal to the sum of the discounted present value of profits from period $t$ onwards:

$$P_{A,t} = \int_t^{\infty} e^{-[r(\iota)-r(t)]}\pi_\iota d\iota,$$

where deriving (3.9) by taking the time derivative of $P_{A,t}$ yields (3.9) as well.

R&D firms develop new varieties of goods by investing efficient units of labour in $F_t$. The production technology is represented as follows:

$$\dot{A}_t = L_{A,t}/F_t. \tag{3.10}$$

The profit of an R&D firm in perfect competition is $\pi_t^A = P_{A,t}\dot{A}_t - w_t L_{A,t}$. As explained in Chap. 2, the free entry condition gives $P_{A,t} = w_t F_t$.

### 3.2.4 Market

Household labour is supplied to firms in the goods and R&D sectors. The market clearing condition for the labour market is $L_{X,t} + L_{A,t} = L$, which can be rewritten as:

$$F_t\dot{A}_t + A_t x_t = L, \tag{3.11}$$

The market clearing condition for the asset market is (3.9) and for the goods market is $A_t q_t = A_t x_t$.

## 3.3 Equilibrium

### 3.3.1 Dynamic System

This book focuses on comparative static analysis in the steady state and does not cover transitional dynamics or comparative dynamic analysis. For transitional dynamics and stability analysis in the present model, see Grossman and Helpman (1991, Chap. 3).

The BGP in the present model is an equilibrium path that satisfies two conditions. First, there is a constant, positive economic growth rate, $g_t = \dot{A}_t/A_t > 0$. Second, the labour allocation between the goods firms and the R&D firms is constant, $L_{X,t} = L_X$ and $L_{A,t} = L_A$. Assuming $F_t = F/A_t$, the positive knowledge spillover from past R&D activities reduces the fixed R&D cost. Hence, (3.10) is rewritten as $L_A = Fg$ and $P_{A,t} = w_t F_t$ becomes $P_{A,t} = w_t F/A_t$. We define expenditure per wage rate as $\varepsilon_t = E_t/w_t$ and construct the law of motion for $\varepsilon_t$.

First, $E_t = \int_0^{A_t} p_{j,t}x_{j,t}dj$ is rewritten as $E_t = p_t x_t A_t$. By combining this expenditure with (3.7) and (3.8), we derive the dividend per unit expenditure as follows:

$$\frac{A_t\pi_t}{E_t} = \frac{(p_t - w_t)A_t x_t}{p_t A_t x_t} = \frac{p_t - w_t}{p_t} = \frac{1}{\sigma}, \tag{3.12}$$

and wage income in the goods sector per unit of expenditure as follows:

$$\frac{w_t L_{X,t}}{E_t} = 1 - \frac{1}{\sigma}, \tag{3.13}$$

where $A_t\pi_t + w_t L_{X,t} = E_t$ holds. Here, by using (3.8), $L_A = Fg$ and $E_t = p_t x_t A_t$, we rewrite (3.11) to obtain $Fg_t + [1 - (1/\sigma)]\varepsilon_t = L$.

Substituting (3.9) into $r_t$ in (3.6) yields the following:

$$\frac{\dot{E}_t}{E_t} = \frac{\pi_t + \dot{P}_{A,t}}{P_{A,t}} - \rho,$$

which is rewritten with (3.12) and $P_{A,t} = w_t F/A_t$ as follows:

$$\frac{\dot{E}_t}{E_t} = \frac{\dot{w}_t}{w_t} - g_t + \frac{1}{\sigma F}\cdot\frac{E_t}{w_t} - \rho,$$

which is further rewritten with $\varepsilon_t = E_t/w_t$ and $Fg_t + [1 - (1/\sigma)]\varepsilon_t = L$ as follows:

$$\frac{\dot{\varepsilon}_t}{\varepsilon_t} = \frac{\varepsilon_t}{F} - \frac{L + \rho F}{F}, \tag{3.14}$$

which is the law of motion for $\varepsilon_t$. $\varepsilon^* = L + \rho F$ holds in the steady state at $\dot{\varepsilon}_t = 0$.

### 3.3.2 Steady State

In (3.14), since $\dot{\varepsilon}_t > 0$ when $\varepsilon_t > \varepsilon^*$ or $\dot{\varepsilon}_t < 0$ when $\varepsilon_t < \varepsilon^*$, this economy diverges from the steady state. Therefore, at any time, this economy jumps to $\varepsilon_t = \varepsilon^*$ and $\dot{\varepsilon}_t = 0$. The equilibrium of this dynamic system is deterministic and stable.

Organising (3.13) with $\varepsilon_t = E_t/w_t$ yields $L_X^*$. Substituting this $L_X^*$ for $L_X^* + L_R^* = L$ in (3.11), we obtain $L_A^*$. Substituting $L_{A,t} = Fg_t$ into $L_A^* + L_X^* = L$ in (3.11) and rearranging, we obtain $g^*$. Each economic variable in a steady state is expressed as follows:

$$L_X^* = \left(1 - \tfrac{1}{\sigma}\right)\varepsilon^*,\ L_R^* = L - \left(1 - \tfrac{1}{\sigma}\right)\varepsilon^*,\ g^* = \tfrac{1}{F}\left[L - \left(1 - \tfrac{1}{\sigma}\right)\varepsilon^*\right], \tag{3.15}$$

where $L_R^* > 0$ and $g^* > 0$ hold under $\sigma/\sigma - 1 > (L + \rho F)/L$.

## 3.4 Growth Effect

When we analyse the impact of economic structure changes, such as household preferences and firm technology, on economic growth, we find that the higher the labour force, the more patient households are and the lower the substitutability of differentiated goods, the higher the economic growth rate. Differentiating $g^*$ in (15) concerning $L$ yields $dg^*/dL = 1/\sigma F > 0$. This growth-enhancing effect implies a scale effect. An increase in the working population expands production in the goods and R&D sectors, increases labour income and raises expenditure per wage.

Differentiating $g^*$ in (3.15) concerning $F$ gives $dg^*/dF = -L/\sigma F^2 < 0$. As shown in (3.10), an increase in fixed R&D costs stagnates R&D activities and lowers the economic growth rate. Since labour moves from the R&D sector to the goods sector, production of goods expands and household expenditure increases.

Differentiating $g^*$ in (3.15) concerning $\rho$ gives $dg^*/d\rho = -(\sigma - 1)/\sigma < 0$. Due to the rise in the subjective discount rate, the interest rate rises from $r_t = \rho$. Households substitute investment in risky assets (stocks) with safe assets. As R&D investment declines, economic growth falls. Since labour moves from the R&D sector to the goods sector, production of differentiated goods and household expenditure increases.

Differentiating $g^*$ in (15) concerning $\sigma$ gives $dg^*/d\sigma = -\varepsilon^*/\sigma^2 F < 0$. The degree of product differentiation increases as the elasticity of substitution increases. Hence, mark-ups decrease and the price of goods falls. The goods firm tries to make up for the decline in sales due to the fall in prices by expanding production. The economic growth rate declines because labour moves from the R&D firm to the goods firm. In (3.12) and (3.13), the increase in labour income is offset by the decrease in dividend income, hence, the elasticity of substitution has no effect on expenditure.

## References

Dixit, A. K., & Stiglitz, J. E. (1977). Monopolistic competition and optimum product diversity. *The American Economic Review*, 67(3), 297–308. https://www.jstor.org/stable/1831401

Ethier, W. J. (1982). National and international returns to scale in the modern theory of international trade. *The American Economic Review*, 72(3), 389–405. https://www.jstor.org/stable/1831539

Grossman, G. M., & Helpman, E. (1991). Innovation and growth in the global economy. MIT press.

Latzer, H., Matsuyama, K., & Parenti, M. (2019). Reconsidering the market size effect in innovation and growth. *Global Poverty Research Lab Working Paper*, (19–106). https://doi.org/10.2139/ssrn.3513610

Romer, P. M. (1990). Endogenous technological change. *Journal of Political Economy*, 98(5, Part 2), S71-S102. https://doi.org/10.1086/261725

# Chapter 4
# Basic Mechanism of Sustainable Development

**Abstract** In this chapter, the variety expansion model is extended to include pollution emitted from the production of goods. To internalise this negative externality, the government introduces environmental tax and emissions trading for goods firms. The environmental tax is passed on to the price, hence, demand for goods decreases. Goods firms reduce production, therefore, pollution is reduced. Labour moves from goods to the R&D sector, hence, varieties are developed and the economy grows. While consumption reduction caused by production contraction worsens welfare, consumption expansion and pollution reduction caused by economic growth improves welfare. Therefore, environmental taxes have a U-shaped welfare effect. The reduction in emission quotas leads to economic growth due to labour transfer from goods to the R&D sector, as emission allowances are passed on to prices. Furthermore, since the emission allowances allocated for free are potential rents, profit increases from rents stimulate incentives for developing variety, leading to economic growth. This is the distribution effect. Since the emission allowances cap production, the economic growth rate depends on population, fixed costs, pollution removal productivity and emission allowances. The emission allowances have an inverted U-shaped welfare effect. Hence, the effects of environmental taxes and emission allowances on pollution and growth are equivalent.

## 4.1 Introduction

As explained in Chap. 1, various R&D-based growth models have elucidated the sustainable development mechanism, which is the simultaneous achievement of pollution reduction and economic growth through environmental policies. However, by introducing pollution functions and environmental policies into the variety expansion model, which includes preferences for the variety of goods developed by Grossman and Helpman (1991, Chap. 3), a simple sustainable development mechanism can be shown. The simple model analysis and main results can be applied to Nash bargaining, industrial location and industrial structure. Hamaguchi (2020, 2021a, 2021b) implicitly applied this mechanism to environmental tax evasion and



Y. Hamaguchi, *Sustainable Development in Economic Growth Theory*,
https://doi.org/10.1007/978-981-96-7639-2_4

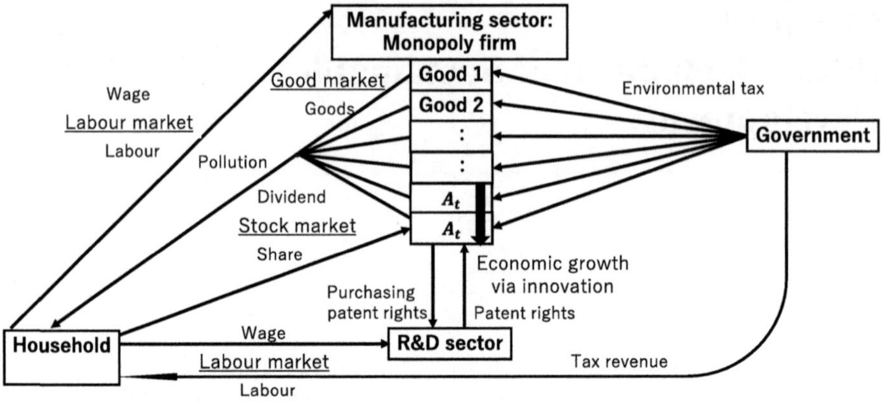


**Fig. 4.1** Structure of the variety expansion model with variety preferences and environmental tax

industrial location, however, did not explicitly explain it. In Hamaguchi (2024), this mechanism was recognised and led to its application to monetary policy and sustainable finance in the next chapter. Therefore, understanding the sustainable development mechanism in the variety expansion model, which includes preferences for varieties of goods, opens pathways to various applied studies.

Since the basic structure of the economic model is the same as in Chap. 3, only the changes are described here. Goods firms emit flow pollution during labour input. This pollution, as a negative externality, worsens household utility. To internalise this externality, the government introduces an environmental tax or opens an emissions trading market. Figure 4.1 illustrates this economic structure.

## 4.2 The Model

### 4.2.1 Household

Households have the following intertemporal utility functions:

$$U_t = \int_0^{\infty} (\log Q_t - \eta_P \log P_t) e^{-\rho t} dt\,, \tag{4.1}$$

where the utility function is assumed to be a logarithmic function. Following Latzer et al. (2019), the composition of differentiated goods in $Q_t$ is expressed as:

$$Q_t = \int_0^{A_t} x_{j,t}^{1-\frac{1}{\sigma}} dj\,, \tag{4.2}$$

where the number of any variety is $j \in [0, A_t]$. Total pollution emissions are defined as follows:

$$P_t = \int_0^{A_t} d_{j,t} dj \,, \tag{4.3}$$

where $d_{j,t}$ is the amount of pollution emitted by the goods-producing firm concerning variate $j$. Household expenditure on the good is $E_t = \int_0^{A_t} p_{j,t} x_{j,t} dj$ and the demand function for the good is (3.4). Constrained by the intertemporal budget of $\dot{W}_t = r_t W_t + w_t L + T_t - E_t$, households decide how much of the goods to consume and how much to save to maximise the utility level in (4.1). Hence, we obtain the Euler equation $\dot{E}_t / E_t = r_t - \rho$ in (3.6).

In the pollution emission function by Gradus and Smulder (1993), the endogenous pollution abatement good is changed to the exogenous pollution abatement productivity parameter $\theta_j$. Hence, the pollution emission function per firm is $d_{j,t} = q_{j,t}/\theta_j$. Since the production of one unit of good emits one unit of pollution, if pollution abatement productivity is improved by an exogenous amount of $\theta_j$, pollution emissions are reduced by the same amount. In this model, an increase in $\theta_j$ implies direct regulation in the form of improved pollution abatement technology. To simplify the analysis, we assume that the productivity is identical across firms, with $\theta_j = \theta$.

## 4.2.2 Goods and Innovation Sectors

A goods firm under monopolistic competition maximises its profits under the constraint of $d_{j,t}$, given the demand for goods. The profit maximisation problem for this firm is as follows:

$$\max_{p_{j,t}} \pi_{j,t} \equiv \left(p_{j,t} - w_t\right) q_{j,t} - \tau d_{j,t} = \left(p_{j,t} - w_t - \tfrac{\tau}{\theta}\right) q_{j,t}, \tag{4.4}$$

where $\tau$ is an environmental tax imposed by the government on the pollution emissions of goods firms, as in $T_t = \tau P_t$. The government distributes the environmental tax revenues to households as a lump-sum subsidy. From the first-order condition of profit maximisation, the following goods prices are obtained:

$$p_{j,t} = \tfrac{\sigma}{\sigma - 1}\left(w_t + \tfrac{\tau}{\theta}\right), \tag{4.5}$$

where $\sigma/(\sigma - 1)$ is the mark-up. Since the RHS of the goods price is common across firms, they are symmetric in equilibrium. Henceforth, the subscript $j$ is omitted unless necessary. By this symmetry, $q_{j,t} = x_{j,t} = x_t = q_t$, thus, $\pi_{j,t} = \pi_t$ holds. Combining the profit function of $\pi_t$ in (4.4) and $p_t x_t A_t = E_t$, the dividend income per expenditure can be expressed as follows:

$$\frac{A_t \pi_t}{E_t} = \frac{p_t - w_t - (\tau/\theta)}{p_t} = \frac{1}{\sigma}, \tag{4.6}$$

where the dividend income per expenditure is equal to the inverse elasticity of substitution. Rewriting (4.6) with $L_{X,t} = A_t x_t$ and $p_t x_t A_t = E_t$ yields the following:

$$\left(w_t + \frac{\tau}{\theta}\right)\frac{L_{Xt}}{E_t} = 1 - \frac{1}{\sigma}, \tag{4.7}$$

where the wage income per expenditure is equal to the inverse mark-up. From (4.4) and (4.5), the gain per unit of goods is obtained as follows:

$$\frac{\pi_t}{x_t} = \frac{1}{\sigma - 1}\left(w_t + \frac{\tau}{\theta}\right),$$

where environmental tax increases increase the profit per unit of goods, as goods firms pass on the tax burden to their prices.

The production technology and behaviour of R&D firms are the same as in Chap. 3. The non-arbitrage condition is $\left(\pi_t + \dot{P}_{A,t}\right)/P_{A,t} = r_t$ in (3.9) and the free entry condition is $P_{A,t} = w_t F_t$.

### 4.2.3 Market and Welfare

The market clearing conditions are the same as in Chap. 3. For the goods market, $Q_t = A_t q_t = A_t x_t$ and, for the labour market, $L = L_{A,t} + L_{X,t} = F_t \dot{A}_t + A_t x_t$ in (3.11). Total pollution emissions depend on the labour input of the goods firm as $P_t = L_{X,t}/\theta$. Substituting $L_{X,t} = A_t x_t$ into (4.2), we obtain $Q_t = A_t^{1/\sigma} L_{X,t}^{-[(1/\sigma)-1]}$. Substituting $P_t$ and $Q_t$ into (4.1) and rearranging them, we obtain the following welfare:

$$U = \left(1 - \frac{1}{\sigma}\right)\frac{\log L_X}{\rho} + \left[\left(\frac{1}{\sigma} - \theta\right)\frac{L - L_X}{\rho^2 F} + \frac{A_0}{\sigma\rho}\right]$$
$$+ \left[\frac{\eta}{\rho}(\log\theta - \log L_X) - \theta\frac{A_0}{\rho}\right],$$

which consists of three components. The first term on the RHS is welfare improvement due to increased goods consumption. The second term is welfare improvement due to an increase in the number of varieties. The third term is welfare improvement due to pollution abatement.

By rewriting this welfare, we obtain the following:

$$U = \left[\left(1 - \frac{1}{\sigma}\right) - \eta_P\right]\frac{\log L_X}{\rho} + \left(\frac{1}{\sigma} - \theta\right)\frac{L - L_X}{\rho^2 F}$$
$$+ \frac{\eta_P}{\rho}\log\theta + \left(\frac{1}{\sigma} - \theta\right)\frac{A_0}{\rho}, \tag{4.8}$$

where $t = 1$ and $(1 - 1/\sigma) > \eta_P$ are assumed. When goods firms reduce labour input, welfare improves because pollution emissions are reduced. However, under $(1 - 1/\sigma) > \eta_P$, welfare deterioration due to reduced goods consumption outweighs the improvement. Hence, a reduction in labour input worsens welfare. Since R&D firms can increase labour input, the number of varieties expands and welfare improves. However, as the number of varieties expands, goods production increases, which increases pollution emissions and worsens welfare. Which effect is relatively larger depends on the parameter conditions of $1/\sigma \gtreqless \theta$. Hence, environmental policies affect welfare through these factors.

## 4.3 Equilibrium

### 4.3.1 *Steady State*

Assuming $F_t = F/A_t$, we obtain $L_{R,t} = F_t\dot{A}_t = Fg_t$. In BGP equilibrium, $g_t = \dot{A}_t/A_t = -\dot{P}_{A,t}/P_{A,t}$ holds, where the growth rate of the new variety is considered as the economic growth rate. We define expenditure per wage rate as $\varepsilon_t \equiv E_t/w_t$ and construct a dynamic system for the $\varepsilon_t$. Note that this $\varepsilon_t$ is a jump variable.

From the Euler equation in (3.6) and the non-arbitrage condition in (3.9), we obtain $\dot{E}_t/E_t = (\pi_t + \dot{P}_{A,t})/P_{A,t} - \rho$. Time differentiation of the free entry condition in $P_{A,t} = w_tF/A_t$ yields $\dot{P}_{A,t}/P_{A,t} = \dot{w}_t/w_t - \dot{A}_t/A_t$. Combining these two equations and organising them using the free entry condition in $P_{A,t} = w_tF/A_t$ and (4.6), we claim the following:

$$\frac{\dot{E}_t}{E_t} = \frac{\dot{w}_t}{w_t} - g_t + \frac{1}{\sigma F}\left(\frac{E_t}{w_t}\right) - \rho,$$

which is rewritten as follows:

$$\frac{\dot{\varepsilon}_t}{\varepsilon_t} = \frac{\varepsilon_t}{\sigma F} - g_t - \rho\,, \tag{4.9}$$

which is used to derive the expenditure per wage rate $\varepsilon_t \equiv E_t/w_t$. By using (4.7), rewriting $L = F_t\dot{A}_t + A_tx_t$ in (3.11) yields the following:

$$L = Fg_t + \left[\frac{1-(1/\sigma)}{1+(\tau/\theta)}\right]\varepsilon_t\,, \tag{4.10}$$

where $w_t = 1$ holds because the wage rate is assumed to be numeraire.

The variety expansion model with preference for a variety of goods by Grossman and Helpman (1991, Chap. 3) yields the expenditure per wage rate in a steady state. Therefore, either the wage rate or household expenditure can be chosen as the numeraire. This choice depends on the analysis of the model and the research question. As the model in this chapter introduces environmental taxes and emission allowances, the wage rate is chosen as the numeraire to derive the BGP equilibrium.

By substituting $g_t$ in (4.10) for $g_t$ in (4.9), the law of motion in this economy can be expressed as:

$$\frac{\dot{\varepsilon}_t}{\varepsilon_t} = \frac{\varepsilon_t}{F}\left[\frac{1}{\sigma} - \frac{1-(1/\sigma)}{1+(\tau/\theta)}\right] - \rho - \frac{L}{F}, \tag{4.11}$$

for $1 + (\tau/\theta) > \sigma - 1$. Under $\dot{\varepsilon}_t > 0$ for $\varepsilon_t > \varepsilon^*$ or $\dot{\varepsilon}_t < 0$ for $\varepsilon_t < \varepsilon^*$, the economy diverges from the equilibrium in $\varepsilon_0 = \varepsilon^*$ and jumps to the equilibrium in $\varepsilon_t = \varepsilon^*$. This transition process is illustrated in Fig. 4.2.

Since $\dot{\varepsilon}_t = 0$ in the steady state, we obtain the following $\varepsilon^*$ in the BGP equilibrium from (4.11):

$$\varepsilon^* = \frac{L+\rho F}{\frac{1}{\sigma} - \frac{1-(1/\sigma)}{1+\tau/\theta}}, \tag{4.12}$$

which implies that an environmental tax increase lowers the $\varepsilon^*$ (See Appendix C). As shown in Appendix C, using this $\varepsilon^*$, the labour, total pollution emissions and economic growth rate of goods and R&D firms in BGP equilibrium can be derived as follows:

$$L_X^* = \frac{\varepsilon^*}{1+\tau/\theta}, L_R^* = L - L_X^*, g^* = \frac{L-L_X^*}{F}, P^* = \frac{L_X^*}{\theta}, \tag{4.13}$$

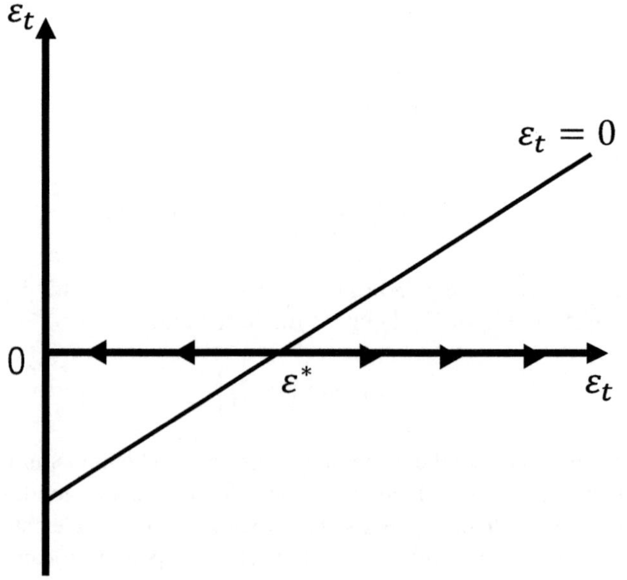


**Fig. 4.2** Transition process

where the expenditure per wage rate determines the amount of labour in goods firms, which further determines the amount of labour and pollution in R&D firms. In addition to its direct effects, environmental taxes indirectly affect the economy and the environment through $\varepsilon^*$.

### 4.3.2 Growth Effect of Environmental Tax

Environmental tax increases reduce expenditure per wage rate, reduce the amount of labour in goods firms and increase the amount of labour in R&D firms, resulting in sustainable development through economic growth and pollution reduction. For proof, see Appendix C. The intuition behind this is as follows.

In (4.5), goods firms pass on the tax burden to the price of the good. This price increase reduces the demand for goods, hence, the firms try to reduce production. As a result, total pollution emissions are reduced. In the labour market, full employment is achieved, as workers laid off from goods firms are employed in R&D firms. The blueprints for new varieties are developed to promote R&D activities. Here, as shown in $\pi/x = [1/(\sigma-1)](1+\tau/\theta)$, the profit per unit of goods increases due to price shift by goods firms. Entrepreneurs who see a positive profit raise R&D funds by selling shares to households. With this money, they purchase the blueprint and enter the goods market. The profits from production are distributed to households as dividends. Hence, higher environmental taxes increase the economic growth rate. However, the increase in the goods prices increases its purchasing cost, hence, households' expenditure per wage rate falls.

### 4.3.3 Welfare Effect of Environmental Tax

Environmental taxes bring about sustainable development through pollution reduction and economic growth. However, will this tax increase lead to a welfare improvement? Differentiating (4.8) concerning the environmental tax yields the following:

$$\frac{dU^*}{d\tau} = \left[\frac{\eta_P}{\rho L_X^*}\left(1-\frac{1}{\sigma}\right) - \frac{1}{\rho^2 F}\left(\frac{1}{\sigma}-\eta_P\right)\right]\underbrace{\frac{dL_X^*}{d\tau}}_{(-)} \gtreqless 0,$$

where the brackets on the RHS are rewritten as follows:

$$\tau \gtreqless \sigma\theta\left[\frac{(L+\rho F)(1/\sigma-\eta_P)}{\rho(1-1/\sigma)-\rho\eta_P} + \left(1-\frac{1}{\sigma}\right)\right] - \theta \equiv \hat{\tau}\,, \tag{4.14}$$

where $\hat{\tau}$ is a welfare-maximising environmental tax rate.

Economic growth through an environmental tax increase expands household consumption through an increase in the number of varieties. Hence, the policy leads to a welfare improvement. However, an increase in the number of varieties due to economic growth increases total pollution due to expanded production. Hence, the policy leads to a welfare deterioration. This is the dynamic welfare effect. Whether the welfare-improving effect dominates the welfare-worsening effect depends on the $1/\sigma \gtreqless \theta$ in (4.8).

If an environmental tax increase shifts labour from goods to R&D firms, it reduces production and leads to welfare deterioration due to lower consumption. However, a production decrease due to an environmental tax increase leads to a welfare improvement due to reduced pollution. This opposing effect is the static welfare effect. Under $(1 - 1/\sigma) > \eta_P$, the welfare worsening effect dominates the welfare improving effect. Therefore, the reduction in the workload of goods firms due to environmental taxes leads to welfare deterioration.

In summary, the relationship between environmental tax rates and welfare levels takes an inverse U-shape depending on whether positive dynamic welfare effects dominate positive static welfare effects and negative dynamic welfare effects. When the government sets a tax rate of $\hat{\tau}$, its welfare is maximised.

## 4.4 Emissions Permit Trade

### 4.4.1 *Firm and Steady State*

In this section, emissions trading is introduced instead of an environmental tax. Since the basic set-up and derivation are the same, only the areas where it differs are described. Figure 4.3 illustrates the economic structure in this case.

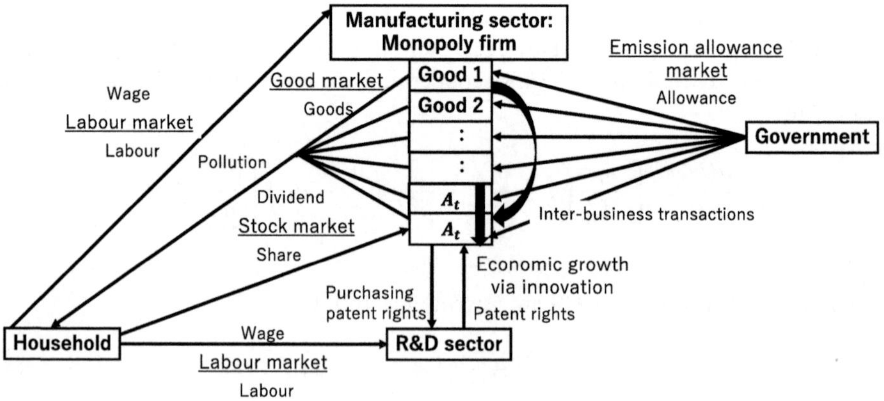


Fig. 4.3 Structure of the variety expansion model with variety preferences and emissions allowance

The government opens an emissions trading market to internalise the negative externalities. Each goods firm is allocated an emissions quota of $s_t$. This quota is the average of the total emission allowance and is the same across firms. Hence, $s_t = \overline{P}/A_t$, where $\overline{P}$ is the total emission allowance. As the number of goods firms increases with increasing variety, the emission allowance allocated per firm decreases.

In a perfectly competitive emissions trading market, firms are free to buy and sell emission allowances at a price of $p_t^e$. A firm that emits more pollution than its allocated emission allowance because of its relatively high labour input has to buy allowances from other firms for the missing $d_t - s_t > 0$. However, firms that emit less pollution than their allocated allowance because of their relatively high pollution abatement productivity can sell their surplus $s_t - d_t > 0$ to other firms. Hence, from $P_t = A_t d_t$ and $A_t s_t = \overline{P}$, this market must be cleared as $P_t = \overline{P}$.

The profit maximisation problem for goods firms is as follows:

$$\begin{aligned}\max_{p_{j,t}} \pi_{j,t} &\equiv \left(p_{j,t} - 1\right) q_{j,t} - p_t^e\left[d_{j,t} - s_t\right] \\ &= \left(p_{j,t} - 1 - \frac{p_t^e}{\theta}\right) x_{j,t} + p_t^e s_t,\end{aligned} \tag{4.15}$$

where $w_t = 1$ is assumed and $p_t^e s_t$ in the second term on the RHS is the allocation rent in Hamaguchi (2020). By selling allocated emission allowances, firms achieve increased profits (Smale et al. 2006) and higher stock prices (Martin et al. 2014; Oestreich and Tsiakas 2015). Here, $P_{A,t} = F/A_t$ in Chap. 3 implies that the stock price falls as the variety expands. In addition, $s_t = \overline{P}/A_t$ and $P_{A,t} = F/A_t$ are combined to obtain $P_{A,t} = \left(F/\overline{P}\right)s_t$. By differentiating this stock price over time, we obtain $\dot{P}_{A,t}/P_{A,t} = \dot{s}_t/s_t$. An increase in emission allowances per firm increases the stock price and generates capital gains. Hamaguchi (2020) was the first to point out that this increase in monopoly profits from quota rents stimulates innovation, leading to economic growth through environmental policy. This is called the distribution effect.

From the first-order condition of profit maximisation, the following goods prices are obtained:

$$p_{j,t} = \tfrac{\sigma}{\sigma-1}\left(1 + \tfrac{p_t^e}{\theta}\right), \tag{4.16}$$

where the subscript $j$ henceforth is omitted unless necessary as the equilibrium is symmetrical between firms. In the case of environmental taxes, dividend income per expenditure is derived as follows:

$$\tfrac{A_t \pi_t}{E_t} = \tfrac{1}{\sigma} + \tfrac{\sigma-1}{\sigma}\left(\tfrac{p_t^e}{1+p_t^e/\theta}\right)\tfrac{s_t}{q_t}, \tag{4.17}$$

where the second term on the RHS is the permit allocation rent. By using output per firm at $q_t = x_t$, average expenditure at $p_t x_t = E_t/A_t$ and labour at $L_{X,t} = A_t x_t$, the profit in (4.15) is rewritten as follows:

$$\frac{A_t \pi_t}{E_t} = 1 - \left(1 + \frac{p_t^e}{\theta}\right) \frac{L_{X,t}}{E_t} + \frac{p_t^e A_t s_t}{E_t}, \tag{4.18}$$

where the third term on the RHS is the permit allocation rent.

Substituting (4.18) into (4.17) and using $s_t = \overline{P}/A_t$ and $L_{X,t} = A_t x_t$, we obtain:

$$\frac{1}{\sigma} + \frac{\sigma - 1}{\sigma}\left[\frac{p_t^e}{1 + p_t^e/\theta}\right]\left(\frac{\overline{P}}{L_{X,t}}\right) = 1 - \left(1 + \frac{p_t^e}{\theta}\right)\frac{L_{X,t}}{E_t} + \frac{p_t^e \overline{P}}{E_t}, \tag{4.19}$$

which implies that the profits generated by goods firms are distributed to households as dividends. From (4.19), the equilibrium emission allowance price is derived. The market clearing condition for the emission allowances market is $p_t^e\left(P_t - \overline{P}\right) = 0$, in which $P_t = \overline{P} = L_{X,t}/\theta$ must hold. Hence, the amount of labour of the goods firm in the steady state is $L_X^* = \theta\overline{P}$, which depends on the emission allowance and pollution abatement productivity, instead of the technology or preference parameters. This is because the emission allowance caps the production of goods firms. By substituting $\varepsilon_t = E_t$ and $L_X^* = \theta\overline{P}$ into (4.19) and rearranging, we obtain the following:

$$\theta + p_t^e = \left(\frac{\sigma - 1}{\sigma\overline{P}}\right)\varepsilon_t, \tag{4.20}$$

where increased production of goods due to increased expenditure increases pollution. Hence, the demand for emission allowance rises, leading to higher emission allowance prices.

After substituting $\dot{P}_{A,t}/P_{A,t} = \dot{w}_t/w_t - \dot{A}_t/A_t$ for $\dot{E}_t/E_t = \left(\pi_t + \dot{P}_{A,t}\right)/P_{A,t} - \rho$, using the free entry condition in $P_{A,t} = w_t F/A_t$ and (4.17) to organise this equation, we obtain the following:

$$\frac{\dot{\varepsilon}_t}{\varepsilon_t} = \frac{\varepsilon_t}{\sigma F}\left[1 + (\sigma - 1)\frac{p_t^e}{\theta + p_t^e}\right] - g_t - \rho, \tag{4.21}$$

which uses $s_t = \overline{P}/A_t$, $q_t = L_{X,t}/A_t$ and $L_X^* = \theta\overline{P}$. From the labour market clearing condition at $L = Fg_t + \theta\overline{P}$, the economic growth rate in the BGP equilibrium is derived as:

$$g^* = \frac{L - \theta\overline{P}}{F}, \tag{4.22}$$

where, unlike environmental taxes, the economic growth rate depends only on population, fixed R&D costs, pollution abatement productivity and emission allowances. Population growth and lower fixed R&D costs increase labour in the R&D sector and improve productivity, leading to economic growth. Lower emission allowances and lower pollution abatement productivity lead to economic growth through labour transfer from the goods to the R&D sector, as it reduces goods production.

Substituting (4.22) into (4.21), we obtain the law of motion for the economy as

$$\frac{\dot{\varepsilon}_t}{\varepsilon_t} = \frac{1}{F}\left(\varepsilon_t - \theta\overline{P}\right) - \frac{L - \theta\overline{P}}{F} - \rho, \tag{4.23}$$

where, under $\dot{\varepsilon}_t > 0$ for $\varepsilon_t > \varepsilon^*$ or $\dot{\varepsilon}_t < 0$ for $\varepsilon_t < \varepsilon^*$, the economy diverges from equilibrium in $\varepsilon_0 = \varepsilon^*$ and jumps to equilibrium in $\varepsilon_t = \varepsilon^*$. Since $\dot{\varepsilon}_t = 0$ in the steady state, from (4.23) we obtain the steady-state value of expenditure per wage rate as:

$$\varepsilon^* = L + \rho F \, , \tag{4.24}$$

where emission allowances have no effect on $\varepsilon^*$. From (4.20) and (4.24), the emission allowance price in the BGP equilibrium is:

$$p^{e*} = \tfrac{\sigma - 1}{\sigma}\left(\tfrac{L+\rho F}{\overline{P}} - \theta\right) - \tfrac{\theta}{\sigma} \, , \tag{4.25}$$

where the permit price in equilibrium falls due to a decrease in allowances as in $dp^{e*}/d\overline{P} = -(\sigma - 1)(L + \rho F)/\sigma\overline{P}^2 < 0$.

Substituting $L_X^* = \theta\overline{P}$ for $Q_t = A_t^{1/\sigma} L_{X,t}^{-[(1/\sigma)-1]}$, we obtain $Q_t = A_t^{1/\sigma}\left(\theta\overline{P}\right)^{-[(1/\sigma)-1]}$. Substituting this $Q_t$ into (4.1) and rearranging it, we obtain the following welfare:

$$\begin{aligned} U = & \left(1 - \frac{1}{\sigma}\right)\frac{\log\theta\overline{P}}{\rho} + \frac{1}{\sigma}\left(\frac{L - \theta\overline{P}}{\rho^2 F} + \frac{A_0}{\rho}\right) \\ & - \frac{\eta_P}{\rho}\left[\log\overline{P} + \frac{L - \theta\overline{P}}{\rho F} + A_0\right], \end{aligned} \tag{4.26}$$

where this welfare consists of three components. The first term on the RHS is the welfare improvement due to increased goods consumption. The second term is welfare improvement due to an increase in the number of varieties. The third term is welfare deterioration due to pollution emissions. By rewriting this welfare, we obtain the following:

$$\begin{aligned} U = & \left[\left(1 - \frac{1}{\sigma}\right) - \eta_P\right]\frac{\log\theta\overline{P}}{\rho} + \left(\frac{1}{\sigma} - \eta_P\right)\frac{L - \theta\overline{P}}{\rho^2 F} \\ & + \frac{\eta_P}{\rho}\log\theta + \left(\frac{1}{\sigma} - \eta_P\right)\frac{A_0}{\rho}, \end{aligned} \tag{4.27}$$

where $t = 1$ and $(1 - 1/\sigma) > \eta_P$ are assumed. The effect of emission allowances on welfare through the three components is almost identical to that of environmental tax. However, the parameter condition that determines the effect of the expansion of the variety on welfare changes to $1/\sigma \gtreqless \eta_P$.

### 4.4.2 Growth Effect of Permit

Reducing emission allowances leads to sustainable development through economic growth and pollution reduction, as it reduces the workload of goods firms and increases the workload of R&D firms, without affecting expenditure per wage rate. The intuition behind this is as follows.

In (4.25), the reduction of emission allowances increases their demand, which increases the permit price. From (4.16), goods firms transfer this price increase to the goods price. The increase in the goods price lowers their demand, hence, goods firms reduce their labour input. Labour transfer from goods to R&D firms stimulates R&D activities and the development of blueprints for new varieties. In (4.17) and (4.18), higher permit prices increase the permit allocation rent and monopoly profits of goods firms. Entrepreneurs sell shares and enter the goods market through the purchase of blueprints, distributing their profits to households as dividends. The increase in stock prices due to the reduction of emission allowances results in capital gains for households, as shown in $P_{A,t} = \left(F/\overline{P}\right)s_t$. A reduction in emission allowances consequently increases the economic growth rate. However, due to general equilibrium effects, emission allowances do not affect households' expenditure per wage.

### 4.4.3 Welfare Effect of Permit

Emission allowances, like environmental taxes, lead to sustainable development. However, will this reduction in allowances lead to improved welfare? Differentiating (4.27) concerning the permit yields the following:

$$\frac{dU^*}{d\overline{P}} = \frac{(1-1/\sigma)-\eta_P}{\rho\overline{P}} - \frac{\theta}{\rho^2 F}\left(\frac{1}{\sigma}-\eta_P\right) \gtreqless 0,$$

where the RHS of this inequality is rewritten as follows:

$$\hat{P} \equiv \tfrac{\rho}{\theta}\left[\tfrac{(1-1/\sigma)-\eta_P}{(1/\sigma)-\eta_P}\right] \gtreqless P, \tag{4.28}$$

where $\hat{P}$ is the welfare-maximising emissions allowance.

Economic growth due to emission allowance reductions has a positive and a negative dynamic welfare effect through an increase in the number of varieties. Whether the welfare-improving effect dominates the welfare-deteriorating effect depends on the $1/\sigma \gtreqless \eta_P$ in (4.27).

Labour migration due to emission allowance reductions leads to welfare deterioration due to lower consumption. However, a production reduction due to emission allowance reductions leads to welfare improvement due to reduced pollution. This opposing effect is the static welfare effect. Under $(1-1/\sigma) > \eta_P$, the welfare worsening effect dominates the welfare improving effect. Therefore, a reduction in the workload of goods firms due to emission allowance reductions leads to welfare deterioration.

In summary, the relationship between the emission allowance and welfare levels is inverted U-shaped, depending on whether the positive dynamic welfare effect dominates the positive static and negative dynamic welfare effects. The welfare is maximised when the government sets a tax rate of $\hat{P}$.

### 4.4.4 Equivalence Between Environmental Taxes and Emission Allowances

Although environmental taxes and emission allowances are different policy instruments, economic variables, such as growth and welfare, remain the same regardless of policy. This point is confirmed in this section.

From (4.13) and $L_X^* = \theta \overline{P}$, the amount of labour of goods firms in environmental taxes and emission allowances is equal at the following emission allowance levels:

$$\overline{P} = \frac{L+\rho F}{\frac{\theta}{\sigma}(1+\frac{\tau}{\theta})-\theta(1-\frac{1}{\sigma})} \equiv \tilde{P}, \tag{4.29}$$

where $\tilde{P}$ is an emission allowance that equalises the quantity of labour of goods firms for environmental tax and emission allowance. From the market clearing condition of the labour market, $L_R^* = L - L_X^*$, therefore, the amount of labour in R&D firms is equal under both policies. Hence, the economic growth rates in (4.13) and (4.22) are identical. Furthermore, $L_X^*$, $L_R^*$, $g^*$ and $P^*$ are the same for both policies. Therefore, the welfare of (4.8) and (4.27) is equal.

In (4.25), if we set $\tau = p^{e*}$, we obtain the following:

$$\tau = \frac{\sigma-1}{\sigma}\left(\frac{L+\rho F}{\overline{P}} - \theta\right) - \frac{\theta}{\sigma}, \tag{4.30}$$

where, if the environmental tax is equal to the permit price and the allocation of emission allowances is abolished, with $\overline{P} = 0$ and $s_t = 0$, the environmental regulatory costs for goods firms are the same. Since the goods prices in (4.5) and (4.16) become equal, the profit functions in (4.4) and (4.15) are equal as well. Hence, the dividend income per expenditure in (4.6) and (4.17) equalises. Given the above results, the law of motion in (4.11) and (4.21) is identical and $\varepsilon^*$ in (4.12) and (4.24). Thus, the equivalence of environmental taxes and emission allowances is proven since the same equilibrium is reached, regardless of the policy instrument.

Since both policies produce the same result, the choice of policy instrument can be according to the analysis task. However, compared to environmental taxes, emission allowances cap the production of goods, which makes equilibrium and comparative statics analysis easier. Hence, they are suitable for application to international and political economy. Later chapters will deal with this applied research.

## References

Gradus, R., & Smulders, S. (1993). The trade-off between environmental care and long-term growth—pollution in three prototype growth models. Journal of Economics, 58(1), 25–51. https://doi.org/10.1007/BF01234800

Grossman, G. M., & Helpman, E. (1991). *Innovation and growth in the global economy*. MIT press.

Hamaguchi Y (2020) Dynamic analysis of bribery firms' environmental tax evasion in an emissions trading market. Journal of Macroeconomics 63. https://doi.org/10.1016/j.jmacro.2019.103169

Hamaguchi, Y. (2021a). Polluting firms' location choices and pollution havens in an R&D-based growth model for an international emissions trading market. *The Journal of International Trade & Economic Development*, 30(4), 625–642. https://doi.org/10.1080/09638199.2021.1889644

Hamaguchi, Y. (2021b). Does the trade of aviation emission permits lead to tourism-led growth and sustainable tourism?. *Transport Policy*, 105, 181–192. https://doi.org/10.1016/j.tranpol.2021.03.012

Hamaguchi Y (2024) Comparative study of environmental and monetary policies in an R&D-based growth model. Journal of Environmental Management 360. https://doi.org/10.1016/j.jenvman.2024.121199

Latzer, H., Matsuyama, K., & Parenti, M. (2019). Reconsidering the market size effect in innovation and growth. *Global Poverty Research Lab Working Paper*, (19–106). https://doi.org/10.2139/ssrn.3513610

Martin R, Muûls M, De Preux LB, Wagner UJ (2014) Industry compensation under relocation risk: A firm-level analysis of the EU emissions trading scheme. The American Economic Review 104(8):2482–2508. https://doi.org/10.1257/aer.104.8.2482

Oestreich AM, Tsiakas I (2015) Carbon emissions and stock returns: Evidence from the EU Emissions Trading Scheme. Journal of Banking & Finance 58:294–308. https://doi.org/10.1016/j.jbankfin.2015.05.005

Smale, R., Hartley, M., Hepburn, C., Ward, J., & Grubb, M. (2006). The impact of $CO_2$ emissions trading on firm profits and market prices. Climate Policy, 6(1), 31–48. https://doi.org/10.1080/14693062.2006.9685587

# Chapter 5
# Sustainable Finance

**Abstract** In Chap. 4, the variety expansion model with a preference for variety and pollution emissions is introduced, along with monetary policy through endogenous money supply and interest rate manipulation. Under the k% rule, the monetary authority supplies money to households and redistributes seigniorage income to them. Households subject to the cash-in-advance (CIA) constraint spend money on goods and lend it to R&D firms. R&D firms subject to the CIA constraint use the borrowed funds to pay researchers' wages. In an environmental tax, a reduction in the nominal interest rate increases the real money supply, as the Fisher effect causes deflation. Therefore, there is an increase in lending. As the demand for labour in the R&D sector rises, there is a labour shift from the goods to the R&D sector. As economic growth increases, pollution is reduced due to a decrease in production and sustainable development is achieved. This nominal interest rate has an inverted U-shaped effect on welfare, however, it inhibits the growth-enhancing effect of environmental taxes. Depending on the emission allowance level and the interest rate, there is a trade-off, win–win or lose-lose relationship between sustainable development and the development of financial markets.

## 5.1 Introduction

Sustainable finance and monetary policy are attracting attention as measures to promote decarbonisation (Drudi et al. 2021). However, there is an ongoing empirical debate about whether the development of financial markets leads to decontamination and decarbonisation. The development of financial markets leads to an increase in green total factor productivity, as it facilitates financing for decarbonisation technologies (Xie et al. 2021; Qian et al. 2022). However, this development leads to an increase in carbon dioxide ($CO_2$) emissions because it leads to the concentration of carbon-intensive firms through a decrease in borrowing costs (Maji et al. 2017; Sethi et al. 2020). Acheampong et al. (2020) argued that the effect of financial market development on $CO_2$ intensity depends on the degree of development.

 
Y. Hamaguchi, *Sustainable Development in Economic Growth Theory*,
https://doi.org/10.1007/978-981-96-7639-2_5

The R&D-based growth model, which includes money, was surveyed by Chu (2022). However, until recently, the relationship between pollution emissions and environmental policy had not been analysed. Afonso (2023) filled this gap and, in a variety expansion model with intermediate goods, showed that a reduction in the nominal interest rate led to deflation and economic growth, yet increased pollution emissions. Hence, there is a trade-off between pollution emissions and economic growth. This result is dependent on the wage effect, that is, the effect of the nominal interest rate on the wage rate changes labour mobility between sectors.

In the model presented in this chapter, the reduction in the nominal interest rate leads to sustainable development, in addition to deflation and economic growth, by reducing pollution emissions. As the wage rate is numeraire, this result does not depend on the wage effect, rather on labour mobility due to the reduction in borrowing costs. The effects of environmental taxes are analysed in this chapter, as in Afonso (2023), however, the effects of emission allowances are taken into account. This emissions trading has various relationships with sustainable development and the development of financial markets. This chapter complements Afonso (2023) and presents the basic relationships between growth, the environment and finance based on the R&D-based growth model and the various effects of financial environmental policies.

## 5.2 The Model

### *5.2.1 Structure of a Variety Expansion Model with Finance*

The financial economy structure is based on the model settings in Chu (2022) and Chu and Cozzi (2014). Monetary authorities supply money to households. Households under the cash-in-advance constraint (CIA) use the money for expenditure on goods and loans to the R&D sector. R&D firms borrow from households to pay wages to researchers. These firms are under the CIA constraint. The monetary authority's tool is to manipulate the nominal interest rate. This economic structure is summarised in Fig. 5.1. The economic model in this chapter is based on Hamaguchi (2024).

### *5.2.2 Household and Firm*

There is a utility function for households in (4.1), a differentiated goods composition in (4.2) and a total pollution emission function in (4.3). The ordinary demand function in (3.4) is obtained under expenditure on goods as $E_t = \int_0^{A_t} p_{j,t}x_{j,t}dj$. In this, the price index of differentiated goods is (3.5). We assume that pollution abatement technology is the same across firms. A firm in monopolistic competition maximises its profits

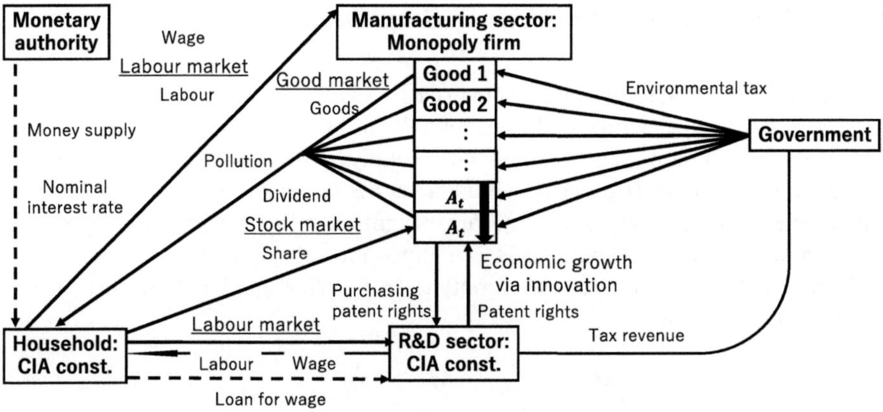


**Fig. 5.1** Structure of the R&D-based growth model with finance

by determining the price of the good, given the demand and accounting for pollution emissions, following the profit function in (4.4). The first-order condition for profit maximisation dictates the price of the good in (4.5). Moreover, dividend income per expenditure in (4.6) and wage income per expenditure in (4.7) are derived.

As in Chap. 3, the non-arbitrage condition in (3.9) holds in the capital market. The production technology of the R&D sector is (3.10). Following Chu and Cozzi (2014), R&D firms borrow money from households to pay wages. Hence, the profit function of the R&D firm is defined as follows:

$$\pi_t^A = P_{A,t}\dot{A}_t - w_t L_{A,t} - i_t o_A w_t L_{A,t},$$

where the third term on the RHS is the additional borrowing cost necessary for wage payment. Here, $o_A \in (0, 1)$ is the share of R&D expenditure in the CIA constraint. The higher the $o_A$, the higher the borrowing cost. By using $\dot{A}_t = L_{A,t}/F_t$ in (3.10), we can rewrite this profit function as follows:

$$\pi_t^A = \left[P_{A,t} - w_t F_t (1 + i_t o_A)\right]\dot{A}_t,$$

and, under the zero-profit condition, the free entry condition is as follows:

$$P_{A,t} = (1 + i_t o_A) w_t F_t, \tag{5.1}$$

where the price of patents rises due to the cost of borrowing. This is because R&D firms with negative profits exit the market, reducing the supply of blueprints for new varieties. The market clearing condition for the labour market is (3.11).

### 5.2.3 Intertemporal Problem of Household

The budget constraint for the household in Chap. 3 is $\dot{W}_t = r_t W_t + w_t L + T_t - E_t$. Since money supply brings income to the household, this budget constraint changes. When $M_t$ is the nominal money supply, the money supply by the monetary authority brings money holdings of $\dot{M}_t / P_{M,t}$. Households earn $i_t B_t$ in loan income from lending to R&D firms. The monetary authority earns seigniorage income from money supply, however, distributes it to households as a lump-sum subsidy of $H_t$.

Here, we define the real money supply as $m_t = M_t / P_{M,t}$. The time derivative of $m_t$ yields the following:

$$\dot{m}_t = \frac{\dot{M}_t}{P_{M,t}} - \frac{\dot{P}_{M,t}}{P_{M,t}} \cdot \frac{M_t}{P_{M,t}} = \frac{\dot{M}_t}{M_t} \cdot m_t - \Pi_t m_t,$$

where $\Pi_t$ is an inflation rate and $H_t = \dot{M}_t / P_{M,t} = \dot{m}_t + \Pi_t m_t$ holds. By using $H_t = \dot{m}_t + \Pi_t m_t$ and the non-arbitrage condition in (3.9), we can rewrite the budget constraint as follows:

$$\dot{W}_t + \dot{m}_t = r_t W_t + w_t L + i_t B_t - \Pi_t m_t + T_t + H_t - E_t, \tag{5.2}$$

where $\Pi_t m_t$ implies a decrease in the purchasing power of money due to inflation. Households are subject to the same CIA constraints as R&D firms:

$$B_t + o_H E_t \leq m_t, \tag{5.3}$$

where $o_H \in (0, 1)$ is the share of consumption expenditure in the CIA constraint. The more $o_H$ increases, the more money must be prepared in advance for expenditure.

The household determines its expenditure to maximise its utility in (4.1) under the constraints of (5.2) and (5.3). The first-order condition of this dynamic utility maximisation problem yields the following:

$$-\tfrac{\dot{\lambda}_t}{\lambda_t} = r_t - \rho = \tfrac{\dot{E}_t}{E_t}, \tag{5.4a}$$

$$\tfrac{1}{\lambda_t} = (1 + i_t o_H) E_t, \tag{5.4b}$$

$$\lim_{T \to \infty} W_T e^{-r_T} \geq 0, \tag{5.4c}$$

where the Fisher equation $i_t = \Pi_t + r_t$ is used to derive the Euler Eq. (5.4a).

### 5.2.4 Monetary Authority

The monetary authority implements monetary policy by manipulating the nominal interest rate, hence, the interest rate is treated as an exogenous parameter, $i_t = i$. In addition, this monetary authority adjusts the money supply following the k% rule. This rule relies on the classical dichotomy and increases the money supply in line with the increase in money demand for transactional motives accompanying economic development. Therefore, the money supply increases at a constant rate, as $\dot{M}_t/M_t = \mu$. This money supply rule yields the following:

$$\frac{\dot{m}_t}{m_t} = \mu - \Pi_t, \tag{5.5}$$

where monetary authorities determine the money supply endogenously by manipulating the nominal interest rate to achieve the target inflation rate.

## 5.3 Equilibrium

### 5.3.1 Dynamic System

In addition to the definition of the balanced growth path and the expenditure per unit wage rate as $\varepsilon_t = E_t/w_t$, the derivation process for the law of motion for $\varepsilon_t$ and the steady state is the same as in Chap. 3. If we replace $P_{A,t} = w_t F/A_t$ in Chap. 4 with $P_{A,t} = (1 \mid i_t o_A) w_t F_t$ in (5.1), we obtain the steady state using the same derivation process as in Chap. 4. Therefore, in this section, we only describe the derivation results.

$\dot{E}_t/E_t$ in Chap. 4, which is obtained by combining (3.6), (3.9) and (4.6), can be rewritten as follows by using $P_{A,t} = (1 + i_t o_A) w_t F_t$ in (5.1):

$$\frac{\dot{E}_t}{E_t} = \frac{\dot{w}_t}{w_t} - g_t + \frac{1}{\sigma F(1 + i o_A)} \left( \frac{E_t}{w_t} \right) - \rho,$$

which is rewritten as follows:

$$\frac{\dot{\varepsilon}_t}{\varepsilon_t} = \frac{\varepsilon_t}{\sigma F(1+i o_A)} - g_t - \rho, \tag{5.6}$$

which derives the expenditure per wage rate $\varepsilon_t \equiv E_t/w_t$. By using (4.7), rewriting $L = F_t \dot{A}_t + A_t x_t$ in (3.11) yields (4.10), where $w_t = 1$ holds because the wage rate is assumed to be numeraire. By substituting $g_t$ in (4.10) for $g_t$ in (5.6), the law of motion in this economy can be expressed as:

$$\frac{\dot{\varepsilon}_t}{\varepsilon_t} = \frac{\varepsilon_t}{F} \left[ \frac{1}{\sigma(1+i o_A)} - \frac{1-(1/\sigma)}{1+(\tau/\theta)} \right] - \rho - \frac{L}{F}, \tag{5.7}$$

for $[1 + (\tau/\theta)]/(1 + io_A) > \sigma - 1$. As shown in the transition process in Fig. 4.2, $\varepsilon_t = \varepsilon^*$ is obtained in the steady state where $\dot{\varepsilon}_t = 0$.

### 5.3.2 Steady State with Money

Chu and Cozzi (2014) and Afonso (2023) derived the inflation rate by substituting $r_t$ in the non-arbitrage condition $\Pi_t = i - r_t$. However, in the present model, the wage rate is assumed to be numeraire, hence, under the condition $\dot{E}_t = 0$, $r_t = \rho$ holds and the inflation rate depends only on the nominal interest rate and subjective discounting. As an alternative approach, Hamaguchi (2024) focused on $P_{M,t} \equiv \left(\int_0^{A_t} p_{j,t}^{1-\sigma} dj\right)^{\frac{1}{1-\sigma}}$ in (3.5). When the wage rate is a numeraire, the price of goods in (4.5) is constant over time. Therefore, the time derivative with respect to $P_{M,t}$ yields the following:

$$\frac{\dot{P}_{M,t}}{P_{M,t}} = -\frac{1}{\sigma - 1} \cdot \frac{\dot{A}_t}{A_t},$$

which is rewritten with $Fg_t + L_{X,t} = L$ in (3.11) as follows:

$$\Pi_t = -\frac{L - L_{X,t}}{F(\sigma - 1)}, \tag{5.8}$$

where an increase in the number of varieties leads to deflation because, in a monopolistic competitive market, an increase in the number of varieties increases the total supply of goods, lowering the price index. Therefore, the monetary policy has a different effect on the inflation rate than Afonso (2023).

By solving $\dot{m}_t = (\mu - \Pi_t)m_t$ as a first-order linear differential equation, we obtain the following:

$$m_t = m_0 \exp\left[\left(\mu + \frac{L - L_{X,t}}{F(\sigma - 1)}\right)t\right], \tag{5.9}$$

where $m_0$ is the initial value of the real money supply. As economic growth leads to deflation, the real money supply increases to boost the purchasing power of money. Substituting (5.9) into (5.3) with $m_t = B_t + o_H \varepsilon_t$, we obtain the following borrowing:

$$B_t = m_0 \exp\left[\left(\mu + \frac{L - L_{X,t}}{F(\sigma - 1)}\right)t\right] - o_H \varepsilon_t, \tag{5.10}$$

where $B_t > 0$ holds under sufficiently large $\mu$ and $m_0$. The increase in the real money supply associated with economic growth increases lending and borrowing.

From (5.7), $\varepsilon^*$ in the steady state is expressed as follows:

$$\varepsilon^* = \frac{\sigma(L + \rho F)}{\frac{1}{1 + io_A} - \frac{\sigma - 1}{1 + \frac{\tau}{\theta}}}, \tag{5.11}$$

where (5.11) is equal to (4.12) when $i = 0$. Here, the nominal interest rate affects the real economy only through stock prices and its effect is concentrated on expenditure per wage. Therefore, the nominal interest rate affects $L_X^*$, $L_A^*$, $g^*$ and $P^*$ in (4.13) through $\varepsilon^*$. By incorporating (5.11) into (4.8), with (4.13) substituted, we can derive welfare in the current model.

### 5.3.3 Growth Effect of Nominal Interest Rate

A decrease in nominal interest rates reduces expenditure per wage rate and the amount of labour in goods firms and expands the amount of labour in R&D firms, resulting in sustainable development through economic growth and pollution reduction. A reduction in the nominal interest rate leads to a fall in the inflation rate and an increase in the real money supply and amount of lending. For proof, see Appendix D. The intuition behind this is as follows.

Through the Fisher effect, a reduction in the nominal interest rate causes the inflation rate to fall. When a fall in the inflation rate is expected, there is an unintended redistribution of income from borrowers to lenders. While the increase in the purchasing power of repayments due to deflation improves bank earnings, the decrease in sales due to deflation worsens corporate earnings. Therefore, a reduction in the nominal interest rate leads to deflation. A fall in the inflation rate increases the purchasing power of money and expands the real money supply. The amount of money held by households increases, hence, it is lent to R&D firms.

Due to the reduction in the nominal interest rate, the supply of blueprints for variety increases and stock prices falls. By using (5.1) and (5.11), we can rewrite (4. 6) as follows:

$$\frac{\pi}{P_A} = \frac{L+\rho F}{1-(1+i\sigma_A)\left(\frac{\sigma-1}{1+(\tau/\theta)}\right)}\left(\frac{1}{F}\right), \tag{5.12}$$

where due to a decrease in dividend income, expenditure per wage decreases. Due to labour transfer from the goods to the R&D sector, production shrinks and pollution emissions decrease.

In the present model, the impact of environmental taxes on the economy and the environment is almost the same as in Chap. 4. An increase in environmental taxes leads to pollution reduction and economic growth through labour mobility between sectors because, when $i = 0$, (5.11) is equal to (4.12). In Afonso (2023), an increase in the environmental tax rate led to pollution reduction and economic growth, as in this chapter; however, unlike this chapter, it led to inflation as well. This is because, in this chapter, the inflation rate is defined as the price index of differentiated goods, hence, an expansion of variety leads to a fall in prices.

A reduction in the nominal interest rate does not eliminate the growth-enhancing and pollution-reducing effects of environmental policy. However, as shown in

Appendix D, since $d\varepsilon^*/d\tau < 0$ and $|d\varepsilon^*/d\tau di| > 0$, the positive effect of environmental taxes on expenditure per wage is reduced through a reduction in the nominal interest rate. In other words, the nominal interest rate reduces the magnitude of the level and growth effects of environmental taxes. When it is difficult to raise environmental tax, it is possible to promote sustainable development by lowering the nominal interest rate, however, the impact on the level effect and growth effect of the environmental tax should be noted.

As shown in Hamaguchi (2024), the relaxation of the CIA constraint on R&D firms through a decline in $o_A$ leads to sustainable development in the same way as a reduction in the nominal interest rate. Nonetheless, it does not affect the growth-enhancing or pollution-reducing effects of environmental financial policy. In contrast, the main result in Afonso (2023) depended on the relative magnitude of the CIA constraint on R&D and intermediate goods firms. In this chapter, the relaxation of the CIA constraint on households through a decline in $o_H$ only increased lending. Therefore, to achieve sustainable development, it may be necessary to prioritise the resolution of the funding constraints of firms over households.

### 5.3.4 *Welfare Effect of Monetary and Environmental Policies*

A reduction in the nominal interest rate brings about sustainable development through economic growth and pollution reduction, however, will it improve welfare? Differentiating welfare in the current model with the nominal interest rate yields:

$$\frac{dU^*}{di} = \left[\frac{\eta_P}{\rho L_X^*}\left(1 - \frac{1}{\sigma}\right) - \frac{1}{\rho^2 F}\left(\frac{1}{\sigma} - \eta_P\right)\right]\underbrace{\frac{\partial L_X^*}{\partial i}}_{(+)} \gtreqless 0,$$

where the brackets on the RHS are rewritten as follows:

$$\hat{i} \equiv \frac{1+(\tau/\theta)}{\beta\sigma}\left[\frac{(L+\rho F)(1/\sigma-\eta_P)}{\rho(1-1/\sigma)-\rho\eta_P} + \left(1 - \frac{1}{\sigma}\right)\right]^{-1} - \frac{1}{\beta} \gtreqless i, \tag{5.13}$$

where $\hat{i}$ is a welfare-maximising nominal interest rate. As with environmental tax in Chap. 4, there is a positive dynamic welfare effect, a positive static welfare effect and a negative dynamic welfare effect associated with a reduction in the nominal interest rate. Through these effects, a U-shaped relationship is created between the nominal interest rate and welfare.

Differentiating (5.13) concerning the environmental tax gives the following:

$$\frac{d\hat{i}}{d\tau} = \frac{1/\theta}{\beta\sigma}\left[\frac{(L+\rho F)(1/\sigma - \eta_P)}{\rho(1-1/\sigma) - \rho\eta_P} + \left(1 - \frac{1}{\sigma}\right)\right]^{-1} > 0,$$

where environmental tax increases reduce the area in which the welfare-improving effects of a welfare-maximising nominal interest rate are realised because they raise the nominal interest rate. Economic growth and pollution reduction through a reduction in the nominal interest rate are compatible with welfare improvement. However, since environmental tax increases reduce the area of welfare improvement, environmental tax reductions complement the welfare effects of monetary policy. The welfare effects of environmental taxes in the current model are almost the same as in Chap. 4. By differentiating welfare in the present model with environmental taxes, the following welfare-maximising environmental tax rate is derived:

$$\frac{dU^*}{d\tau} \gtreqless 0 \text{ for } \tau \gtreqless \sigma\theta(1+io_A)\left[\frac{(L+\rho F)(1/\sigma - \eta_P)}{\rho(1-1/\sigma) - \rho\eta_P} + \left(1 - \frac{1}{\sigma}\right)\right] - \theta \equiv \hat{\tau}_i,$$

which is differentiated concerning $i$ and yields $d\hat{\tau}_i/di > 0$ (Hamaguchi 2024).

A reduction in the nominal interest rate decreases the area in which the welfare-improving effects of environmental taxes are realised, therefore, an increase in the nominal interest rate complements the welfare effects of environmental policies. When promoting sustainable development through monetary policy, we should be careful of the interdependence with environmental policies.

## 5.4 Emissions Permit Trade

### 5.4.1 Growth Effect of Nominal Interest Rate

The economic structure, when considering the emissions trading market, is the same as in Chap. 4 and the structure of the monetary economy is the same as in Sect. 2. Therefore, the law of motion in this economy can be expressed as:

$$\frac{\dot{\varepsilon}_t}{\varepsilon_t} = \frac{\varepsilon_t}{\sigma F(1+io_A)}\left[1 + (\sigma - 1)\frac{p_t^e}{\theta + p_t^e}\right] - g_t - \rho,$$

which is rewritten with (4.22) as follows:

$$\frac{\dot{\varepsilon}_t}{\varepsilon_t} = \frac{\varepsilon_t - \theta\overline{P}}{F(1+io_A)} - \frac{L - \theta\overline{P}}{F} - \rho, \quad (5.14)$$

where, as depicted in the transition process in Fig. 4.2, $\varepsilon_t = \varepsilon^*$ is obtained in the steady state where $\dot{\varepsilon}_t = 0$. Next, $\dot{\varepsilon}_t = 0$ in (5.14) yields the following:

$$\varepsilon^* = (1 + io_A)\big(L + \rho F - \theta\overline{P}\big) + \theta\overline{P}, \quad (5.15)$$

which is substituted for (4.20) to derive the following:

$$p^{e*} = (1 + io_A)\left(\frac{\sigma - 1}{\sigma}\right)\left(\frac{L + \rho F}{\overline{P}} - \theta\right) - \frac{\theta}{\sigma}, \tag{5.16}$$

where a reduction in the nominal interest rate lowers the price of emission allowances through a reduction in expenditure per unit of wage. Here, by substituting $L_X^* = L - \theta\overline{P}$ into (5.8)–(5.10), we obtain the following:

$$\Pi^* = -\frac{L - \theta\overline{P}}{F(\sigma - 1)}, \tag{5.17}$$

$$m^* = m_0 \exp\left[\left(\mu + \frac{L - \theta\overline{P}}{F(\sigma - 1)}\right)t\right], \tag{5.18}$$

$$B^* = m_0 \exp\left[\left(\mu + \frac{L - \theta\overline{P}}{F(\sigma - 1)}\right)t\right] - o_H \varepsilon^*, \tag{5.19}$$

In general, the nominal interest rate affects the inflation rate through the Fisher effect, however, in (5.17), it does not affect the inflation rate. This is because the nominal interest rate has no effect on goods production or R&D activities, as the emission allowance caps the amount of goods produced. Therefore, the nominal interest rate has no effect on the real money supply or the amount of loans, which are affected by the inflation rate. However, emissions trading may interfere with the general effects of monetary policy.

When emission allowances cap the production of goods, monetary policy has no effect on labour mobility. In emissions trading, the nominal interest rate loses its growth-enhancing effect. Since production depends only on emission allowances and pollution abatement productivity, the pollution-reducing effect of the nominal interest rate disappears. As a result, the nominal interest rate has no effect on welfare. Here, the first term on the RHS of (4.21) implies the following dividend per share:

$$\frac{\pi^*}{P_A^*} = \frac{\varepsilon^*}{\sigma F}\left[1 + (\sigma - 1)\frac{p^{e*}}{\theta + p^{e*}}\right],$$

which is rewritten by using (5.1) and (5.15) as follows:

$$\frac{\pi^*}{P_A^*} = \frac{(L + \rho F - \theta\overline{P}) + \theta\overline{P}/(1 + io_A)}{\sigma F}\left[1 + (\sigma - 1)\frac{1}{1 + (\theta/p^{e*})}\right], \tag{5.20}$$

where the second term in brackets on the RHS implies the allowance allocation rent. A reduction in the nominal interest rate increases the dividend per share through a direct effect, however, decreases it through an indirect effect of a fall in the price of emission allowances. As this indirect effect dominates the direct effect, the monetary policy reduces expenditure per wage through a decrease in dividend income.

### 5.4.2 Growth and Welfare Effects of Permit

As explained in Chap. 4, the reduction in emissions allowances stimulates economic growth by shifting labour from the goods to the R&D sector. The increase in variety causes the price index of goods to fall, therefore, the inflation rate falls and the real money supply increases through deflation. This deflation increases the amount of money held by households and the amount of lending expands. In (5.20), the reduction in the emission allowance increases the dividend per share due to its direct effect and its indirect effect of increasing the price of emission allowances. This dividend income increases expenditure per wage, decreasing the loan amount. Therefore, the emission allowance has a non-monotonic effect on the loan amounts.

Differentiating (5.19) with respect to $\overline{P}$ yields the following:

$$\frac{dB^*}{d\overline{P}} = -\frac{tm_0}{F(\sigma-1)}\exp\left[\left(\mu + \frac{L-\theta\overline{P}}{F(\sigma-1)}\right)t\right] + io_A o_H \theta \gtreqless 0,$$

which is rewritten by logarithmically transformation as follows:

$$P \gtreqless \frac{F(\sigma-1)}{t\theta}\left[\log\left(\frac{tm_0}{F(\sigma-1)}\right) - \log io_A o_H + \mu\right] \equiv \check{P},$$

where there is an inverted U-shaped relationship between the emission allowance and the loan amounts. Even in the current model, by differentiating (4.27) for the emission allowance, we obtain $\widehat{P}$ in (4.28) and there is an inverted U-shaped relationship between the emission allowance and welfare. Here, in $\hat{P} \gtreqless \check{P}$, a reduction in the emission allowance leads to welfare improvement or deterioration and loan increase or decrease, in addition to sustainable development.

When the loan amount is considered to be the credit amount, its expansion can be interpreted as the development of financial markets. Hamaguchi (2024) classified sustainable development and financial market development into four cases according to the nominal interest rate level. Under $\overline{P} < \check{P} = \hat{P}$, an emission allowance reduction leads to welfare deterioration and credit expansion, while under $\overline{P} < \check{P} = \hat{P}$, emissions allowances lead to improved welfare and reduced credit. Therefore, there is a trade-off between sustainable development and financial market development. In contrast, under $\hat{P} < \overline{P} < \check{P}$, depending on the nominal interest rate, emissions allowances lead to improved welfare and increased credit or deteriorated welfare and reduced credit. Therefore, there is a win–win or lose-lose relationship. This theoretical relationship supports the empirical results of Acheampong et al. (2020) and others. The nominal interest rate level should be carefully determined to promote a sustainable environment and finance through emissions trading.

## References

Acheampong, A. O., Amponsah, M., & Boateng, E. (2020). Does financial development mitigate carbon emissions? Evidence from heterogeneous financial economies. *Energy Economics*, 88, 104768. https://doi.org/10.1016/j.eneco.2020.104768

Afonso, O. (2023). Fiscal and monetary effects on environmental quality, growth, and welfare. *Research in Economics*, 77(1), 202–219. https://doi.org/10.1016/j.rie.2023.02.002

Chu, A. C. (2022). Patent policy and economic growth: A survey. *The Manchester School*, 90(2), 237–254. https://doi.org/10.1111/manc.12392

Chu, A. C., & Cozzi, G. (2014). R&D and economic growth in a cash-in-advance economy. *International Economic Review*, 55(2), 507–524. https://doi.org/10.1111/iere.12059

Drudi, F., Moench, E., Holthausen, C., Weber, P. F., Ferrucci, G., Setzer, R., ... & Ouvrard, J. F. (2021). Climate change and monetary policy in the euro area. ECB Occasional Paper No. 2021/271, Available at SSRN: https://ssrn.com/abstract=3928292

Hamaguchi, Y. (2024). Comparative study of environmental and monetary policies in an R&D-based growth model. *Journal of Environmental Management*, 360, 121199. https://doi.org/10.1016/j.jenvman.2024.121199

Maji, I. K., Habibullah, M. S., & Saari, M. Y. (2017). Financial development and sectoral CO 2 emissions in Malaysia. *Environmental Science and Pollution Research*, 24, 7160–7176. https://doi.org/10.1007/s11356-016-8326-1

Qian, Y., Liu, J., & Forrest, J. Y. L. (2022). Impact of financial agglomeration on regional green economic growth: evidence from China. *Journal of Environmental Planning and Management*, 65(9), 1611–1636. https://doi.org/10.1080/09640568.2021.1941811

Sethi, P., Chakrabarti, D., & Bhattacharjee, S. (2020). Globalization, financial development and economic growth: Perils on the environmental sustainability of an emerging economy. *Journal of Policy Modeling*, 42(3), 520–535. https://doi.org/10.1016/j.jpolmod.2020.01.007

Xie, R., Fu, W., Yao, S., & Zhang, Q. (2021). Effects of financial agglomeration on green total factor productivity in Chinese cities: Insights from an empirical spatial Durbin model. *Energy Economics*, 101, 105449. https://doi.org/10.1016/j.eneco.2021.105449

# Part II
# The Importance of Household Preferences

# Chapter 6
# Endogenous Labour Supply

**Abstract** Leisure time is introduced in the variety expansion model in Chap. 2 to endogenize the labour supply. While pollution is emitted through physical capital input, pollution is reduced through the input of pollution abatement goods. To internalise this negative externality, the government introduces emissions trading. A reduction in the emissions allowance brings about economic growth and improves welfare through the substitution effect. Due to the demand for pollution abatement goods, final goods firms increase the production of final goods by investing in intermediate goods. The rise in the price of intermediate goods encourages the development of new varieties, as it increases monopoly profits. The demand for labour in the R&D sector increases the wage rate, increasing the opportunity cost of leisure and substituting leisure for labour. As a result, the economy grows due to the development of varieties. When the preference parameter for pollution is high, welfare improvement due to increased consumption, economic growth and reduced pollution dominates welfare deterioration due to reduced leisure time, hence, welfare improves. In case there is no leisure time, the growth-enhancing effect of emission allowances disappears, therefore, this growth effect depends on the preference for leisure time.

## 6.1 Introduction

Since ancient times, people have spent their leisure time in environments rich in nature. Based on this observation, leisure time likely increases in areas with a better environment. If leisure time reduces working hours, labour supply to the R&D sector will decrease and economic growth will likely stagnate. However, leisure time will likely increase in areas with poor environmental conditions. This is because deteriorating health due to air pollution reduces working hours due to absenteeism and hospital visits (Yang et al. 2013; Hanna and Oliva 2015; Wu et al. 2023). Furthermore, air pollution worsens workers' productivity (Graff Zivin and Matthew 2012; Chang et al. 2019). In this case, if environmental policies reduce air pollution, the economy would grow as working hours and labour productivity in the R&D sector would

 
Y. Hamaguchi, *Sustainable Development in Economic Growth Theory*,
https://doi.org/10.1007/978-981-96-7639-2_6

increase. This channel can be analysed in an endogenous growth model that internalises labour supply because the marginal rate of substitution between consumption and leisure gives rise to leisure's opportunity cost. Environmental policies bring about economic growth and pollution reduction through this opportunity cost, resulting in substitution from leisure to education in the Uzawa-Lucas model (Hettich 1998) and from leisure to labour in the AK model with indeterminacy (Itaya 2008). These theoretical mechanisms have been empirically confirmed by Xu et al. (2024). The economic model in this chapter applies this channel to the variety expansion model and provides useful insights into such a discussion.

## 6.2 The Model

### *6.2.1 Structure of the Variety Expansion Model with Leisure*

As the basic structure of the economic model is the same as in Chap. 2, only the changes are described here. Final goods firms emit flow pollution when inputting aggregate intermediate goods (physical capital). This pollution, as a negative externality, worsens household utility. Governments, therefore, open emissions trading markets to internalise this externality. In addition to the consumption of final goods, households derive positive utility from leisure. The above economic structure is illustrated in Fig. 6.1. The economic model in this chapter is based on Hamaguchi (2021b) and Hamaguchi et al. (2022).

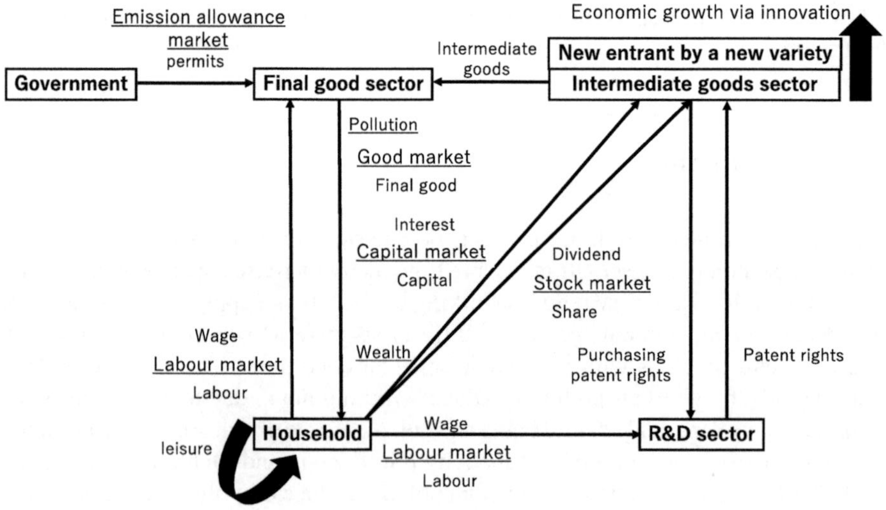


**Fig. 6.1** Structure of the variety expansion model with leisure

### 6.2.2 Household

Households obtain utility from leisure in addition to consumption of final goods. The utility function of a household (representative individual) living for an infinite period of time is expressed as:

$$U_t = \int_0^\infty \left[\beta \log C_t + (1-\beta)\log l_t - \eta_P \log P_t\right] e^{-\rho t} dt, \tag{6.1}$$

where a Cobb–Douglas type utility function is assumed. Note that $l_t \in (0, 1)$ is leisure and $P_t$ is the pollution level. In addition, $\beta \in (0, 1)$, $1-\beta \in (0, 1)$ and $\eta_P$ are the relative weights of consumption, leisure and pollution in utility, respectively.

Households allocate a given amount of time to work and leisure. Standardising the population $L$ to 1, the time constraint equation becomes $L_{Y,t} + L_{A,t} + l_t = 1$.. Hence, the household budget constraint equation in (2.3) is rewritten as:

$$\dot{W}_t = r_t W_t + w_t(1-l_t) - C_t, \tag{6.2}$$

where increased leisure decreases wage income and asset accumulation.

The households' intertemporal utility maximisation problem can be formulated as follows:

$$\max_{C_t, l_t} U_t = \int_0^\infty \left[\beta \log C_t + (1-\beta)\log l_t - \eta_P \log P_t\right] e^{-\rho t} dt,$$

$$\text{s.t. } \dot{W}_t - r_t W_t + w_t(1-l_t) - C_t,$$

The first-order conditions for utility maximisation between different points in time assert the following:

$$\frac{\beta}{C_t} = \lambda_t, \tag{6.3}$$

$$\frac{1-\beta}{l_t} = w_t \lambda_t, \tag{6.4}$$

where, in the first-order condition for leisure of (6.4), the marginal utility is equal to the marginal cost of leisure as the wage rate multiplied by the cointegrating variable. When $(1-\beta)/l_t > w_t\lambda_t$ and $\lambda_t$ is assumed to be constant, the household's utility increases by substituting labour for leisure, because its marginal utility is greater than its marginal cost. Hence, the law of diminishing marginal utility dictates that the marginal utility of leisure decreases. However, when $(1-\beta)/l_t < w_t\lambda_t$, household utility increases by substituting leisure for labour because its marginal cost is greater than its marginal utility. Hence, the law of diminishing marginal utility dictates that the marginal utility of leisure increases. Hence, (4) holds.

Substituting (6.3) into (6.4), we obtain the following:

$$\frac{(1-\beta)/l_t}{\beta/C_t} = w_t \Leftrightarrow w_t = \frac{1-\beta}{\beta}\left(\frac{C_t}{l_t}\right), \tag{6.5}$$

where the marginal rate of substitution between consumption and leisure equals the wage rate. When $[(1-\beta)/l_t]/[\beta/C_t] < w_t$, substituting leisure for labour increases consumption due to wage income increase. In this case, (5) holds because the marginal utility of leisure increases while the marginal utility of consumption decreases. (6.5) implies that the wage rate is an opportunity cost of leisure.

The shadow price of the asset is (2.6) and the transversality condition is (2.7). From (2.6) and (6.3), we obtain the Euler equation for consumption in (2.8).

### 6.2.3 *Final Good Sector*

Following Gradus and Smulders (1993), the emission mechanism for net pollution flows is assumed as follows:

$$P_t = \frac{\int_0^{A_t} x_{j,t}dt}{Z_t}, \tag{6.6}$$

where $Z_t$ is a pollution abatement good produced from final goods and is an end-of-pipe abatement technology. While final goods firms emit pollution when inputting aggregate intermediate goods (physical capital), they reduce pollution by inputting abatement goods.

The government opens an emissions trading market. Firms are allocated emission allowances of $\overline{P}$ for each period. In the emissions trading market, a fully competitive market, firms are free to buy and sell emission allowances at a permit price of $p_t^e$. A firm that emits more pollution than its allocated allowance because it inputs a relatively large amount of intermediate goods has to buy allowances from other firms for the missing $P_t - \overline{P} > 0$. However, a firm that emits lesser polluting emissions than its allocated allowance because it inputs relatively more polluting abatement goods can sell its surplus emission allowance of $\overline{P} - P_t > 0$ to another firm. Hence, this market has to be cleared as $P_t = \overline{P}$.

Under production function in (2.9), the profit function of this firm is formulated as follows:

$$\Pi_t = Y_t - w_t L - p_{j,t}x_{j,t} - p_t^e\left(P_t - \overline{P}\right), \tag{6.7}$$

where $p_t^e\left(P_t - \overline{P}\right) > 0$ is the cost of purchasing emission allowances and $p_t^e\left(\overline{P} - P_t\right) > 0$ is the profit from selling emission allowances. The first-order condition of profit maximisation yields:

$$\alpha\left(\frac{L_{Y,t}}{x_{j,t}}\right)^{1-\alpha} = p_{j,t} + \frac{p_t^e}{Z_t}, \tag{6.8}$$

$$\frac{p_t^e}{Z_t}\left(\frac{\int_0^{A_t} x_{j,t}dt}{Z_t}\right) = 1, \tag{6.9}$$

where, on the RHS of (6.8), the marginal cost of intermediate goods increases due to the cost of purchasing emission allowances. The first-order condition for profit maximisation regarding labour is (2.11).

Substituting $P_t = \overline{P}$ into (6.9), we obtain $p_t^e = Z_t/\overline{P}$. Under this permit price, the profit function in (6.7) converges to a constant value if the permit price diverges to infinity at $t \to \infty$. However, Hettich (1998) considered an environmental tax under a pollution emission function of $P_t = K_t/Z_t$, where a coefficient of elasticity of 1 is assumed. In this case, (6.9) becomes $\tau_t^P = K_t/P_t^2$. Under this environmental tax, the profit function in (6.7) does not converge to a constant value at $t \to \infty$, unless the environmental tax rate diverges to infinity. Since hyperinflation is observed, it is rational regarding the permit price, however, not when regarding the tax rate diverging to infinity. Hence, when considering the pollution emission function of (6.6) in the dynamic general equilibrium model, emission allowances are more consistent than environmental taxes. See Hamaguchi (2021a) for a detailed explanation on this point.

### 6.2.4 Intermediate Good Sector and R&D Sector

As monopolies, intermediate goods firms determine their output, accounting for the demand behaviour of firms in the final goods sector. Permit price, therefore, affects the production and profits of intermediate goods firms through intermediate goods prices. The profit function of the $j$ th intermediate goods firm is defined as follows:

$$\pi_{j,t} = p_{j,t}x_{j,t} - r_t x_{j,t}, \text{ s.t. } p_{j,t} = \alpha\left(\frac{L_{Y,t}}{x_{j,t}}\right)^{1-\alpha} - \frac{p_t^e}{Z_t}, \tag{6.10}$$

for $j = 1, 2, \cdots, A_t$. The first-order condition of profit maximisation yields the following:

$$\alpha^2\left(\frac{L_{Y,t}}{x_{j,t}}\right)^{1-\alpha} - \frac{p_t^e}{Z_t} = r_t \Leftrightarrow p_t = \frac{1}{\alpha}\left(r_t + \frac{1}{\overline{P}}\right), \tag{6.11}$$

where a reduction in emission allowances results in an increase in the intermediate goods prices. In the inverse demand function in (6.10), holding others constant, an increase in the prices of emission allowances decreases the prices of intermediate goods, resulting in a decrease in $p_{j,t}x_{j,t}$ sales. However, if firms in the final goods sector reduce the input of intermediate goods to reduce the purchasing cost of emission allowances, intermediate goods' prices and sales increase. The former effect is considered dominant, hence, (6.11) holds.

By substituting (6.11) into the monopoly profit in (6.10), we obtain the monopoly profit of the intermediate goods firm as:

$$\pi_t = \tfrac{1-\alpha}{\alpha}\left(r_t + \tfrac{1}{\overline{P}}\right)x_t, \tag{6.12}$$

where, due to the general equilibrium effect of the permit price, a reduction in emission allowances increases monopoly profits, holding others constant. Substituting (2.14) into (2.12) and rearranging it, we obtain $x_t = L_{Y,t}\left[\alpha\overline{P}/\left(r_t\overline{P} + 1 + \alpha\right)\right]$. This equation implies that the output of each intermediate good is identical across firms. The R&D sector is the same as in Chap. 2. An R&D firm under perfect competition chooses (2.17) as the free entry condition under the production technology in (2.16).

### 6.2.5 Market

In addition to capital, stock, labour and goods markets, there is an emissions trading market. The total emission allowances issued by the government are $\overline{P}$. Due to emissions trading between firms, the total pollution emitted by firms in the final goods sector is equal to the total emissions allowance. Hence, the market clearing condition for the emissions trading market is $P_t = \overline{P}$. Since the population is standardised to 1, the market clearing condition for the labour market is (6.2).

In the capital market, $\int_0^{A_t} x_{j,t}dj = A_t x_t = K_t$ holds. Using $P_t = \overline{P}$ and $A_t x_t = K_t$, we rewrite (6.6) to obtain $K_t = \overline{P}Z_t$. This relationship implies that emission allowances and pollution abatement goods are substitutive in keeping the level of physical capital (the pollution source) constant. If the emission allowance is lowered, the input of pollution abatement goods must be increased accordingly: substituting $K_t = \overline{P}Z_t$ for $Y_t = K_t^{\alpha}\left(A_t L_{Y,t}\right)^{1-\alpha}$, $Y_t = \left(\overline{P}Z_t\right)^{\alpha}\left(A_t L_{Y,t}\right)^{1-\alpha}$ is obtained. $\overline{P}Z_t$, in this production function, implies the pollution-saving technology in Bovenberg and Smulders (1995). In the present model, $A_t L_{Y,t}$ implies that the improvement in labour productivity due to the expansion of varieties leads to a pollution-saving production expansion.

The market clearing conditions for goods markets are as follows:

$$Y_t = C_t + Z_t + \dot{K}_t, \tag{6.13}$$

where the final goods produced by the final goods sector are distributed for consumption and investment by households and abatement by firms.

## 6.3 Equilibrium

### 6.3.1 Dynamic System

This section constructs the dynamic system in this economy and derives its steady state, with final goods per capital as $y_t \equiv Y_t/K_t$, consumption per capital as $z_t \equiv C_t/K_t$ and average capital as $\omega_t \equiv K_t/A_t$.[1] Note that $y_t$ and $z_t$ are jump variables and $\omega_t$ is a state variable.

In Appendix E, the above results can be used to construct a three-dimensional dynamic system as follows:

$$\frac{\dot{y}_t}{y_t} = \frac{1-\alpha}{\alpha}\left(\alpha\delta y_t^{\frac{1}{1-\alpha}}\omega_t + \frac{1}{\overline{P}} - \alpha^2 y_t\right), \tag{6.14}$$

$$\frac{\dot{z}_t}{z_t} = z_t - \left(1-\alpha^2\right)y_t - \rho, \tag{6.15}$$

$$\frac{\dot{\omega}_t}{\omega_t} = y_t - z_t - \frac{1}{\overline{P}} - \delta\left(L - y_t^{\frac{1}{1-\alpha}}\omega_t - \frac{1-\beta}{\beta(1-\alpha)}y_t^{\frac{1}{1-\alpha}}z_t\omega_t\right), \tag{6.16}$$

where, compared to the economic model in Chap. 2, the RHS of (14) includes emission allowances and that of (6.16) includes leisure.

In a BGP equilibrium, $g = \dot{C}_t/C_t = \dot{K}_t/K_t = \dot{A}_t/A_t = \dot{Y}_t/Y_t$ because $\dot{y}_t = \dot{z}_t = \dot{\omega}_t = 0$. From (6.14)–(6.16), the steady state can be derived as follows:

$$\omega^* = \frac{\alpha^2 y^* - 1/\overline{P}}{\alpha\delta y^{*\frac{1}{1-\alpha}}}, \tag{6.17}$$

$$z^* = \left(1-\alpha^2\right)y^* + \rho, \tag{6.18}$$

$$y^* = \frac{\beta}{2\alpha(1+\alpha)}\left[B_1 + \sqrt{B_1^2 + \frac{4\alpha(1+\alpha)}{\beta}B_2}\right], \tag{6.19}$$

where

$$B_1 \equiv \delta + \frac{\beta-\alpha}{\beta(1-\alpha)}\rho + \frac{1+\alpha}{\alpha\beta\overline{P}}, \quad B_2 \equiv \frac{\rho(1-\beta)}{\alpha\beta(1-\alpha)\overline{P}}.$$

Using the steady-state values of (6.17)–(6.19), the various variables in equilibrium can be expressed in terms of parameters and the real interest rate. As in Appendix F, working and leisure hours in equilibrium can be derived as follows:

$$l^* = \frac{1-\beta}{\alpha\beta\delta(1-\alpha)}\left(1-\alpha^2 + \frac{\alpha^2\rho}{r^*+1/\overline{P}}\right)r^*, \tag{6.20}$$

[1] For a detailed derivation process, see the Appendix in Hamaguchi et al. (2022).

$$L_Y^*\left(\overline{P}\right)=\tfrac{r^*}{\alpha\delta}, \tag{6.21}$$

$$L_A^*=\delta-\tfrac{r^*}{\alpha}-\tfrac{1-\beta}{\alpha\beta(1-\alpha)}\left(1-\alpha^2+\tfrac{\alpha^2\rho}{r^*+1/\overline{P}}\right)r^*, \tag{6.22}$$

where working and leisure time depend on the real interest rate in equilibrium. This interest rate is expressed as follows:

$$r^*=\tfrac{\alpha}{2\beta(1-\alpha^2)}\left[r_1+\sqrt{r_1^2+\tfrac{4\beta(1-\alpha^2)r_2}{\alpha}}\right], \tag{6.23}$$

$$r_1\equiv\beta(1-\alpha)(\rho+\delta)-\alpha\rho(1-\beta)-\frac{1-\alpha^2}{\alpha}\left(1-\beta+\frac{\beta}{\overline{P}}\right)>0,$$

$$r_2\equiv\frac{1}{\overline{P}}\left[\beta(1-\alpha)(\rho+\delta)-\frac{\left(1-\alpha^2\right)(1-\beta)}{\alpha}\right]>0,$$

where the following parameter condition is assumed to hold $r_1>0$ and $r_2>0$:

$$\hat{\alpha}<\delta<\delta+\rho,\ P_1<\overline{P},$$

for

$$\hat{\alpha}\equiv\frac{(1+\alpha)(1-\beta)}{\alpha\beta},\ P_1\equiv\frac{\beta\left(1-\alpha^2\right)}{\rho\alpha(\beta-\alpha)}.$$

Substituting (6.22) into (2.16), we obtain the economic growth rate as:

$$g^*=\delta-\tfrac{r^*}{\alpha}-\tfrac{1-\beta}{\alpha\beta(1-\alpha)}\left(1-\alpha^2+\tfrac{\alpha^2}{r^*+1/\overline{P}}\right)r^*, \tag{6.24}$$

where the second term on the RHS is labour in the final goods sector and the third term is leisure. If emission allowance reductions lead to an increase in working hours due to labour transfer from the final goods to the R&D sector and a decrease in leisure time, the development of varieties and economic growth will increase.

The welfare level in this economy is the household utility. Using $C_t=z^*K_0e^{gt}$ and rewriting (6.1), welfare can be expressed as:

$$U=\tfrac{\beta}{\rho}\log z^*+\left[\tfrac{\beta}{\rho}\log K_0+\tfrac{\beta g^*}{\rho^2}\right]+\tfrac{(1-\beta)}{\rho}\log l^*-\tfrac{\eta_P}{\rho}\log\overline{P}, \tag{6.25}$$

where welfare depends on four factors. First, on the RHS, is the increase in utility due to consumption. Second, is the increase in utility due to increased consumption associated with economic growth. Third, is the utility increase due to leisure. Fourth, is the utility decrease due to increased pollution. The second factor is the dynamic welfare effect, while the other factors are static welfare effects.

For this economic model, it is necessary to analyse the stability of the dynamic system locally in the vicinity of the steady state. For this stability analysis, see Hamaguchi (2021b).

### 6.3.2 Comparative Statics

Differentiating (6.17)–(6.24) by the emission allowance $\overline{P}$, we obtain:

$$\frac{dy^*}{d\overline{P}} < 0,\ \frac{dz^*}{d\overline{P}} < 0,\ \frac{d\omega^*}{d\overline{P}} > 0,\ \frac{dr^*}{d\overline{P}} > 0,$$

$$\frac{dg^*}{d\overline{P}} < 0,\ \frac{dL_Y^*}{d\overline{P}} > 0,\ \frac{dL_A^*}{d\overline{P}} < 0,\ \frac{dl^*}{d\overline{P}} > 0,$$

which are used to derive the following:

$$\frac{d\left(p^* + 1/\overline{P}\right)}{d\overline{P}} < 0,\ \frac{d\left(\pi^*/x^*\right)}{d\overline{P}} < 0,\ \frac{d\left(P_A^*/x^*\right)}{d\overline{P}} < 0,\ \frac{d\left(w^*/K^*\right)}{d\overline{P}} < 0,$$

which imply that the reduction in emission allowances decreases the marginal cost of intermediate goods, profit per intermediate good, stock price per intermediate good and wage rate per capital, respectively. The derivation of these comparative statics analyses is highly technical. See Hamaguchi et al. (2022) for a proof. Based on these results, an intuitive explanation of the effects of emission allowance reductions is provided.

The RHS of $p_t^e/Z_t = 1/\overline{P}$, obtained by rewriting (6.9), represents the marginal cost of the pollution abatement good. Differentiating this equation by $\overline{P}$, we obtain $d\left(p_t^e/Z_t\right)/d\overline{P} = -\left(1/\overline{P}^2\right) < 0$. When emission allowances are reduced, their demand and prices increase. Hence, if pollution emissions are not reduced, the cost of purchasing emission allowances reduces profits. Firms in the final goods sector increase inputs of pollution abatement goods, hence, their marginal costs rise. For reduced emissions, firms increase their intermediate goods inputs, increasing production. Hence, the price of intermediate goods rises ($d\left(p^* + 1/\overline{P}\right)/d\overline{P} < 0$) due to an increase in the demand for intermediate goods and an increase in the price of emission allowances. This increases the sales of the intermediate goods firms and their profits ($d(\pi^*/x^*)/d\overline{P} < 0$). Entrepreneurs can obtain a blueprint for a new variety through R&D funding and earn positive profits in a new market. Therefore, the demand for the new variety increases and the share prices rise ($d\left(P_A^*/x^*\right)/d\overline{P} < 0$). This increase in labour demand increases the wage rate ($d(w^*/K^*)/d\overline{P} < 0$). Hence, in (6.5), households substitute leisure for work ($dl^*/d\overline{P} > 0$) because the opportunity cost of leisure increases. Furthermore, due to general equilibrium effects, labour migration occurs from the final goods to the R&D sector ($dL_Y^*/d\overline{P} > 0$). Hence, labour supply to the R&D sector increases and, as a result of the promotion of R&D activities, the economic growth rate increases ($dL_A^*/d\overline{P} < 0, dg^*/d\overline{P} < 0$).

Hettich (1998) showed that in the Uzawa-Lucas model, the substitution of leisure for education by environmental taxes resulted in economic growth and pollution reduction through human capital accumulation. Ricci (2007) called this growth-enhancing effect the substitution effect. In other words, under $p_t = \left(L_{Y,t}/x_t\right)^{1-\alpha} - \left(p_t^e/Z_t\right)$ in (6.8), when the emission allowance is lowered, final goods firms invest in pollution abatement goods to reduce pollution. Hence, with others constant, the price of intermediate goods rises. This price increase reduces the demand for intermediate goods, reducing their input and output of final goods (direct effect). However, as the abatement good is produced from the final good, the demand for the intermediate good increases to increase its production (indirect effect). Under the parameter conditions in (6.26), the indirect effect dominates the direct effect. In this case, the production of final goods expands and consumption increases ($dy^*/d\overline{P} < 0, dz^*/d\overline{P} < 0$). As a result, the economic growth rate increases due to substitution from leisure to labour, as the profits of intermediate goods firms increase and the demand for new varieties expands. Furthermore, the average capital decreases due to the relative increase in the number of varieties ($d\omega^*/d\overline{P} > 0$).

Here, the following parameter conditions are further assumed to obtain a monotonic welfare effect of the emission allowance:

$$\hat{\delta} < \hat{\alpha}, \ \hat{\eta} < \eta_P,$$

for

$$\hat{\delta} \equiv \frac{\alpha(1+\alpha)}{\beta(1-\alpha)}, \ \hat{\eta} \equiv \frac{2\alpha(1+\alpha)^2(1-\beta)}{\delta(1-\alpha)^2[\beta-\alpha+2\alpha(1-\beta)]}.$$

Differentiating (6.25) by the emission allowance $\overline{P}$, as in Hamaguchi et al. (2022), we obtain the following welfare effects:

$$\frac{dU}{d\overline{P}} = \left[\frac{\beta}{\rho z^*}\underbrace{\frac{\partial z^*}{\partial \overline{P}}}_{(-)} + \frac{\beta}{\rho^2}\underbrace{\frac{\partial g^*}{\partial \overline{P}}}_{(-)}\right] - \left[\frac{\eta_P}{\rho \overline{P}} - \frac{1-\beta}{\rho l^*}\underbrace{\frac{\partial l^*}{\partial \overline{P}}}_{(+)}\right] < 0,$$

where the second term in brackets on the RHS is positive due to the parameter condition, even if $\partial l^*/\partial \overline{P} > 0$. The environmental policy monotonically improves welfare because consumption increase, economic growth and pollution reduction due to the reduction of emission allowances dominate the decrease in leisure due to their reduction.

## 6.4 Determinant of a Growth-Enhancing Effect

### 6.4.1 Importance of Leisure

Assuming $\beta = 1$ in (6.1), we can analyse the growth effect of emission allowances under exogenous labour supply. Substituting $\beta = 1$ in (6.19)–(6.24) yields the following:

$$y^* = \frac{1}{\alpha(1+\alpha)}\left(\delta + \rho + \frac{1+\alpha}{\alpha \overline{P}}\right), \tag{6.26}$$

$$l^* = 0, L_Y^* = \frac{r^*}{\alpha}, \; L_A^* = \delta - \frac{r^*}{\alpha}, \tag{6.27}$$

where working hours depend on the real interest rate in equilibrium. Substituting (6.26) for $r^* = \alpha^2 y^* - \left(1/\overline{P}\right)$ in Appendix F, we obtain $r^* = \alpha(\delta + \rho)/(1+\alpha)$. Substituting this interest rate into (2.8), we obtain the economic growth rate under exogenous labour supply as $g^* = \alpha(\delta + \rho)/(1+\alpha) - \rho$.

When labour supply is exogenous, the growth effect of emission allowances disappears. The $\partial y^*/\partial \overline{P} < 0$ in (6.26) implies an increase in the production of final goods due to an increase in demand for pollution abatement goods. However, $\partial r^*/\partial \overline{P} > 0$ in $r^* = \alpha^2 y^* - \left(1/\overline{P}\right)$ implies the following. The real interest rate falls because intermediate goods firms reduce their capital rentals due to lower demand for intermediate goods following the reduction in emission allowances. Under $\beta = 1$, the growth effect of the emission allowance disappears because these two opposing effects cancel each other out. This suggests that, in the variety expansion model, households' preferences determine the growth-enhancing effects of environmental policy. This is investigated again in Chap. 7 concerning social status preferences and Chap. 8 concerning non-homothetic preferences.

### 6.4.2 Importance of Labour in the R&D Sector

The growth-enhancing effect of environmental policies in the variety expansion model depends on the production technology of the R&D sector. This is confirmed in the lab-equipment model. Note that intermediate goods are produced here through the input of capital rented from households, following Haruyama and Itaya (2006). The above economic structure is illustrated in Fig. 6.2.

The profit function of an R&D firm with an input of final goods in $\upsilon$ units is $\pi_t^A = P_{A,t}\dot{A}_t - \upsilon \dot{A}_t$ and the zero-profit condition for profit maximisation yields $P_A = \upsilon$. Substituting $P_A = \upsilon$ into $y_t = \left[(1-\alpha)/\left(\delta P_{A,t}\right)\right]^{\frac{1-\alpha}{\alpha}}$ in Appendix F, we obtain the output per capital in the steady state as follows:

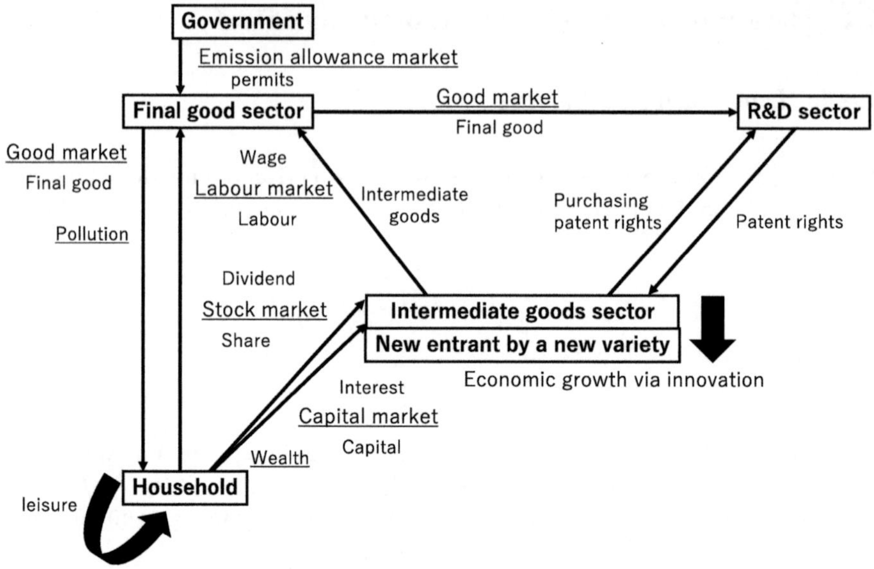


**Fig. 6.2** Structure of the lab-equipment model with capital and allowance

$$y^* = \left(\frac{1-\alpha}{\delta \upsilon}\right)^{\frac{1-\alpha}{\alpha}}, \tag{6.28}$$

where $y^*$ is independent of the emission allowance. Substituting (6.28) for $r^* = \alpha^2 y^* - (1/\overline{P})$ in (F.1) of Appendix F, we obtain $r^* = \alpha^2[(1-\alpha)/\delta\upsilon]^{\frac{1-\alpha}{\alpha}} - (1/\overline{P})$. Substituting this interest rate into (2.8), the economic growth rate in the lab-equipment model is expressed as:

$$g^* = \alpha^2\left(\frac{1-\alpha}{\delta \upsilon}\right)^{\frac{1-\alpha}{\alpha}} - \left(\frac{1}{\overline{P}}\right) - \rho, \tag{6.29}$$

where, from $dg^*/d\overline{P} = 1/\overline{P}^2 > 0$, the reduction in emission allowances decreases the economic growth rate.

As shown in (A.6) of Appendix A, capital gains equalise the rates of return on risky and safe assets. However, under this present model, this effect disappears because the stock price is constant. In this case, $y^*$ is independent of the emission allowance, hence, from $r^* = \alpha^2 y^* - (1/\overline{P})$, we have $\partial r^*/\partial \overline{P} > 0$. When demand for intermediate goods falls due to emissions allowance reduction, intermediate goods firms decrease their capital rentals from households. The real interest rate falls and households' capital accumulation decreases, resulting in a lower economic growth rate. Hence, labour input in the R&D sector is essential for the development of growth-enhancing effects in environmental policy.

## References

Bovenberg, A. L., & Smulders, S. (1995). Environmental quality and pollution-augmenting technological change in a two-sector endogenous growth model. *Journal of public Economics*, 57(3), 369-391. https://doi.org/10.1016/0047-2727(95)80002-Q

Chang, T. Y., Graff Zivin, J., Gross, T., & Neidell, M. (2019). The effect of pollution on worker productivity: evidence from call center workers in China. *American Economic Journal: Applied Economics*, 11(1), 151–172. https://doi.org/10.1257/app.20160436

Gradus, R., & Smulders, S. (1993). The trade-off between environmental care and long-term growth—pollution in three prototype growth models. *Journal of Economics*, 58(1), 25–51. https://doi.org/10.1007/BF01234800

Graff Zivin, J., & Matthew N. (2012). The impact of pollution on worker productivity. *American Economic Review*, 102(7), 3652–3673. https://doi.org/10.1257/aer.102.7.3652

Hamaguchi, Y. (2021a). Environmental policy and social status preference for education in an Uzawa–Lucas model. *Bulletin of Economic Research*, 73(3), 456–468. https://doi.org/10.1111/boer.12259

Hamaguchi, Y. (2021b). Environmental policy effects: an R&D-based economic growth model with endogenous labour supply. *Journal of Economic Policy Reform*, 24(2), 236–252. https://doi.org/10.1080/17487870.2019.1631598

Hamaguchi, Y., Bhuiyan, M. A., & Rahman, M. K. (2022). Analytical method to derive environmental policy effects in an endogenous growth model with leisure. *MethodsX*, 9, 101840. https://doi.org/10.1016/j.mex.2022.101840

Hanna, R., & Oliva, P. (2015). The effect of pollution on labor supply: Evidence from a natural experiment in Mexico City. *Journal of Public Economics*, 122, 68–79. https://doi.org/10.1016/j.jpubeco.2014.10.004

Haruyama, T., & Itaya, J. I. (2006). Do distortionary taxes always harm growth?. *Journal of Economics*, 87, 99–126. https://doi.org/10.1007/s00712-005-0163-5

Hettich, F. (1998). Growth effects of a revenue-neutral environmental tax reform. *Journal of Economics*, 67, 287–316. https://doi.org/10.1007/BF01234647

Itaya, J. I. (2008). Can environmental taxation stimulate growth? The role of indeterminacy in endogenous growth models with environmental externalities. *Journal of Economic Dynamics and Control*, 32(4), 1156–1180. https://doi.org/10.1016/j.jedc.2007.05.002

Ricci, F. (2007). Channels of transmission of environmental policy to economic growth: A survey of the theory. *Ecological Economics*, 60(4), 688–699. https://doi.org/10.1016/j.ecolecon.2006.11.014

Wu, B., Yan, T., & Elahi, E. (2023). The impact of environmental pollution on labor supply: empirical evidence from China. *Environmental Science and Pollution Research*, 30(10), 25764–25772. https://doi.org/10.1007/s11356-022-23720-3

Xu, S., Huang, J., & Zheng, K. (2024). Create or squeeze out? The effect of environmental protection tax on labor demand and labor demand transfer: evidence from China. *Clean Technologies and Environmental Policy*, 1–16. https://doi.org/10.1007/s10098-024-03059-8

Yang, J., Beirne, J., Liu, G., & Sheng, P. (2013). Labour supply and pollution in China. *Applied Economics Letters*, 20(10), 949–952. https://doi.org/10.1080/13504851.2013.765539

# Chapter 7
# Social Status Preferences

**Abstract** Taking the variety expansion model with pollution emissions and emissions trading in Chap. 6, the preference of households for leisure time is replaced by a preference for social status. Households perceive utility from social status when they have more personal assets than the average assets in society. A reduction in the total emission allowances reduces pollution emissions through pollution abatement goods and affects the economic growth rate through the marginal rate of substitution (MRS) for assets and consumption. This is known as the substitution effect and is dependent on the crowding-out effect and the resource reallocation effect. The complementary impact of the crowding-out effect on the substitution effect leads to multiple steady states. In a high steady state, under specific conditions, the resource reallocation effect dominates the crowding-out effect, hence, the reduction in emission allowances improves welfare by growing the economy through the substitution effect. However, in a low steady state, which is a poverty trap, environmental policy reduces the economic growth rate and has a non-monotonic effect on welfare. When there is no social status preference, status goods are consumer goods, in the lab-equipment model, the growth-enhancing effect of emission allowances disappears.

## 7.1 Introduction

Max Weber's hypothesis that the spirit of capitalism promotes economic development is well-known. In endogenous growth models, early research revealed that social status preferences regarding assets promoted economic growth (Weiss and Fershtman 1998). In particular, Pan et al. (2018) revealed that this social status preference had a growth-enhancing effect on strengthening intellectual property rights in the lab-equipment model. Furthermore, with the development of behavioural economics, other-referenced behaviours, such as social status preferences, are updating the conventional findings of environmental economics (Gsottbauer and van den Bergh 2011). Howarth (1996) and Wendner (2003) found that in an economy where consumption goods are a pollution source, it is necessary to raise Pigovian taxes when considering social status preferences regarding consumption. This is because

 
Y. Hamaguchi, *Sustainable Development in Economic Growth Theory*,
https://doi.org/10.1007/978-981-96-7639-2_7

the status-seeking behaviour that leads to increased consumption leads to increased pollution as well. This is known as the status effect.

A pioneering study analysing the impact of this status effect on the environment and growth was conducted by Brekke and Howarth (2002), who found that while the strengthening of social status preferences for assets can lead to economic growth and environmental improvement, it results in inefficiencies in resource allocation due to excessive asset accumulation. Nguyen-Van and Pham (2013) found numerically that in economies with sufficiently high social status preferences for assets, status-seeking led to lower economic growth and poorer environmental quality. Nonetheless, the impact of environmental policy on growth and the environment through innovation and social status preferences has not been analysed. Hamaguchi (2019) fills this gap. This chapter presents the reasons why behavioural economics factors give environmental policy a growth-promoting effect.

## 7.2 The Model

### 7.2.1 *Structure of the Variety Expansion Model with Social Status Preference*

Households accumulate assets to increase future consumption and perceive utility from the asset level. There is heterogeneity among households regarding asset levels. If the asset level rises, households feel a higher social status and utility level. However, if the average asset level in society rises, households feel a low social status and utility level. The more their assets exceed the average asset level, the more their utility rises through social status preference. Leisure time, from Chap. 6, is replaced here by social status preference regarding assets, keeping the other economic structures the same. This economic structure is summarised in Fig. 7.1. The economic model in this chapter is based on Hamaguchi (2019).

### 7.2.2 *Firms and Market*

In the final goods sector, under perfect competition, the production function is (2.9), the pollution emission function is (6.6) and the firms trade in emission allowances. From the profit function in (6.7), the factor demand functions for intermediate goods and pollution abatement goods in (6.8 and 6.9) can be obtained, respectively. The intermediate goods firm, which is a monopoly, determines the intermediate goods price that maximises the profit function in (6.10), subject to the constraint in (6.8) as (6.11). Its profit is (6.12) and the quantity of intermediate goods produced is $x_t = L_{Y,t}\left[\alpha\overline{P}/\left(r_t\overline{P} + 1 + \alpha\right)\right]$. In the R&D sector, under perfect competition, (2.17) is determined by the R&D firm that maximises profits under the production

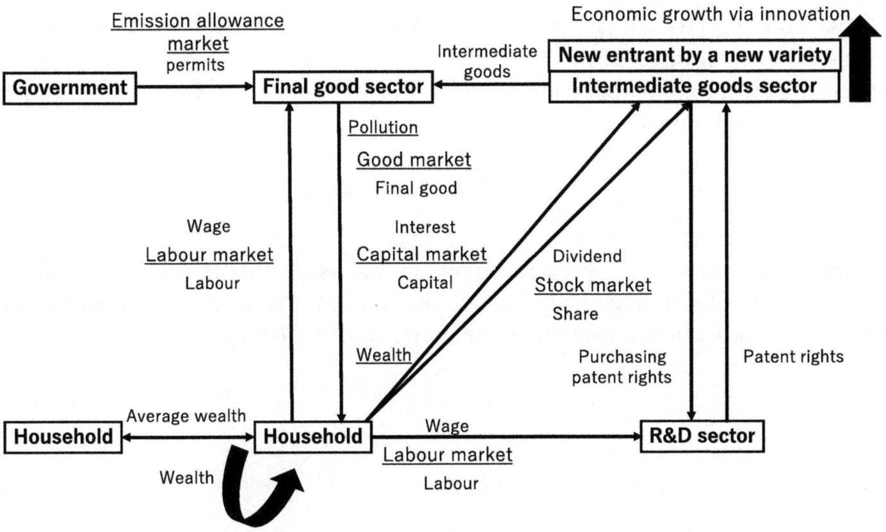


**Fig. 7.1** Structure of the variety expansion model with social status preference

technology in (2.16). The non-arbitrage condition is (2.4). The respective market clearing conditions are as follows: $P_t = \overline{P}$ in the emissions trading market, $\int_0^{A_t} x_{j,t}dj = A_t x_t = K_t$ in the capital market, (2.18) in the labour market and (6.13) in the goods market.

### 7.2.3 Household

To simplify the analysis, the population is normalised to 1, with $L = 1$. The utility function of household $h$ is expressed as follows:

$$U_t = \int_0^{\infty}\left[\beta \log C_{h,t} + \eta_W \log V_{h,t}\left(\frac{W_{h,t}}{\overline{W}_t}\right) - \eta_P \log P_t\right]e^{-\rho t}dt, \tag{7.1}$$

where $W_{h,t}$ is the asset of household $h$, $\overline{W}_t$ is the average asset in the economy and $\eta_W > 0$ is the relative weight of social status preference on utility. Households in this economy prefer social status relative to their assets. Following Futagami and Shibata (1998), the social status function, defined as $V_{h,t}\left(W_{h,t}/\overline{W}_t\right)$, is a non-monotonic increasing function of $W_{h,t}/\overline{W}_t$ and satisfies the concavity condition as follows:

$$\frac{dV_{h,t}}{dW_{h,t}/\overline{W}_t} > 0, \quad \frac{d^2V_{h,t}}{d\left(W_{h,t}/\overline{W}_t\right)^2} < 0,$$

where, while $V_{h,t}(W_{h,t}/\overline{W}_t)$ increases in response to an increase in $W_{h,t}$, it decreases in response to an increase in $\overline{W}_t$. The choice of status goods affects the growth-enhancing effect of environmental policies. We discuss this in Sect. 4. The budget constraint of household $h$ is as follows from (2.3):

$$\dot{W}_{h,t} = r_t W_{h,t} + w_t - C_{h,t}. \tag{7.2}$$

Given $\overline{W}$, household $h$ chooses consumption and assets that maximise the utility level in (7.1), subject to the budget constraint in (7.2). The first-order condition for the dynamic utility maximisation problem yields the following:

$$\frac{\beta}{C_{h,t}} = \lambda_{h,t}, \tag{7.3}$$

$$-\dot{\lambda}_{h,t} + \rho\lambda_{h,t} = r_t\lambda_{h,t} + \eta_W \frac{V_{h,t}{}'(W_{h,t}/\overline{W}_t)}{V_{h,t}(W_{h,t}/\overline{W}_t)} \cdot \frac{1}{\overline{W}_t}, \tag{7.4}$$

$$\lim_{T\to\infty} \lambda_{h,T} W_{h,T} e^{-\rho T} = 0, \tag{7.5}$$

where (7.5) is TVC and the second term on the RHS in (7.4) expresses the effect of social status preference.

Futagami and Shibata (1998) performed an analysis, accounting for the heterogeneity between households in terms of assets, however, this complicates the present analysis. Therefore, we assume symmetry between households, following Pan et al. (2018). In this case, the assets of household $h$ are equal to the assets of society, as follows:

$$W_{h,t} = K_{h,t} + P_{A,t}A_{h,t} = K_t + P_{A,t}A_t = W_t,$$

where $W_{h,t}/\overline{W}_t = 1$ holds. Assets, consumption and labour are aggregated as follows:

$$\int_0^1 W_{h,t}dh = K_t + P_{A,t}A_t,$$

$$\int_0^1 C_{h,t}dh = C_t = C_{h,t},$$

$$\int_0^1 (L^Y_{h,t} + L^A_{h,t})dh = L_{Y,t} + L_{A,t} = L^Y_{h,t} + L^A_{h,t}.$$

Here, following Futagami and Shibata (1998), we define the social status preference of household $h$ as $\theta_{W,h} \equiv \eta_W V_h'(1)/\beta V_h(1)$. Under a symmetric equilibrium, $\theta_W \equiv \eta_W V_h'(1)/\beta V_h(1)$, an increase in $\theta_W$ implies an increase in social status preference. Using (7.3), (7.4) can be rewritten to derive the Euler equation, including social status preference, as follows:

$$\frac{\dot{C}_t}{C_t} = (r_t - \rho) + \theta_W \frac{C_t}{W_t}, \tag{7.6}$$

where the $\theta_W(C_t/W_t)$ in the third term on the RHS is the marginal rate of substitution between assets and consumption. Holding all other parameters as constant, an increase in $\theta_W$ raises the consumption growth rate because households work harder to accumulate capital to improve their social status. This status-seeking increases their future assets, which, in turn, increases future consumption. Pan et al. (2018) called the growth effect through $\theta_W C_t/W_t$ as the substitution effect. The reduction in emission allowances affects economic growth through this substitution effect.

## 7.3 Equilibrium

### 7.3.1 Dynamic System

The dynamic system in the present model is constructed from the jump variables $y_t \equiv Y_t/K_t$ and $z_t \equiv C_t/K_t$ and the static variable $\omega_t \equiv K_t/A_t$, similar to Chap. 6.[1]

Using $W_t = K_t + P_{A,t}A_t$, $P_{A,t}\delta A_t = w_t$ in (2.17) and $L_{Y,t} = y_t^{\frac{1}{1-\alpha}}\omega_t$ in Appendix A.5, we rewrite $\theta_W(C_t/W_t)$ in (7.6) as follows:

$$\theta_W \frac{C_t}{W_t} = \frac{\theta_W C_t}{K_t + P_{A,t}A_t} = \frac{\theta_W z_t}{1 + \left(\frac{1-\alpha}{\delta}\right)\frac{1}{y_t^{\alpha/(1-\alpha)}\omega_t}}, \tag{7.7}$$

where $\theta_W(C_t/W_t)$ depends on $y_t$, $z_t$ and $\omega_t$. The complexity of this variable gives rise to multiple steady states (explained later). In Appendix F, the three-dimensional dynamical system for the present model is derived as follows:

$$\frac{\dot{y}_t}{y_t} = \frac{1-\alpha}{\alpha}\left(\alpha\delta y_t^{\frac{1}{1-\alpha}}\omega_t + \frac{1}{P} - \alpha^2 y_t\right), \tag{6.14}$$

$$\frac{\dot{z}_t}{z_t} = z_t - (1-\alpha^2)y_t - \left(\rho - \frac{\delta\theta_W y_t^{\frac{\alpha}{1-\alpha}} z_t\omega_t}{\delta y_t^{\frac{\alpha}{1-\alpha}} + 1 - \alpha}\right), \tag{7.8}$$

$$\frac{\dot{\omega}_t}{\omega_t} = y_t - z_t - \frac{1}{P} - \delta\left(L - y_t^{\frac{1}{1-\alpha}}\omega_t\right), \tag{7.9}$$

where the RHS of (7.8) includes the status effect of $\theta_W(C_t/W_t)$ and the RHS of (6.14) and (7.9) include the emission allowance, compared to the economic model in Chap. 2.

In a BGP equilibrium, $g = \dot{C}_t/C_t = \dot{K}_t/K_t = \dot{A}_t/A_t = \dot{Y}_t/Y_t$ because $\dot{y}_t = \dot{z}_t = \dot{\omega}_t = 0$. In the steady state, from (6.14), the multiple steady states can be derived as follows:

---

[1] For a detailed derivation process, see the appendix in Hamaguchi (2019).

$$y_l^* = \frac{B_3 - \sqrt{B_3^2 - B_4}}{2\alpha(1+\alpha)(1+\theta_W)},\ y_h^* = \frac{B_3 + \sqrt{B_3^2 - B_4}}{2\alpha(1+\alpha)(1+\theta_W)}, \tag{7.10}$$

and $y_h^* > y_l^* > 0$ for

$$B_3 \equiv \delta + \rho + \alpha\delta\theta_W + \frac{(1+\alpha)^2(1+\theta_W)}{\alpha\overline{P}},$$

$$B_4 \equiv 4\alpha(1+\alpha)(1+\theta_W)\left[B_3 - \frac{(1+\alpha)(1+\theta_W)}{\overline{P}}\right],$$

where $B_4 > 0$ and $B_3^2 - B_4 > 0$ hold under following parameters:

$$\frac{2+\delta+\rho+\alpha\delta\theta_W}{4\alpha(1+\alpha)} \geq 1+\theta_W,\ \frac{\delta}{2\alpha} \geq 1+\theta_W,\ 1 \geq \alpha(1+\alpha)^2,$$

$$\frac{1+\alpha}{\alpha} \geq \overline{P},\ \frac{1+\theta_W}{\alpha(\delta+\rho+\alpha\delta\theta_W)} \geq \overline{P},$$

which guarantees the non-negativity of $y_l^*$, the locally saddle-point stability of the steady state and the effect of the emission allowance. These parameter conditions are satisfied under the numerical values based on previous research (Hamaguchi 2019). In addition, $(2+\delta+\rho+\alpha\delta\theta_W)/[4\alpha(1+\alpha)] \geq 1+\theta_W$ guarantees $y_l^* > 0$. In the steady state, from (7.9) and (7.10), multiple steady states can be derived as follows:

$$\omega_l^* = \frac{\alpha^2 y_l^* - 1/\overline{P}}{\alpha\delta y_l^{*\frac{1}{1-\alpha}}},\ \omega_h^* = \frac{\alpha^2 y_h^* - 1/\overline{P}}{\alpha\delta y_h^{*\frac{1}{1-\alpha}}}, \tag{7.11}$$

and

$$z_l^* = (1+\alpha)y_l^* - \left(\tfrac{1+\alpha}{\alpha}\right)\tfrac{1}{\overline{P}} - \delta,\ z_h^* = (1+\alpha)y_h^* - \left(\tfrac{1+\alpha}{\alpha}\right)\tfrac{1}{\overline{P}} - \delta. \tag{7.12}$$

In the appendix, Hamaguchi (2019) rigorously proved the local stability of the dynamical system consisting of (6.14), (7.9) and (7.10). Under $1 \geq \alpha(1+\alpha)^2$ and $(1+\theta_W)/[\alpha(\delta+\rho+\alpha\delta\theta_W)] \geq \overline{P}$, the high steady state of $\left(y_h^*, z_h^*, \omega_h^*\right)$ and $\left(y_l^*, z_l^*, \omega_l^*\right)$ are equilibria with locally saddle-point stable paths, respectively. Since $y_h^* > y_l^* > 0$, $\left(y_l^*, z_l^*, \omega_l^*\right)$ implies a poverty trap, Antoci et al. (2011) derived multiple steady states by assuming an externality effect. Their numerical analysis shows that a three-dimensional dynamic system in continuous time can exhibit chaos and limit cycles in its transfer dynamics. In the present model, which does not assume an externality effect, there is a possibility that limit cycles and exhibits chaos. However, a rigorous numerical analysis is awaited.

### 7.3.2 Growth and Welfare

(7.7) can be rewritten as follows by using a steady value:

$$\theta_W \frac{C_l^*}{W_l^*} = \frac{\theta_W z_l^*}{1+\frac{1-\alpha}{\alpha-\left(\frac{1}{\alpha P y_l^*}\right)}},\ \theta_W \frac{C_h^*}{W_h^*} = \frac{\theta_W z_h^*}{1+\frac{1-\alpha}{\alpha-\left(\frac{1}{\alpha P y_h^*}\right)}}, \tag{7.13}$$

which is used to derive the following economic growth rates in Appendix F:

$$g_l^* = \frac{1}{1+\alpha}\left[\alpha\delta - \left(\rho - \theta_W \frac{C_l^*}{W_l^*}\right)\right],\ g_h^* = \frac{1}{1+\alpha}\left[\alpha\delta - \left(\rho - \theta_W \frac{C_h^*}{W_h^*}\right)\right], \tag{7.14}$$

where $\rho - \theta_W(C_t/W_t)$ is an effective discount rate in Futagami and Shibata (1998). Emission allowances affect the economic growth rate through MRS regarding assets and consumption in $\theta_W(C_t/W_t)$.

The welfare level in this economy is the household utility. Using $C_t = z^* K_0 e^{gt}$ and rewriting (7.1), welfare can be expressed as:

$$U_l = \frac{\beta}{\rho}\log z_l^* + \left[\frac{\beta}{\rho}\log K_0 + \frac{\beta g_l^*}{\rho^2}\right] + \frac{\eta_W}{\rho}\log V(1) - \frac{\eta_P}{\rho}\log \overline{P}, \tag{7.15a}$$

$$U_h = \frac{\beta}{\rho}\log z_h^* + \left[\frac{\beta}{\rho}\log K_0 + \frac{\beta g_h^*}{\rho^2}\right] + \frac{\eta_W}{\rho}\log V(1) - \frac{\eta_P}{\rho}\log \overline{P}, \tag{7.15b}$$

where the third term on the RHS is the static welfare improvement effect due to social status preference. As explained in (6.25), the welfare effects of the first, second and fourth terms on the RHS are the same as in Chap. 6.

### 7.3.3 Comparative Statics

Differentiating (7.10)–(7.14) by the emission allowance $\overline{P}$, we obtain:

$$\frac{dy_l^*}{d\overline{P}} > 0,\ \frac{dz_l^*}{d\overline{P}} > 0,\ \frac{d}{d\overline{P}}\left(\theta_W \frac{C_l^*}{W_l^*}\right) > 0,\ \frac{dg_l^*}{d\overline{P}} = \frac{1}{1+\alpha}\frac{\partial}{\partial\overline{P}}\left(\theta_W \frac{C_l^*}{W_l^*}\right) > 0,$$

and

$$\frac{dy_h^*}{d\overline{P}} < 0,\ \frac{dz_h^*}{d\overline{P}} < 0,\ \frac{d}{d\overline{P}}\left(\theta_W \frac{C_h^*}{W_h^*}\right) < 0,\ \frac{dg_h^*}{d\overline{P}} = \frac{1}{1+\alpha}\frac{\partial}{\partial\overline{P}}\left(\theta_W \frac{C_h^*}{W_h^*}\right) < 0,$$

where, in the low steady state, a reduction in the emission allowance lowers the economic growth rate through a decrease in the MRS for assets and consumption, while, in the high steady state, a reduction in the emission allowance raises the economic growth rate through an increase in the MRS for assets and consumption.

Furthermore, the level effect of the emission allowance on $\omega^*$ and the growth effect of social status preference are difficult to prove analytically due to their complexity. For the derivation process, refer to Hamaguchi (2019).

The effect of emission allowances on economic growth rates through MRS regarding assets and consumption is the substitution effect. This effect depends on the crowding-out and the resource reallocation effects. First, let us explain the crowding-out effect. In a low steady state, due to the reduction of emission allowances, final goods firms must reduce pollution by inputting pollution abatement goods. When the quantity of final goods produced remains unchanged, as $(1+\alpha)/\left(\alpha\overline{P}\right)$ in (7.12), the final goods used for consumption are substituted for pollution abatement goods and $z_l^*$ decreases (crowding-out effect). As a result, $\theta_W C_l^*/W_l^*$ in (7.13) decreases. The rate of economic growth falls through the substitution effect, in which consumption is substituted for assets.

In a high steady state, the reduction in the emission allowance increases $z_h^*$, despite the crowding-out effect, because the production of the final good increases due to the resource reallocation effect and $y_h^*$ rises. Under certain parameter conditions, the resource reallocation effect dominates the crowding-out effect. Therefore, due to the increase in $y_h^*$, the pollution abatement goods at $(1+\alpha)/\alpha\overline{P}$ but $z_h^*$ increase. Due to the increase in $z_h^*$, $\theta_W C_h^*/W_h^*$ in (7.13) increases. The economic growth rate increases through the substitution effect, in which assets are substituted for consumption.

Next, we explain the resource reallocation effect. As shown in (6.9), $p_t^e = Z_t/\overline{P}$, a reduction in the emission allowance increases its price through demand. As shown in (6.8), $\alpha\left(L_{Y,t}/x_t\right)^{1-\alpha} = p_t + \left(p_t^e/Z_t\right)$, the marginal cost of the intermediate good increases, keeping all other factors the same. When the amount of pollution abatement goods input remains unchanged, final goods firms reduce pollution emissions by reducing intermediate goods input. As a result, the production of final goods decreases. Hence, firms substitute intermediate goods input for labour input. Using (6.8), (2.11) can be rewritten as a wage rate per variety as follows:

$$\frac{w_t}{A_t} = (1-\alpha)\left[\frac{\alpha}{p_t + (p_t^e/Z_t)}\right]^{\frac{\alpha}{1-\alpha}},$$

where a reduction in the emission allowance raises $w_t/A_t$ through an increase in the price of emission allowances. This is because the substitution of intermediate goods for labour increases labour demand, which, in turn, increases the production of final goods without increasing pollution emissions. In a low steady state, the decrease in dirty inputs $x_t = K_t/A_t$ due to the reduction in emission allowances dominates the increase in clean inputs $L_{Y,t}$, hence, the production of final goods decreases and $y_l^*$ falls. However, in a high steady state, the increase in clean input $L_{Y,t}$ due to the reduction in emission allowances dominates the decrease in dirty input $x_t = K_t/A_t$, hence, the production of final goods increases and $y_h^*$ rises.

In a low steady state, as shown $1/\alpha\overline{P}y_l^*$ in (7.13), the resource reallocation effect decreases $\theta_W\left(C_l^*/W_l^*\right)$ in (7.13) through a decrease in $y_l^*$. The economic growth rate falls through the substitution effect, in which consumption is substituted for assets. In a high steady state, as in $1/\left(\alpha\overline{P}y_h^*\right)$ in (7.13), the resource reallocation effect increases $\theta_W C_h^*/W_h^*$ in (7.13) through an increase in $y_h^*$. The economic growth rate increases through the substitution effect, in which assets are substituted for consumption.

Under the parameter conditions of $(\delta/2\alpha) \geq 1+\theta_W$ and $(1+\alpha)/\alpha \geq \overline{P}$, emission allowances have a monotonic effect on economic growth rates through substitution effects consisting of crowding-out and resource reallocation effects. However, under $(\delta/2\alpha) < 1+\theta_W$, even in a high steady state, a decrease in dirty inputs $x_t = K_t/A_t$ due to a reduction in emission allowances dominates an increase in clean inputs $L_{Y,t}$. Hence, there is the possibility that production of the final good decreases and $dy_h^*/d\overline{P} > 0$. In this case, under the condition $(1+\alpha)/\alpha < \overline{P}$, there is a possibility that $dz_h^*/d\overline{P} > 0$ through the crowding-out and the resource reallocation effects. Therefore, the reduction of the emission allowance reduces $\theta_W\left(C_h^*/W_h^*\right)$ in (7.13) through the decrease of $y_h^*$ and $z_h^*$, declining the economic growth rate. Under these conditions, in a high steady state, the non-monotonic relationship between emission allowances, assets and consumption may produce non-monotonic growth effects. However, due to its analytical complexity, it is difficult to prove. For details, see Hamaguchi (2019).

Differentiating (7.15b) by the emission allowance $\overline{P}$, we obtain the following welfare effects:

$$\frac{dU_h}{d\overline{P}} = \left[\frac{\beta}{\rho z_h^*}\underbrace{\frac{\partial z_h^*}{\partial \overline{P}}}_{(-)} + \frac{\beta}{\rho^2}\underbrace{\frac{\partial g_h^*}{\partial \overline{P}}}_{(-)}\right] - \frac{\eta_P}{\rho \overline{P}} < 0,$$

where, in a high steady state, the reduction of emission allowances monotonically improves welfare through increased consumption, economic growth and pollution reduction.

Differentiating (7.15a) by the emission allowance $\overline{P}$, we obtain the following welfare effects;

$$\frac{dU_l}{d\overline{P}} = \left[\frac{\beta}{\rho z_l^*}\underbrace{\frac{\partial z_l^*}{\partial \overline{P}}}_{(+)} + \frac{\beta}{\rho^2}\underbrace{\frac{\partial g_l^*}{\partial \overline{P}}}_{(+)}\right] - \frac{\eta_P}{\rho \overline{P}} \gtreqless 0,$$

where, in a low steady state, a reduction in the emission allowance leads to welfare deterioration due to decreased consumption and economic growth and welfare improvement due to pollution reduction. The welfare effect of the emission allowance is determined depending on whether the positive welfare effect dominates the negative welfare effect. Since $z_l^*$ and $g_l^*$ do not include $\eta_P$, we obtain $dU_l/d\overline{P} \gtreqless 0$ for

$$\hat{\eta}_P \equiv \rho\overline{P}\left[\frac{\beta}{\rho z_l^*}\frac{\partial z_l^*}{\partial \overline{P}} + \frac{\beta}{\rho^2}\frac{\partial g_l^*}{\partial \overline{P}}\right] \gtrless \eta_P,$$

where $\hat{\eta}_P$ is the threshold value for the welfare effect of emission allowances. When households place more importance on pollution than on consumption, a reduction in emission quotas in the low steady state monotonically improves welfare.

## 7.4 Determinant of a Growth-Enhancing Effect

### *7.4.1 Importance of Social Status Preference*

By assuming $\theta_W = 0$, the Euler equation for consumption in (7.6) can be rewritten as $g_C = \dot{C}_t/C_t = r_t - \rho$. In this, the economic growth rate is no longer dependent on the substitution effect of $\theta_W(C_t/W_t)$. Hence, as shown in Appendix A of Chap. 2, the variety growth rate is $g_A = \dot{A}_t/A_t = \delta - (r_t/\alpha)$. In the steady state, from $g_C = g_A$, the economic growth rate is derived as $g^* = \alpha(\delta + \rho)/(1 + \alpha) - \rho$. This economic growth rate is the same as in the case where leisure is not considered, with $\beta = 1$, in Chap. 6. In this case, the steady-state values $y^*$ in (6.26), $L_Y^*$ and $L_A^*$ in (6.27) and $r^* = \alpha(\delta + \rho)/(1 + \alpha)$ in (6.27) are obtained. Therefore, the multiple steady states for $y^*$, which were obtained in the previous section, become a single steady state. When $\theta_W = 0$ and social status preferences are not taken into account, as was explained in the case of leisure time, $\partial y^*/\partial \overline{P} < 0$ in (6.26) and $\partial r^*/\partial \overline{P} > 0$ in $r^* = \alpha^2 y^* - \left(1/\overline{P}\right)$ cancel each other out, hence, the environmental policy loses its growth effect.

### *7.4.2 Importance of Status Good*

When analysing the growth effects of environmental policies through social status preferences, the choice of status goods affects these growth effects. As in Howarth (1996) and Wendner (2003), households feel that their social status is higher when their consumption and utility levels increase, while they feel that it is lower when the average consumption in society increases and their utility level decreases. Hence, the utility function in (7.1) is as follows:

$$U_t = \int_0^\infty \left[\beta \log C_{h,t} + \eta_C \log V_{h,t}\left(\frac{C_{h,t}}{\overline{C}_t}\right) - \eta_P \log P_t\right] e^{-\rho t} dt, \tag{7.16}$$

where $\overline{C}_t$ is average consumption in the economy and $\theta_C > 0$ is a degree of social status preference for consumption. Given $\overline{C}$, the household $h$ chooses consumption and assets that maximise the utility level in (7.16), subject to the budget constraint in (7.2), as follows:

$$\frac{\beta}{C_{h,t}} + \eta_C \frac{V_{h,t}{}'(C_{h,t}/\overline{C}_t)}{V_{h,t}(C_{h,t}/\overline{C}_t)} \cdot \frac{1}{\overline{C}_t} = \lambda_{h,t}, \tag{7.17a}$$

$$-\dot{\lambda}_{h,t} + \rho\lambda_{h,t} = r_t\lambda_{h,t}, \tag{7.17b}$$

$$\lim_{T\to\infty} \lambda_{h,T} W_{h,T} e^{-\rho T} = 0, \tag{7.17c}$$

where (7.17c) is TVC and the second term on the LHS of (7.17a) expresses the effect of social status preference.

Under a symmetric equilibrium, the social status preference of household $h$ is $\theta_W \equiv \eta_W V_h'(1)/\beta V_h(1)$. Hence, (7.17a) can be rewritten as follows:

$$\frac{\beta}{C_t} + \frac{\theta_C}{C_t} = \lambda_t,$$

which is used with (7.17b) to derive the Euler equation as $\dot{C}_t/C_t = r_t - \rho$. An increase in $\theta_C$ leads to a consumption decrease, as it increases the marginal utility of consumption at present. However, as shown in $-[(\beta + \theta_C)/C_t]\big(\dot{C}_t/C_t\big) = \dot{\lambda}_t$, an increase in $\theta_C$ leads to a consumption increase, as it decreases the marginal utility of consumption between different times. As these two effects cancel each other out, social status preferences regarding consumption do not affect the Euler equation. In this case, the steady state is the same as in 4.1, environmental policies do not affect economic growth and there are no multiple steady states.

### 7.4.3 Reason for Multiple Steady States

When $\theta_W > 0$, multiple steady states for $y^*$ arise due to the complementary effect of $y_t$ in $\theta_W(C_t/W_t)$. Substituting $z^*$ in (7.12) into (7.13) asserts the following:

$$\theta_W \frac{C^*}{W^*} = \frac{\theta_W\left[(1+\alpha)y^* - \left(\frac{1+\alpha}{\alpha}\right)\frac{1}{\overline{P}} - \delta\right]}{1 + \frac{1-\alpha}{\alpha - \left(\frac{1}{\alpha\overline{P}y^*}\right)}},$$

where, as shown in $1/\alpha\overline{P}y^*$, an increase in $y^*$ increases $\theta_W(C^*/W^*)$ through the substitution effect, which causes assets to be substituted for consumption. Hence, an increase in $y^*$ stimulates this substitution effect through an increase in $z^*$, which indirectly further increases $\theta_W(C^*/W^*)$. This mutually complementary effect promotes economic growth and, through asset accumulation, future production increases, creating a high steady state. However, a fall in $y^*$ reduces $\theta_W(C^*/W^*)$ through the substitution effect, which causes consumption to be substituted for assets. Hence, a fall in $y^*$ inhibits this substitution effect through a fall in $z^*$ and indirectly further reduces $\theta_W(C^*/W^*)$. This mutually complementary effect causes economic growth to stagnate and, through a slowdown in asset accumulation, future production decreases, creating a low steady state. This low steady state is an equilibrium with a locally saddle-point stable path, hence, it implies a poverty trap because $y_h^* > y_l^* > 0$.

### 7.4.4 Importance of Labour in the R&D Sector

When considering the lab-equipment model in Chap. 6, what is the impact of the growth effect through social status preference? As shown in Chap. 6, the output per unit of capital is $y = [(1-\alpha)/\delta v]^{(1-\alpha)/\alpha}$ in (6.28) and, from $y = \alpha^2 r - \left(1/\overline{P}\right)$, $r = \alpha^2[(1-\alpha)/\delta \upsilon]^{\frac{1-\alpha}{\alpha}} - \left(1/\overline{P}\right)$ holds. If $L_{Y,t} = L = 1$ in the production function, we obtain $Y_t = K_t^{\alpha}(A_t)^{1-\alpha}$, which can be rewritten as $y_t = \omega_t^{\alpha-1}$. Using $y = [(1-\alpha)/\delta v]^{(1-\alpha)/\alpha}$, we obtain $\omega = [\delta v/(1-\alpha)]^{1/\alpha}$. Substituting $p_t^e = Z_t/\overline{P}$ in (6.9) and $p_t = (1/\alpha)\left[r + \left(1/\overline{P}\right)\right]$ and $L_{Y,t} = L = 1$ into (6.8) gives $x = \left[\alpha^2/\left\{r + (1+\alpha)/\overline{P}\right\}\right]^{1/(1-\alpha)}$, which is rewritten by using $r = \alpha^2[(1-\alpha)/\delta \upsilon]^{\frac{1-\alpha}{\alpha}} - \left(1/\overline{P}\right)$ as follows:

$$x = \left[\frac{\alpha}{\alpha[(1-\alpha)/\delta \upsilon]^{\frac{1-\alpha}{\alpha}} + 1/\overline{P}}\right]^{\frac{1}{1-\alpha}}, \tag{7.18}$$

where $dx/d\overline{P} > 0$ implies that a reduction in the emission allowance reduces the production of intermediate goods, because the rise in the price of emission allowances increases the marginal cost of intermediate goods input for final goods firms, reducing the intermediate goods input. From $x = K_t/A_t$, we obtain $\dot{K}_t = \dot{A}_t$ and $K_t = xA_t$. Using these, the labour market clearing condition $Y_t = C_t + Z_t + \dot{K}_t + \upsilon\dot{A}_t$ can be rewritten as follows:

$$\frac{\dot{K}_t}{K_t} = \frac{1}{1+v}\left[\left(\frac{1-\alpha}{\delta v}\right)^{\frac{1-\alpha}{\alpha}} - z_t - \frac{1}{\overline{P}}\right]. \tag{7.19}$$

By using $P_A = \upsilon$ and $\omega = [\delta v/(1-\alpha)]^{1/\alpha}$, (7.7) can be rewritten as follows:

$$\theta_W \frac{C_t}{W_t} = \frac{\theta_W z_t}{1+v[(1-\alpha)/\delta v]^{1/\alpha}}, \tag{7.20}$$

which is used to rewrite (7.8) with (7.6) and $r^* = \alpha^2[(1-\alpha)/\delta \upsilon]^{\frac{1-\alpha}{\alpha}} - \left(1/\overline{P}\right)$ as follows:

$$\frac{\dot{C}_t}{C_t} = -\left(1-\alpha^2\right)\left(\frac{1-\alpha}{\delta v}\right)^{\frac{1-\alpha}{\alpha}} - \left(\rho - \frac{\theta_W z_t}{1+v[(1-\alpha)/\delta v]^{1/\alpha}}\right), \tag{7.21}$$

which is used with (7.19) to derive the following dynamic system:

$$\frac{\dot{z}_t}{z_t} = z_t + \frac{1}{\overline{P}} - \left(1 - \alpha^2 + \frac{1}{1+v}\right)\left(\frac{1-\alpha}{\delta v}\right)^{\frac{1-\alpha}{\alpha}} - \left(\rho - \frac{\theta_W z_t}{1+v[(1-\alpha)/\delta v]^{1/\alpha}}\right). \tag{7.22}$$

At $\dot{z}_t = 0$, we obtain the consumption per unit of capital in the steady state as follows:

$$z^* = \frac{\left(\rho - \frac{1}{\overline{P}}\right) + \left(1-\alpha^2+\frac{1}{1+v}\right)\left(\frac{1-\alpha}{\delta v}\right)^{\frac{1-\alpha}{\alpha}}}{1+\frac{\theta_W}{1+v[(1-\alpha)/\delta v]^{1/\alpha}}}, \tag{7.23}$$

which implies that the reduction in the emission allowance lower $z^*$ through the crowding-out effect. Substituting (7.23) into (7.21) gives the following economic growth rate:

$$g^* = -\left(1 - \alpha^2\right)\left(\frac{1-\alpha}{\delta v}\right)^{\frac{1-\alpha}{\alpha}} - \rho + \frac{\left(\rho - \frac{1}{\overline{P}}\right) + \left(1-\alpha^2+\frac{1}{1+v}\right)\left(\frac{1-\alpha}{\delta v}\right)^{\frac{1-\alpha}{\alpha}}}{(1/\theta_W)+v[(1-\alpha)/\delta v]^{1/\alpha}+1}, \tag{7.24}$$

where $dg^*/d\overline{P} > 0$ and $dg^*/d\theta_W > 0$ holds.

In the MRS for assets and consumption in (7.20), there is a crowding-out effect through $z_t$, however, the resource reallocation effect through $y_t$ disappears due to $P_A = \upsilon$. As this complementary effect through $y_t$ disappears, the steady state becomes unique. In addition, in this lab-equipment model, an increase in social status preference for assets promotes economic growth through a substitution effect.

In (7.18), a reduction in the emission allowance reduces the production of final goods, as final goods firms reduce their input of intermediate goods through an increase in the price of emission allowances. In addition, due to the reduction in emission allowances, firms increase their input of pollution abatement goods. Therefore, due to the decrease in production and the increase in pollution abatement goods, consumption per unit of capital decreases. In (7.20), the economic growth rate decreases due to the substitution effect, in which consumption is substituted for assets. Regarding social status preference, the labour input in the R&D sector affects the growth-enhancing effect of environmental policy.

## References


Antoci, A., Galeotti, M., & Russu, P. (2011). Poverty trap and global indeterminacy in a growth model with open-access natural resources. *Journal of Economic Theory*, 146(2), 569–591. https://doi.org/10.1016/j.jedc.2020.103929

Brekke, K. A., & Howarth, R. B. (2002). Status, growth and the environment: goods as symbols in applied welfare economics. In Status, Growth and the Environment. Edward Elgar Publishing. https://doi.org/10.4337/9781035335558

Futagami, K., & Shibata, A. (1998). Keeping one step ahead of the Joneses: Status, the distribution of wealth, and long run growth. *Journal of Economic Behavior & Organization*, 36(1), 109–126. https://doi.org/10.1016/S0167-2681(98)00072-9

Gsottbauer, E., & van den Bergh, J. C. (2011). Environmental policy when pollutive consumption is sensitive to advertising: Norms versus status. *Ecological Economics*, 107, 39–50. https://doi.org/10.1016/j.ecolecon.2014.07.001

Hamaguchi, Y. (2019). Positive effect of pollution permits in a variety expansion model with social status preference. *The Manchester School*, 87(4), 591–606. https://doi.org/10.1111/manc.12270

Howarth, R. B. (1996). Status effects and environmental externalities. *Ecological Economics*, 16(1), 25–34. https://doi.org/10.1016/0921-8009(95)00076-3

Nguyen-Van, P., & Pham, T. K. C. (2013). Endogenous fiscal policies, environmental quality, and status-seeking behavior. *Ecological Economics*, 88, 32–40. https://doi.org/10.1016/j.ecolecon.2012.10.021

Pan, S., Zhang, M., & Zou, H. F. (2018). Status preference and the effects of patent protection: Theory and evidence. *Macroeconomic Dynamics*, 22(4), 837–863. https://doi.org/10.1017/S1365100516000420

Weiss, Y., & Fershtman, C. (1998). Social status and economic performance: A survey. https://doi.org/10.1016/S0014-2921(97)00137-2

Wendner, R. (2003). Status, environmental externality, and optimal tax programs. *Economics Bulletin*, 8(5), 1–10. http://www.economicsbulletin.com/2003/volume8/EB-02H20005A.pdf

# Chapter 8
# Non-Homothetic Preferences

**Abstract** The variety expansion model with constant substitution elasticity in Chap. 4 is extended to the Direct Explicitly Additivity (DEA) model, in which the direct utility function is explicitly added. This non-homothetic preference creates competition between goods sector firms and alters the growth effects of environmental policy. When the mark-up rate rises with goods production, environmental tax leads to pollution reduction and economic growth through imperfect pass-through effects. However, when the mark-up rate falls with goods production, the environmental tax increases pollution emissions and decreases the economic growth rate through perfect pass-through effects. To pass on the environmental tax to the price, the production volume of the goods company temporarily decreases, however, the mark-up rate increases. Due to this increase, the goods company increases production and pollution emissions. In addition, due to the stagnation of variety development accompanying the labour transfer from the R&D to the goods sector, the economic growth rate decreases. Therefore, the growth promotion effect of environmental policy can change depending on the demand composition.

## 8.1 Introduction

In the variety expansion model developed by Grossman and Helpman (1991, Chap. 3), the elasticity of substitution between varieties was an important parameter. This is because it implies the degree of product differentiation and influences household preferences for varieties. As explained in Chap. 3, an increase in substitution elasticity leads to a decrease in the mark-up rate and, consequently, lowers the economic growth rate. This mark-up rate affects the profits of good firms through price pass-through and the economic growth rate through labour mobility. Therefore, endogenous changes in substitution elasticity have the potential to bring about new growth effects.

Latzer et al. (2019) focused on this point and considered Direct Explicitly Additivity (DEA), in which the direct utility function is explicitly additive. This non-homothetic preference produces counterintuitive results because it creates competition between goods firms. When the effect of mark-up price pass-through is weak, the

 
Y. Hamaguchi, *Sustainable Development in Economic Growth Theory*,
https://doi.org/10.1007/978-981-96-7639-2_8

economic growth rate falls despite population growth. This contradicts the scale effect when substitution elasticity is constant. Although it is not an R&D-based growth model, Alonso-Carrera et al. (2019), applied non-homothetic preferences and showed that when the income elasticity of pollution abatement is greater than 1, the majority of the increased income is used for pollution abatement. Hence, pollution emissions decrease in line with income. This chapter applies this result to environmental policy.

In the simple variety expansion model in Chap. 4, an environmental tax leads to sustainable development through pollution reduction and economic growth. However, regarding non-homothetic preferences, this growth-enhancing effect may disappear. The variety expansion model in Grossman and Helpman (1991, Chap. 3) is applied to the location of firms and industrial structure in the following chapters, hence, the results obtained may vary depending on the demand composition.

## 8.2 The Model

### 8.2.1 *Structure of the Variety Expansion Model with Non-Homothetic Preferences*

The basic structure of the economic model is the same as in Chap. 3. However, in Chap. 3, the substitution elasticity, which is assumed to be constant between any two varieties, changes. As in Latzer et al. (2019), the intratemporal preference satisfies DEA when the direct utility function is explicitly additive. This non-homothetic preference creates competition between goods firms and alters the growth effect of environmental policy. The economic model in this chapter is an extension of the R&D-based growth model by Latzer et al. (2019) and is summarised in Fig. 8.1.

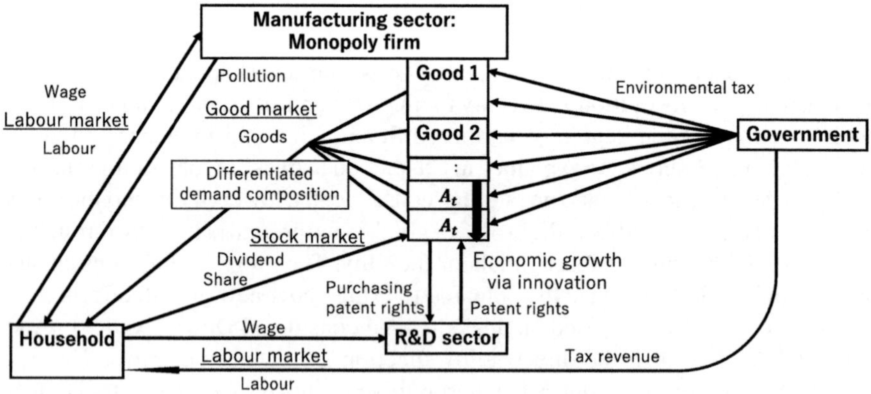


**Fig. 8.1** Structure of the variety expansion model with non-homothetic preferences

### 8.2.2 Household Under DEA Preference

Intertemporal preferences of each household are represented as follows:

$$u_t = \int_0^\infty \log U(Q_t, P_t)e^{-\rho t}dt, \tag{8.1}$$

where $U(Q_t, P_t)$ is the intertemporal utility function. For simplicity in analysis, we assume $L = 1$. We describe the intertemporal budget constraint. Each household holds its asset $W_t = P_{A,t}A_t$, which is the shares of R&D firms as the return for funding. They obtain labour income $w_t$ and share income $\pi_t A_t$ and receive a lump sum subsidy $T_t$ from the government. Using these incomes, they spend $E_t = p_t x_t A_t$ for consumption and purchase $P_{A,t}\dot{A}_t$ for saving. Thus, the flow budget constraint is represented as follows:

$$P_{A,t}\dot{A}_t + E_t = w_t + \pi_t A_t + T_t,$$

where $T_t \equiv \tau P_t$ is the lump sum covered by environmental tax revenue. Summing the capital gains $\dot{P}_{A,t}A_t$ on both sides, this equation is rewritten as follows:

$$W_t + E_t = w_t + r_t W_t + T_t,$$

which is derived using the non-arbitrage condition in (3.9) and $W_t = P_{A,t}A_t$. Integrating it with $t = 0$ to infinity, yields the following intertemporal budget constraint:

$$\int_0^\infty E_t e^{-Rt}dt \leq W_0 + \int_0^\infty w_t e^{-Rt}dt + \int_0^\infty T_t e^{-Rt}dt, \tag{8.2}$$

where $\lim_{t\to\infty} W_t e^{-Rt} \geq 0$ is the transversality condition and $R_t$ is the cumulated instantaneous real interest rate.

Under broader DEA preferences, CES preferences are a knife-edge case. We consider the following direct explicitly additive preferences:

$$U(Q_t, P_t) \equiv \int_0^{A_t} u(x_{j,t})dj,$$

where the sub-utility function of $u(\cdot)$ is assumed to be thrice-differentiable and $u_0 = 0$, $u'(x) > 0$ and $u''(x) < 0$. The households maximise this intratemporal utility subject to $\int_0^{A_t} p_{j,t}x_{j,t}dj = E_t$. Solving this utility maximisation problem yields the following demand function per capita for each good:

$$p_{j,t} = \frac{u'(x_{j,t})E_t}{\Theta_t}, \tag{8.3}$$

where

$$\Theta_t \equiv \int_0^{A_t} u'\left(x'_{j,t}\right)x_{j',t}dj',$$

which implies the effects of firms competing in the market.

### 8.2.3 Firms and Market Under DEA Preference

Taking $P_{M,t}$ in (3.5) as given, each firm chooses the price $p_{j,t}$, subject to $d_{j,t} = q_{j,t}/\theta_j$, $\theta = \theta_j$ and (8.3), to maximise the following profit:

$$\max_{p_{j,t}} \pi_{j,t} = \left[p_{j,t} - \iota_t\left(1 + \frac{\tau}{\theta}\right)\right]q_{j,t}, \text{ s.t. } p_{j,t} = \frac{u'\left(x_{j,t}\right)E_t}{\Theta_t},$$

which is used to derive the following optimal price via the first-order condition for the profit maximisation problem:

$$\frac{u'\left(x_{j,t}\right)E_t}{\Theta_t}\left[1 - \frac{1}{\sigma\left(x_{j,t}\right)}\right] = p_{j,t}\left(1 - \frac{1}{\sigma\left(x_{j,t}\right)}\right) = \iota_t\left(1 + \frac{\tau}{\theta}\right),$$

which is rewritten as follows:

$$\frac{u'\left(x_{j,t}\right)}{Z\left(x_{j,t}\right)} \cdot \frac{E_t}{\Theta_t} = \iota_t\left(1 + \frac{\tau}{\theta}\right), \tag{8.4}$$

where $Z\left(x_{j,t}\right) \equiv \sigma\left(x_{j,t}\right)/\left(\sigma\left(x_{j,t}\right) - 1\right)$ is the mark-up rate in direct explicitly additive preferences.

Under monopolistic competition, each firm faces the price elasticity of demand, which is an exogenously constant parameter under CES preferences. However, under DEA preferences, the price elasticity of demands impacts only consumption per capita of the good. For any differentiable price elasticity function $\sigma\left(x_{j,t}\right) > 1$, sub-utility function is defined as $u(x) = \int_0^x \exp\left[-\int_{\overline{x}_0}^{\overline{x}} \frac{dz}{z\sigma(z)}\right]dx$, where $u_0 = 0$, $u'(x) > 0$, $u''(x) < 0$ hold and the function is thrice-differentiable. This implies that the price elasticity function $\sigma\left(x_{j,t}\right)$ is regarded as the primitive DEA preference. Moreover, CES preferences are a special case of the DEA preferences, where $\sigma\left(x_{j,t}\right) = \sigma > 1$ leads to $u(x) = \overline{U}(x)^{1-(1/\sigma)}$ for $\overline{U}(x) > 0$.

The non-arbitrage condition is $\left(\pi_t + \dot{P}_{A,t}\right)/P_{A,t} = r_t$ in (3.9) and the free entry condition is $P_{A,t} = w_t F_t$. From (3.11), the labour market clearing condition, including the knowledge spillover effect in the manufacturing sector, is $L = L_{A,t} + L_{X,t} = F_t\dot{A}_t + \iota_t A_t x_t$.

### 8.2.4 Subclass of DEA Preference

Here, the subclass of DEA preferences is assumed as follows:

$$\frac{1}{\sigma(x_t)} + \frac{x_t Z'(x_t)}{Z(x_t)} > 0, \tag{D.1}$$

which implies that $u'(x_t)/Z(x_t)$ decreases according to $x_t$. Namely, the LHS of (8.4) represents the firm's marginal revenue, which decreases according to $x_{j,t}$. This leads to a unique equilibrium as $x_{j,t} = x_t$, which decreases in $\iota_t[1 + (\tau/\theta)](\Theta_t/E_t)$. Thus, this yields the symmetry of equilibrium among firms and goods, where $p_{j,t} = p_t$, $q_{j,t} = q_t$ and $\pi_{j,t} = \pi_t$. Under (D.1), the balanced growth path is held as the only equilibrium path of the economy.

In addition, the two alternative conditions are defined as follows:

$$\sigma(x_t)' < 0 \Leftrightarrow \mathrm{Z}(\mathrm{x_t})' > 0, \tag{D.2}$$

which implies Marshall's Second Law of Demand—price elasticity of demand for each good becomes higher as one moves up along the demand curve in (8.3). In other words, substitution elasticity between any two varieties, which is measured at $x_{j1,t} = x_{j2,t} = x_t$, decreases according to $x_t$ or (D.2) increases the Relative Love for Variety (RLV), similar to Zhelobodkho et al. (2012).

Here, (D.2) implies (D.1) while (D.1) does not imply (D.2). This yields the following condition:

$$\frac{1}{\sigma(x_t)} > -\frac{x_t Z(x_t)'}{Z(x_t)} > 0, \tag{D.3}$$

where (D.1) and the opposite of (D.2) hold. This states a violation of Marshall's Second Law of Demand and (D.3) increases RLV. Thus, CES preferences are represented as a borderline case between two DEA subclasses holding (D.2) or (D.3). Note that whether (D.2) or (D.3) holds determines the comparative static results.

The symmetry of equilibrium under (D.1) yields the following pricing rule:

$$p_{j,t}\left(1 - \frac{1}{\sigma(x_t)}\right) = \iota_t\left(1 + \frac{\tau}{\theta}\right) \Leftrightarrow p_t = \iota_t Z(x_t)\left(1 + \frac{\tau}{\theta}\right),$$

which is used to rewrite the ratio of the firms' profits to aggregate expenditure in (4. 6) as follows:

$$\frac{A_t \pi_t}{E_t} = \frac{1}{\sigma(x_t)} = 1 - \frac{1}{Z(x_t)}, \tag{8.5}$$

and the ratio of the wage payment in manufacturing sector to aggregate expenditure in (4.7) is rewritten as follows:

$$\left(w_t + \frac{\tau}{\theta}\right)\frac{L_{Xt}}{E_t} = 1 - \frac{1}{\sigma(x_t)} = \frac{1}{Z(x_t)},$$

where changes from CEA to DEA do not affect the relationship between these shares and the mark-up rate. However, the mark-up increases in $x_t$ under (D.1) and (D.2) or decreases in $x_t$ under (D.3). Thus, these shares become endogenous under DEA.

### 8.2.5 Euler Equation Under DEA Preference

Intertemporal utility function under DEA is represented as follows:

$$u_0 = \int_0^\infty \log\left[A_t u\left(\frac{E_t}{p_t A_t} \cdot \frac{1}{P_t^{\eta_P}}\right)\right] e^{-\rho t} dt,$$

where each household chooses each manufactured good to maximise their utility function subject to the intertemporal budget constraint in (8.2). This leads to the first-order condition of the utility maximisation problem:

$$\frac{\zeta(x_t)}{E_t} e^{-\rho t} = \lambda_0 e^{-Rt},$$

where $\zeta(x_t) \equiv x_t u(x_t)'/u(x_t)$ holds. Differentiating the logarithm first-order condition with time yields the following Euler equation:

$$\frac{\dot{E}_t}{E_t} = r_t - \rho + \frac{\dot{\zeta}(x_t)}{\zeta(x_t)} = r_t - \rho + \left(1 - \frac{1}{\sigma(x_t)} - \zeta(x_t)\right)\frac{\dot{x}_t}{x_t}, \tag{8.6}$$

where the last term is an additional term generated by DEA preferences and disappears under CES, with $\sigma(x_t) = \sigma$.

## 8.3 Equilibrium

### 8.3.1 Dynamic System

Similar to the BGP equilibrium under CES, we can define the BGP equilibrium under DEA. A constant $x_t$ leads to a constant mark-up rate. By substituting $\iota_t = \iota/A_t$ into $L_{X,t} = \iota_t x_t A_t$, we obtain $L_{X,t} = \iota x_t$. Since $x_t$ is constant, $L_{X,t}$ is constant as well. In the present model, a positive knowledge spillover effect on the manufacturing sector is necessary to exist in the BGP equilibrium.

Following the calculation to derive (4.9) in the CES case, the law of motion for the economy in the DEA case is represented as follows:

$$\frac{\dot{\varepsilon}_t}{\varepsilon_t} = \frac{\varepsilon_t}{\sigma(x_t)F} - g_t - \rho + \left(1 - \frac{1}{\sigma(x_t)} - \zeta(x_t)\right)\frac{\dot{x}_t}{x_t}, \tag{8.7}$$

which is derived from (8.6) and where $\varepsilon_t \equiv E_t$ is the expenditure per wage rate. By integrating (8.7) with (8.5), $\varepsilon_t = \iota x_t Z(x_t)(1 + \tau/\theta)$ and $L = F_t\dot{A}_t + \iota x_t$, the following is derived:

$$\left[\zeta(x_t) + \frac{1}{\sigma(x_t)} + \frac{x_t Z(x_t)'}{Z(x_t)}\right]\frac{\dot{x}_t}{x_t} = \frac{\iota}{F}\left(1 + \frac{\tau}{\theta}\right)x_t Z(x_t) - \left(\frac{L}{F} + \rho\right), \tag{8.8}$$

where (D.1) implies that the positive bracket term $[\cdot] > 0$ in the LHS of (8.8) and $dx_t Z(x_t)/dx_t > 0$. This leads to $\dot{x}_t > 0$ for $x_t > x^*$ and $\dot{x}_t < 0$ for $x_t < x^*$, where $x^*$ is implicitly defined as follows:

$$x^* Z(x^*) = \frac{L+\rho F}{\iota\left(1+\frac{\tau}{\theta}\right)}. \tag{8.9}$$

### 8.3.2 Steady State

The economy in (8.8) diverges from equilibrium. However, the economy immediately jumps $x_0 = x^*$ and stays at $x_t = x^*$ as equilibrium. This leads to labour employment in manufacturing and R&D sectors, an economic growth rate and total pollution emissions in BGP equilibrium. The LHS of (8.9), as in (D.1), increases according to $x^*$. This is equal to $\iota Z(1 + \tau/\theta) > L + \rho F$. Under the condition of $\iota Z(1 + \tau/\theta) > L + \rho F$, each variable in the BGP equilibrium is represented as follows:

$$L_X^* = \left[\frac{\sigma(x^*)-1}{\sigma(x^*)}\right]\left(\frac{L+\rho F}{1+\tau/\theta}\right) = \frac{L+\rho F}{Z(x^*)\left(1+\frac{\tau}{\theta}\right)},\ L_R^* = L - L_X^*,\ g^* = \frac{L-L_X^*}{F}, \tag{8.10}$$

where $x^*$ is implicitly defined in (8.9).

Labour demand in the manufacturing sector decreases in response to price pass-through because firms increase sales by raising prices through production cuts. This price pass-through relies on two effects. First is the direct effect of environmental tax, where the regulatory cost is passed on to prices. Second is the indirect effect of the endogenous mark-up rate, where the mark-up rate is passed on to prices.

Since we are considering $L_X = \iota x$ according to $\iota_t = \iota/A_t$, we assume that the total pollution emissions in (4.3) are the pollution emissions in the following efficient unit:

$$P_t^e = \frac{P_t}{A_t} = \frac{1}{A_t}\left(\int_0^{A_t} d_{j,t}dj\right), \tag{8.11}$$

where the positive knowledge spillover effect reduces pollution per unit of efficiency. Substituting (8.10) into (8.11) gives the following pollution emission at BGP equilibrium:

$$P^* = \frac{L_X^*}{\theta}. \tag{8.12}$$

## 8.4 Comparative Statics

### *8.4.1 The Case of (D.1) and (D.2)*

Differentiating (8.9) concerning the environmental tax yields the following:

$$\frac{dx^*}{d\tau} = -\frac{1}{\left[Z(x^*) + x^*Z(x^*)'\right]} \cdot \frac{L + \rho F}{(1 + \tau/\theta)^2} \cdot \frac{1}{\iota\theta} < 0,$$

which is rewritten as follows:

$$\frac{dx^*}{d\tau} = -\frac{1}{\theta\left[Z(x^*)+x^*Z(x^*)'\right]} \cdot \frac{x^*Z(x^*)}{1+\tau/\theta} < 0, \tag{8.13}$$

where $Z(x^*) + x^*Z(x^*)' > 0$ and $Z(x^*)' > 0$ hold for (D.1) and (D.2). Under DEA preferences with (D.1) and (D.2), (8.4) has the unique solution of $x^*$, which strictly decreases according to $\iota(1 + \tau/\theta)$. Thus, this leads to $dZ(x^*)/d\tau < 0$ in (D.1) and (D.2) and an increase in environmental tax rate raises the mark-up rate. Manufacturing firms pass on the environmental tax increase to goods prices, hence, the production volume decreases. Moreover, since the mark-up rate falls due to this decrease, the production volume decreases further.

Differentiating $L_X^*$ in (8.10) concerning the environmental tax yields the following:

$$\frac{dL_X^*}{d\tau} = -\frac{\iota}{\theta} \cdot \frac{x^*}{(1+\tau/\theta)^2} + \left(\frac{\iota}{1+\tau/\theta}\right)\frac{\partial x^*}{\partial \tau}, \tag{8.14}$$

where the first term in the RHS represents direct price pass-on effect of environmental taxes and the second term in the RHS represents indirect price pass-on effect due to mark-up rate. Using (8.13), (8.14) is rewritten as follows:

$$\frac{dL_X^*}{d\tau} = -\frac{\iota}{\theta} \cdot \frac{x^*}{(1 + \tau/\theta)^2}\left(\frac{1}{1 + \frac{x^*Z(x^*)'}{Z(x^*)}} + 1\right) < 0,$$

which implies that the passing on of prices and the reduction in mark-up rates reduce the amount of goods produced, decreasing the amount of work in the industrial sector. Differentiating $L_R^*$, $g^*$ and $P^*$ in (8.10) and (8.11) concerning the environmental tax yields the following:

$$\frac{dL_A^*}{d\tau} = -\frac{\partial L_X^*}{\partial \tau} > 0, \quad \frac{dg^*}{d\tau} = -\frac{1}{F} \cdot \frac{\partial L_X^*}{\partial \tau} > 0, \quad \frac{dP^*}{d\tau} = \frac{1}{\theta} \cdot \frac{\partial L_X^*}{\partial \tau} < 0.$$

Under DEA with (D.1) and (D.2), environmental tax has growth-enhancing and pollution-reducing effect via the imperfect pass-through effect. In $p_t = \iota_t Z(x_t)(1 + \tau/\theta)$, an increase in environmental tax leads to a rise in the marginal cost of manufacturing goods. Thus, manufacturing firms reduce production. This leads to a decrease in the mark-up rate $Z(x^*)$. Thus, firms imperfectly pass incremental cost of environmental tax to price of manufacturing good. The policy reduces production and reallocates labour from manufacturing to R&D sectors. This expands economic growth rate and reduces pollution emissions.

### 8.4.2 *The Case of (D.3)*

Unlike DEA preferences with (D.1) and (D.2), the growth-enhancing and pollution-reducing effects of environmental taxes disappear in DEA preferences with (D.3). Differentiating (8.9) for the environmental tax yields the following:

$$\frac{dx^*}{d\tau} = -\frac{1}{\left[Z(x^*) + x^* Z(x^*)'\right]} \cdot \frac{L + \rho F}{(1 + \tau/\theta)^2} \cdot \frac{1}{\iota\theta} > 0,$$

which is rewritten as follows:

$$\frac{dx^*}{d\tau} = -\frac{1}{\theta\left[Z(x^*) + x^* Z(x^*)'\right]} \cdot \frac{x^* Z(x^*)}{1 + \tau/\theta} > 0, \tag{8.15}$$

where $Z(x^*) + x^* Z(x^*)' < 0$ and $Z(x^*)' < 0$ hold for (D.3). Under DEA preferences with (D.3), (8.4) has the unique solution of $x^*$, which strictly decreases according to $\iota(1 + \tau/\theta)$. Thus, this leads to $dZ(x^*)/d\tau > 0$ in (D.3) and an increase in the environmental tax rate decreases the mark-up rate. To pass on the environmental tax increase to goods prices, the production volume is temporarily decreased. However, as shown by $Z(x^*)' < 0$ in (D.3) with DEA preferences, the mark-up rate increases due to this production decrease. The indirect price pass-through effect of the mark-up rate dominates the direct price pass-through effect of the environmental tax. Hence, an increase in the environmental tax rate increases the production volume through an increase in the mark-up rate.

Using (8.15), (8.14) is rewritten as follows:

$$\frac{dL_X^*}{d\tau} = -\frac{\iota}{\theta} \cdot \frac{x^*}{(1+\tau/\theta)^2}\left(\frac{1}{1+\frac{x^*Z(x^*)'}{Z(x^*)}} + 1\right),$$

which is further rewritten with $Z(x^*) + x^*Z(x^*)' < 0$ and $2Z(x^*) + x^*Z(x^*)' > 0$ as follows:

$$\frac{dL_X^*}{d\tau} = -\frac{\iota}{\theta} \cdot \frac{x^*}{(1+\tau/\theta)^2} \cdot \underbrace{\frac{2Z(x^*) + x^*Z(x^*)'}{Z(x^*) + x^*Z(x^*)'}}_{(-)} > 0,$$

which implies that the increase in the mark-up rate due to the environmental tax reduces the amount of labour in the manufacturing sector to increase the production volume. Differentiating $L_R^*$, $g^*$ and $P^*$ in (8.10) and (8.11) regarding the environmental tax yields the following:

$$\frac{dL_A^*}{d\tau} = -\frac{\partial L_X^*}{\partial \tau} < 0, \quad \frac{dg^*}{d\tau} = -\frac{1}{F} \cdot \frac{\partial L_X^*}{\partial \tau} < 0, \quad \frac{dP^*}{d\tau} = \frac{1}{\theta} \cdot \frac{\partial L_X^*}{\partial \tau} > 0.$$

Under DEA with (D.3), environmental tax has growth-reducing and pollution-expanding effect due to the perfect pass-through effect. In $p_t = \iota_t Z(x_t)(1 + \tau/\theta)$, an increase in environmental tax leads to a rise in the marginal cost of manufacturing goods. Thus, manufacturing firms reduce production. However, a mark-up rate $Z(x^*)$ increases under (D.3). The former effect is dominated by the latter. Thus, firms perfectly pass incremental cost via environmental tax to the price of manufacturing goods. The policy results in expanding production and reallocating labour from R&D to manufacturing sectors. This reduces the economic growth rate and expands pollution emissions.

As explained in Chap. 1, in the AK model, where capital accumulation is the source of economic growth, environmental policies can achieve sustainable development through externality effects. However, as the taste effect suggests, the substitutability of different periods affects the growth-enhancing effect. Under $\overline{\sigma} = 1$, the economic growth due to the taste effect disappears. In the economic model explained in Chap. 4, the substitution elasticity between varieties does not affect the growth-enhancing effect of environmental policies. However, when the elasticity changes endogenously under non-homothetic preferences, the growth-enhancing effect is undermined. Therefore, household preferences play a crucial role in sustainable development through environmental policies.

## References

Alonso-Carrera et al. (2019) Alonso-Carrera, J., de Miguel, C., & Manzano, B. (2019). Economic growth and environmental degradation when preferences are non-homothetic. *Environmental and Resource Economics*, 74(3), 1011–1036. https://doi.org/10.1007/s10640-019-00357-4

Grossman, G. M., & Helpman, E. (1991). Quality ladders in the theory of growth. *The Review of Economic Studies*, 58(1), 43–61. https://doi.org/10.2307/2298044

Latzer, H., Matsuyama, K., & Parenti, M. (2019). Reconsidering the market size effect in innovation and growth. *Global Poverty Research Lab Working Paper*, (19–106). https://doi.org/10.2139/ssrn.3513610

Zhelobodko, E., Kokovin, S., Parenti, M., & Thisse, J. F. (2012). Monopolistic competition: Beyond the constant elasticity of substitution. *Econometrica*, 80(6), 2765–2784. https://doi.org/10.3982/ECTA9986

# Part III
# The International Economy

# Chapter 9
# R&D-Based Location Model

**Abstract** Martin and Ottaviano (1999) extended the variety expansion model, which accounted for households' preferences for varieties of goods, to a firm location model. In this case, an agricultural sector that produces numerous goods is introduced and the wage rate is standardised to 1. When goods firms export goods to the partner country, they incur additional transport costs. Hence, through the home market effect in Krugman (1980), good firms are concentrated in countries with larger market sizes between the North and South. Transport cost reduction due to trade liberalisation leads to the concentration of firms in the North, with a large market size. The amount and direction of foreign direct investment, defined as the difference between the number of firms located in a country and the number of shares held in that country, is affected by trade liberalisation. In global spillovers, where global variety lowers fixed R&D costs, trade liberalisation and the number of firms in a country do not affect economic growth rates. In local spillovers, where the variety in the North lowers fixed costs, trade liberalisation increases economic growth rates through an increase in the number of firms in a country. This growth-enhancing effect is called the location effect.

## 9.1 Structure of R&D-Based Location Model

The economic model explained in Chap. 3 is extended to a two-country North–South model. Household preferences and the technology of firms in the North and South are the same as those in the economic model in Chap. 3. The North and the South trade with each other. They only differ in the initial household endowments, the rest being identical. The initial endowment in the North is $W_0$ and in the South is $W_0^*$, where $W_0 > W_0^*$. As they are almost symmetrical, we describe only the North's economy unless necessary and add an asterisk to the variables of the South. There is a representative household with population $L$ in the North and South and the world population is $2L$. Households in the North and South supply labour to the agriculture, manufacturing and R&D sectors in their countries, however, there is no labour migration. This economic structure is illustrated in Fig. 9.1.

 
Y. Hamaguchi, *Sustainable Development in Economic Growth Theory*,
https://doi.org/10.1007/978-981-96-7639-2_9

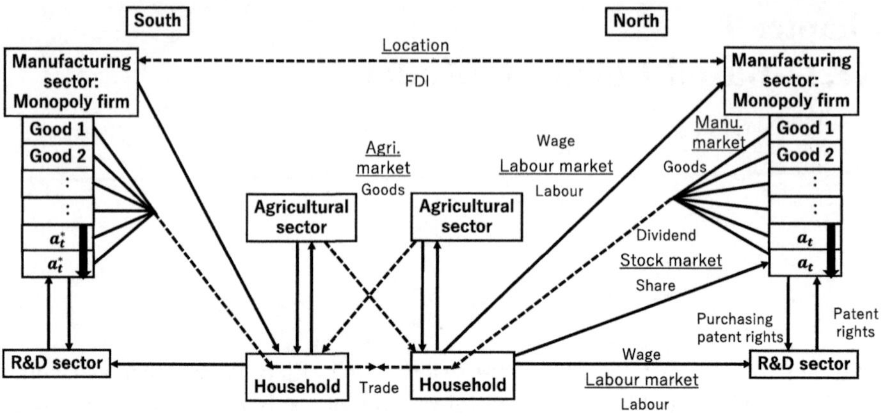


**Fig. 9.1** Structure of the R&D-based location model

## 9.2 The Model

### 9.2.1 *Household*

The utility function of a representative household in the North over different periods can be expressed as a logarithmic function as follows:

$$U_t = \int_0^{\infty} \log\left(Q_t^{\nu} D_t^{1-\nu}\right) e^{-\rho t} dt, \tag{9.1}$$

where $D_t$ is the agricultural goods as numeraire. In accordance with Dixit and Stiglitz (1977), the composition of differentiated goods in $Q_t$ is expressed as a CES-type function as follows:

$$Q_t = \left( \int_0^{A_t} x_{j,t}^{\frac{\sigma-1}{\sigma}} dj \right)^{\frac{\sigma}{\sigma-1}}, \tag{9.2}$$

where the number of any variety is $j \in [0, A_t]$ and $\sigma > 1$ is the substitution elasticity between any two varieties. $A_t$ is the total number of varieties produced in both the North and the South.

Household expenditure in the North is expressed as follows:

$$\int_0^{a_t} p_{j,t} x_{j,t} dj + \int_0^{a_t^*} t p_{i,t}^* x_{i,t} di + P_{D,t} D_t = E_t, \tag{9.3}$$

where $p_{j,t}$ and $p_{i.t}^*$ are the prices of variety $j$ in the North and variety $i$ in the South, respectively. The agricultural goods price is assumed to be numeraire, with $P_{D,t} = 1$. In addition, $a_t$ and $a_t^*$ are the number of varieties in the North and South, respectively, and $a_t + a_t^* = A_t$ holds. Following Samuelson (1954), when a household in the North purchases a manufactured good from the South, it incurs an iceberg-type transportation cost of $t > 1$. In contrast, this transportation cost does not apply to the numeraire agricultural goods.

The household's expenditure is (3) and assets are $W_t = P_{A,t}A_t$. From (2.3), the household's budget constraint is $\dot{W}_t = r_t W_t + w_t L - E_t$. In the static utility maximisation problem, given the expenditure, the household decides how much of each good to purchase and the following demand function is obtained:

$$P_{M,t}Q_t = \nu E_t,\ D_t = (1-\nu)E_t, \tag{9.4}$$

where the price index for differentiated goods is defined as follows:

$$P_{M,t} \equiv \left(\int_0^{a_t} p_{j,t}^{1-\sigma} dj + \int_0^{a_t^*} t^{1-\sigma} p_{i,t}^{*1-\sigma} di\right)^{\frac{1}{1-\sigma}}. \tag{9.5}$$

By solving the first-order conditions of this utility maximisation problem, the demand functions for manufactured goods in the North and South can be derived as follows:

$$x_{j,t} = p_{j,t}^{-\sigma} P_{M,t}^{\sigma-1} \nu E_t,\ x_{i,t} = t^{-\sigma} p_{i,t}^{*-\sigma} P_{M,t}^{\sigma-} \nu E_t, \tag{9.6}$$

where households in the South have a symmetrical demand function.

By substituting (9.4) into (9.2) and incorporating it into (9.1), we obtain the indirect utility function $U_t = \int_0^{\infty} \log\left[(\nu E_t/P_{M,t})^{\nu}[(1-\nu)E_t]^{1-\nu}\right] e^{-\rho t} dt$. In the dynamic utility maximisation problem, the household chooses expenditures that maximise this indirect utility under budget constraints and the following Euler equation is obtained in the North:

$$\frac{\dot{E}_t}{E_t} = r_t - \rho,$$

where under free capital movement between the North and South, their Euler equations are equalised through the real interest rate as follows:

$$\frac{\dot{E}_t}{E_t} = \frac{\dot{E}_t^*}{E_t^*} = r_t - \rho, \tag{9.7}$$

where $r_t = \rho$ holds when the expenditure in the North and South is constant in a steady state. Henceforth, unless necessary, subscript $t$ will be omitted. Furthermore, since $W_0 > W_0^*$, $E > E^*$ holds.

### 9.2.2 Manufacturing Sector

As Dixit and Stiglitz (1977) showed, the manufacturing sector is in a monopolistic competitive market and produces horizontally differentiated goods. Each firm holds a patent on a single unique variety. This patent is freely traded between the North and South, hence, the country of patent development does not need to be the same as the country of actual production. As in Martin and Rogers (1995), each firm can locate its production base in either the North or South for free, hence, the cost of relocating the factory and repatriating profits is zero. The technology of the manufacturing firms is constant returns to scale (CRS) and the same across firms. This firm invests $L_j^X$ units of labour to produce one unit of industrial goods. Its production function is $q_j = L_j^X$.

Given the inverse demand function in (9.6), manufacturing firms choose the price of goods that maximises the profit function:

$$\max_{p_j} \pi_j = (p_j - w)q.$$

The first-order condition for profit maximisation yields the following:

$$p_j = \left(\tfrac{\sigma}{\sigma-1}\right)w, \ p_i^* = tp_j, \tag{9.8}$$

where $\sigma/(\sigma - 1)$ is the mark-up. In (9.8), the mark-up and wage rate are the same across firms, hence, all firms are symmetric. Henceforth, unless necessary, we omit the subscripts $i$ and $j$. By substituting (9.8) into the profit function, the optimal profit of a manufacturing firm in the North is expressed as follows:

$$\pi = \left(\tfrac{w}{\sigma-1}\right)q. \tag{9.9}$$

Agricultural firms operate in a perfectly competitive market and there are no transport costs involved in the trade of agricultural goods. The technology of agricultural firms is CRS and the same for all firms. They produce one unit of agricultural goods by inputting $L_D$ units of labour. Since the price of agricultural goods is numeraire, from the zero-profit condition, $P_A = w = 1$ is obtained.

Rewriting (9.6), using (9.5) and (9.8), we obtain the following demand function for the manufactured goods of the North and South from the North's household:

$$x_j = \left(\tfrac{\sigma-1}{\sigma}\right)\tfrac{\nu E}{a+\varphi a^*}, \ x_i = \left(\tfrac{\sigma-1}{\sigma}\right)\left(\tfrac{1}{t^\sigma}\right)\tfrac{\nu E}{a+\varphi a^*}, \tag{9.10}$$

and, using (9.4), the demand function for agricultural goods for the North's household can be obtained as follows:

$$D = (1 - \nu)E, \tag{9.11}$$

where $\varphi \equiv 1/t^{\sigma-1}$ measures the degree of trade liberalisation and an increase in $\varphi$ due to a decrease in $t$ implies a decrease in transport costs due to trade liberalisation.

### 9.2.3 R&D Sector

An R&D firm, in a perfectly competitive market, develops a new variety of goods by investing $F_t$ units of efficient labour. Its production technology is $\dot{A}_t = L_{A,t}/F_t$ in (3.10). The free entry condition yields $P_{A,t} = w_t F_t$. By assuming $F_t = F/A_t$, the global knowledge spillover from past R&D activities reduces the fixed R&D costs in the North and South. Thus, $P_A = F/A$ holds. Due to global spillovers, the patent prices in the North and South become the same.

Households in both places either save in a risk-free asset with a rate of return $r$ or invest in the stock market, buying shares in companies (risky assets). Here, $W$ is the stock asset held by the household in the North and $W^*$ is in the South. The share price is equal to the sum of the discounted present value of profits from period $t$ onwards as $P_{A,t} = \int_t^{\infty} e^{-[r(\iota)-r(t)]}\pi_\iota d\iota$. By taking the time derivative of $P_{A,t}$, the non-arbitrage condition is obtained as $\pi + \dot{P}_A = rP_A$ in (3.9).

### 9.2.4 Market

In this economy, there are markets for manufactured goods, labour and capital. Under the market clearing conditions for manufactured goods, the supply and demand of manufactured goods in the North and South are equal, including transport costs. From (9.10), this condition is expressed as follows:

$$x = \nu L\left(\frac{\sigma-1}{\sigma}\right)\left(\frac{E}{a+\varphi a^*} + \frac{\varphi E^*}{a^*+\varphi a}\right), \tag{9.12a}$$

$$x^* = \nu L\left(\frac{\sigma-1}{\sigma}\right)\left(\frac{\varphi E}{a+\varphi a^*} + \frac{E^*}{a^*+\varphi a}\right), \tag{9.12b}$$

where household demand in (9.10) is aggregated by population. Keeping all other factors constant, demand for manufactured goods increases due to increased expenditure, increased preference for manufactured goods, population growth, trade liberalisation and a fall in mark-ups. Here, $a + \varphi a^*$ $(a^* + \varphi a)$ implies that the price index falls due to an increase in the variety supplied to the North (South) and that market share falls due to a decrease in the supply of any given variety.

The market production conditions of the capital market are $\pi + \dot{P}_A = rP_A$. The number of manufactured goods firms is fixed to the number of varieties and is held by households in the North and South. Therefore, the following relationship holds:

$$a + a^* = W + W^* = A. \tag{9.13}$$

In a capital market where capital movements are not restricted, when the operating profit of either the North or South is high, arbitrage behaviour occurs through the firms' location, hence, their profits are equalised at equilibrium as follows:

$$\pi = \pi^*, \tag{9.14}$$

where this location behaviour results in $x = x^*$. Households supply labour to the industrial, agricultural and R&D sectors of their country. Therefore, the clearing conditions of the labour market are as follows:

$$L_A + L_M + L_D = 2L. \tag{9.15}$$

The number of manufacturing firms located in the North is defined as the number of manufacturing firms worldwide located in the North and is expressed as $\gamma \equiv a/A$. Using the third term on the RHS of (9.12a) and (9.13), the number of manufacturing firms located in the North is derived as follows, as shown in Appendix H:

$$\gamma = \frac{a}{A} = \frac{E-\varphi E^*}{(1-\varphi)(E+E^*)}, \tag{9.16a}$$

and the number of manufacturing firms located to the South derived is as follows:

$$1-\gamma = \frac{a^*}{A} = \frac{E^*-\varphi E}{(1-\varphi)(E+E^*)}, \tag{9.16b}$$

where the location of manufacturing firms depends on the relative market size in $(E - \varphi E^*)/(E + E^*)$ and manufacturing firms are located in countries with larger market sizes and higher expenditure levels. This can save on transport costs and, under the technology of increasing CRS, production expansion can increase profits. This result implies the home market effect of Krugman (1980). With all conditions constant, an increase in $\varphi$ due to trade liberalisation raises $1/(1 - \varphi)$ in $\gamma$ and $1 - \gamma$, strengthening the impact of relative market size on the firms' location. This is because, due to the reduction in transport costs, firms can make more profits by producing in countries with large markets and exporting to partner countries. However, in $\varphi E^*$ and $\varphi E$, as exports to partner countries increase, the relative size of the home market shrinks, hence, the number of firms located in the home country decreases.

## 9.3 Equilibrium

### *9.3.1 Dynamic System in Global Spillover*

The BGP in the present model is an equilibrium path that satisfies three conditions. First, there is a constant, positive economic growth rate $g_{A,t} = \dot{A}_t/A_t > 0$. Second, the labour allocation of manufactured goods, R&D and agricultural firms is constant, as $L_{X,t} = L_X$, $L_{A,t} = L_A$ and $L_{D,t} = L_D$, respectively. Third, the aggregate expenditure is constant, as $E_t + E_t^* = E + E^*$. We construct the law of motion for $E_t + E_t^*$.

By using (9.13) and (9.14), (9.12a) and (9.12b) can be rewritten as follows:

$$x = x^* = \nu L\left(\frac{\sigma-1}{\sigma}\right)\left(\frac{E+E^*}{A}\right), \tag{9.17}$$

which is used with (9.11) and $L_A = Fg_A$ to rewrite (9.15) as follows:

$$Fg_A + L\left(\frac{\sigma-\nu}{\sigma}\right)(E+E^*) = 2L. \tag{9.18}$$

By differentiating $P_{A,t} = F/A_t$ with respect to time, we obtain $g_A = -\left(\dot{P}_{A,t}/P_{A,t}\right) = -g_{PA}$, which implies that capital loss occurs as the number of varieties increases. Using (9.14), we rewrite (9.9) to yield the following:

$$\pi = \frac{\nu L}{\sigma}\left(\frac{E+E^*}{A}\right), \tag{9.19}$$

where, as the number of varieties increases, the supply of manufactured goods expands and the market share shrinks, causing the profits of manufacturing firms to decline. This decline discourages entrepreneurs from entering the market. However, under global spillovers, the increase in the number of varieties lowers the fixed cost of future R&D and reduces the price of patent rights, encouraging entrepreneurs to enter the market. Therefore, R&D activities are carried out at equilibrium. Using (9.19) and $r = \rho$, we can rewrite $\pi + \dot{P}_A = rP_A$ as follows:

$$\frac{\nu L}{\sigma F}(E+E^*) = \rho - g_{PA},$$

which is further rewritten with $g_A = -g_{PA}$ as follows:

$$\frac{\nu L}{\sigma F}(E+E^*) = \rho + g_A. \tag{9.20}$$

While $g_A$ in (9.18) is a decreasing function of $E_t + E_t^*$, $g_A$ in (9.20) is an increasing function of $E_t + E_t^*$. As $E_t + E_t^*$ moves along (9.18), this economy diverges from the steady state. Therefore, at any time, it jumps to the steady state, where $g = g_A = -g_{PA}$. The equilibrium of this dynamical system is deterministic and stable. For a detailed explanation of the dynamics and stability analysis, see Grossman and Helpman (1991, Ch3).

### 9.3.2 Steady State

Under $g = g_A$, from (9.18) and (9.20), the equilibrium economic growth rate is expressed as follows:

$$g = \frac{2L}{F}\left(\frac{\nu}{\sigma}\right) - \left(1 - \frac{\nu}{\sigma}\right)\rho, \tag{9.21}$$

where, under global spillover, the reduction in transport costs due to trade liberalisation does not affect the economic growth rate.

Using $r = \rho$, $W_t = P_{A,t}A_t$, $P_{A,t} = F/A_t$ and $\dot{W}_t/W_t = g_A - g_{PA} = 0$, we can rewrite $\dot{W}_t = r_t W_t + w_t L - E_t$ as follows:

$$E + E^* = 2 + \tfrac{\rho F}{L}, \tag{9.22}$$

which is derived from the budget constraint for the South. Here, the 2 in (9.22) is the labour income of the North and South. The stock income owned by households in the North and South is $rW = rP_A a$ and $rW^* = rP_A a^*$, respectively, and using $P_A = F/A$, it can be rewritten as $(rFa)/A$ and $(rFa^*)/A$. From (9.13) and $r = \rho$, the stock income worldwide is $(rFa)/A + (rFa^*)/A = \rho F$. The per capita expenditure of households in the North and South consists of labour income ($w = 1$) and stock income ($\rho F/L$). Therefore, the expenditure in the North and South increases at a constant rate. From (9.22), the expenditure in both locations is expressed as follows:

$$E = 1 + \left(\tfrac{\rho F}{L}\right)k,\ E^* = 1 + \left(\tfrac{\rho F}{L}\right)(1 - k), \tag{9.23}$$

where $k \equiv W/A > 1/2$ is the number of firms owned by the North household, which amounts to more than half of the world's firms because $W > 1/2 > W^*$ holds.

Using (9.22) and (9.23), the number of firms located in the North in (9.16a) can be rewritten as follows:

$$\gamma = \tfrac{a}{A} = \frac{(1-\varphi)+\left(\frac{\rho F}{L}\right)[k-\varphi(1-k)]}{(1-\varphi)\left(2+\frac{\rho F}{L}\right)}, \tag{9.24}$$

where $0 < \gamma \leq 1$ holds and $\gamma = 1$ for

$$k = \left(\frac{1-\varphi}{1+\varphi}\right)\frac{1}{(\rho F)/L} \equiv \bar{k}.$$

The number of firms located in the North depends on population, subjective discount rate, fixed R&D cost, per capita assets in the North and South and transportation cost. Since households in the North have more initial assets than households in the South, they spend more through stock income. Hence, more labour is employed in the manufacturing sector, with increasing CRS, making the number of firms in the North more than in the South through the home market effect.

The impact of changes in the economic structure on $\gamma$ is a short-term accumulation effect. The long-term accumulation effect is determined by foreign direct investment (FDI). By transforming (9.13), we obtain $a - W = W^* - a^*$, however, since the initial assets held by the households in the North are not enough to buy up all the shares in the North, the households in the South, who have some initial assets left over after buying shares in the South, are buying shares in the North. The opposite occurs in $W - a = a^* - W^*$. By differentiating this equation with respect to time, we obtain $\dot{a} - \dot{W} = \dot{W}^* - \dot{a}^*$. In a given time interval $dt$, the number of firms located in the North increases as $da/dt$, while those firms are purchased by households in the North as $dW/dt$. When the former is greater than the latter, the number of firms in the North increases more than the purchases by households in the South, hence, the purchases of firms in the North by households in the South are made as FDI. These equations are defined as follows:

$$\dot{a} - \dot{W} = g(a - W),$$

which is rewritten with (9.13) and (9.24) as follows:

$$\dot{a} - \dot{W} = \frac{gA\left(k-\frac{1}{2}\right)[\varphi\rho F - L(1-\varphi)]}{2L(1-\varphi)\left(1+\frac{\rho F}{2L}\right)}, \tag{9.25}$$

which implies that the direction of FDI net flows, which depend on the sign of $a - W$, is affected by the following parameter condition: $\dot{a} - \dot{W} \gtreqless 0$.

$$\frac{\rho F}{L} \gtrless \frac{1-\varphi}{\varphi} \equiv \hat{\varphi}, \tag{9.26}$$

where FDI from South to North occurs in $(\rho F)/L > \hat{\varphi}$ because $\dot{a} - \dot{W} > 0$, while FDI from North to South occurs in $(\rho F)/L \leq \hat{\varphi}$ because $\dot{a} - \dot{W} \leq 0$. This FDI amount increases through the economic growth rate $g$.

This long-term accumulation effect depends on the capital income effect on the LHS and the competition effect on the RHS of (9.26). The capital income effect encourages FDI from the South to the North as follows. Through a larger $\rho$ and a smaller $F$ and $L$, the per capita stock income of $\rho F/L$ increases. Since households in the North have more initial assets than those in the South, they spend more through stock income. Due to the home market effect, manufacturing firms have an incentive to locate in the North, however, due to the increase in asset income, households in the South begin to purchase industrial firms in the North, hence, FDI from the South enters the North. However, the competition effect encourages FDI from the North to the South as follows. The rise in $\hat{\varphi}$ due to trade liberalisation implies that the transport costs of exporting goods produced in the South to the North decrease. In addition, there are fewer firms located in the South, hence, competition between firms is less intense. Therefore, operating in the South allows more profits, moving FDI from the North to the South.

The decline in fixed R&D costs weakens the capital income effect and encourages FDI from the North to the South. This decline encourages the development of new varieties (9.21), reducing the monopoly of existing firms. The decline in stock income causes households to reduce expenditure, however, since the expenditure reduction in the North is greater than in the South, the relative market size shrinks. As a result, the decline in fixed costs encourages FDI from the North to the South. An increase in the subjective discount rate has the opposite effect as it increases stock income.

### 9.3.3 Comparative Statics

Differentiating (9.21)–(9.25) with respect to $L$ yields the following:

$$\frac{dg}{dL} = \frac{2}{F}\left(\frac{\nu}{\sigma}\right) > 0, \quad \frac{dE+E^*}{dL} = -\frac{\rho F}{L^2} < 0, \quad \frac{dE}{dL} = -\left(\frac{\rho F}{L^2}\right)k < 0,$$

$$\frac{dE^*}{dL} = -\left(\frac{\rho F}{L^2}\right)(1-k) < 0, \quad \frac{d\gamma}{dL} = -\frac{2(1+\varphi)(k-\frac{1}{2})\left(\frac{\rho F}{L^2}\right)}{(1-\varphi)\left(2+\frac{\rho F}{L}\right)^2} < 0,$$

$$\frac{d\dot{a}-\dot{W}}{dL} = \frac{gA(k-\frac{1}{2})}{2(1-\varphi)\left(1+\frac{\rho F}{2L}\right)^2}\left[\varphi\left(\frac{\rho F}{L}\right)^2 - (1-\varphi)\left(1+\frac{3\rho F}{2L}\right)\right] \gtreqless 0,$$

where population growth has a non-monotonic effect on FDI. Although population growth reduces per capita expenditure, since $dAx/dL > 0$ in (9.17), demand for manufactured goods increases. Moreover, since $dA\pi/dL > 0$ in (9.19), profits for manufacturing firms increase. This increases the incentive for entrepreneurs to enter the market. Through economies of scale, the development of new varieties accelerates, increasing the production of manufactured goods due to entrepreneurs purchasing blueprints. Therefore, the economy grows. Although population expansion leads to a per capita expenditure decrease, households in the North, who hold more shares, decrease their expenditure more than the households in the South. Therefore, the number of firms located in the North decreases, as the relative market size shrinks. The decline in per capita expenditure due to population growth weakens the capital income effect, decreasing the amount of FDI. However, when the relative market size of the North increases due to a decline in per capita global expenditure, the amount of FDI increases, as manufacturing firms are located in the North.

Differentiating (9.21)–(9.25) with $\varphi$ yields the followings:

$$\frac{dg}{d\varphi} = 0, \quad \frac{dE+E^*}{d\varphi} = 0, \quad \frac{dE}{d\varphi} = 0, \quad \frac{dE^*}{d\varphi} = 0,$$

$$\frac{d\gamma}{d\varphi} = \frac{2\left(\frac{\rho F}{L}\right)(k-\frac{1}{2})}{(1-\varphi)^2\left(2+\frac{\rho F}{L}\right)} > 0,$$

$$\frac{d\dot{a}-\dot{W}}{d\varphi} = \frac{gA(k-\frac{1}{2})(\varphi+L)}{2(1-\varphi)\left(1+\frac{\rho F}{2L}\right)} + \frac{\gamma}{(1-\varphi)} > 0,$$

where, under global spillover, the decrease in transport costs due to trade liberalisation does not affect expenditure, hence, the production volume of manufactured goods and the profits of manufacturing firms do not change. Trade liberalisation does not affect the economic growth rate. However, due to the home market effect, the number of firms located in the North increases, increasing the purchase of their stocks and the amount of FDI.

## 9.4 The Case of Local Spillover

### 9.4.1 Fixed Costs Related to R&D

In this section, we will analyse the case of local spillovers in R&D. In this case, the fixed R&D cost at a given location is $F_t = F/a_t$ in the North and $F_t^* = F/a_t^*$ in the South. While global spillover is an externality effect based on Marshall-Arrow-Romer (MAR), local spillover is an externality effect based on Jacobs (1969).

Local spillovers in R&D imply that researchers can discover ways to develop new goods by observing the production process. In areas with more firms, the development of new varieties is promoted through positive local spillovers. Households in the North have more initial assets and purchase more stocks, hence, firms are located in the North. Therefore, researchers conduct research activities in the North, where the fixed R&D costs are low due to local spillovers, however, not in the South. The blueprints for the varieties developed in the North and the shares of firms are traded internationally without transaction costs, hence, the R&D departments in the South are replaced by those in the North. The number of firms located in the North determines the level of R&D in the area, which determines the economic growth rate worldwide.

### 9.4.2 Steady State

Since the fixed R&D cost is local spillover, as $F_t = F/a_t$, the stock price is $P_A = F/a$ due to the zero-profit condition in the R&D sector. By substituting $\gamma = a/A$, the stock price becomes $P_A = F/(A\gamma)$. Next, $P_A = F/(A\gamma)$ is obtained by differentiating with respect to time and $\dot{P}_A/P_A = -g_A$ implies that the stock price falls as the economy grows. Since the stock price depends on the number of firms located in the area, the expenditure in (9.22) and (9.23) is as follows:

$$E + E^* = 2 + \left(\frac{\rho F}{L}\right)\frac{1}{\gamma},\ E = 1 + \left(\frac{\rho F}{L}\right)\frac{k}{\gamma},\ E^* = 1 + \left(\frac{\rho F}{L}\right)\frac{1-k}{\gamma}, \qquad (9.27)$$

where, under local spillover, the concentration of firms in the North reduces stock prices and household stock income due to the decline in fixed costs.

The clearing conditions of the labour market in (9.18) are rewritten as follows:

$$F\left(\frac{g_A}{\gamma}\right) + L\left(\frac{\sigma-\nu}{\sigma}\right)(E+E^*) = 2L, \tag{9.28}$$

which is used with (9.20) and (9.27) to derive the following economic growth rate:

$$g = \frac{2L}{F}\left(\frac{\nu}{\sigma}\right)\gamma - \left(1 - \frac{\nu}{\sigma}\right)\rho, \tag{9.29}$$

where, under local spillover, the concentration of firms in the North reduces the fixed cost and promotes economic growth. By substituting (9.27) into (9.16a), the number of firms located in the North can be obtained as follows:

$$\gamma = \frac{(1-\varphi)+\left(\frac{\rho F}{L}\right)\left(\frac{1}{\gamma}\right)[k-\varphi(1-k)]}{(1-\varphi)\left[2+\left(\frac{\rho F}{L}\right)\left(\frac{1}{\gamma}\right)\right]}, \tag{9.30}$$

where $\gamma = 1$ holds for $k = \bar{k}$. The number of firms located in the North affects household expenditure through stock income, hence, changes in the relative market size affect the number of firms located in the North.

By organising (9.30), we obtain the following quadratic equation for $\gamma$:

$$f(\gamma) = 2L(1-\varphi)\gamma^2 + (1-\varphi)(\rho F - L)\gamma - \rho F[k - \varphi(1-k)],$$

where, by solving $f(\gamma) = 0$, we obtain two different real solutions as $\gamma^- < 0 < \gamma^+$. Note that $\gamma^- < 0$ is a solution that has no economic significance and is excluded because it results in $g < 0$ in (9.29). The number of firms located in the North in the case of local spillovers is as follows:

$$\gamma^+ = \frac{1}{4L}\left[L - \rho F + \sqrt{(L-\rho F)^2 + 8L\left(\frac{\rho F}{1-\varphi}\right)[k - \varphi(1-k)]}\right], \tag{9.31}$$

where $f(1/2) < 0$ on $1/2 < k + \varphi k$ yields $1/2 < \gamma^+$ and $\gamma < 1$ in (9.30) holds on $\rho F[(1+\varphi)k - 1] < (1-\varphi)L$ as $\gamma = 1$. Thus, $1/2 < \gamma^+ < 1$ implies that, under local spillover, the number of firms in the South is smaller than those in the North because the initial assets of households in the South are smaller than those in the North. However, not all firms are located in the North. The case of the endpoint solution at $\gamma = 1$ is excluded.

Some of the firms that hold patents for new varieties developed in the North may be located in the South. In this case, the number of firms located in the South is expressed as follows:

$$\dot{W} - \dot{a} = gA\left(1 - \gamma^+\right), \tag{9.32}$$

As there is no R&D activity in the South, only FDI from the North to the South takes place.

### 9.4.3 Comparative Statics

Differentiating (9.27), (9.29) and (9.31) with $\varphi$ yields the following:

$$\frac{d\gamma^+}{d\varphi} = \frac{1}{L}\sqrt{\frac{\rho FL}{(1-\varphi)^2}}\left(k - \frac{1}{2}\right) > 0, \quad \frac{dg}{d\varphi} = \frac{2L}{F}\left(\frac{\nu}{\sigma}\right)\frac{\partial\gamma^+}{\partial\varphi} > 0,$$

$$\frac{dE + E^*}{d\varphi} = -\left(\frac{\rho F}{L}\right)\left(\frac{1}{\gamma}\right)^2\frac{\partial\gamma^+}{\partial\varphi} < 0, \quad \frac{dE}{d\varphi} = -k\left(\frac{\rho F}{L}\right)\left(\frac{1}{\gamma}\right)^2\frac{\partial\gamma^+}{\partial\varphi} < 0,$$

$$\frac{dE^*}{d\varphi} = -(1-k)\left(\frac{\rho F}{L}\right)\left(\frac{1}{\gamma}\right)^2\frac{\partial\gamma^+}{\partial\varphi} < 0,$$

where, as in the case of global spillovers, trade liberalisation increases the number of firms located in the North through the home market effect. This concentration of firms lowers the fixed costs and promotes innovation, hence, the economic growth rate increases. This growth-enhancing effect is called the location effect by Martin and Ottaviano (1999). Due to the concentration of firms and economic growth, stock prices fall, hence, expenditure decreases. Therefore, trade liberalisation reduces the income gap between the North and South. Expenditure decline caused by falling stock prices reduces the market size in the North, hence, the number of firms located in the North may decrease. However, as a result, the number of firms located in the North increases due to the home market effect. The fixed costs and the rise in the subjective discount rate reduce the economic growth rate, however, there is a possibility that economic growth is promoted through the location effect.

Differentiating (9.32) with respect to $\varphi$ asserts the following:

$$\frac{d\dot{W} - \dot{a}}{d\varphi} = A(1-\gamma^+)\frac{\partial g}{\partial\varphi} - gA\frac{\partial\gamma^+}{\partial\varphi},$$

which is rewritten by using (9.29) and (9.32) as follows:

$$\frac{d\dot{W} - \dot{a}}{d\varphi} = A\left[\left(1 - \frac{\nu}{\sigma}\right)\rho - \frac{4L}{F}\left(\frac{\nu}{\sigma}\right)\left(\gamma^+ - \frac{1}{2}\right)\right]\frac{\partial\gamma^+}{\partial\varphi} \gtreqless 0,$$

where the sign of $[\cdot]$ on the RHS determines the effect of trade liberalisation on the amount of FDI. When the industrial structure between the North and South is similar at $\gamma^+$ sufficiently close to $1/2$, $d(\dot{W} - \dot{a})/d\varphi > 0$ and trade liberalisation promotes economic integration through relocating to the South. This is because, even if a new variety of patents is developed in the North, entrepreneurs choose to locate in the South due to economic integration. However, if the industrial structure between the North and South is not similar at $\gamma^+$ close to 1, then $d(\dot{W} - \dot{a})/d\varphi \leq 0$ and trade liberalisation promotes industrial concentration in the North. Finally, the welfare effects of trade liberalisation are complex and it is difficult to provide a fully analytical proof. For an analysis of the welfare effects using numerical examples, see Martin and Ottaviano (1999).

## References

Dixit, A. K., & Stiglitz, J. E. (1977). Monopolistic competition and optimum product diversity. *The American Economic Review*, 67(3), 297–308. https://doi.org/https://www.jstor.org/stable/1831401.

Grossman, G. M., & Helpman, E. (1991). Quality ladders in the theory of growth. *The Review of Economic Studies*, 58(1), 43–61. https://doi.org/10.2307/2298044

Jacobs, J. (1969). The economy of cities. Vintage, New York.

Krugman, P. (1980). Scale economies, product differentiation, and the pattern of trade. *The American Economic Review*, 70(5), 950–959. https://doi.org/https://www.aeaweb.org/aer/top20/70.5.950-959.pdf.

Martin, P., & Ottaviano, G. I. (1999). Growing locations: Industry location in a model of endogenous growth. *European Economic Review*, 43(2), 281–302. https://doi.org/10.1016/S0014-2921(98)00031-2

Martin, P., & Rogers, C. A. (1995). Industrial location and public infrastructure. *Journal of international Economics*, 39(3–4), 335–351. https://doi.org/10.1016/0022-1996(95)01376-6

Samuelson, P. A. (1954). The transfer problem and transport costs, II: Analysis of effects of trade impediments. *The Economic Journal*, 64(254), 264–289. https://doi.org/10.2307/2226834

# Chapter 10
# Pollution Haven Hypothesis

**Abstract** In the R&D-based location model, pollution emissions by manufacturing firms and emissions trading are introduced. Through internationally coordinated emissions trading, the emission allowances allocated to manufacturing firms in the North and South are the same. As this allowance generates an allowance allocation rent, a reduction in the total emission allowance leads to economic growth due to the distribution effect. In addition, this rent affects the home market effect. In global spillovers, a reduction in the total emissions allowance and trade liberalisation leads to a green haven effect, with pollution reduction in the South and pollution increase in the North, through the firms' locations. Pollution abatement and productivity improvement lead to a pollution haven effect, with pollution increase in the South, pollution reduction in the North and a decrease in economic growth rates. The interaction between local spillovers and allowance allocation rent leads to a poverty trap. Furthermore, when the pollution abatement productivity is standardised to 1, the total emission allowance does not affect the location. In the steady state of excessive accumulation in the North, trade liberalisation leads to the pollution haven hypothesis and economic growth, resulting in increased pollution in the South and reduced pollution in the North.

## 10.1 Introduction

As economic globalisation accelerates, debates continue about whether environmental policies and trade liberalisation will reduce or increase global emissions of pollutants and $CO_2$. This hypothesis is known as the pollution haven hypothesis. Copeland and Taylor (2004) defined the pollution haven effect and the pollution haven hypothesis. The pollution haven effect implies that the pollution emissions of the host country increase when a polluting firm from a country with strict environmental regulations relocates to a country with relatively lax regulations. The pollution haven hypothesis implies that pollution emissions in developing countries increase as a result of trade liberalisation, as pollution-intensive firms from developed countries locate themselves in developing countries. As Acheampong et al. (2019) and

 
Y. Hamaguchi, *Sustainable Development in Economic Growth Theory*,
https://doi.org/10.1007/978-981-96-7639-2_10

Dauda et al. (2021) showed, the pollution haven hypothesis has been observed in African countries, however, as Erdogan (2014) pointed out, its statistical significance is low. Therefore, the discovery of variables that affect the pollution haven hypothesis through theoretical analysis can contribute to increasing the empirical significance of the hypothesis.

In early theoretical analysis, Copeland and Taylor (1994, 1995) showed that trade liberalisation increased global pollution, while Antweiler et al. (2001) showed that trade liberalisation decreased global pollution. An analysis of agglomeration models highlight that income inequality and environmental policies are factors in the pollution haven hypothesis (Elbers and Withagen 2003; Lange and Quaas 2007; Zeng and Zhao 2009; Forslid et al. 2017). Analyses based on the monopolistic competition model in Dixit and Stiglitz (1977) included Plüger (2001) and Benarroch and Weder (2006).

Dauda et al. (2021) empirically demonstrated the pollution haven hypothesis in African countries by explicitly considering innovation. Copeland and Taylor (2005) and Silva and Zhu (2009) pointed out the pollution haven hypothesis through emissions trading and Ishikawa and Okubo (2017) performed a model analysis. Grandfathering-type emission quotas are potential rents, hence, firms may consider locating in countries or regions with more emission quotas. Hence, the emission quota levels affect the concentration of firms. The economic model in this chapter explains the pollution haven hypothesis from the perspective of a dynamic agglomeration model that includes innovation by incorporating pollution emissions and emission trading into the R&D-based growth model.

## 10.2 The Model

### *10.2.1 Structure of R&D-Based Location Model with Pollution*

The emissions trading scheme described in Chap. 4 is introduced into the economic model in Chap. 9. The governments of the North and South allocate emission allowances to firms in their manufacturing sectors. In a single international emissions trading market, manufacturing firms in the North and South can trade emission allowances with manufacturing firms in their own countries and other countries. Since the manufacturing firms in the North and South emit cross-border pollution, households in their countries suffer from negative externalities from pollution emissions from other countries. Household preferences and firm technologies are the same as in Chaps. 4 and 9. This economic structure is illustrated in Fig. 10.1. The economic model in this chapter is based on Hamaguchi (2021, 2023).

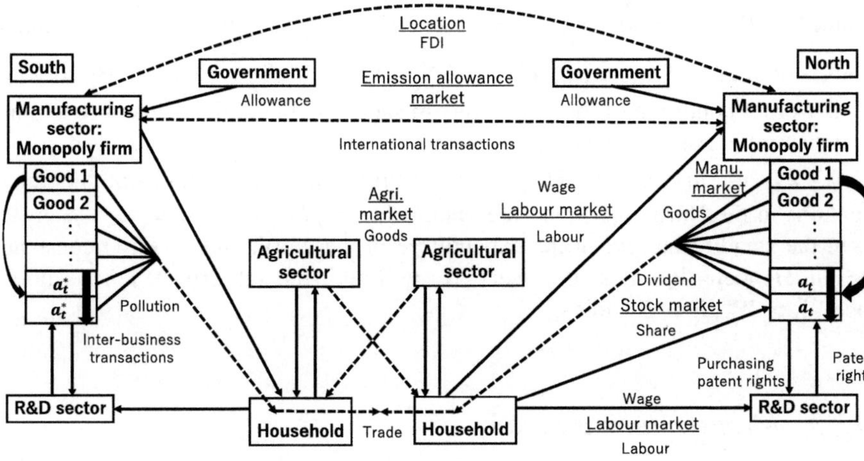


**Fig. 10.1** Structure of the R&D-based location model with pollution

## 10.2.2 Household

The utility function of a representative household in the North over different periods can be expressed as a logarithmic function as follows:

$$U_t = \int_0^\infty \log\left[\frac{Q_t^\nu D_t^{1-\nu}}{(P_t+P_t^*)^{\eta P}}\right] e^{-\rho t} dt, \tag{10.1}$$

where $P_t^*$ is the pollution emitted by manufacturing firms in the South. The composition of differentiated goods in $Q_t$ is (9.2). The total pollution emissions in the North are expressed as follows:

$$P_t = \int_0^{a_t} d_{j,t} dj, \tag{10.2}$$

where $d_{j,t}$ is the pollution emitted by manufacturing firms in the North that produce variety $j$. As with the economic model in Chap. 4, the pollution emission function per firm is $d_{j,t} = q_{j,t}/\theta_j$. To simplify the analysis, we assume that the productivity is identical across firms, with $\theta_j = \theta$.

Household expenditure in the North is (9.3) $\int_0^{a_t} p_{j,t}x_{j,t}dj + \int_0^{a_t^*} tp_{i,t}^* x_{i,t}di + P_{D,t}D_t = E_t$ and, in this, agricultural goods are numeraire, with $P_{D,t} = 1$. As in Chap. 9, firms in the agricultural sector in the perfect competition market produce agricultural goods by inputting $L_{D,t}$. In the zero-profit condition, $w_t = P_{D,t} = 1$. From (2.3) and the household's asset holdings $W_t = P_{A,t}A_t$, the household's budget constraint is $\dot{W}_t = r_t W_t + L - E_t$.

In the static utility maximisation problem, given the expenditures, households decide the quantity of each good to purchase and the demand functions in (9.4) are obtained as $P_{M,t}Q_t = \nu E_t$ and $D_t = (1-\nu)E_t$. The price index for differentiated goods is defined as $P_{M,t} \equiv \left(\int_0^{a_t} p_{j,t}^{1-\sigma} dj + \int_0^{a_t^*} t^{1-\sigma} p_{i,t}^{*1-\sigma} di\right)^{\frac{1}{1-\sigma}}$ in (9.5). By solving the first-order condition of the utility maximisation problem, the demand functions for industrial goods in the North and South become $x_{j,t} = p_{j,t}^{-\sigma} P_{M,t}^{\sigma-1} \nu E_t$ and $x_{i,t} = t^{-\sigma} p_{i,t}^{*-\sigma} P_{M,t}^{\sigma-} \nu E_t$ in (9.6). From the dynamic utility maximisation problem, the Euler equations in the North and South are obtained as $\dot{E}_t/E_t = \dot{E}_t^*/E_t^* = r_t - \rho$ in (9. 7). In the steady state, when the expenditure in the North and South is constant, $r_t = \rho$. Henceforth, unless necessary, we will omit the subscript $t$. Furthermore, since $W_0 > W_0^*$, $E > E^*$ holds.

### 10.2.3 Manufacturing Sector

The governments of the North and South have established a single international emissions trading market. The governments allocate grandfathered emissions allowances $s_j$ ($s_i^*$) to firms in the manufacturing sector of the North (South). Under a perfectly competitive emissions trading market, manufacturing firms buy and sell emissions allowances with manufacturing firms in their country or partner countries at an emissions allowance price of $p^e$. Manufacturing firms in the North (South) that emit more pollution than their allocated allowance must purchase emission allowances from other manufacturing firms, with a value of $d_j - s_j > 0$ ($d_i^* - s_i^* > 0$). However, North (South) manufacturing firms that emit less pollution than their allocated emission allowance can sell their emission allowance of $s_j - d_j > 0$ ($s_i^* - d_i^* > 0$). In equilibrium, this emissions market must be cleared. As shown in $\overline{P} = \int_0^a s_j dj + \int_0^{a^*} s_i^* di$, the total global emissions allowance is the sum of the allowances allocated to the North and South.

It is assumed that the governments are implementing a coordinated environmental policy. Each government allocates the average emission allowance of $s = s_j = s_i^* = \overline{P}/A$ to its manufacturing firms. As the number of manufacturing firms increases with increasing variety, the emission allowance allocated per firm decreases. The total emission allowance allocated to the manufacturing sector of the North is $as_j = (a/A)\overline{P}$ and of the South is $a^* s_i^* = (a^*/A)\overline{P}$. Thus, $as_j + a^* s_i^* = \overline{P}$ holds by $s = s_j = s_i^*$. The global pollution emission is capped by $\overline{P}$, however, the relative pollution emission between the North and South changes according to the number of firms in both places.

A manufacturing firm under monopolistic competition maximises its profits under the constraint of $d_{j,t}$, given the demand for manufacturing goods. The profit maximisation problem for this firm is as follows:

$$\max_{p_j} \pi_j \equiv p_j q_j - q_j - p^e (d_j - s_j), \tag{10.3}$$

where $p^e(d_j - s_j) > 0$ is the purchase cost of the emission allowance while $p^e(s_j - d_j) > 0$ is the gain on the sale of emission allowances. The first-order condition for profit maximisation yields the following:

$$p_j = \frac{\sigma}{\sigma-1}\left(1 + \frac{p^e}{\theta}\right),\ p_i^* = tp_j, \tag{10.4}$$

where the environmental regulation costs of $p^e/\theta$ are passed on to the price of the manufactured goods. Since the RHS of the manufacturing goods price is common across firms by $s = s_j = s_i^*$, all the firms are symmetric in equilibrium. Henceforth, subscript $j$ is omitted unless necessary.

By substituting (10.4) and $d_{j,t} = q_{j,t}/\theta$ into (10.3), the optimal profit of a manufacturing firm producing in the North is expressed as follows:

$$\pi = \frac{1}{\sigma-1}\left(1 + \frac{p^e}{\theta}\right)q + p^e s, \tag{10.5}$$

where the profit depends on revenue and allocation rent, similar to Hamaguchi (2020). The soaring price of emission allowances increases profits through increased sales due to price pass-on and through allocation rent from the sale of grandfathered emission allowances. This allocation rent is the driving force for the establishment of new business locations due to environmental policies.

### 10.2.4 R&D Sector

The production technology of an R&D firm in a perfectly competitive market is $\dot{A}_t = L_{A,t}/F_t$ in (3.10). From $F_t = F/A_t$ in global knowledge spillover and the free entry condition, $P_A = F/A$ is obtained. The share price is equal to the sum of the discounted present value of profits from period $t$ onwards as $P_{A,t} = \int_t^\infty e^{-[r(\iota)-r(t)]}\pi_\iota d\iota$. By taking the time derivative of $P_{A,t}$, the non-arbitrage condition is obtained as $\pi + \dot{P}_A = rP_A$ in (3.9).

### 10.2.5 Market

This economy has markets for manufactured goods, agricultural goods, labour, capital and emissions trading. The market clearing conditions for manufactured goods are such that the supply and demand of manufactured goods from the North and the South are equal, including the transport costs. From the demand function in (9.10), this condition is expressed as follows:

$$x = \nu L\left(\frac{\sigma-1}{\sigma}\right)\left(\frac{1}{1+(p^e/\theta)}\right)\left(\frac{E}{a+\varphi a^*} + \frac{\varphi E^*}{a^*+\varphi a}\right), \tag{10.6a}$$

$$x^* = \nu L\left(\tfrac{\sigma-1}{\sigma}\right)\left(\tfrac{1}{1+(p^e/\theta)}\right)\left(\tfrac{\varphi E}{a+\varphi a^*} + \tfrac{E^*}{a^*+\varphi a}\right), \tag{10.6b}$$

where, in (9.10), household demand is aggregated by population. An increase in $\varphi$ implies a decrease in transport costs due to trade liberalisation. Price pass-through due to the price of emission allowances reduces demand for manufactured goods in both places. From $D = (1-\nu)E$, the global demand for agricultural goods is $D^* = L(1-\nu)(E+E^*)$.

The market production conditions for the capital market are $\pi + \dot{P}_A = rP_A$. The number of manufacturing firms worldwide is fixed to the number of varieties worldwide and is owned by households in the North and South. Therefore, $a + a^* = W + W^* = A$ in (9.13) holds. In a capital market where capital movements are unrestricted, when the operating profit of either the North or South is high, arbitrage behaviour occurs through the firms' location, hence, from the non-arbitrage condition, the profits of manufacturing firms are equal at equilibrium, as $\pi = \pi^*$. This location behaviour results in $x = x^*$. Households supply labour to the industrial, agricultural and R&D sectors of their country and the clearing condition of the labour market in (9.15) is obtained as $L_A + L_M + L_D = 2L$.

As derived in Appendix H of Chap. 9, the number of manufacturing firms located in the North is expressed as follows:

$$\gamma = \tfrac{a}{A} = \tfrac{E-\varphi E^*}{(1-\varphi)(E+E^*)}, \tag{9.16a}$$

and in the South is as follows:

$$1-\gamma = \tfrac{a^*}{A} = \tfrac{E^*-\varphi E}{(1-\varphi)(E+E^*)}, \tag{9.16b}$$

where the home market effect in Krugman (1980) implies that the location of industrial firms depends on the relative market size in $(E-\varphi E^*)/(E+E^*)$ and industrial firms locate themselves in countries with larger market sizes and higher expenditure levels. The clearing condition in the emissions trading market is $a^*p^e(s-d^*) - ap^e(d-s) = 0$. Using (9.16a, 9.16b) and (9.16b), we have $as = (a/A)\overline{P} = \gamma\overline{P}$, $a^*s = (a^*/A)\overline{P} = (1-\gamma)\overline{P}$ and $as + a^*s = \overline{P}$ holds. From the symmetry between manufacturing firms, $\int_0^a d_j dj + \int_0^{a^*} d_i^* di = ad + a^*d^*$ holds. Using these relationships, the market clearing condition for emissions trading can be rewritten as follows:

$$P + P^* = ad + a^*d^* = \overline{P}. \tag{10.7}$$

## 10.3 Equilibrium

### 10.3.1 Dynamic System

The BGP in the present model is an equilibrium path that satisfies three conditions. First, there is a constant, positive economic growth rate $g_{A,t} = \dot{A}_t/A_t > 0$. Second, the labour allocation of manufacturing, R&D and agricultural firms is constant, as $L_{X,t} = L_X$, $L_{A,t} = L_A$, and $L_{D,t} = L_D$, respectively. Third, the aggregate expenditure is constant, as $E_t + E_t^* = E + E^*$. We construct the law of motion for $E_t + E_t^*$.

By using $a + a^* = W + W^* = A$ and $\pi = \pi^*$, (10.6a) and (10.6b) can be rewritten as follows:

$$x = x^* = \nu L\left(\tfrac{\sigma-1}{\sigma}\right)\left(\tfrac{1}{1+(p^e/\theta)}\right)\tfrac{E+E^*}{A}, \tag{10.8}$$

which is used with $D + D^* = L(1-\nu)(E + E^*)$ and $L_A = Fg_A$ to rewrite $L_A + L_M + L_D = 2L$ as follows:

$$Fg_A + L\left[1 - \nu + \nu\left(\tfrac{\sigma-1}{\sigma}\right)\left(\tfrac{1}{1+(p^e/\theta)}\right)\right](E + E^*) = 2L, \tag{10.9}$$

where passing on the price increase due to the price of emission allowances reduces manufactured goods demand and, subsequently, labour demand in the manufacturing sector.

Using $s = \overline{P}/A$ and (10.8), we can rewrite (10.5) to yield the following:

$$\pi = \tfrac{\nu L}{\sigma}\left(\tfrac{E+E^*}{A}\right) + p^e\left(\tfrac{\overline{P}}{A}\right), \tag{10.10}$$

where the expansion of the allowance allocation rent due to the price surge of emission allowances increases the profits of manufacturing firms. This expansion incentivises entrepreneurs to enter the market.

Substituting (10.10), $r = \rho$ and $g_A = -g_{PA}$ into $\pi + \dot{P}_A = rP_A$, we yield the following:

$$\tfrac{\nu L}{\sigma F}(E + E^*) + p^e\left(\tfrac{\overline{P}}{F}\right) = \rho + g_A, \tag{10.11}$$

where, as shown by Hamaguchi (2021), the dynamical system consisting of (10.9) and (10.11) has a deterministic and stable equilibrium. In this steady state, $g = g_A = -g_{PA}$ holds.

### 10.3.2 Steady State

By using (9), $d = q/\theta$ and $a + a^* = A$, we can rewrite (8) as follows:

$$\overline{P} = \left(\frac{\nu L}{\theta}\right)\left(\frac{\sigma-1}{\sigma}\right)\frac{E+E^*}{1+(p^e/\theta)}, \quad (10.12)$$

where, when the total emission allowance caps the amount of pollution emissions, the increase in demand for manufactured goods and expenditure expands pollution emissions through production expansion. Hence, the price of emission allowances rises due to demand for emission allowances, decreasing the demand for manufactured goods due to price pass-on. The amount of pollution emissions in the manufacturing sector falls within the total emission allowance, as the amount of pollution emissions decreases through production contraction.

Substituting (10.12) for (10.11) and rearranging gives the following claim about the economic growth rate:

$$g = \frac{\sigma p^e+\theta}{\sigma-1}\left(\frac{\overline{P}}{F}\right) - \rho, \quad (10.13)$$

where the profit per share depends on the allowance allocation rent. As the distribution effect in Hamaguchi (2020) described, this rent expansion promotes economic growth. We define $b \equiv \left[(\sigma p^e + \theta)/(\sigma - 1)\right]\left[\overline{P}/(2L)\right]$ as the allowance allocation rent per population.

By substituting (10.13) and $g = g_A$ into (10.9), we obtain the following expression for per capita expenditure in the world:

$$E + E^* = \frac{2(1-b)+\frac{\rho F}{L}}{1-\nu+\nu\left(\frac{\sigma-1}{\sigma}\right)\left[\frac{1}{1+(p^e/\theta)}\right]}, \quad (10.14)$$

where the household budget, which consists of labour income in 2 and stock income in $\rho F/L$, suffers an income loss of $-b$ due to the allowance allocation rent. This is because the price of manufactured goods rises as a result of the pass-through of the emissions allowance price. Furthermore, as shown in $1 + (p^e/\theta)$, the increase in the emissions allowance price expands household expenditure, leading to an expansion in the production of manufactured goods and settling the emissions allowance trade in (10.12). The expenditure in the North and South increases at a constant rate. Hence, from (14), expenditure in the North and South can be expressed as follows:

$$E = \frac{1-b+\frac{\rho F}{L}k}{1-\nu+\nu\left(\frac{\sigma-1}{\sigma}\right)\left[\frac{1}{1+(p^e/\theta)}\right]}, \quad (10.15a)$$

$$E^* = \frac{1-b+\frac{\rho F}{L}(1-k)}{1-\nu+\nu\left(\frac{\sigma-1}{\sigma}\right)\left[\frac{1}{1+(p^e/\theta)}\right]}, \quad (10.15b)$$

where $k \equiv W/A > 1/2$ is the number of firms owned by the North household, who own more than half of the world's firms.

By substituting (10.14) into (10.12), the equilibrium emission price is derived as follows:

$$p^e = \nu L\left(\frac{\sigma-1}{\sigma}\right)\left(2+\frac{\rho F}{L}\right)\left(\frac{1}{\overline{P}}\right)-\theta, \tag{10.16}$$

where an increase in the preference for manufactured goods, a decrease in markups and an increase in household income stimulate production expansion through the demand for manufactured goods. The price of emission allowances rises because its demand increases due to the increase in pollution emissions. From $dp^e/d\overline{P} = -\nu L[(\sigma-1)/\sigma][2+(\rho F)/L]\left(1/\overline{P}^2\right) < 0$, a reduction in the total emission allowance increases demand for emission allowances, causing its price to rise. Improvements in pollution abatement productivity reduces the pollution emitted per unit of production, which reduces the demand for emission allowances, causing its price to fall. Rewriting $b$ in this $p^e$ gives the following:

$$b = \frac{\overline{P}}{2L}\left(\frac{\sigma p^e+\theta}{\sigma-1}\right) = \left(1+\frac{\rho F}{2L}\right)\nu - \frac{\theta\overline{P}}{2L}, \tag{10.17}$$

where, as $db/d\overline{P} = -\theta/(2L) < 0$, the reduction in the total emission allowance increases the allowance allocation rent through a rise in the price of emission allowances.

By substituting (10.17) for (10.13), we obtain the following economic growth rate at equilibrium:

$$g = \frac{2L}{F}\left(\frac{\nu}{\sigma}\right) - \frac{\theta\overline{P}}{F} - (1-\nu)\rho, \tag{10.18}$$

where the reduction in expenditure due to the pass-through of the price reduces profits and economic growth rate. However, as can be seen in $dg/d\overline{P} = -(\theta/F) < 0$, the expansion of the allowance allocation rent at $b$ due to the reduction in the total emission allowance enhanced economic growth, which dominates the effect of the reduction in expenditure inhibiting economic growth. Hence, in equilibrium, the environmental policy raises the economic growth rate.

By substituting (10.14), (10.15a) and (10.15b) into (9.16a), the number of firms located in the North at equilibrium is expressed as follows:

$$\gamma = \frac{(1-\varphi)(1-b)+\frac{\rho F}{L}[k-\varphi(1-k)]}{2(1-\varphi)\left(1-b+\frac{\rho F}{2L}\right)}, \tag{10.19}$$

where the concentration of firms in the North is affected by the allowance allocation rent in $b$. Furthermore, $\gamma \geq 0$ holds for

$$(1-\varphi)(1-b) + \frac{\rho F}{L}[k-\varphi(1-k)] \geq 0,$$

and $\gamma = 1$ holds for

$$1 - b = \frac{\rho F}{L(1-\varphi)}[k - \varphi(1-k)],$$

where we assume that the solution is an interior point with $0 < \gamma < 1$ in the present model.

In $a - W = W^* - a^*$, the household in the North cannot buy up all the shares in the North with its initial assets, hence, the household in the South, which has some initial assets left over after buying shares in the South, buys shares in the North. The opposite happens in $W - a = a^* - W^*$. By taking the time derivative of this formula, we get $\dot{a} - \dot{W} = \dot{W}^* - \dot{a}^*$. The amount of FDI between North and South is defined as follows:

$$\dot{a} - \dot{W} = g(n - W),$$

which is rewritten with $a + a^* = W + W^* = A$, (15a) and (15b) as follows:

$$\dot{a} - \dot{W} = \frac{gA\left(k-\frac{1}{2}\right)[\varphi\rho F - L(1-\varphi)(1-b)]}{2L(1-\varphi)\left(1-b+\frac{\rho F}{2L}\right)}, \tag{10.20}$$

which implies that the direction of FDI net flows is dependent on the sign of $a - W$ and $\dot{a} - \dot{W} \gtreqless 0$ is affected by the following parameter conditions:

$$\overline{\varphi} \equiv \left(\frac{\varphi}{1-\varphi}\right)\frac{\rho F}{L} \gtrless 1 - b, \tag{10.21}$$

where FDI from the South to the North occurs in $\overline{\varphi} > 1 - b$ because $\dot{a} - \dot{W} > 0$, while from the North to the South occurs in $\overline{\varphi} \leq 1 - b$ because $\dot{a} - \dot{W} \leq 0$. The amount of FDI increases through the economic growth rate $g$. The direction of FDI is affected by the allowance allocation rent at $b$.

By using (Eqs. 16a and 16b, Chap. 9), (2), $d = q/\theta$, $as = (a/A)\overline{P}$ and $a^*s = (a^*/A)\overline{P}$, the total pollution emissions of the North, the South and total amount of pollution emitted by the North as a percentage of the South, respectively, are derived as follows:

$$P = \gamma\overline{P},\ P^* = (1-\gamma)\overline{P},\ \frac{P}{P^*} = \frac{1}{(1/\gamma)-1}, \tag{10.22}$$

where the total pollution emissions of the North and South are expressed as the pollution share, which is the total emission allowance multiplied by the number of firms located there. The total pollution emissions of the North in the South depend on the concentration of firms in the North. While the total emission allowance caps the pollution worldwide, the emission allowances allocated to manufacturing firms in the North and South are the same. Hence, the number of manufacturing firms located there will affect the pollution emissions in the North and South. Although the total emission allowance levels are the same, the amount of pollution emitted in the North is greater than in the South because manufacturing firms that emit pollution are located in the North rather than the South. Therefore, even if the emission allowance levels are the same, stricter environmental regulations are imposed on manufacturing firms in the North.

Finally, the following parameter conditions are imposed:

$$L > \frac{1-\nu}{2\nu}\left(\frac{\theta\overline{P}}{1-\nu} + \rho F\right), \quad \frac{\sigma-1}{\sigma}\left(\frac{\nu\rho}{\theta}\right) > \overline{P},$$

where these parameter conditions guarantee $g > 0$ and $p^e > 0$.

## 10.4 Comparative Statics

### *10.4.1 Pollution Haven Hypothesis Via Emission Allowance*

In Appendix I, the effect of the total emission allowance on the steady state is shown as follows:

$$\frac{dE + E^*}{d\overline{P}} \gtreqless 0, \quad \frac{dE}{d\overline{P}} \gtreqless 0, \quad \frac{dE^*}{d\overline{P}} \gtreqless 0, \quad \frac{d\gamma}{d\overline{P}} < 0, \quad \frac{d\dot{a} - \dot{W}}{d\overline{P}} < 0,$$

and

$$\frac{dP}{d\overline{P}} = \overline{P}\frac{\partial\gamma}{\partial\overline{P}} + \gamma > 0, \quad \frac{dP^*}{d\overline{P}} = -\overline{P}\frac{\partial\gamma}{\partial\overline{P}} + (1-\gamma), \quad \frac{d}{d\overline{P}}\left(\frac{P}{P^*}\right) = \frac{1}{(1-\gamma)^2}\frac{\partial\gamma}{\partial\overline{P}} > 0,$$

where a reduction in the total emissions allowance increases the allowance allocation rent due to an increase in the price of emissions allowances, which boosts economic growth. Due to the pass-through of the price of emissions allowances, the price of manufactured goods rises and expenditure decreases. However, due to the increase in the price of emissions allowances, demand for manufactured goods as a proportion of expenditure decreases in $[\cdot](E + E^*)$ in (10.9) and expenditure increases. Regardless of the change in expenditure, since the households in the North have more initial assets, the relative market size in the North is large. Hence, the home market effect promotes the concentration of firms from the South to the North and the amount of FDI increases. When the reduction in allowance allocation rent leads to $\overline{\varphi} < 1 - b$ in (10.21), the reduction in the total emission allowance induces the direction of FDI from the South to the North. As manufacturing firms that emit pollution are concentrated in the North, the total amount of pollution emitted in the North increases and the total amount of pollution emitted in the North as a proportion of the total in the South decreases. Although the total emissions allowance in the North and South is the same, the environmental regulation level is stricter in the North because the North, with more manufacturing firms, has a relatively higher level of pollution emissions. The concentration of polluting firms in countries with relatively strict environmental regulations implies the green haven effect, as shown by Poelhekke and Van der Ploeg (2015).

### 10.4.2 Effects of Abatement Productivity and Trade Liberalisation

In the present model, the pollution haven from the South to the North due to the reduction of the total emission allowance does not imply the pollution haven hypothesis. However, the improvement of pollution abatement productivity due to $\theta \uparrow$, which implies direct regulation, leads to pollution haven from the North to South. In Appendix I, the effect of the improvement of pollution abatement productivity on the steady state is shown as follows:

$$\frac{dE+E^*}{d\theta} > 0, \ \frac{dE}{d\theta} > 0, \ \frac{dE^*}{d\theta} > 0, \ \frac{d\gamma}{d\theta} < 0, \ \frac{d\dot{a}-\dot{W}}{d\theta} < 0,$$

and

$$\frac{dP}{d\theta} = \overline{P}\frac{\partial \gamma}{\partial \theta} < 0, \ \frac{dP^*}{d\theta} = -\overline{P}\frac{\partial \gamma}{\partial \theta} > 0, \ \frac{d}{d\theta}\left(\frac{P}{P^*}\right) = \frac{1}{(1-\gamma)^2}\frac{\partial \gamma}{\partial \theta} < 0,$$

where, from (10.17), $dp^e/d\theta = -1 < 0$, the amount of pollution emitted per unit of production decreases. Hence, the price of emission allowances falls due to a decrease in demand for emission allowances. From (10.17), $db/d\theta = -\overline{P}/(2L) < 0$, the allowance allocation rent shrinks, lowering the economic growth rate. As a result of the pass-through of the price of emission allowances, the price of manufactured goods drops and expenditure increases. While expenditure increases in both the North and South, the relative market size in the North shrinks, even though households in the North have more initial assets than those in the South. Due to the home market effect, the concentration of firms from the North to the South increases and the amount of FDI shrinks. When the reduction in allowance allocation rent leads to $\overline{\varphi} \geq 1 - b$ in (10.21), the improvement in pollution abatement productivity induces FDI to flow from the North to the South. Since manufacturing firms that emit pollution are concentrated in the South, the total amount of pollution emitted in the North is reduced and the total amount of pollution emitted in the South by the North is increased. This result implies the pollution haven hypothesis.

In Appendix I, the effect of the reduction in transport costs due to trade liberalisation on the steady-state value is shown as follows:

$$\frac{dE+E^*}{d\varphi} = 0, \ \frac{dE}{d\varphi} = 0, \ \frac{dE^*}{d\varphi} > 0, \ \frac{d\gamma}{d\varphi} > 0, \ \frac{d\dot{a}-\dot{W}}{d\varphi} > 0,$$

and

$$\frac{dP}{d\varphi} = \overline{P}\frac{\partial\gamma}{\partial\varphi} > 0, \quad \frac{dP^*}{d\varphi} = -\overline{P}\frac{\partial\gamma}{\partial\varphi} < 0, \quad \frac{d}{d\varphi}\left(\frac{P}{P^*}\right) = \frac{1}{(1-\gamma)^2}\frac{\partial\gamma}{\partial\varphi} > 0,$$

where, since stock income is not dependent on transportation costs, trade liberalisation does not affect expenditure. Instead, through the home market effect, transportation costs reduction due to trade liberalisation encourages the location of firms in the North. Furthermore, from $d\overline{\varphi}/d\varphi > 0$ in (10.21), when trade liberalisation leads to $\overline{\varphi} < 1 - b$, trade policy induces the direction of FDI from the South to the North. While the concentration of firms in the North increases the total pollution emissions of the North, the deconcentration of firms in the South reduces the pollution emissions of the South. As a result, trade liberalisation increases the pollution emissions of the North as a proportion of the South.

## 10.5 The Case of Local Spillover

### 10.5.1 Steady State

Under global spillover, trade liberalisation leads to a pollution haven from the South to the North. However, under local spillover, transport costs affect the price of emission allowances, hence, trade liberalisation leads to a pollution haven from the North to the South through the allowance allocation rent. In this section, $\theta = 1$ is assumed to clarify the role of pollution abatement productivity in the growth and agglomeration effects of the total emission allowance.

In local spillover, the fixed R&D costs in the North and South are $F_t = F/a_t$ and $F_t^* = F/a_t^*$, respectively. The zero-profit condition in the R&D sector yields the stock price $P_A = F/a$, which can be rewritten as $P_A = F/(A\gamma)$ by using $\gamma = a/A$. Hence, (10.11), under the non-arbitrage condition, can be rewritten as follows:

$$\tfrac{\gamma}{F}\left[\tfrac{\nu L}{\sigma}(E+E^*) + p^e\overline{P}\right] = \rho + g_A, \tag{10.23}$$

where, on the LHS, the decrease in R&D costs due to local spillovers increases the supply of a variety of blueprints, increasing the price of patents and the dividend per share. The market clearing conditions of the labour market in (10.9) are rewritten as follows:

$$g_A\left(\tfrac{F}{\gamma}\right) + L\left[1 - \nu + \nu\left(\tfrac{\sigma-1}{\sigma}\right)\left(\tfrac{1}{1+p^e}\right)\right](E+E^*) = 2L, \tag{10.24}$$

where the number of firms located in the North affects stock prices and household expenditure.

The expenditure in (10.14), (10.15a) and (10.15b) is rewritten as follows:

$$E + E^* = \frac{2 - \frac{\overline{P}(1+p^e)}{L} + \frac{\rho F}{\gamma L}}{1 - \nu + \nu\left(\frac{\sigma - 1}{\sigma}\right)}, \tag{10.25}$$

and

$$E = \frac{1 - \frac{\overline{P}(1+p^e)}{L} + \frac{\rho F}{\gamma L}k}{1 - \nu + \nu\left(\frac{\sigma - 1}{\sigma}\right)}, \quad E^* = \frac{1 - \frac{\overline{P}(1+p^e)}{L} + \frac{\rho F}{\gamma L}(1-k)}{1 - \nu + \nu\left(\frac{\sigma - 1}{\sigma}\right)}, \tag{10.26}$$

where, in local spillover, the concentration of firms in the North leads to a drop in stock prices and a fall in stock income leads to a fall in expenditure. Under the assumption of local spillover and $\theta = 1$, $b$ in (10.17) changes to $\left[\overline{P}(1+p^e)\right]/L$. Furthermore, under this assumption, the emission allowance price in the denominator in (10.25) and (10.26) disappears.

By substituting (10.25) into (10.11), the price of emission allowances in local spillovers is as follows:

$$p^e = \nu L\left(\frac{\sigma - 1}{\sigma}\right)\left(2 + \frac{\rho F}{\gamma L}\right)\left(\frac{1}{\overline{P}}\right) - 1, \tag{10.27}$$

where the concentration of firms in the North reduces expenditure and demand for manufactured goods. Manufacturing firms reduce pollution emissions by reducing production and the price of emission allowances falls due to a drop in demand for emission allowances. By substituting (10.12) into (10.25) and using (10.27), the following economic growth rate is derived:

$$g = \left(2\nu L - \overline{P}\right)\frac{\gamma}{F} - (1 - \nu)\rho, \tag{10.28}$$

where, similar to global spillovers, in local spillovers, lowering the total emissions allowance increases the economic growth rate through the expansion of the allowance allocation rent in $\overline{P}/F$.

By substituting (10.27), the expenditure in (10.25) and (10.26) becomes as follows:

$$E + E^* = \hat{\sigma}\left(2 + \frac{\rho F}{\gamma L}\right), \; E = \hat{\sigma}\left(1 + \frac{\rho F}{\gamma L}k\right), \; E^* = \hat{\sigma}\left[1 + \frac{\rho F}{\gamma L}(1 - k)\right],$$

for $\hat{\sigma} \equiv [\sigma(1 - \nu) + \nu]/(\sigma - \nu)$. By assuming $\theta = 1$, the effect of the total emission allowance on expenditure disappears. The amount of FDI and its direction are $\dot{W} - \dot{a} = gA(1 - \gamma)$ in (9.32).

### *10.5.2 Poverty Trap*

By substituting (10.25) and (10.26) into (9.16a), the number of firms located in the North in a local spillover can be derived as follows:

$$\gamma = \frac{(1-\varphi)\left[1-\frac{\overline{P}(1+p^e)}{2L}\right]+\frac{\rho F}{\gamma L}[k-\varphi(1-k)]}{2(1-\varphi)\left(1-\frac{\overline{P}(1+p^e)}{2L}+\frac{\rho F}{2\gamma L}\right)}, \tag{10.29}$$

which is substituted for (10.27) to derive the quadratic function of $\gamma$ as $f(\gamma) \equiv 2\gamma^2 - f_4\gamma + \rho F f_5 = 0$ for

$$f_4 \equiv \frac{L}{\sigma}[(1-\nu)\sigma+\nu] - \frac{\rho F}{L} > 0,\ f_5 \equiv \frac{\nu}{2}\left(\frac{\sigma-1}{\sigma}\right) - \frac{k-\varphi(1-k)}{1-\varphi} > 0.$$

By solving this quadratic equation, the following distinct positive real solutions are derived:

$$\gamma_l = \frac{f_4-\sqrt{f_4^2-8\rho F f_5}}{4} > 0,\ \gamma_h = \frac{f_4+\sqrt{f_4^2-8\rho F f_5}}{4} > 0, \tag{10.30}$$

where, as shown in Appendix I, under certain parameter conditions, $0 < 1/2 < \gamma_l < \gamma_h < 1$ holds in Fig. 10.2. The combination of local spillovers and emissions trading creates a poverty trap for firm location.

Notice that $(\nu/2)[(\sigma-1)/\sigma]$ in $f_5$ is the term for emissions trading at $\theta = 1$. When there is no emissions trading, $\overline{f}_5 = -[k-\varphi(1-k)]/(1-\varphi) < 0$, and medium-level agglomeration in the North is expressed as a positive real number solution in $f(\gamma)$. This solution is $\gamma_m = (1/4)\left[f_4 + \sqrt{f_4^2 - \rho F \overline{f}_5}\right]$. When there is emissions trading in global spillover, the number of firms located in the North is the unique solution in (10.19). When there is no emissions trading, the number of firms located

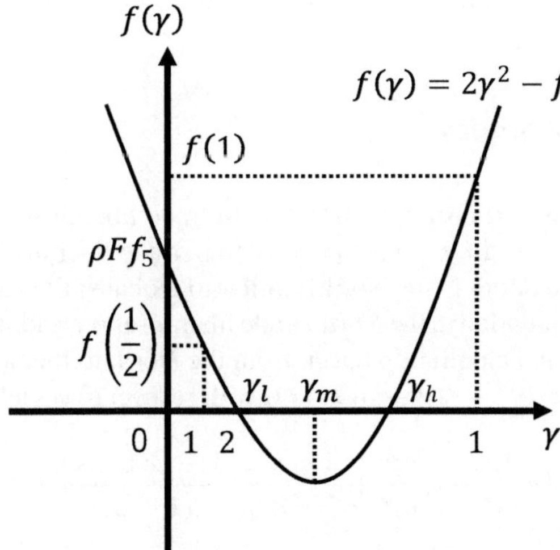


**Fig. 10.2** The relationship between the number of firms located in the North and the quadratic function

in the North is the unique solution in both global and local spillover, as shown in (9.24) and (9.31). Therefore, the poverty trap regarding the number of firms located is caused by the combination of local spillover and emissions trading.

In (10.27), $1 + p^e$ is $\left(\nu L/\overline{P}\right)[(\sigma - 1)/\sigma]\left[(\rho F)/\gamma L\right]$, which becomes $(\nu/2)[(\sigma - 1)/\sigma]$ in $f_5$. This $1 + p^e$ affects the allowance allocation rent through $\left[\overline{P}(1 + p^e)\right]/L$ in (10.28). Due to the reduction in the total emissions allowance, the price surge of emission allowances is passed on to the price of manufactured goods, reducing expenditure. Keeping all factors constant, the relative market size in the North shrinks, hence, the number of firms in the North decreases. The deconcentration of firms in the North raises the fixed R&D cost through local spillovers, the development of variety stagnates and the number of firms located in the North decreases further. In addition, as the price of emission allowances rises due to the decrease in the number of firms in the North, expenditure decreases due to further price pass-through. Through this interaction, a poverty trap occurs concerning the number of firms located in the North.

Under global spillover, a reduction in the total emissions allowance reduces the number of firms in the North. However, under local spillover, $\gamma$ in (10.29) is not affected by the total emission allowance, as shown in (10.27) by $\overline{P}(1 + p^e) = \nu L[(\sigma - 1)/\sigma]\left[(\rho F)/\gamma L\right]$. This change occurs by assuming $\theta = 1$ for $\theta \neq 1$. It has been pointed out that the cost of pollution reduction, such as the cost of pollution abatement activities and their productivity, significantly impacts the statistical significance of the pollution haven hypothesis (Keller and Levinson 2002; Forslid et al. 2017). Therefore, when we change the pollution abatement productivity, which is assumed to be an exogenous parameter, into an endogenous variable that requires the input of goods and labour, the effects of total emissions allowances and trade liberalisation on the location of firms and pollution havens may change.

### 10.5.3 Comparative Statics

In the present model, transport cost reduction due to trade liberalisation leads to a decrease in $\gamma_h$ and an increase in $\gamma_l$. In the poverty trap, trade liberalisation leads to a pollution haven from the South to the North, similar to global spillovers. However, regarding excessive accumulation in the North, trade liberalisation leads to a decrease in economic growth rate and a pollution haven from the North to the South.

Differentiating $f(\gamma) \equiv 2\gamma^2 - f_4\gamma + \rho F f_5 = 0$ with respect to $\varphi$ yields:

$$\frac{\partial f(\gamma)}{\partial \gamma}\frac{\partial \gamma}{\partial \varphi} = 4\gamma\frac{\partial \gamma}{\partial \varphi} - f_4\frac{\partial \gamma}{\partial \varphi} + \frac{1-k}{1-\varphi} - \frac{k - \varphi(1-k)}{(1-\varphi)^2} = 0,$$

which is rewritten with (10.29) as follows:

$$\frac{d\gamma_l}{d\varphi} = \frac{2k-1}{(1-\varphi)^2}\cdot\frac{1}{f_4^2 - 8\rho F f_5} > 0, \quad \frac{d\gamma_h}{d\varphi} = -\frac{2k-1}{(1-\varphi)^2}\cdot\frac{1}{f_4^2 - 8\rho F f_5} < 0, \tag{10.31}$$

where trade liberalisation leads to the agglomeration of firms in the North in the poverty trap and the deagglomeration of firms in the North in over-agglomeration.

In Appendix I, the effect of transport cost decrease on the steady state is shown as follows: $d(E+E^*)/d\varphi = 0$, $dE/d\varphi = 0$, $dE^*/d\varphi = 0$ hold. In the poverty trap, the following effects are derived:

$$\frac{dp_l^e}{d\varphi} = -\frac{\nu L}{\overline{P}}\left(\frac{\sigma-1}{\sigma}\right)\left(\frac{\rho F}{\gamma_l^2 L}\right)\frac{\partial \gamma_l}{\partial \varphi} < 0, \quad \frac{dg_l}{d\varphi} = \frac{\left(2\nu L - \overline{P}\right)}{F}\frac{\partial \gamma_l}{\partial \varphi} > 0,$$

$$\frac{dP_l}{d\varphi} = \overline{P}\frac{\partial \gamma_l}{\partial \varphi} > 0, \quad \frac{dP_l^*}{d\varphi} = -\overline{P}\frac{\partial \gamma_l}{\partial \varphi} < 0, \quad \frac{d}{d\varphi}\left(\frac{P_l}{P_l^*}\right) = \frac{1}{(1-\gamma_l)^2}\frac{\partial \gamma_l}{\partial \varphi} > 0,$$

$$\frac{d\left(\dot{a} - \dot{W}\right)\big|_{\gamma=\gamma_l}}{d\varphi} = A(1-\gamma_l)\frac{\partial g_l}{\partial \varphi} - gA\frac{\partial \gamma_l}{\partial \varphi},$$

where trade liberalisation encourages the concentration of manufacturing firms in the North and the reduction in fixed R&D costs leads to an increase in the economic growth rate. As the location and agglomeration effects are contradictory, the dominant effect determines the effect of trade liberalisation on the FDI amount. As a result of the decline in stock prices, household expenditure and the production of manufactured goods declines and the price of emission allowances falls due to a decrease in its demand. Hence, there is a pollution haven from the South to the North, that is, the total amount of pollution emissions increases in the North and decreases in the South. As a result, the amount of pollution emissions from the North as a proportion of the total in the South increases.

The following effects are derived from excessive accumulation:

$$\frac{dp_h^e}{d\varphi} = -\frac{\nu L}{\overline{P}}\left(\frac{\sigma-1}{\sigma}\right)\left(\frac{\rho F}{\gamma_h^2 L}\right)\frac{\partial \gamma_h}{\partial \varphi} > 0, \quad \frac{dg_h}{d\varphi} = \frac{\left(2\nu L - \overline{P}\right)}{F}\frac{\partial \gamma_h}{\partial \varphi} < 0,$$

$$\frac{dP_h}{d\varphi} = \overline{P}\frac{\partial \gamma_h}{\partial \varphi} < 0, \quad \frac{dP_h^*}{d\varphi} = -\overline{P}\frac{\partial \gamma_h}{\partial \varphi} > 0, \quad \frac{d}{d\varphi}\left(\frac{P_h}{P_h^*}\right) = \frac{1}{(1-\gamma_h)^2}\frac{\partial \gamma_h}{\partial \varphi} < 0,$$

$$\frac{d\left(\dot{a} - \dot{W}\right)\big|_{\gamma=\gamma_h}}{d\varphi} = A(1-\gamma_h)\frac{\partial g_h}{\partial \varphi} - gA\frac{\partial \gamma_h}{\partial \varphi},$$

where trade liberalisation encourages the concentration of firms in the South and an increase in fixed R&D costs decreases the economic growth rate. The effect of trade liberalisation on the FDI amount is influenced by the location and agglomeration effects. As a result of the increase in household expenditure through the rise in stock prices and in the production of manufactured goods, the price of emission allowances rises due to an increase in demand. Hence, there is pollution haven from the North to the South, that is, the total amount of pollution emissions increases in the South and decreases in the North. As a result, the amount of pollution emitted by the North in the South decreases. This implies the pollution haven hypothesis due to trade liberalisation.

The above discussion highlights that the spillover effect of R&D technology determines whether the pollution haven hypothesis due to environmental and trade policies is successful.

## References


Acheampong, A. O., Adams, S., & Boateng, E. (2019). Do globalization and renewable energy contribute to carbon emissions mitigation in Sub-Saharan Africa? *Science of the Total Environment*, 677, 436–446. https://doi.org/10.1016/j.scitotenv.2019.04.353

Antweiler, W., Copeland, B. R., & Taylor, M. S. (2001). Is free trade good for the environment?. *The American Economic Review*, 91(4), 877–908. https://doi.org/10.1257/aer.91.4.877

Benarroch, M., & Weder, R. (2006). Intra-industry trade in intermediate products, pollution and internationally increasing returns. *Journal of Environmental Economics and Management*, 52(3), 675–689. https://doi.org/10.1016/j.jeem.2006.05.001

Copeland, B. R., & Taylor, M. S. (2004). Trade, growth, and the environment. *Journal of Economic literature*, 42(1), 7–71. https://doi.org/10.1257/002205104773558047

Copeland, B. R., & Taylor, M. S. (2005). Free trade and global warming: a trade theory view of the Kyoto protocol. *Journal of Environmental Economics and Management*, 49(2), 205–234. https://doi.org/10.1016/j.jeem.2004.04.006

Erdogan, A. M. (2014). Foreign direct investment and environmental regulations: a survey. *Journal of Economic Surveys*, 28(5), 943–955. https://doi.org/10.1111/joes.12047

Forslid, R., Okubo, T., & Sanctuary, M. (2017). Trade liberalization, transboundary pollution, and market size. *Journal of the Association of Environmental and Resource Economists*, 4(3), 927–957. https://doi.org/10.1086/693562

Hamaguchi, Y. (2020). Do pollution havens restrict tourism-led growth? Achieving sustainable tourism via a mix of environmental and tourism policies. *Tourism Economics*, 26(7), 1175-1196. https://doi.org/10.1177/1354816619868086

Hamaguchi, Y. (2021). Polluting firms' location choices and pollution havens in an R&D-based growth model for an international emissions trading market. *The Journal of International Trade & Economic Development*, 30(4), 625–642. https://doi.org/10.1080/09638199.2021.1889644

Hamaguchi, Y. (2023). Pollution havens and agglomeration: The effect of globalization and technological spillover. *Applied Economics*, 56(19), 2223–2240. https://doi.org/10.1080/00036846.2023.2186361

Ishikawa, J., & Okubo, T. (2017). Greenhouse-gas emission controls and firm locations in north–south trade. *Environmental and Resource Economics*, 67, 637–660. https://doi.org/10.1007/s10640-015-9991-0

Plüger, M. (2001). Ecological dumping under monopolistic competition. *Scandinavian Journal of Economics*, 103(4), 689–706. https://doi.org/10.1111/1467-9442.00266

Poelhekke, S., & Van der Ploeg, F. (2015). Green havens and pollution havens. *The World Economy*, 38(7), 1159–1178. https://doi.org/10.1111/twec.12219

Silva, E. C., & Zhu, X. (2009). Emissions trading of global and local pollutants, pollution havens and free riding. *Journal of Environmental Economics and Management*, 58(2), 169–182. https://doi.org/10.1016/j.jeem.2009.04.001

Zeng, D. Z., & Zhao, L. (2009). Pollution havens and industrial agglomeration. *Journal of Environmental Economics and Management*, 58(2), 141–153. https://doi.org/10.1016/j.jeem.2008.09.003

Krugman, P. (1980). Scale economies, product differentiation, and the pattern of trade. *The American economic review*, 70(5), 950-959. https://www.jstor.org/stable/1805774

Keller, W., & Levinson, A. (2002). Pollution abatement costs and foreign direct investment inflows to US states. *Review of Economics and Statistics*, 84(4), 691–703. https://doi.org/10.1162/003465302760556503

Copeland, B, R., & Taylor, M. S., (1994). North-South Trade and the Environment, *The Quarterly Journal of Economics*, 109(3), 755–787, https://doi.org/10.2307/2118421

Copeland, B, R., & Taylor, M. S., (1995). Trade and Transboundary Pollution. *The American Economic Review*, 85(4), 716–737. http://www.jstor.org/stable/2118228

Dauda, L., Long, X., Mensah, C. N., Salman, M., Boamah, K. B., Ampon-Wireko, S., & Dogbe, C. S. K. (2021). Innovation, trade openness and $CO_2$ emissions in selected countries in Africa. *Journal of Cleaner Production*, 281, 125143. https://doi.org/10.1016/j.jclepro.2020.125143

Dixit, A. K., & Stiglitz, J. E. (1977). Monopolistic competition and optimum product diversity. *The American Economic Review*, 67(3), 297–308. https://www.jstor.org/stable/1831401

Elbers, C., & Withagen, C. (2003). Environmental policy, population dynamics and agglomeration. *Contributions in Economic Analysis & Policy*, 3(2). https://doi.org/10.2202/1538-0645.1286

Lange, A., & Quaas, M. F. (2007). Economic geography and the effect of environmental pollution on agglomeration. *The BE Journal of Economic Analysis & Policy*, 7(1). https://doi.org/10.2202/1935-1682.1724

# Chapter 11
# Sustainable Tourism

**Abstract** In the R&D-based location model, including emissions, global environmental quality is introduced along with the tourism sector and tourism mobility. In addition to pollution emissions, the environmental quality deteriorates due to the crowding effect at tourist destinations. Through externality effects, it deteriorates the productivity of the tourism sector. Reduced total emissions allowance brings economic growth and tourism mobility. It expands tourism consumption due to a pollution haven from the South to the North and the improvement of the global environmental quality. This environmental policy achieves tourism-led growth and sustainable tourism. Reduction in low airfares leads to decreased tourism consumption due to the rise in the price of tourism goods based on tourism pollution and externalities. Therefore, while it promotes industrialisation and economic growth in the North, it causes environmental degradation and tourism decline, hindering sustainable tourism. Reduction in high airfares brings about industrialisation and improved environmental quality in the South at the expense of low growth and reduced tourism. Therefore, it promoted industrialisation in developing countries that rely on tourism. The externality effects of tourism lead to a malfunctioning of environmental policy, as the high price of emission allowances undermine the incentive for manufacturing firms to reduce pollution.

## 11.1 Introduction

The tourism industry accounts for around 10% of global GDP and around 7% of global exports. Some countries aim to achieve economic development by becoming a tourist nation. The hypothesis that economic growth through the development of the tourism sector is tourism-led growth was proposed by Balagner and Catavela-Jordá (2002) through an empirical analysis of Spain. Despite some biases, the hypothesis is supported in empirical studies to this day (Brida et al. 2016; Nunkoo et al. 2020; Song and Wu 2022).

However, while the tourism industry is dependent on the natural environment, it has the potential to cause irreversible environmental damage through climate change

 
Y. Hamaguchi, *Sustainable Development in Economic Growth Theory*,
https://doi.org/10.1007/978-981-96-7639-2_11

(Buckey 2011). As the tourism industry is growing steadily, it is increasing its carbon footprint. There is concern that it will become a carbon-intensive industry if appropriate environmental policies are not introduced (Lenzen et al. 2018). Since sustainable tourism aims to balance tourism development and environmental conservation, several related studies have been conducted (Liu 2003) and a dynamic model of sustainable tourism has been constructed by Johnston and Tyrrell (2005).

Analyses of the relationship between tourism and environment in endogenous economic growth models include externalities (Lozano Ibáñez et al. 2004), pollution abatement through tourism tax revenue (Cerina 2007), the crowding-out effect (Gómez et al. 2008; Marsiglio 2015), migration dynamics (Ouattara et al. 2019), tourism investment for congestion mitigation (Schubert and Schamel 2021) and the tourist destination life cycle hypothesis (Lozano et al. 2008; Hernánddez and León 2013). For a survey of previous research on sustainable tourism in endogenous growth models, see Hamaguchi (2024). In particular, Albaladejo and Martínez-García (2015) were aware of the role of innovation in international tourism as it improves the carrying capacity of tourist destinations and brings economic growth through tourism development.

However, in Cristea et al. (2013), international transport accounted for a relatively high proportion of global $CO_2$ emissions and, in Gössling et al. (2007), air travel, a means of international tourism, negatively impacts the environment. Wang and Wang (2018) pointed out that improving energy efficiency promoted the decarbonisation of the aviation industry and led to sustainable tourism. Furthermore, Lenzen et al. (2018) argued for the introduction of environmental taxes and emissions trading into the tourism and aviation industries. By introducing the tourism sector and tourism mobility into the R&D-based location model, which includes emissions trading, it is possible to understand the mechanisms of the tourism-led growth hypothesis and sustainable tourism through environmental policies.

## 11.2 The Model

### *11.2.1 Structure of R&D-Based Location Model with Tourism*

Under perfect competition, firms in the tourism sector produce tourism goods by investing one unit of labour. Here, environmental quality has a positive externality effect on the tourism firms' productivity. Improving environmental quality expands the production of tourism goods through increased labour productivity. Within the carrying capacity of the environment, environmental quality improves through self-regeneration. However, in addition to pollution emissions from the manufacturing sector, the congestion effect of tourism consumption worsens environmental quality. Households in the North and South perceive positive utility from environmental quality, which is considered a global public good. Households in their country can

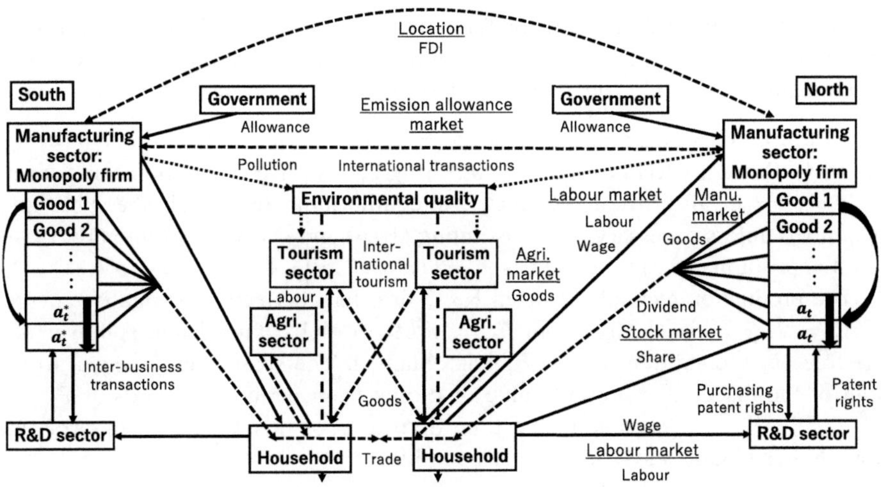


**Fig. 11.1** Structure of the R&D-based location model with tourism

make temporary tourism trips to consume tourism goods in the partner country by paying exogenous airfare. However, they cannot move to the partner country to supply labour. This economic structure is illustrated in Fig. 1.1. The economic model in this chapter is based on Hamaguchi (2020b).

## *11.2.2 Manufacturing and R&D Sector*

In the Euler equation, $r_t = \rho$ at equilibrium, hence, unless necessary, we omit the subscript $t$. The agricultural good is numeraire, with $P_{D,t} = 1$. As in Chap. 10, the firms in the agricultural sector in the perfectly competitive market produce agricultural goods by inputting $L_{D,t}$. From the zero-profit condition, $w_t = P_{D,t} = 1$.

In the international emissions trading market, the government of the North (South) allocates grandfathered emission allowances $s_j$ ($s_i^*$) to firms in the manufacturing sector of the North (South). As shown in $\bar{P} = \int_0^a s_j dj + \int_0^{a^*} s_i^* di$, the total global allowance is the sum of the allowances allocated to the North and South. It is assumed that the governments of the North and South are implementing coordinated environmental policies. Each government allocates an average allowance of $s = s_j = s_i^* = \overline{P}/A$ to its manufacturing firms. Under a perfectly competitive emissions trading market, manufacturing firms buy and sell allowances with manufacturing firms in their country or in other countries at an emissions allowance price of $p^e$. Manufacturing firms in the North (South) that emit more pollution than the allowance allocated to them must purchase quotas from other manufacturing firms that emit less pollution than the allowance allocated to them, where $d_j - s_j > 0$ ($d_i^* - s_i^* > 0$). In equilibrium, this emissions market must be cleared.

Considering the demand function for manufactured goods and the pollution emission function, a manufacturing firm in a monopolistic competition chooses a price that maximises $\max_{p_j} \pi_j \equiv p_j q_j - q_j - p^e\left(d_j - s_j\right)$ in (10.3). From the first-order condition for profit maximisation, we obtain $p_j = [\sigma/(\sigma-1)]\left[1+(p^e/\theta)\right]$ and $p_i^* = \tau p_j$ in (10.4). Since the RHS of the manufacturing goods price is common across firms by $s = s_j = s_i^*$, all firms are symmetric in equilibrium. Henceforth, the subscript $j$ is omitted unless necessary. By substituting (10.4) and $d_{j,t} = q_{j,t}/\theta$ into (10.3), the optimal profit in (10.5) is derived as $\pi = [1/(\sigma-1)]\left[1+(p^e/\theta)\right]q + p^e s$.

The production technology of an R&D firm in a perfectly competitive market is $\dot{A}_t = L_{A,t}/F_t$ in (3.10). From $F_t = F/A_t$ in global knowledge spillover and the free entry condition, $P_A = F/A$ is obtained. The share price is equal to the sum of the discounted present value of profits from period $t$ onwards as $P_{A,t} = \int_t^{\infty} e^{-[r(\iota)-r(t)]}\pi_\iota d\iota$. By taking the time derivative of this $P_{A,t}$, the non-arbitrage condition is obtained as $\pi + \dot{P}_A = rP_A$ in (3.9).

### 11.2.3 Tourism Sector

The tourism sector is covered by perfect competition. Tourism firms produce tourism goods $Y$ by inputting labour $L_T$. According to Brida et al. (2016), the tourism sector is a labour-intensive industry and relies on the natural environment and resources. Therefore, environmental quality has a positive externality effect on labour productivity. The production function of a tourism firm is $Y = NL_T$, where $N$ is the quality of the environment. Under $w = 1$ and the zero-profit condition, $P_T = 1/N$ is obtained. As the environmental quality improves, the production of tourism goods increases through externality effects, hence, their prices drop.

### 11.2.4 Households

The utility functions of representative households in the North and South at different times are expressed as logarithmic functions as follows:

$$U_t = \int_0^{\infty} \log\left[Q_t^{\nu} D_t^{1-\chi_N-\chi_S-\eta_N} Y_t^{\chi_N} Y_t^{*\chi_S} N_t^{\eta_N}\right] e^{-\rho t} dt, \tag{11.1a}$$

and

$$U_t^* = \int_0^{\infty} \log\left[Q_t^{*\nu} D_t^{*1-\chi_N-\chi_S-\eta_N} Y_t^{*\chi_N} Y_t^{\chi_S} N_t^{\eta_N}\right] e^{-\rho t} dt, \tag{11.1b}$$

where $Y_t$ and $Y_t^*$ are the consumption of tourism goods produced in the North and South, respectively, and $Q_t$ is the environmental quality. In addition, $\chi_N \in (0, 1)$,

$\chi_S \in (0, 1)$ and $\eta_N \in (0, 1)$ are the weights of the tourism goods produced in the North, produced in the South and environmental quality, respectively, in the utility. Following Zeng and Zhao (2011), we assume that households in the North must temporarily move to the South to consume the tourism goods produced in the South. The composition of differentiated goods in $Q_t$ is (9.2).

The expenditure of households in the North is expressed as follows:

$$\int_0^a p_j x_j dj + \int_0^{a^*} tp_i^* x_i di + D + P_T Y + \hat{t} P_T^* Y^* = E, \tag{11.2}$$

where $\hat{t}$ is the airfare with alien tax. Domestic tourists must pay an exogenous airfare $\hat{t}$ when travelling to a partner country for tourism.[1] Notice that $P_T = P_T^* = 1/N$. Household expenditure is $E_t = \int_0^{A_t} p_{j,t} x_{j,t} dj$ and its assets are $W_t = P_{A,t} A_t$. From (2. 3), the budget constraint for the household is $\dot{W}_t = r_t W_t + L - E_t$.

In the static utility maximisation problem, given the expenditure, the household decides how much of each good to purchase and the following demand function is obtained:

$$P_M Q = \nu E, \; D = (1 - \chi_N - \chi_S - \eta_N) E, \; P_T Y = \chi_N E, \; \hat{t} P_T^* Y^* = \chi_S E, \tag{11.3}$$

where the price index of differentiated goods is defined as $P_{M,t} \equiv \left( \int_0^{a_t} p_{j,t}^{1-\sigma} dj + \int_0^{a_t^*} t^{1-\sigma} p_{i,t}^{*1-\sigma} di \right)^{\frac{1}{1-\sigma}}$ in (9.5). By solving the first-order condition of the utility maximisation problem, the demand functions for manufactured goods in the North and South become $x_{j,t} = p_{j,t}^{-\sigma} P_{M,t}^{\sigma-1} \nu E_t$ and $x_{i,t} = t^{-\sigma} p_{i,t}^{*-\sigma} P_{M,t}^{\sigma-} \nu E_t$, respectively, in (9.6). From the dynamic utility maximisation problem, the Euler equations in the North and South are obtained as $\dot{E}_t / E_t = \dot{E}_t^* / E_t^* = r_t - \rho$ in (9.7). In the steady state, when the expenditure in both places is constant, $r_t = \rho$. Furthermore, since $W_0 > W_0^*$, $E > E^*$ holds.

### 11.2.5 Sightseeing Transport

Following Albaladejo and Martínez-García (2015), the number of tourists travelling from their home country to the destination country can be expressed as a logistic function as follows:

$$\dot{L}_M = L_M \left( \frac{1}{\hat{t} P_T^*} - L_M \right), \; \dot{L}_M^* = L_M^* \left( \frac{1}{\hat{t} P_T} - L_M^* \right), \tag{11.4}$$

[1] Hamaguchi (2021) internalised tourism mobility by considering the aviation sector. Based on the empirical results in Brida and Scuderi (2013) and Abbruzzo et al. (2014) that the distance of tourism travel is proportional to tourism expenditure and consumption, it is assumed that consumption of air goods implies that tourism travel improves utility through consumption of tourism goods in the partner country. This is because it is possible to consume tourism goods in more distant regions through air goods.

where $L_M$ and $L_M^*$ are the number of tourists travelling from North to South and from South to North, respectively. When $1/\left(2\hat{\iota}P_T^*\right) < L_M$, the rate of increase in the number of tourists travelling from North to South slows down and when $L_M = 1/\left(2\hat{\iota}P_T^*\right)$, $\dot{L}_M = 0$. Here, $1/\left(\hat{\iota}P_T^*\right)$ and $1/\left(\hat{\iota}P_T\right)$ represent the carrying capacity of tourist destinations in the North and South, respectively. In the present model, the number of mobile tourists is a flow variable, hence, in the steady state, $\dot{L}_M = \dot{L}_M^* = 0$ holds.

Albaladejo and Martínez-García (2015) considered that this tourist accommodation capacity is dependent on the production and consumption of tourism goods through the congestion effect. In the present model, the decrease in capacity due to consumption of tourism goods is offset by the increase in capacity due to production of tourism goods. However, Gössling (1999) pointed out that the carrying capacity of a tourist destination depends on environmental quality and tourism cost. In the present model, in addition to airfare decrease, the carrying capacity of a tourist destination increases due to the decrease in the price of tourism goods caused by the improvement in environmental quality.

### 11.2.6 Market

This economy has markets for manufactured goods, agricultural goods, tourism goods, labour, capital and emissions trading. The market clearing conditions for manufactured goods are expressed as follows:

$$x = \nu L\left(\tfrac{\sigma-1}{\sigma}\right)\left(\tfrac{1}{1+(p^e/\theta)}\right)\left(\tfrac{E}{a+\varphi a^*} + \tfrac{\varphi E^*}{a^*+\varphi a}\right), \tag{10.7a}$$

$$x^* = \nu L\left(\tfrac{\sigma-1}{\sigma}\right)\left(\tfrac{1}{1+(p^e/\theta)}\right)\left(\tfrac{\varphi E}{a+\varphi a^*} + \tfrac{E^*}{a^*+\varphi a}\right), \tag{10.7b}$$

where, in (11.3), household demand is aggregated by population. Here, an increase in $\varphi$ implies a decrease in transport costs due to trade liberalisation. From $D = (1 - \chi_N - \chi_S - \eta_N)E$, the global demand for agricultural goods is $D + D^* = L(1 - \chi_N - \chi_S - \eta_N)(E + E^*)$. Similarly, the demand for tourism goods is $Y = L(\chi_N/P_T)(E + E^*)$ and $Y^* = L\left[\chi_S/\left(\hat{\iota}P_T^*\right)\right](E + E^*)$. The market production condition for the capital market is $\pi + \dot{P}_A = rP_A$. Under free capital movement, with $a + a^* = W + W^* = A$ in (9.13) and $\pi = \pi^*, x = x^*$ holds. The clearing condition for the labour market is obtained as $L_A + L_M + L_D + L_T = 2L$.

As derived in Appendix H of Chap. 9, the number of manufacturing firms located in the North is expressed as follows:

$$\gamma = \tfrac{a}{A} = \tfrac{E-\varphi E^*}{(1-\varphi)(E+E^*)}, \tag{9.16a}$$

where the home market effect in Krugman (1980) implies that the location of manufacturing firms depends on the relative market size in $(E - \varphi E^*)/(E + E^*)$.

Manufacturing firms located themselves in countries with larger market sizes and higher expenditure levels. The clearing condition in the emissions trading market as $a^*p^e(s - d^*) - ap^e(d - s) = 0$ can be rewritten as $P + P^* = ad + a^*d^* = \overline{P}$ in (10.8).

Environmental quality regenerates itself through the logistic curve as $\dot{N} = N(\hat{N} - N)$, where $\hat{N}$ is the carrying capacity of the environment. When $1/(2\hat{N}) < N$, the pace of increase in environmental quality slows down and when $N = 1/(2\hat{N})$, $\dot{N} = 0$ holds. In Gómez et al. (2008), tourism activities worsened environmental quality and, in Cerina (2007), pollution emissions further worsened it. Assuming that tourism pollution and pollution emissions complementarily worsen environmental quality, Hamaguchi (2020b) formed the following accumulation equation for environmental quality:

$$\dot{N} = N(\hat{N} - N) - (P + P^*)(L_M + L_M^*), \tag{11.5}$$

where, in the present model, environmental quality is considered a flow variable, hence, $\dot{N} = 0$ holds in the steady state.

## 11.3 Equilibrium

### 11.3.1 Dynamic System

The BGP in the present model is an equilibrium path that satisfies three conditions. First, there is a constant and positive economic growth rate $g_{A,t} = \dot{A}_t/A_t > 0$. Second, the labour allocation of manufacturing, R&D, agricultural and tourism firms is constant, as $L_{X,t} = L_X$, $L_{A,t} = L_A$, $L_{D,t} = L_D$ and $L_{T,t} = L_T$, respectively. Third, aggregate expenditure is constant as $E_t + E_t^* = E + E^*$. We construct the law of motion for $E_t + E_t^*$.

By using $a + a^* = W + W^* = A$ and $\pi = \pi^*$, (10.7a) and (10.7b) can be rewritten as $x = x^* = \nu L[(\sigma - 1)/\sigma][1/(1 + (p^e/\theta))][(E + E^*)/A]$ in (10.9). Using this manufactured goods production volume, $D + D^* = L(1 - \chi_N - \chi_S - \eta_N)(E + E^*)$ and $L_A = F g_A$, $L_A + L_M + L_D + L_T = 2L$ can be rewritten as follows:

$$Fg_A + L\Big[\overline{\chi} + \overline{N} + \nu\big(\tfrac{\sigma-1}{\sigma}\big)\Big(\tfrac{1}{1+(p^e/\theta)}\Big)\Big](E + E^*) = 2L, \tag{11.6}$$

for $\overline{\chi} \equiv 1 - \chi_N - \chi_S - \eta_N$. In $\overline{N} \equiv N[\chi_N + (\chi_S/\hat{t})]$, which implies the share of expenditure on tourism goods, the improvement of environmental quality encourages labour transfer from other sectors to the tourism sector to promote the production of tourism goods.

By using $s = \overline{P}/A$ and (10.4), (10.5) can be rewritten as (10.11) by yielding $\pi = [(\nu L)/\sigma][(E + E^*)/A] + p^e(\overline{P}/A)$. In this, the expansion of the allowance allocation rent due to the soaring price of emission allowances increases the profits of manufacturing firms and incentivises new entrants. Substituting (10.11), $r = \rho$ and $g_A = -g_{PA}$ into $\pi + \dot{P}_A = rP_A$ asserts $[(\nu L)/(\sigma F)](E + E^*) + p^e(F) = \rho + g_A$ in (10.12). As Hamaguchi (2020b) showed, the dynamical system consisting of (10.10) and (10.12) is deterministic and stable. In this steady state, $g = g_A = -g_{PA}$ holds.

## 11.3.2 Steady State

By using (10.9), $d = q/\theta$ and $a + a^* = A$, (10.8) can be rewritten as $\overline{P} = [(\nu L)/\theta][(\sigma - 1)/\sigma]\big[(E + E^*)/(1 + (p^e/\theta))\big]$ in (10.13). When the total emission allowance caps pollution emissions, the increase in demand for manufactured goods that accompanies the increase in expenditure expands pollution emissions. The price of emission allowances rises as a result of price pass-through. Hence, as the demand for manufactured goods and pollution emissions decrease, pollution emissions in the manufacturing sector are kept within the total emission allowance. Substituting (10.13) for (10.12) and rearranging gives the following claim about economic growth rates:

$$g = \tfrac{\sigma p^e + \theta}{\sigma - 1}\left(\tfrac{\overline{P}}{F}\right) - \rho, \tag{10.14}$$

where, as the distribution effect in Hamaguchi (2020a) described, rent as profit per share of stock promotes economic growth. Here, $b \equiv \big[(\sigma p^e + \theta)/(\sigma - 1)\big]\big[\overline{P}/(2L)\big]$ is defined as the allowance allocation rent per population.

By using $P_T = P_T^* = 1/N$ in $\dot{L}_M = 0$ in (11.4), $L_M = L_M^* = N/\hat{t}$ is obtained. By incorporating $L_M = L_M^* = N/\hat{t}$ and $P + P^* = \overline{P}$ into $\dot{N} = 0$ in (11.5), we yield environmental quality in the following equilibrium:

$$N = \hat{N} - 2\left(\tfrac{\overline{P}}{\hat{t}}\right),$$

where, as shown in $dN/d\overline{P} = -\big(2/\hat{t}\big) < 0$ and $dN/d\hat{t} = -2\big(\overline{P}/\hat{t}^2\big) > 0$, the reduction in the total emissions allowance and increase in airfares reduce the number of tourists, improving environmental quality. Using environmental quality at equilibrium, the expenditure share of tourism goods, $\overline{N}$, can be rewritten as follows:

$$\overline{N} \equiv \left[\hat{N} - 2\left(\tfrac{\overline{P}}{\hat{t}}\right)\right]\left(\chi_N + \tfrac{\chi_S}{\hat{t}}\right), \tag{11.7}$$

which is differentiated with respect to $\hat{t}$ as $d\overline{N}/d\hat{t} \gtreqless 0$ for

$$\bar{t} \equiv \frac{4}{\frac{\hat{N}}{\overline{P}} - 2\left(\frac{\chi_N}{\chi_S}\right)} \gtreqless \hat{t},$$

where $\bar{t} \gtreqless 0$ for $(\chi_S \hat{N})/(2\chi_N) \gtreqless \bar{P}$. Under $\bar{t} > \hat{t} > 0$, airline fare increases expand $\overline{N}$ via improved accommodation capacity of tourist destinations. Under $\hat{t} > \bar{t} > 0$, the increase in airfares reduces $\overline{N}$ due to a decrease in expenditure on tourism goods in the partner country. Therefore, while airfares have an inverted U-shaped effect on $\overline{N}$ in $(\chi_S \hat{N})/(2\chi_N) > \overline{P}$, they have a monotonically negative effect on $\overline{N}$ in $(\chi_S \hat{N})/(2\chi_N) \leq \overline{P}$.

By substituting (10.15) and $P_T = P_T^* = 1/N$ into $Y = L(\chi_N/P_T)(E + E^*)$ and $Y^* = L[\chi_S/(\hat{t}P_T^*)](E + E^*)$, the demand for tourism goods at equilibrium is as follows:

$$Y = \chi_N L\left[\hat{N} - 2\left(\frac{\overline{P}}{\hat{t}}\right)\right](E + E^*), \ Y^* = \frac{\chi_S L}{\hat{t}}\left[\hat{N} - 2\left(\frac{\overline{P}}{\hat{t}}\right)\right](E + E^*), \tag{11.8}$$

where, in addition to increased expenditure, improvements in environmental quality increases tourism expenditure. By substituting (11.7) into $L_M = L_M^* = N/\hat{t}$, we can assert the following equilibrium for the number of mobile tourists:

$$L_M = L_M^* = \frac{1}{\hat{t}}\left[\hat{N} - 2\left(\frac{\overline{P}}{\hat{t}}\right)\right],$$

which is differentiated concerning $\hat{t}$ as $dL_M/d\hat{t} = 2(\overline{P}/\hat{t}^3) - (L_M/\hat{t}) \gtreqless 0$ for $4(\overline{P}/\hat{N}) \gtreqless \hat{t}$. In $4(\overline{P}/\hat{N}) > \hat{t}$, raising airfares increases the number of tourists travelling to the destination, as it improves the destination's carrying capacity by restoring environmental quality. However, when $4(\overline{P}/\hat{N}) \leq \hat{t}$, the congestion at tourist destinations, caused by increasing airfares, reduces the number of tourists travelling due to the congestion effect. Therefore, airfares have an inverted U-shaped effect on the number of tourists.

By substituting (10.14) and $g = g_A$ into (11.6), we obtain the following per capita expenditure worldwide:

$$E + E^* = \frac{2(1-b) + \frac{\rho F}{L}}{\chi + \overline{N} + \nu\left(\frac{\sigma-1}{\sigma}\right)\left[\frac{1}{1+(p^e/\theta)}\right]}, \tag{11.9}$$

where the household budget, which consists of labour income in 2 and stock income in $\rho F/L$, has an income loss of $-b$ due to the allowance allocation rent. From (11.9), the expenditure of the North and South can be expressed as follows:

$$E = \frac{1-b+\frac{\rho F}{L}k}{\chi + \overline{N} + \nu\left(\frac{\sigma-1}{\sigma}\right)\left[\frac{1}{1+(p^e/\theta)}\right]}, \tag{11.10a}$$

$$E^* = \frac{1-b+\frac{\rho F}{L}(1-k)}{\chi + \overline{N} + \nu\left(\frac{\sigma-1}{\sigma}\right)\left[\frac{1}{1+(p^e/\theta)}\right]}, \tag{11.10b}$$

for $k \equiv W/A > 1/2$.

By substituting (10.13) into (11.9), the equilibrium price of emission allowances is derived as follows:

$$p^e = \frac{\frac{\nu L}{\overline{P}}\left(\frac{\sigma-1}{\sigma}\right)\left(2+\frac{\rho F}{L}\right)-\frac{\nu\theta}{\sigma}(2L+\sigma-1)-\theta\left(\overline{\chi}+\overline{N}\right)}{\left(\overline{\chi}+\overline{N}\right)+2\nu L}, \tag{11.11}$$

which is differentiated concerning $\overline{P}$ as follows:

$$\frac{dp^e}{d\overline{P}} = \frac{1}{\left(\overline{\chi}+\overline{N}\right)+2\nu L}\left[\left(\theta+p^e\right)\underbrace{\frac{\partial\overline{N}}{\partial\overline{P}}}_{(-)}-\frac{\nu L}{\overline{P}^2}\left(\frac{\sigma-1}{\sigma}\right)\left(2+\frac{\rho F}{L}\right)\right],$$

where, in (11.4), when the carrying capacity of the tourist destination does not depend on the price of the tourism good, the total emission allowance has no effect on $\overline{N}$ through environmental quality. Thus, $d\overline{N}/d\overline{P} = 0$ holds. In this case, as in Chap. 10, $dp^e/d\overline{P} < 0$ and the reduction of the total emission allowance increases its demand, leading to an increase in the price of emission allowances. However, when the carrying capacity of a tourist destination depends on the price of tourism goods, a reduction in the total emission allowance increase $\overline{N}$ through improved environmental quality. In this case, the demand for tourism goods as a proportion of expenditure increases in $[\cdot](E+E^*)$ in (11.6) and expenditure decreases, with $2-b+[(\rho F)/L]$ in (11.9) held constant. This decrease reduces demand for manufactured goods and as their production shrinks, the price of emission allowances falls. Hence, $dp^e/d\overline{P} \geq 0$ implies that the lowering of emission allowances impedes firms from reducing pollution through an increase in the price of emission allowances. Therefore, the externality effects of the tourism sector lead to a malfunctioning of environmental policy. However, since it is analytically difficult to prove that $dp^e/d\overline{P} \geq 0$, we will assume that $dp^e/d\overline{P} < 0$.

Differentiating (11.11) with respect to $\hat{t}$ yields the following:

$$\frac{dp^e}{d\hat{t}} = -\frac{\theta+p^e}{\left(\overline{\chi}+\overline{N}\right)+2\nu L}\frac{\partial\overline{N}}{\partial\hat{t}} \gtreqless 0,$$

for $d\overline{N}/d\hat{t} \gtreqless 0$ in $\bar{t} \gtreqless \hat{t}$ and $\left(\chi_S\hat{N}\right)/(2\chi_N) > \overline{P}$.

Airline ticket prices affect the price of emission allowances through the carrying capacity of tourist destinations. Under $\bar{t} > \hat{t} > 0$, an increase in ticket prices increases the demand for tourist goods as a proportion of expenditure, as $[\cdot](E+E^*)$ in (11.6) increases $\overline{N}$ due to an improvement in the carrying capacity of tourist destinations. Since expenditure decreases, production shrinks due to a fall in demand for manufactured goods and the price of emission allowances falls. However, under $\hat{t} > \bar{t} > 0$, an increase in airfares reduces $\overline{N}$ due to a fall in the expenditure on tourism goods in the partner country. In (11.6), $[\cdot](E+E^*)$ causes demand for tourism goods to decrease as a proportion of expenditure and expenditure to increase. As a result, production expands due to an increase in demand for manufactured goods, raising the price of emission allowances. Here, when $(\chi_S \hat{N})/(2\chi_N) \leq \overline{P}$ due to an increase in the total emission allowance, $d\overline{N}/d\hat{t} < 0$ because $\overline{t} < 0 < \hat{t}$. In this case, a reduction in airfares reduces the price of emission allowances due to an increase in $\overline{N}$. Depending on the level of emission allowances, a reduction in airfares discourages firms from reducing pollution through an increase in the price of emission allowances.

By rewriting $b$ in (11.11), we obtain the following:

$$b = \frac{\nu(\sigma-1)\left(2+\frac{\rho F}{L}\right)-\frac{\nu\theta\overline{P}}{L}\left[\sigma-1+2L\left(\frac{1+\theta}{\theta}\right)\right]-\frac{\theta\overline{P}}{L}(\sigma-1)\left(\overline{\chi}+\overline{N}\right)}{2(\sigma-1)\left[\left(\overline{\chi}+\overline{N}\right)+2\nu L\right]}, \tag{11.12}$$

where, as shown in Appendix J, $db/d\overline{P} < 0$ holds when $d\overline{N}/d\overline{P} = 0$ and the reduction in the total emissions allowance increases the allowance allocation rent through the emissions allowance price. However, when $d\overline{N}/d\overline{P} > 0$, there is a possibility that $db/d\overline{P} > 0$ due to the rise in the emissions allowance price. By substituting (11.12) into (10.14), the economic growth rate at equilibrium becomes $g = b(2L/F) - \rho$, with $dg/d\overline{P} = (2L/F)db/d\overline{P} > 0$. The increase in allowance allocation rent due to the reduction in the total emissions allowance incentivises entrepreneurs to enter the market, raising the economic growth rate.

Differentiating (11.12) with respect to $\hat{t}$ yields:

$$\frac{db}{d\hat{t}} = -\frac{\theta\overline{P}+2bL}{2L\left[\left(\overline{\chi}+\overline{N}\right)+2\nu L\right]}\frac{\partial\overline{N}}{\partial\hat{t}} \gtreqless 0,$$

$d\overline{N}/d\hat{t} \gtreqless 0$ for $\overline{t} \gtreqless \hat{t}$ and $(\chi_S \hat{N})/(2\chi_N) > \overline{P}$.

An increase in airfares, in the case of $\overline{t} > \hat{t} > 0$, reduces the allowance allocation rent because an increase in $\overline{N}$ causes the price of emission allowances to fall. In the case of $g = b(2L/F) - \rho$, $dg/d\hat{t} = (2L/F)db/d\hat{t} < 0$ holds. The reduction in the allowance allocation rent, caused by an airfare increase, reduces the incentive for entrepreneurs to enter the market, dropping the economic growth rate. Furthermore, an increase in airfares, in the case of $\hat{t} > \overline{t} > 0$, increases the allowance allocation rent, as the decrease in $\overline{N}$ increases the price of emission allowances. In $g = b(2L/F)-\rho, dg/d\hat{t} = (2L/F)db/d\hat{t} < 0$ holds and an airfare increase increases the economic growth rate.

By substituting (11.9), (11.10a) and (11.10b) into (9.16a), the number of firms located in the North at equilibrium is expressed as follows:

$$\gamma = \frac{(1-\varphi)(1-b)+\frac{\rho F}{L}[k-\varphi(1-k)]}{2(1-\varphi)\left(1-b+\frac{\rho F}{2L}\right)}, \tag{10.20}$$

where the concentration of firms in the North is affected by the allowance allocation rent in $b$.

As in Chap. 10, the amount of FDI between the North and South is defined as $\dot{a} - \dot{W} = g(n - W)$, which is rewritten with $a + a^* = W + W^* = A$, (11.10a) and (11.10b) as follows:

$$\dot{a} - \dot{W} = \frac{gA\left(k-\frac{1}{2}\right)[\varphi\rho F - L(1-\varphi)(1-b)]}{2L(1-\varphi)\left(1-b+\frac{\rho F}{2L}\right)}, \tag{10.21}$$

which implies the direction of FDI net flows, which depend on the sign of $a - W$; $\dot{a} - \dot{W} \gtreqless 0$ is affected by the following parameter conditions:

$$\overline{\varphi} \equiv \left(\frac{\varphi}{1-\varphi}\right)\frac{\rho F}{L} \gtreqless 1 - b, \tag{10.22}$$

where, in $\overline{\varphi} > 1 - b$, $\dot{a} - \dot{W} > 0$ holds, hence, FDI occurs from the South to the North, while, in $\overline{\varphi} \leq 1 - b$, $\dot{a} - \dot{W} \leq 0$ holds, hence, FDI occurs from the North to the South.

By using $P_t = \int_0^{a_t} d_{j,t} dj,$, $d = q/\theta$, $as = (a/A)\overline{P}$ and $a^*s = (a^*/A)\overline{P}$ in (9.16a), (9.16b) and (10.2), the total amount of pollution emissions from the North and South, respectively, are $P = \gamma\overline{P}$, $P^* = (1-\gamma)\overline{P}$ and $P/P^* = 1/\left[(1/\gamma) - 1\right]$ in (10.23). The total pollution emissions of the North and South are expressed as the pollution share obtained by multiplying the total emission allowance by the number of firms located there. Hence, the total pollution emissions of the North in the South depend on the concentration of firms in the North.

## 11.4 Effect of Environmental Policy

In Appendix J, the effect of the total emissions allowance on the steady state is shown as follows:

$$\frac{dE+E^*}{d\overline{P}} \gtreqless 0, \quad \frac{dE}{d\overline{P}} \gtreqless 0, \quad \frac{dE^*}{d\overline{P}} \gtreqless 0, \quad \frac{d\gamma}{d\overline{P}} < 0, \quad \frac{d\dot{a} - \dot{W}}{d\overline{P}} < 0,$$

and

$$\frac{dP}{d\overline{P}} = \overline{P}\frac{\partial\gamma}{\partial\overline{P}} + \gamma, \quad \frac{dP^*}{d\overline{P}} = -\overline{P}\frac{\partial\gamma}{\partial\overline{P}} + (1-\gamma), \quad \frac{d}{d\overline{P}}\left(\frac{P}{P*}\right) = \frac{1}{(1-\gamma)^2}\frac{\partial\gamma}{\partial\overline{P}} > 0,$$

and

$$\frac{dY}{d\overline{P}} = \frac{Y}{E+E^*}\frac{\partial E+E^*}{\partial\overline{P}} - \frac{2\chi_N L}{\hat{t}}(E+E^*), \quad \frac{dY}{d\overline{P}} = \frac{Y}{E+E^*}\frac{\partial E+E^*}{\partial\overline{P}} - \frac{2\chi_S L}{\hat{t}}(E+E^*),$$

where $dp^e/d\overline{P} < 0$ and $db/d\overline{P} < 0$ are assumed. The reduction in the total emissions allowance has the same effect as in Chap. 10, as the increase in the price of emissions allowances expands the allowance allocation rent. The increase in the allowance allocation rent causes the economy to grow, however, the rise in the price of manufactured goods due to price pass-through reduces expenditure. Nonetheless, the increase in the price of emissions allowances expands expenditure as the manufactured demand for expenditure decreases in (11.6) due to $[\cdot](E+E^*)$. Regardless of the change in expenditure, the home market effect increases the concentration of firms from the South to the North and the FDI amount. Due to the expansion of the allowance allocation rent, under $\overline{\varphi} > 1-b$ in (10.22), the reduction in the total emission allowance leads to a change in the direction of FDI from the South to the North. As a result, the total amount of pollution emitted by the North towards the South decreases.

Reducing the total emission allowance decreases pollution emissions worldwide and improves global environmental quality. Hence, the carrying capacity of tourist destinations improves and the number of tourists travelling between the North and South increases. When $d(E+E^*)/d\overline{P} < 0$, the consumption of tourism goods in the North and South increases. However, if $d(E+E^*)/d\overline{P} > 0$, then the consumption decreases. Although the reduction of the total emission allowance leads to a pollution haven from the South to the North, it will likely lead to economic growth and tourism migration and expand tourism consumption through pollution reduction and global environmental improvement. Therefore, this environmental policy will achieve sustainable tourism in addition to tourism-led growth. However, in the case of $dp^e/d\overline{P} > 0$ and $db/d\overline{P} > 0$, it may lead to a pollution haven from the North to the South and a stagnation of economic growth, hence, a detailed verification using numerical analysis is necessary.

## 11.5 Effect of Airfare

In Appendix J, the effect of airfares on the steady-state value is shown as follows:

$$\frac{dE+E^*}{d\hat{t}} \gtreqless 0, \quad \frac{dE}{d\hat{t}} \gtreqless 0, \quad \frac{dE^*}{d\hat{t}} \gtreqless 0,$$

and

$$\frac{dY}{d\hat{t}} = \frac{Y}{E+E^*}\frac{\partial E+E^*}{\partial \hat{t}} + \frac{2\chi_N L}{\hat{t}^2}(E+E^*),$$

$$\frac{dY^*}{d\hat{t}} = \frac{Y^*}{E+E^*}\frac{\partial E+E^*}{\partial \hat{t}} + \frac{2\chi_S L}{\hat{t}^2}(E+E^*) - \frac{Y^*}{\hat{t}},$$

and

$$\frac{d\gamma}{d\hat{t}} \gtreqless 0, \quad \frac{d\dot{a}-\dot{W}}{d\hat{t}} \gtreqless 0,$$

$$\frac{dP}{d\hat{t}} = \overline{P}\frac{\partial\gamma}{\partial\hat{t}} \gtreqless 0, \quad \frac{dP^*}{d\hat{t}} = -\overline{P}\frac{\partial\gamma}{\partial\hat{t}} \gtreqless 0, \quad \frac{d}{d\hat{t}}\left(\frac{P}{P^*}\right) = \frac{1}{(1-\gamma)^2}\frac{\partial\gamma}{\partial\hat{t}} \gtreqless 0,$$

for $db/d\hat{t} \gtreqless 0$ in $\bar{t} \gtreqless \hat{t}$ and $(\chi_S \hat{N})/(2\chi_N) > \overline{P}$.

We will explain the case where airfares are low in $\bar{t} > \hat{t} > 0$. Airfare decrease reduces $\overline{N}$ due to the deterioration of the tourist destination's carrying capacity, increasing the price of emission allowances. The increase in allowance allocation rent increases the economic growth rate. The change in expenditure due to allowance allocation rent increases the relative market size in the North. The home market effect leads to the concentration of firms from the South to the North and increases the FDI amount. Hence, the total amount of pollution emitted by the North to the South increases due to pollution expansion in the North and pollution reduction in the South. While expenditure decreases due to the increase in allowance allocation rent, the demand for tourism goods and manufactured goods decreases in $[\cdot](E + E^*)$ in (11.6), however, expenditure increases due to the reduction in the expenditure share.

A temporary increase in the number of tourists due to lower airfares deteriorates environmental quality through tourism pollution. Due to a decrease in the supply of tourism resources through externality effects, the price of tourism resources increases, while their consumption decreases. If $d(E + E^*)/d\hat{t} > 0$, in addition to a decrease in expenditure, the price increase causes a decrease in consumption of tourism resources in the North. However, since airfare reduction increases the consumption of tourism goods in the South, the tourism sector shrinks more in the North than in the South. Under the condition $4(\overline{P}/\hat{N}) > \bar{t} > \hat{t} > 0$, the number of tourists decreases because deterioration in environmental quality worsens the carrying capacity of the tourist destination. When airfares are low, industrialisation and economic growth improve in the North, however, it leads to environmental degradation and a decline in tourism. Therefore, the spread of budget airlines may hinder sustainable tourism.

If airfares are high in $\hat{t} > \bar{t} > 0$, a decrease will increase $\overline{N}$ due to improvements in the capacity of tourist destinations and drop the price of emission allowances. The decrease in allowance allocation rent reduces the economic growth rate. The change in expenditure due to allowance allocation rent reduces the relative market size in the North. The home market effect leads to the concentration of firms from the North to the South, reducing the FDI amount. Simultaneously, the total amount of pollution emitted by the North to the South decreases due to pollution reduction in the North and pollution expansion in the South. While expenditure increases due to the decrease in allowance allocation rent, the demand for tourism goods and manufactured goods increases in $[\cdot](E + E^*)$ in (11.6), decreasing expenditure due to increased expenditure share.

Similar to low airfares, if $d(E + E^*)/d\hat{t} > 0$, in addition to a reduction in expenditure, the price hike leads to a decrease in consumption of tourism goods in the North compared to the South. Under the conditions $\hat{t} > \bar{t} > 4(\overline{P}/\hat{N}) > 0$, the number of tourists increases because the capacity of the tourist destination improves through environmental quality. When airfares are high, their reduction, although at a low growth rate, leads to industrialisation in the South due to a contraction in tourism and improved environmental quality. Therefore, it promotes industrialisation in developing countries that rely on the tourism industry.

Since the total emission allowance allocated to the North and South is the same, the North, which has a relatively large number of manufacturing firms, emits more pollution, hence, environmental regulations are stricter than in the South. Therefore, airfare reduction implies the pollution haven hypothesis. In the present model, environmental policies are more likely to lead to sustainable tourism than aviation policies.

## References

Abbruzzo, A., Brida, J. G., & Scuderi, R. (2014). Determinants of individual tourist expenditure as a network: Empirical findings from Uruguay. *Tourism Management*, 43, 36–45. https://doi.org/10.1016/j.tourman.2014.01.014

Albaladejo, I. P., & Martínez-García, M. P. (2015). An R&D-based endogenous growth model of international tourism. *Tourism Economics*, 21(4), 701–719. https://doi.org/10.5367/te.2014.0379

Balaguer, J., & Cantavella-Jorda, M. (2002). Tourism as a long-run economic growth factor: the Spanish case. *Applied Economics*, 34(7), 877–884. https://doi.org/10.1080/00036840110058923

Brida, J. G., Cortes-Jimenez, I., & Pulina, M. (2016). Has the tourism-led growth hypothesis been validated? A literature review. *Current Issues in Tourism*, 19(5), 394–430. https://doi.org/10.1080/13683500.2013.868414

Brida, J. G., & Scuderi, R. (2013). Determinants of tourist expenditure: A review of microeconometric models. *Tourism Management Perspectives*, 6, 28–40. https://doi.org/10.1016/j.tmp.2012.10.006

Buckley, R. (2011). Tourism and environment. *Annual Review of Environment and Resources*, 36(1), 397–416.

Cerina, F. (2007). Tourism specialization and environmental sustainability in a dynamic economy. *Tourism Economics*, 13(4), 553–582. https://doi.org/10.5367/000000007782696032

Cristea, A., Hummels, D., Puzzello, L., & Avetisyan, M. (2013). Trade and the greenhouse gas emissions from international freight transport. *Journal of Environmental Economics and Management*, 65(1), 153–173. https://doi.org/10.1016/j.jeem.2012.06.002

Gómez z, C. M., Lozano, J., & Rey-Maquieira, J. (2008). Environmental policy and longterm welfare in a tourism economy. *Spanish Economic Review*, 10(1), 41–62. https://doi.org/10.1007/s10108-007-9028-0

Gössling, S., & Peeters, P. (2007). 'It Does Not Harm the Environment!' An Analysis of Industry Discourses on Tourism, Air Travel and the Environment. *Journal of Sustainable Tourism*, 15(4), 402–417. https://doi.org/10.2167/jost672.0

Hamaguchi, Y. (2020a). Dynamic analysis of bribery firms' environmental tax evasion in an emissions trading market. *Journal of Macroeconomics*, 63, 103169. https://doi.org/10.1016/j.jmacro.2019.103169

Hamaguchi, Y. (2020b). Do pollution havens restrict tourism-led growth? Achieving sustainable tourism via a mix of environmental and tourism policies. *Tourism Economics*, 26(7), 1175–1196. https://doi.org/10.1177/1354816619868086

Hamaguchi, Y. (2021). Does the trade of aviation emission permits lead to tourism-led growth and sustainable tourism?. *Transport Policy*, 105, 181–192. https://doi.org/10.1016/j.tranpol.2021.03.012

Hamaguchi, Y. (2024). Environmental and Tourism Policies for the Decarbonization of the Tourism Sector. In: Walker, T., Demir, E., Machnik-Kekesi, G., Kelly, V. (eds) Sustainable Tourism. Palgrave Macmillan, Cham. https://doi.org/10.1007/978-3-031-43528-7_11

Hernández, J. M., & León, C. J. (2013). Welfare and environmental degradation in a tourism-based economy. *Tourism Economics*, 19(1), 5–35. https://doi.org/10.5367/te.2013.0191

Johnston, R. J., & Tyrrell, T. J. (2005). A Dynamic Model of Sustainable Tourism. *Journal of Travel Research*, 44(2), 124–134. https://doi.org/10.1177/0047287505278987

Lenzen, M., Sun, Y.-Y., Faturay, F., Ting, Y.-P., Geschke, A., & Malik, A. (2018). The carbon footprint of global tourism. *Nature Climate Change*, 8(6), 522–528. https://doi.org/10.1038/s41558-018-0141-x

Lozano Ibáñez, J., Rey-Maquieira, J., & Gomez, C. (2004). Land, Environmental Externalities and Tourism Development. SSRN Electronic Journal. https://doi.org/10.2139/ssrn.504423

Lozano, J., Gómez, C. M., & Rey-Maquieira, J. (2008). The TALC Hypothesis and Economic Growth Theory. *Tourism Economics*, 14(4), 727–749. https://doi.org/10.5367/000000008786440166

Liu, Z. (2003). Sustainable tourism development: A critique. *Journal of Sustainable Tourism*, 11(6), 459–475. https://doi.org/10.1080/09669580308667216

Marsiglio, S. (2015). Economic Growth and Environment: Tourism as a Trigger for Green Growth. *Tourism Economics*, 21(1), 183–204. https://doi.org/10.5367/te.2014.0411

Nunkoo, R., Seetanah, B., Jaffur, Z. R. K., Moraghen, P. G. W., & Sannassee, R. V. (2020). Tourism and Economic Growth: A Meta-regression Analysis. *Journal of Travel Research*, 59(3), 404–423. https://doi.org/10.1177/0047287519844833

Ouattara, B., Pérez-Barahona, A., & Strobl, E. (2019). Dynamic implications of tourism and environmental quality. *Journal of Public Economic Theory*, 21(2), 241–264. https://doi.org/10.1111/jpet.12330

Schubert, S. F., & Schamel, G. (2021). Sustainable tourism development: A dynamic model incorporating resident spillovers. *Tourism Economics*, 27(7), 1561–1587. https://doi.org/10.1177/1354816620934552

Song, H., & Wu, D. C. (2022). A Critique of Tourism-Led Economic Growth Studies. *Journal of Travel Research*, 61(4), 719–729. https://doi.org/10.1177/00472875211018514

Wang, M.-C., & Wang, C.-S. (2018). Tourism, the environment, and energy policies. *Tourism Economics*, 24(7), 821–838. https://doi.org/10.1177/1354816618781458

Zeng, D. Z., & Zhu, X. (2011). Tourism and industrial agglomeration. *The Japanese Economic Review*, 62(4), 537–561. https://doi.org/10.1111/j.1468-5876.2010.00518.x

# Part IV
# Quality of Political Institutions

# Chapter 12
# Dual Regulation and Tax Evasion

**Abstract** The variety expansion model, including pollution emissions, is extended to an overlapped double regulation. The impact of corruption and tax evasion, which are determined through negotiations between bureaucrats and manufacturing firms, is analysed. Besides reducing pollution, lowering the emission allowance boosts the economy through the distribution effect. However, raising the environmental tax lowers the economic growth rate because it hinders this distribution effect. Furthermore, since emission allowances cap production volume, environmental taxes do not affect the amount of pollution. Reduced environmental tax rate due to tax evasion increases the allowance allocation rent through a rise in the emission allowance prices, hence, the economic growth rate rises. An increase in the environmental tax rate increases the tax evasion rate, therefore, the economic growth rate falls through a drop in the emission allowance prices and an increase in bribes. Therefore, a reduced tax rate promotes sustainable development. Improving the quality of the political system by reducing the fines and the negotiating power of bureaucrats improves the sustainability of society through an increased economic growth rate. While environmental taxes cannot improve the welfare of households and bureaucrats, there is room for total emissions allowances to improve the welfare of both.

## 12.1 Introduction

As the EU Emissions Trading System (EU ETS) was established during the process of the carbon tax, introduced mainly in the Nordic countries and spreading to EU member states, there was a temporary overlap in the imposition of different environmental regulations, such as environmental taxes and emission allowances, on firms that emitted the same pollutants (Sorell 2002; IETA 2015). This overlapped double regulation was studied as it undermined the efficiency of the environmental policy (Böhringer et al. 2008; Mandell 2008; Eichner and Pethig 2009). Furthermore, the additional regulatory costs of overlapped double regulation incentivise polluting firms to evade environmental taxes.

 
Y. Hamaguchi, *Sustainable Development in Economic Growth Theory*,
https://doi.org/10.1007/978-981-96-7639-2_12

To commit tax evasion, polluting firms pay bribes to government officials. Pellegrini and Gerlagh (2006) pointed out that this bribery could weaken environmental regulatory standards, leading to economic stagnation and increased pollution emissions. There is a positive empirical relationship between pollution and corruption (Welsch 2004; Farzin and Bond 2006; Fredriksson and Wollached 2008). Even if environmental policies promote sustainable development, if corruption and tax evasion undermine them, they fail to achieve their aim. Hence, the importance of analysing environmental policies from a political-economic perspective is important (Oates and Portney 2003; Aidt 2011).

A pioneering analysis of corruption for environmental tax evasion was conducted by Damania (2002), who pointed out that to prevent the under-reporting of pollution emissions due to tax evasion, it was necessary to increase the fines. In contrast to the static analysis by Cerqueti and Coppier (2016), Lapatinas et al. (2019) conducted a dynamic analysis. In Iskandar et al. (2016), the theoretical result that environmental tax evasion encouraged by corruption is dependent on the tax rate has been confirmed in an empirical analysis of Indonesia. Liu (2013) is a valuable empirical analysis of environmental tax evasion. In China, it has been empirically confirmed that strict environmental tax increases encourage corporate tax evasion (Yu et al. 2021; Geng et al. 2021). However, as most of the environmental tax evasion models are static analyses, the theoretical relationship between environmental tax evasion and pollution emissions is unclear. Therefore, it is debatable how environmental tax evasion impedes sustainable development. The economic model in this chapter fills this gap by utilising a variety expansion model with dual regulation.

## 12.2 The Model

### *12.2.1 Structure of Variety Expansion Model with Dual Regulation*

The economic structure in this chapter is the same as the economic model in Chap. 4. However, since the agricultural sector is introduced, the construction of the dynamic system adopts the method in Chap. 10. Environmental taxes are imposed on manufacturing firms that participate in the emissions trading market. The imposition of different environmental regulations on the same pollutant is called overlapped regulation or double regulation. Hamaguchi (2020) argued that this double regulation incentivises tax evasion. Some firms offer to pay a portion of their tax bill to government officials as a bribe. If the bribe is discovered, the official is arrested and fined. If the bribe negotiation is successful, the firm can evade the tax. The impact of this

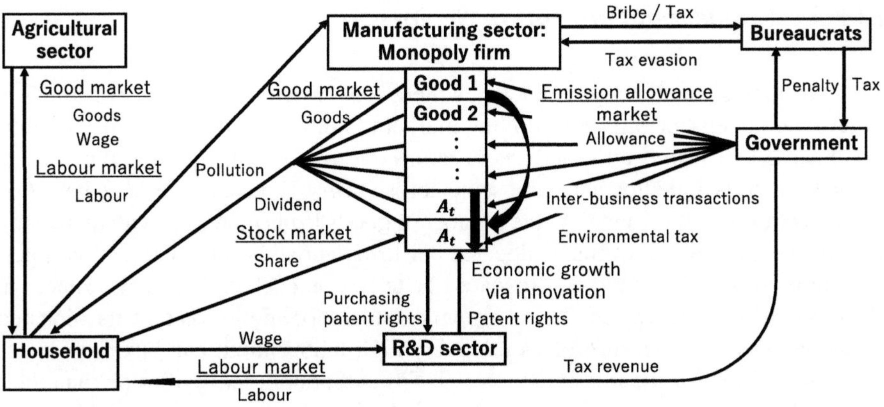


**Fig. 12.1** Structure of the variety expansion model with dual regulation

evasion on economic growth and pollution emissions is analysed. This evasion negotiation is based on Harstad and Svensson (2011). The economic structure is illustrated in Fig. 12.1. The economic model in this chapter is based on Hamaguchi (2020).[1]

## 12.2.2 Household

The intertemporal utility function of the household is $U_t = \int_0^\infty \log\left[\left(Q_t^\upsilon D_t^{1-\upsilon}\right)/P_t^{\eta_P}\right]e^{-\rho t}dt$ in (4.1). The structure of differentiated goods is $Q_t = \int_0^{A_t} x_{j,t}^{1-\frac{1}{\sigma}}dj$ in (4.2). The pollution emission function is expressed as $P_t = \int_0^{A_t} d_{j,t}dj$ in (4.3). Household expenditure on goods is $E_t = \int_0^{A_t} p_{j,t}x_{j,t}dj + P_{D,t}D_{,t}$ and the demand function for the goods is (3.4). Constrained by the intertemporal budget of $\dot{W}_t = r_t W_t + w_t L + T_t - E_t$, households decide how much of the goods to consume and how much to save to maximise the utility level in (4.1). Hence, we obtain the Euler equation $\dot{E}_t/E_t = r_t - \rho$ in (3.6). When expenditure is constant in a steady state, $r_t = \rho$. Henceforth, unless necessary, the subscript $t$ is omitted. As explained in Chap. 9, agricultural goods are numeraire with $P_{D,t} = 1$, therefore, from the zero-profit condition, $w_t = P_{D,t} = 1$. The pollution emission function per firm is $d_j = q_j/\theta_j$, where $\theta_j = \theta$ is assumed to simplify the analysis.

[1] In this chapter, the implications of the economic model are made clearer by deriving the stationary values and performing a comparative static analysis in a more precise manner than Hamaguchi (2020).

### 12.2.3 Goods and Innovation Sectors

First, we analyse double regulation when there is no environmental tax evasion. The government opens an emissions trading market to internalise the negative externalities. Each goods firm is allocated an emissions quota of $s_t$. This quota is the average of the total emission allowance and same across firms. Hence, $s = \overline{P}/A$, where $\overline{P}$ is the total emission allowance. As the number of goods firms increases with increasing variety, the emission allowance allocated per firm decreases. In a perfectly competitive emissions trading market, firms are free to buy and sell emission allowances at an emission allowance price of $p^e$. A firm that emits more pollution than its allocated emission allowance because of its relatively high labour input can buy allowances from other firms for the missing $d - s > 0$. Firms that emit less pollution than their allocated allowance because of their relatively high pollution abatement productivity can sell their surplus $s - d > 0$ to other firms. Hence, from $P = Ad$ and $As = \overline{P}$, this market must be cleared as $P = \overline{P}$.

The government imposes an environmental tax on manufacturing firms participating in the emissions trading market as a form of double regulation. The profit maximisation problem for goods firms is as follows:

$$\max_{p_j} \pi_j \equiv (p_j - 1)q_j - \tau d_j - P^e(d_j - s) = \left(p_j - 1 - \tfrac{\tau + p^e}{\theta}\right)x_j + p^e s, \qquad (12.1)$$

where $p^e s$, in the second term on the RHS, is the allocation rent in Hamaguchi (2020). The government distributes the environmental tax revenues to households as a lump-sum subsidy, as in $T = \tau P$.

From the first-order condition of profit maximisation, the following goods prices are obtained:

$$p = \tfrac{\sigma}{\sigma - 1}\left(1 + \tfrac{\tau + p^e}{\theta}\right), \qquad (12.2)$$

where the subscript $j$ is omitted as the equilibrium is symmetrical between firms. The pass-through of emission credit prices to the price of goods is strengthened by environmental taxes. By substituting (12.2) and $d = q/\theta$ into (12.1), the optimal profit of the manufacturing firm is expressed as follows:

$$\pi = \tfrac{1}{\sigma - 1}\left(1 + \tfrac{\tau + p^e}{\theta}\right)q + p^e s, \qquad (12.3)$$

where the profit depends on revenue and the allocation rent in Hamaguchi (2020).

The production technology and behaviour of R&D firms are the same as in Chap. 3. The non-arbitrage condition is $(\pi + \dot{P}_A)/P_A = r$ in (3.9) and the free entry condition is $P_A = F/A$.

### 12.2.4 Market

This economy has a market for manufacturing goods, agricultural goods, emissions trading, a labour market and a capital market. From the clearing conditions of the goods market and the demand function in (3.4), we obtain the following:

$$q = x = \nu L\left(\tfrac{\sigma-1}{\sigma}\right)\left[\tfrac{1}{1+(\tau+p^e)/\theta}\right]\left(\tfrac{E}{A}\right), \tag{12.4}$$

where household demand is aggregated according to population. From the clearing conditions of the goods market and the demand function in (3.4), we further obtain $D = (1-\nu)LE$. The clearing conditions of the labour market, $L = L_A + L_X = Fg_A + Ax$, can be rewritten as follows:

$$Fg_A + \left[1 - \nu + \nu\left(\tfrac{\sigma-1}{\sigma}\right)\left[\tfrac{1}{1+(\tau+p^e)/\theta}\right]\right]LE = L, \tag{12.5}$$

where, passing on the price reduces the demand for manufacturing goods, which, in turn, reduces labour demand in the manufacturing sector. Moreover, environmental taxation further reduces that labour demand.

Using $s = \overline{P}/A$ and (12.4), we can rewrite (12.3) to assert the following:

$$\pi = \tfrac{\nu L}{\sigma}\left(\tfrac{E}{A}\right) + p^e\left(\tfrac{\overline{P}}{A}\right), \tag{12.6}$$

where the expansion of allowance allocation rent due to price surge in emission allowances increases the profits of manufacturing firms. This profit expansion stimulates entrepreneurs to enter the market.

Substituting (12.6), $r = \rho$ and $g_A = -g_{PA}$ into $\pi + \dot{P}_A = rP_A$ yields the following:

$$\tfrac{\nu L}{\sigma F}E + p^e\left(\tfrac{\overline{P}}{F}\right) = \rho + g_A, \tag{12.7}$$

where the dynamic system, consisting of (12.6) and (12.7), is deterministic and stable. In this steady state, $g = g_A = -g_{PA}$ holds.

### 12.2.5 Equilibrium

By using (12.4) and $d = q/\theta$, we can rewrite $P = \overline{P}$ as follows:

$$\overline{P} = \left(\tfrac{\nu L}{\theta}\right)\left(\tfrac{\sigma-1}{\sigma}\right)\tfrac{E}{1+(\tau+p^e)/\theta}, \tag{12.8}$$

where, when the total emissions allowance caps the amount of pollution emissions, the increase in demand for manufacturing goods accompanying the increase in expenditure expands the amount of pollution emissions through production expansion. The price of emissions allowances rises due to their demand, hence, the demand for manufacturing goods falls due to price pass-on. The amount of pollution emissions in the manufacturing sector falls within the total emissions cap as the amount of pollution emissions falls due to production contraction.

By substituting (12.5) into (12.8), we obtain the following:

$$g = \frac{L-\theta\overline{P}-(1-\nu)LE}{F}, \tag{12.9}$$

where a reduction in the total emissions allowance increases the economic growth rate, as it encourages labour migration from the manufacturing to the R&D sector. However, unlike Chap. 4, this economy has an agricultural sector. As a result of the increase in expenditure, the demand for agricultural goods expands, causing labour migration from the R&D to the agricultural sector and dropping the economic growth rate. An environmental tax under dual regulation may affect economic growth through this expenditure.

Substituting (12.9) for (12.7) yields the following expenditure:

$$E = \frac{\sigma}{\nu+\sigma(1-\nu)}\left[1 + \frac{\rho F}{L} - (\theta + p^e)\frac{\overline{P}}{L}\right], \tag{12.10}$$

where household expenditure depends on wage income and the allowance allocation rent, which is equal to $(\rho F)/L = (rP_A A)/L$. This expenditure decreases because the price of emission allowances is passed on to the price of manufactured goods.

By substituting (12.10) into (12.8), the equilibrium emission price is expressed as follows:

$$p^e = \frac{\nu L}{\overline{P}}\left(\frac{\sigma-1}{\sigma}\right)\left(1 + \frac{\rho F}{L}\right) - \left[\left(1 + \frac{1}{\sigma}\right)\theta + \tau\left(\frac{\nu}{\sigma} + 1 - \nu\right)\right], \tag{12.11}$$

where, from $dp^e/d\overline{P} = \left[(\nu L)/\overline{P}^2\right][(\sigma - 1)/\sigma][1 + (\rho F)/L]<0$, reduced total emissions allowance lowers the price of emission allowances. In addition, since $dp^e/d\tau = -[(\nu/\sigma) + 1 - \nu] < 0$, an increase in the environmental tax rate lowers the price of emission allowances. This is because when the demand for manufacturing goods falls and production shrinks due to the environmental tax being passed on in the price, the amount of pollution emissions is reduced and the demand for emission allowances falls. Under dual regulation, while the environmental tax encourages pollution reduction, it undermines the incentive for pollution reduction provided by the price of emission allowances. Therefore, it leads to a malfunctioning of the emission allowance trading system. In addition, since the total emission allowance caps total pollution emissions, the environmental tax cannot further reduce total pollution emissions.

By substituting (12.11) for (12.10), the expenditure is rewritten as follows:

$$E = \left(1 + \frac{\rho F}{L}\right) + \frac{\overline{P}}{L}\left[\tau + \frac{\theta}{\nu+\sigma(1-\nu)}\right], \tag{12.12}$$

where increasing the environmental tax rate increases expenditure, which mitigates the pass-through effect through a drop in the price of emission allowances. (12.11) and (12.12) show that a drop in the total emission allowance and environmental tax increases expenditure and the price of emission allowances, which increases consumption of manufacturing and agricultural goods in (12.4) and $D = (1 - \nu)LE$.

Using (12.3), (12.4) and (12.8), the dividend per share is expressed as:

$$\frac{\pi}{P_A} = \frac{\nu L}{\sigma}\left(1 + \frac{\sigma-1}{F}\right)\left(1 + \frac{\rho F}{L}\right) - \frac{\nu\overline{P}}{\sigma}\left[(\overline{\nu} - 1)\tau + \theta\frac{(\sigma+1)\nu_0-1}{\nu+\sigma(1-\nu)}\right], \tag{12.13}$$

where $\nu_0 \equiv [\nu + \sigma(1-\nu)]/(\nu F) > 1$ holds. As in $d(\pi/P_A)/d\overline{P} < 0$ and $d(\pi/P_A)/d\tau < 0$, the reduction in the total emissions allowance and environmental tax rate increases the allowance allocation rent through a rise in the price of emissions allowances and expenditure through an increase in dividend income. This expansion of rent stimulates economic growth.

By substituting (12.9) for (12.12), the economic growth rate is rewritten as follows:

$$g = \frac{\nu L}{F} - (1-\nu)\rho - \frac{\theta\overline{P}}{F}\left[(1-\nu)\frac{\tau}{\theta} + \frac{1+\sigma(1-\nu)}{\nu+\sigma(1-\nu)}\right], \tag{12.14}$$

where, as in $dg/d\overline{P} < 0$ and $dg/d\tau < 0$, the expansion of the rent allocated through environmental policy stimulates entrepreneurs to enter the market. Labour transfer from the agricultural and manufacturing to the R&D sector brings about economic growth through innovation. Hence, $g = \left(L - \theta\overline{P}\right)/F$ holds when we assume $\nu = 1$ and the environmental tax has no effect on economic growth. In dual regulation, the agricultural sector determines the growth effect of the environmental tax. Here, while emissions trading brings about sustainable development, the environmental tax does not.

## 12.3 Tax Evasion and Corruption

### *12.3.1 Timing*

In the previous section, we saw that double regulation imposed an environmental tax on the emission of pollutants that are subject to emissions trading. This encourages manufacturing firms to evade taxes. In this section, we analyse the impact of environmental tax evasion on pollution emissions and economic growth.

Figure 12.2 shows the timing of the negotiations between manufacturing firms and bureaucrats regarding tax evasion and corruption. After purchasing a new variety of blueprints from an R&D firm, an entrepreneur enters the manufacturing goods market. It decides on its production volume without knowing the quality of the bureaucrats. Once production begins, pollution is emitted and the bureaucrats demand an environmental tax. Depending on the quality of the bureaucrat, the manufacturing

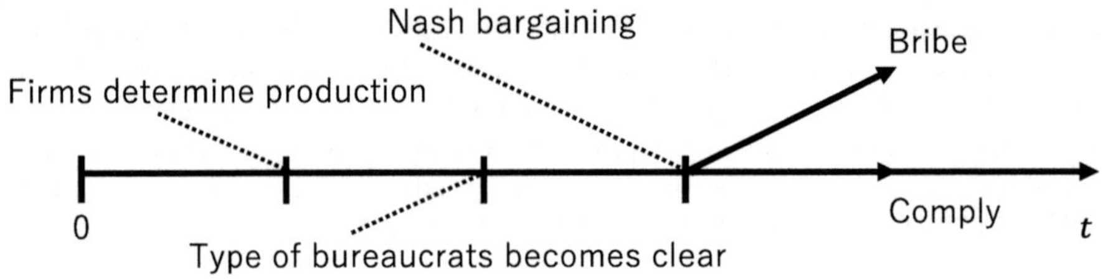


**Fig. 12.2** Timing

firm decides whether to pay or evade taxes. If the quality is low, the manufacturing firms pay a bribe to cover a part of the tax amount and evade the rest. If the quality is high, the manufacturing firms pay the environmental tax without a bribe.

### *12.3.2 Bureaucrats*

While the bureaucrat $o$ perceive positive utility from receiving bribes from manufacturing firm $j$, they perceive negative utility due to externalities, such as pollution emissions, similar to households. The more manufacturing firms produce, the more pollution emitted and the heavier the tax burden. Therefore, the amount of bribes paid by manufacturing firms is proportional to their production volume. The utility of bureaucrat $o$ is $u_{o,t} = \left(h_{o,t} - e_{o,t}\right)d_{j,t}$, where $h_{o,t}$ and $e_{o,t}$ are the bribe and the degree of externality of pollution emissions at bureaucrat $o$, respectively.

The bureaucrat $o$ regards $e_{o,t}$ as the expected fine rate. The government keeps track of the amount of pollution emitted by manufacturing firm $j$ through reports from the bureaucrat $o$ assigned to that firm. Some bureaucrats under-report the pollution emitted for bribes. This allows manufacturing firms to evade environmental taxes. Bureaucrat $o$ is subject to a fine of $\xi_{o,t}\varpi_{o,t}$, if caught by the government. In this, $\xi_{o,t}$ and $\varpi_{o,t} \in (0, 1)$ are the arrest probability and the fine rate for bureaucrat $o$, respectively. Thus, $e_{o,t} = \xi_{o,t}\varpi_{o,t}$ holds. Note that $\xi_{o,t}$ is independent and identically distributed over [0, 1]. This assumption implies different arrest probabilities among bureaucrats. The fine amount for a corrupt bureaucrat $o$ as $e_{o,t}d_{j,t} = \xi_{o,t}\varpi_{o,t}d_{j,t}$ increases in proportion to the pollution emissions associated with production expansion. The larger the production scale, the more pollution emissions and the higher the tax evasion. Hence, the government actively conducts surprise audits of manufacturing firms with high production volumes.

### *12.3.3 Nash Bargaining*

During the production process, manufacturing firm $j$ observes the quality of the bureaucrat as $\xi_{o,t} \in (0, 1)$. Depending on the quality, manufacturing firm $j$ decides, through negotiation, whether to evade taxes by bribing the bureaucrat $o$ or pay taxes and comply with the law. In this negotiation, the manufacturing firm and the bureaucrat do not have private information. Using $\tau \in (0, \varpi_{o,t})$, we define the threshold for tax evasion and payment as follows: when $\xi_{o,t} < \tau/\varpi_{o,t}$, a manufacturing firm pays a bribe, while when $\xi_{o,t} \geq \tau/\varpi_{o,t}$, a manufacturing firm does not pay a bribe. The bribe amount is negotiated between manufacturing firm $j$ and bureaucrat $o$. This negotiated solution is Pareto efficient. For $h_{o,t} \in (\xi_{o,t}\varpi_{o,t}d_{j,t}, \tau d_{j,t})$, manufacturing firm $j$ and bureaucrat $o$ are better off with the bribe paid by manufacturing firm $j$.

By considering negotiations with manufacturing firm $j$, bureaucrats maximise their bribes through the following:

$$\max_{h_{o,t}} \left(h_{o,t} - \xi_{o,t}\varpi_{o,t}d_{j,t}\right)^{\varrho}\left(\tau d_{j,t} - h_{o,t}\right)^{\varrho-1},$$

where $\varrho \in (0, 1)$ is the bureaucrat's bargaining surplus weight. This first-order condition yields the following:

$$h_{o,t} = \varrho\tau d_{j,t} + (1-\varrho)\xi_{o,t}\varpi_{o,t}d_{j,t}, \tag{12.15}$$

where $h_{o,t}$ increases according to $\xi_{o,t}$, $\varpi_{o,t}$, and $d_{j,t}$, keeping all other factors constant. The increased tax burden due to pollution emissions encourages manufacturing firms to bribe the bureaucracy. The probability of arrest and the rate of fines are raised to increase the cost of tacit approval of environmental tax evasion and the bureaucracy demands more bribes from manufacturing firms.

### 12.3.4 Manufacturing Sector

Newly entering manufacturing firms do not know the quality of the bureaucrats until they begin production. Therefore, they decide on their production volume based on the assumption that either a corrupt or non-corrupt bureaucrat is assigned. In the probability of $\xi_{o,t}\varpi_{o,t} < \tau$, the manufacturing firm $j$ that is assigned a corrupt bureaucrat pays a bribe and evades tax. However, in the probability of $\xi_{o,t}\varpi_{o,t} \geq \tau$, the manufacturing firm $j$ that is assigned a non-corrupt official, complies with the law and pays the tax. The expected bribe cost for manufacturing firm $j$ becomes:

$$\mathbb{E}\left[\tau d_{j,t}, h_{o,t}\right] \equiv \left(1 - \frac{\tau}{\varpi_{o,t}}\right)\tau d_{j,t} + \left(\frac{\tau}{\varpi_{o,t}}\right)h_{o,t},$$

which implies the ratio of manufacturing firms that pay tax and evade tax.

By using (12.15), this cost can be rewritten as follows:

$$\mathbb{E}\left[\tau d_{j,t}, h_{o,t}\right] = \overline{\tau}\left(\tau, \varrho, \xi_{o,t}, \varpi_{o,t}\right) d_{j,t},$$

for

$$\overline{\tau}\left(\tau, \varrho, \xi_{o,t}, \varpi_{o,t}\right) \equiv \tau\left[1 - (1-\varrho)\left(\frac{\tau}{\varpi_{o,t}} - \xi_{o,t}\right)\right],$$

where $\overline{\tau}\left(\tau, \varrho, \xi_{o,t}, \varpi_{o,t}\right)$ is an efficient environmental tax rate. The second term on the RHS implies a tax rate. Here, $0 < \tau < \varpi_{o,t}$ and $0 < \varpi_{o,t} < 1$ hold. From the $i.i.d.$ of $\xi_{o,t}$, the average arrest probability is defined as $\xi_{o,t} = \xi = \tau/(2\varpi)$ and the arrest probability among bureaucrats is equal on average. Using $\xi_{o,t} = \xi = \tau/(2\varpi)$, $\mathbb{E}\left[\tau d_{j,t}, h_{o,t}\right]$ can be rewritten as follows:

$$\mathbb{E}\left[\tau d_{j,t}, h_t\right] = \overline{\tau}(\tau, \varrho, \varpi) d_{j,t},$$

for

$$\overline{\tau}(\tau, \varrho, \varpi) = \tau\left[1 - \tfrac{\tau(1-\varrho)}{2\varpi}\right] = \tau\left(1 - \tfrac{\tau}{\tilde{\tau}}\right), \tag{12.16}$$

where $\tilde{\tau} \equiv (2\varpi)/(1-\varrho) > \tau$. Note that $\tau/\tilde{\tau}$ is the tax evasion rate; the higher the environmental tax rate, the higher the tax evasion rate by $1/\tilde{\tau}$. As shown in $d\tilde{\tau}/d\varpi = 2/(1-\varrho) > 0$ and $d\tilde{\tau}/d\varrho = 2\varpi/(1-\varrho)^2 > 0$, a decrease in the fine and a high bargaining power of the bureaucracy raises the tax evasion rate. From $d\overline{\tau}/d\tau = 1-(2\tau/\tilde{\tau}) > 0$, $d\overline{\tau}/d\varpi = (\tau/\tilde{\tau})^2 d\tilde{\tau}/d\varpi > 0$ and $d\overline{\tau}/d\varrho = (\tau/\tilde{\tau})^2 d\tilde{\tau}/d\varrho > 0$, raising the environmental tax, the fine rate and the increase in the negotiating power of bureaucrats raise the efficient environmental tax rate. The relationship between the environmental tax rate and the tax rate is depicted in Fig. 12.3.

Before learning about the quality of bureaucrats, manufacturing firm $j$ choose the price of manufactured goods that maximises the expected profit, as follows:

$$\max_{p_j} \mathbb{E}\left[\pi_j\right] \equiv (p_j - 1)q_j - \mathbb{E}\min\left[\tau d_j, h_o\right] - P^e\left(d_j - s\right), \tag{12.17}$$

and the first-order condition for profit maximisation yields the following:

$$\mathbb{E}\left[p_j\right] = \tfrac{\sigma}{\sigma-1}\left[1 - \tfrac{1}{\sigma}\left(\tfrac{p_i}{q_j}\right)\tfrac{\partial \mathbb{E}\left[\tau d_j, h_o\right]}{\partial p_i} + \tfrac{p^e}{\theta}\right], \tag{12.18a}$$

which is used with (12.17) to derive

$$\mathbb{E}\left[\pi_j\right] = \tfrac{q_j}{\sigma-1}\left[1 - \left(\tfrac{p_i}{q_j}\right)\tfrac{\partial \mathbb{E}\left[\tau d_j, h_o\right]}{\partial p_i} + \tfrac{p^e}{\theta}\right] - \mathbb{E}\left[\tau d_j, h_o\right] + p^e s. \tag{12.18b}$$

After the manufacturing firm $j$ decides on its production, the quality of the bureaucrat $o$ dispatched to this firm is revealed. Hence, by substituting (12.16) into (12.18a) and (12.18b), we obtain the following manufactured goods prices and profits:

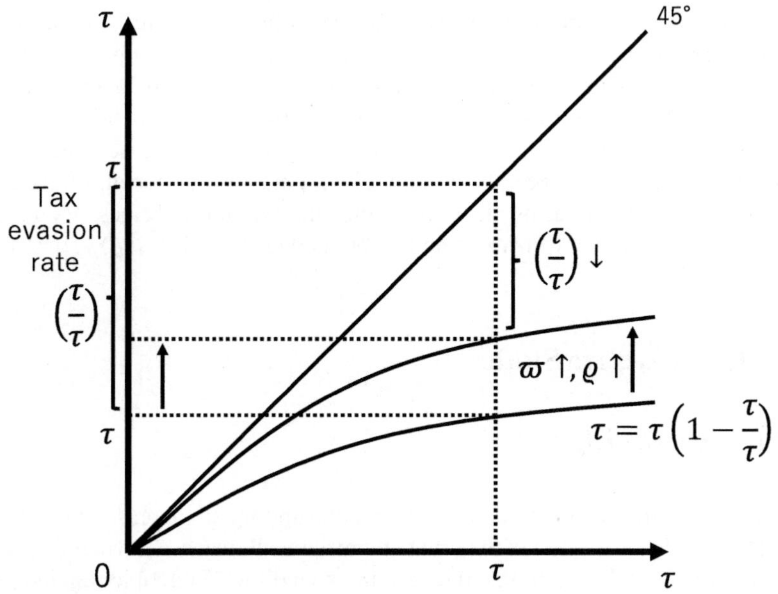


**Fig. 12.3** Tax evasion rate

$$p = \frac{\sigma}{\sigma - 1}\left(1 + \frac{\overline{\tau} + p^e}{\theta}\right), \tag{12.19a}$$

and

$$\pi = \frac{1}{\sigma - 1}\left(1 + \frac{\overline{\tau} + p^e}{\theta}\right)q + p^e s. \tag{12.19b}$$

Note that by replacing $\tau$ in (12.2)–(12.14) with $\overline{\tau}$, the steady-state values, accounting for environmental tax evasion, are derived, hence, the remaining derivation process is omitted. A comparative static analysis is performed based on these steady-state values.

### *12.3.5 Corruption*

By substituting (12.15) into $d = q/\theta$, (12.4) and (12.8), the bribe per bureaucrat at equilibrium is derived as follows:

$$h = \frac{1+\varrho}{2}\left(\frac{\tau \overline{P}}{A}\right), \tag{12.20}$$

which depends on the bargaining power of the bureaucrats, environmental taxes, total emission quotas and the number of varieties. The stronger the bargaining power of the bureaucrats, the more bribes from the manufacturing firms. In addition, the increase in pollution emissions due to the increase in total emission allowances and the increase in environmental taxes increases the amount of tax paid and the benefits of tax evasion. Manufacturing firms try to evade tax by paying more bribes. However, as the number of varieties increases, production per firm decreases and pollution emissions are reduced. Hence, the amount of tax paid and the benefit of tax evasion decrease, with manufacturing firms reducing the amount of bribes. By rewriting (12.20), the total amount of bribes can be obtained as $Ah = \left[(1+\varrho)/2\right]\left(\tau\overline{P}\right)$.

## 12.4 Comparative Statics

### *12.4.1 Growth Effect*

In double regulation without tax evasion and corruption, an increase in the environmental tax rate leads to a fall in the price of emission allowances, dividends per share and economic growth rate, yet an increase in expenditure. In double regulation with tax evasion and corruption, as $d\overline{\tau}/d\tau > 0$, an increase in the environmental tax rate raises the efficient environmental tax rate, however, the tax rate of $\tau/\tilde{\tau}$ increases. Furthermore, since $d\overline{\tau}/d\varpi = (\tau/\tilde{\tau})^2 d\tilde{\tau}/d\varpi > 0$ and $d\overline{\tau}/d\varrho = (\tau/\tilde{\tau})^2 d\tilde{\tau}/d\varrho > 0$, reducing the fine and the bureaucrat's bargaining power further increases the tax rate. Therefore, although the environmental tax rate is raised, the actual tax rate is lower without tax evasion. In summary, environmental tax undercuts dual regulation without tax evasion and corruption can be interpreted as the effect of tax evasion on the economy and environment.

A decrease in the environmental tax rate due to tax evasion leads to an increase in the price of emission allowances, dividends per share and the economic growth rate, yet a decrease in expenditure. An increase in the environmental tax rate raises the efficient environmental tax rate and the tax evasion rate. In this case, the environmental policy decreases the price of emission allowances, dividends per share and the economic growth rate, yet increases expenditure, however, the amount of change is smaller than when there is no tax evasion. In addition, the environmental tax increase increases the bribes per bureaucrat.

Paradoxically, since the total pollution emissions are capped by the total emission allowance, tax rate reduction due to tax evasion promotes sustainable development by increasing the price of emission allowances and economic growth rate. If the environmental tax is increased, sustainable development is hindered due to the decrease in the price of emission allowances and economic growth rate. Under these circumstances, improving the quality of the political system will lead to sustainable development. If the bargaining power of bureaucrats is reduced through administrative reform, the number of bureaucrats who demand bribes would decrease. As a result, the quality of bureaucrats improves because the number of bribes decreases. As the number of good bureaucrats increases, the government can reduce the fine. With these, the effective environmental tax rate is reduced. The price of emission allowances and the economic growth rate increase, hence, the sustainability of society increases.

When the growth-promoting effects of environmental policies are undermined by tax evasion and corruption, the original growth-promoting effects are realised through improvements in the quality of the political system. To achieve sustainable development, it is important to increase transparency in the implementation of environmental policies and the policy process.

### 12.4.2 Welfare Effect

By the derivation process of (4.27) in Chap. 4, we obtain the following:

$$U = \left[\left(1 - \tfrac{1}{\sigma}\right)\nu - \eta_P\right]\tfrac{\log\theta\overline{P}}{\rho} + \tfrac{1-\nu}{\rho}\log E + \left(\tfrac{\nu}{\sigma} - \eta_P\right)\tfrac{g}{\rho^2 F} + \tfrac{\eta_P}{\rho}\log\theta + \nu_1, \quad (12.21)$$

where $\nu_1 \equiv \log(1-\nu) + [(\nu/\sigma) - \eta_P](A_0/\rho)$ and $(1 - 1/\sigma) > \eta_P$ are assumed. The second term on the RHS, $\log E$, is the improvement in welfare due to consumption of agricultural goods. The utility of the bureaucrat as $u = (h-e)d$ can be rewritten as follows by using (12.20), $e = \tau/2$, $d = q/\theta$ and $\overline{P} = Aq$:

$$u = \tfrac{1+\varrho}{2}\left(\tfrac{\tau\overline{P}}{A}\right), \quad (12.22)$$

where the utility of bureaucrats improves because the bribes increase in proportion to the negotiation power of the bureaucrats, the environmental tax rate and the total emissions allowance.

Since raising the environmental tax rate lowers the economic growth rate, household consumption decreases due to a decrease in the number of varieties and welfare deteriorates. However, the utility of bureaucrats improves because the bribes increase due to higher tax evasion. In contrast, a decrease in the environmental tax rate due to tax evasion leads to an improvement in household welfare due to economic growth and a deterioration in the utility of bureaucrats.

A decrease in the total emissions allowance reduces tax evasion, leading to decreased bribes and a deterioration in the utility of the bureaucrats. This environmental policy improves household welfare through economic growth, yet worsens household utility due to lower consumption of manufactured and agricultural goods. Whether the dynamic welfare effect of the former dominates the static welfare effect of the latter determines the welfare effect of the total emissions allowance. If the reduction of the total emissions allowance improves household welfare, the result is the same as the welfare effect of tax evasion. If the reduction of the total emissions allowance worsens household welfare, the environmental policy brings about sustainable development, yet does not improve social welfare.

It has been suggested that corruption is a hindrance to economic development in developing countries. However, as Mauro (1995) pointed out, bribes to government officials can facilitate the use of administrative services and promote economic growth. The result that economic growth through tax evasion improves household welfare but worsens the utility of government officials provides theoretical support for such a claim. The relationship between political bribery and sustainable development will require further analysis.

## References

Aidt, T. S. (2011). "Chapter 1: Corruption and Sustainable Development". In International Handbook on the Economics of Corruption, Volume Two. Cheltenham, UK: Edward Elgar Publishing. https://doi.org/10.4337/9780857936523.00007

Böhringer, C., Koschel, H., & Moslener, U. (2008). Efficiency losses from overlapping regulation of EU carbon emissions. *Journal of Regulatory Economics*, 33, 299–317. https://doi.org/10.1007/s11149-007-9054-8

Cerqueti, R., & Coppier, R. (2016). Corruption, evasion and environmental policy: a game theory approach. *IMA Journal of Management Mathematics*, 27(2), 235–253. https://doi.org/10.1093/imaman/dpu019

Damania, R. (2002). Environmental controls with corrupt bureaucrats. *Environment and Development Economics*, 7(3), 407–427. https://doi.org/10.1017/S1355770X02000256

Eichner, T., & Pethig, R. (2009). Efficient CO2 emissions control with emissions taxes and international emissions trading. *European Economic Review*, 53(6), 625–635. https://doi.org/10.1016/j.euroecorev.2009.02.002

Farzin, Y. H., & Bond, C. A. (2006). Democracy and environmental quality. *Journal of Development Economics*, 81(1), 213–235. https://doi.org/10.1016/j.jdeveco.2005.04.003

Fredriksson, P. G., & Wollscheid, J. R. (2008). The political economy of investment: The case of pollution control technology. *European Journal of Political Economy*, 24(1), 53–72. https://doi.org/10.1016/j.ejpoleco.2007.06.009

Geng, Y., Liu, W., Li, K., & Chen, H. (2021). Environmental regulation and corporate tax avoidance: A quasi-natural experiment based on the eleventh Five-Year Plan in China. *Energy Economics*, 99, 105312. https://doi.org/10.1016/j.eneco.2021.105312

Hamaguchi, Y. (2020). Dynamic analysis of bribery firms' environmental tax evasion in an emissions trading market. *Journal of Macroeconomics*, 63, 103169. https://doi.org/10.1016/j.jmacro.2019.103169

Harstad, B., & Svensson, J. (2011). Bribes, lobbying, and development. *American Political Science Review*, 105(1), 46–63. https://doi.org/10.1017/S0003055410000523

IETA (2015) Overlapping policies with the EU ETS. 1–13. Available at https://www.ieta.org/resources/EU/IETA_overlapping_policies_with_the_EU_ETA.pdf.

Iskandar, D. D., Bhaduri, A., & Wunscher, T. (2016). The determinants of compliance with environmental tax: Behavioural study motivated by the case of Indonesia. *African Journal of Agricultural and Resource Economics*, 11(1), 33–46. https://doi.org/10.22004/ag.econ.233847

Lapatinas, A., Litina, A., & Sartzetakis, E. S. (2019). Environmental projects in the presence of corruption. *International Tax and Public Finance*, 26, 103–144. https://doi.org/10.1007/s10797-018-9503-6

Liu, A. A. (2013). Tax evasion and optimal environmental taxes. *Journal of Environmental Economics and Management*, 66(3), 656–670. https://doi.org/10.1016/j.jeem.2013.06.004

Mandell, S. (2008). Optimal mix of emissions taxes and cap-and-trade. *Journal of Environmental Economics and Management*, 56(2), 131–140. https://doi.org/10.1016/j.jeem.2007.12.004

Mauro, P. (1995). Corruption and growth. *The Quarterly Journal of Economics*, 110(3), 681–712. https://doi.org/10.2307/2946696

Oates, W. E., & Portney, P. R. (2003). The political economy of environmental policy. In Handbook of environmental economics (Vol. 1, pp. 325–354). Elsevier. https://doi.org/10.1016/S1574-0099(03)01013-1

Pellegrini, L., & Gerlagh, R. (2006). Corruption, Democracy, and Environmental Policy: An Empirical Contribution to the Debate. *The Journal of Environment & Development*, 15(3), 332–354. https://doi.org/10.1177/1070496506290960

Sorrell, S. (2002). The climate confusion: implications of the EU emissions trading directive for the UK climate change levy and climate change agreements. Science and Technology Policy Research. University of Sussex, Brighton. Available at http://www.sussex.ac.uk/spru/environment/research/ccrf.pdf

Welsch, H. (2004). Corruption, growth, and the environment: a cross-country analysis. *Environment and Development Economics*, 9(5), 663–693. https://doi.org/10.1017/S1355770X04001500

Yu, H., Liao, L., Qu, S., Fang, D., Luo, L., & Xiong, G. (2021). Environmental regulation and corporate tax avoidance: A quasi-natural experiments study based on China's new environmental protection law. *Journal of Environmental Management*, 296, 113160. https://doi.org/10.1016/j.jenvman.2021.113160

# Chapter 13
# Corruption and Globalisation

**Abstract** The variety expansion model, including environmental tax, is extended to the R&D-based location model, including emissions trading. More manufacturing firms in the North bribe government officials to avoid environmental taxes than in the South. The decline in the price of emission allowances due to the North's tax increase lowers economic growth rates through the distribution effect. Expenditure changes reduce the number of firms in the North and FDI, reducing pollution in the North and increasing in the South. As the tax rate gap widens, the total bribe in the North decreases due to the decrease in the number of firms. However, political and economic factors cause the pollution haven hypothesis. The tax rate decrease due to tax evasion raises the economic growth rate through the soaring price of emission allowances and moves manufacturing firms from the South to the North, increasing the total bribe amount in the North. This implies the green haven effect. Therefore, environmental tax evasion in developed countries may hinder the pollution haven hypothesis. Reducing the fine rate changes the direction of pollution haven from the South to the North and brings about sustainable development through pollution reduction and economic growth in the South.

## 13.1 Introduction

In the EU ETS, there are concerns that the waterbed effect is undermining the decarbonisation effect of emissions trading. Branger and Quirion (2014) pointed to the location behaviour of polluting firms as a factor in this waterbed effect. This location behaviour is influenced by various factors, such as tax evasion, corruption and rent. Grandfathering-type emission allowances are potential rents, hence, they raise the profits and stock prices of firms that are allocated more allowances (Smale et al., 2006; Martin et al., 2014; Oestreich and Tsiakas, 2015). Hamaguchi (2020) called the expansion of allowance allocation rents the distribution effect, which leads to economic growth. In the EU ETS, the mechanism by which the distribution effect

 
Y. Hamaguchi, *Sustainable Development in Economic Growth Theory*,
https://doi.org/10.1007/978-981-96-7639-2_13

and the home market effect provides location incentives for polluting firms was analysed by Hamaguchi (2021, 2023). As pointed out by Sorrell (2002) and IETA (2015), there is a temporary overlap of double regulation in the EU ETS, with environmental taxes and emissions trading. This additional regulatory cost affects the location behaviour. Polluting firms increase profits by locating in countries where it is easy to evade taxes through bribes.

The lowering of environmental regulatory standards due to corruption has been empirically confirmed (Fredriksson et al., 2003; Cole et al., 2006; Cole and Fredriksson, 2009). Candau and Dienesch (2017) analysed the impact of a decrease in the environmental tax due to corruption on pollution avoidance using a simple location model. They showed that polluting firms cluster in countries with a high incidence of corruption. They call this a corruption paradise and empirically confirm its existence within the EU. However, the increase in corruption costs in the host country of FDI may reduce the profits of its firms and hinder the accumulation of firms (Wei and Shleifer, 2000; Wei, 2000; Smarzynka and Wei, 2000). Hence, Smarzynka and Wei (2003) argued for the concept of a 'dirty secret', in which the cost of corruption regarding environmental policy in the host country prevents the accumulation of firms in that country. Therefore, there is an ongoing theoretical and empirical debate regarding the impact of corruption on the pollution haven hypothesis.

As Winkler (2022) pointed out, there are a lot of lobbying activities in the EU ETS in pursuit of rents from grandfathering-type emission allowances. Therefore, corruption occurs. In addition, environmental tax evasion through corruption in Candau and Dienesch (2017) was an exogenous setting for corruption, hence, endogenous tax evasion negotiations between bureaucrats and firms are not considered. The economic model in this chapter applies the environmental tax evasion through corruption in Hamaguchi (2020) to the R&D-based location model including emissions trading in Hamaguchi (2021). This analysis shows that the political-economic factors cause the pollution haven hypothesis. The results of Candau and Dienesch (2017) and Smarzynska and Wei (2003) are included.

## 13.2 The Model

### *13.2.1 Structure of R&D-Based Location Model with Tax Evasion*

The economic model in Chap. 12 is extended to the North–South model through the R&D-based firm location model in Chap. 10. In this case, manufacturing firms located in the North evade environmental taxes because the higher environmental tax rate provides an incentive to evade taxes. This model setting makes it possible to relate political factors, such as tax evasion and corruption, to the pollution haven hypothesis. This economic structure is illustrated in Fig. 13.1. The economic model in this chapter is based on Hamaguchi (2022).

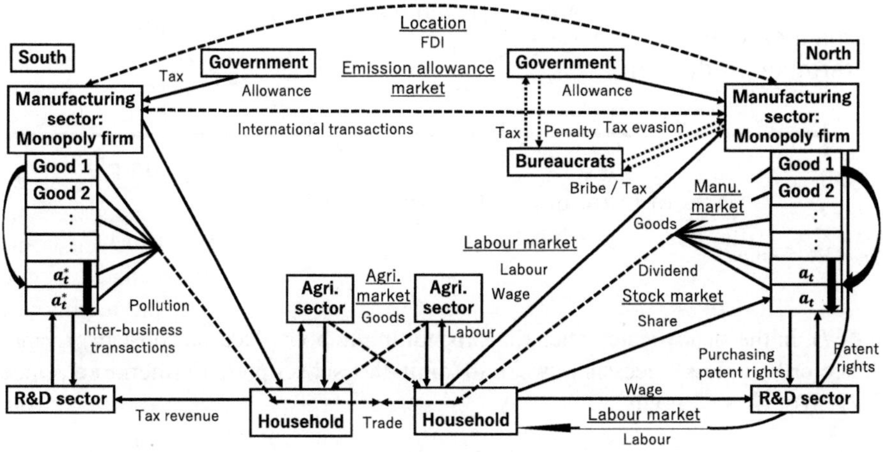


**Fig. 13.1** Structure of the R&D-based location model with tax evasion

## 13.2.2 Household

The intertemporal utility function of the household is $U_t = \int_0^\infty \log\left[\left(Q_t^\nu D_t^{1-\nu}\right)/\left(P_t + P_t^*\right)^{\eta P}\right]e^{-\rho t}dt$ in (10.1). The differentiated good is given by $Q_t = \left(\int_0^{A_t} x_{j,t}^{\frac{\sigma-1}{\sigma}} dj\right)^{\sigma/\sigma-1}$ in (9.2). The pollution emission function is given by $P_t = \int_0^{a_t} d_{j,t}dj$. Household expenditure on the good is $\int_0^{a_t} p_{j,t}x_{j,t}dj + \int_0^{a_t^*} tp_{i,t}^* x_{i,t}di + P_{D,t}D_t = E_t$ and the demand function for the good is (3.4). The intertemporal budget constraint is represented as $\dot{W}_t = r_t W_t + w_t L + T_t - E_t$. Since the agricultural good is numeraire with $P_{D,t} = 1$, from the zero-profit condition, $w_t = P_{D,t} = 1$ and $w_t^* = P_D^* = 1$. The pollution emission function per firm is $d_j = q_j/\theta_j$, where $\theta_j = \theta = 1$ is assumed to simplify the analysis.

In the static utility maximisation problem, given the expenditure, the household decides the quantity of each good to purchase and the demand functions in (9.4) are obtained as $P_{M,t}Q_t = \nu E_t$ and $D_t = (1-\nu)E_t$. The price index for differentiated goods is defined in (9.5) as $P_{M,t} \equiv \left(\int_0^{a_t} p_{j,t}^{1-\sigma}dj + \int_0^{a_t^*} t^{1-\sigma}p_{i,t}^{*1-\sigma}di\right)^{\frac{1}{1-\sigma}}$. By solving the first-order condition of the utility maximisation problem, the demand functions for industrial goods in the North and South become $x_{j,t} = p_{j,t}^{-\sigma}P_{M,t}^{\sigma-1}\nu E_t$ and $x_{i,t} = t^{-\sigma}p_{i,t}^{*-\sigma}P_{M,t}^{\sigma-}\nu E_t$ in (9.6). From the dynamic utility maximisation problem, the Euler equations in the North and South are obtained as $\dot{E}_t/E_t = \dot{E}_t^*/E_t^* = r_t - \rho$

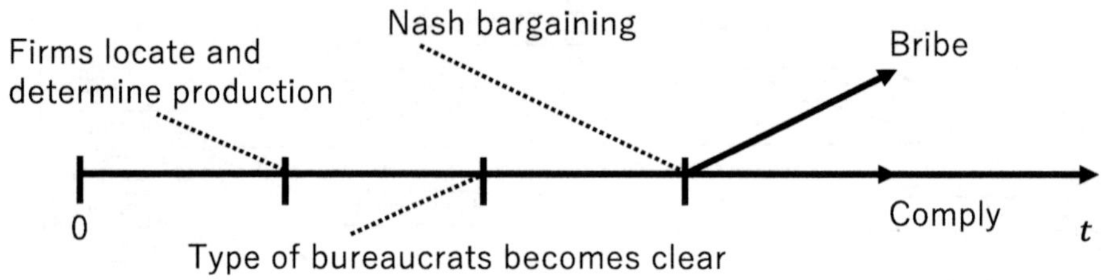


**Fig. 13.2** Timing

in (9.7). In the steady state, when the expenditure in both places is constant, $r_t = \rho$. Henceforth, unless necessary, we will omit the subscript $t$. Furthermore, since $W_0 > W_0^*$, $E > E^*$ holds.

### *13.2.3 Timing*

Figure 13.2 shows the negotiation timing between manufacturing firms and bureaucrats in the North over tax evasion and corruption. After purchasing a new variety of blueprints from an R&D firm, an entrepreneur enters the manufactured goods market. They choose the location. Without knowing the quality of the bureaucrats in the North, the new manufacturing firm located in the North decides on its production volume. After production begins, the manufacturing firm observes the quality of the bureaucrats as they demand an environmental tax. The manufacturing firm's decision to pay or evade the tax depends on the quality of the bureaucrats. If the quality is low, the manufacturing firm pays a bribe and evades the tax. If the quality is high, the manufacturing firm pays the tax. As the government sends bureaucrats to the manufacturing firm in each period, this negotiation is repeated.

### *13.2.4 Bureaucrats*

The utility of a bureaucrat $o$ is $u_o = (h_o - e_o)d_j$, where $h_o$ is the amount of pollution emitted by the manufacturing firm and $e_o$ is the amount of pollution emitted by the bureaucrats. Some bureaucrats accept bribes for under-reporting the amount of pollution emitted by the firms. This allows the manufacturing firms to evade taxes. When the corruption is discovered, the official pays a fine of $\xi_o \varpi_o$. The amount of the fine for a corrupt bureaucrat $o$ as $e_o d_j = \xi_o \varpi_o d_j$ increases in proportion to the pollution emissions associated with increased production.

A manufacturing firm observes the quality of bureaucrats in the production process and decides whether to pay a bribe or pay tax. Under $\tau \in (0, \varpi_o)$, a manufacturing firm with $\xi_o < \tau/\varpi_o$ pays a bribe. However, a manufacturing firm with $\xi_o \geq \tau/\varpi_o$ does not pay bribes. For $h_o \in \left(\xi_o \varpi_o d_j, \tau d_j\right)$, a Pareto-efficient negotiated solution is determined. The first-order condition of $\max_{h_o}(h_o - \xi_o \varpi_o d_j)^{\varrho}(\tau d_j - h_o)^{\varrho-1}$ in (12.15) yields that $h_o = \varrho \tau d_j + (1-\varrho)\xi_o \varpi_o d_j$ and that $h_o$ increases according to $\xi_o$, $\varpi_o$ and $d_j$, keeping all other factors constant.

## *13.2.5 Manufacturing Sector*

The governments of the North and South have established a single international emissions trading market. The governments allocate grandfathered emissions allowances $s_j$ ($s_i^*$) to the manufacturing firms. Under a perfectly competitive emissions trading market, emission allowances are bought and sold at the price of $p^e$ and, at equilibrium, this emissions market is cleared as $\overline{P} = \int_0^a s_j dj + \int_0^{a^*} s_i^* di$. The governments allocate the average allowance of emissions, $s = s_j = s_i^* = \overline{P}/A$, to their manufacturing firms, so that $as_j + a^* s_i^* = \overline{P}$ holds by $s = s_j = s_i^*$.

Manufacturing firm $j$, in a monopolistic competitive market, decides its production volume in anticipation of a corrupt or non-corrupt bureaucrat. In $\xi_o \varpi_o < \tau$, a manufacturing firm $j$ evades tax, while in $\xi_o \varpi_o \geq \tau$, a manufacturing firm $j$ pays tax. The expected bribe cost of manufacturing firm $j$ is $\mathbb{E}[\tau d_j, h_o] \equiv [1 - (\tau/\varpi_o)]\tau d_j + (\tau/\varpi_o)h_o$, which is rewritten with (12.15) as follows: $\mathbb{E}[\tau d_j, h_o] = \overline{\tau}(\tau, \varrho, \xi_o, \varpi_o)d_j$ for $\overline{\tau}(\tau, \varrho, \xi_o, \varpi_o) \equiv \tau[1 - (1-\varrho)\{(\tau/\varpi_o) - \xi_o\}]$, where $\overline{\tau}(\tau, \varrho, \xi_o, \varpi_o)$ is the efficient environmental tax rate and the second term on the RHS implies the tax rate. Here, $0 < \tau < \varpi_o$ and $0 < \varpi_o < 1$ hold.

By using $\xi_o = \xi = \tau/(2\varpi)$, $\mathbb{E}[\tau d_j, h_o]$ is given by $\mathbb{E}[\tau d_j, h] = \overline{\tau}(\tau, \varrho, \varpi)d_j$ for $\overline{\tau}(\tau, \varrho, \varpi) = \tau[1 - (\tau/\tilde{\tau})]$, where $\tilde{\tau} \equiv (2\varpi)/(1-\varrho) > \tau$. Note that $\tau/\tilde{\tau}$ is the tax rate; the higher the environmental tax rate, the more the ratio of tax evasion increases by $1/\tilde{\tau}$. We obtain $d\tilde{\tau}/d\varpi = 2/(1-\varrho) > 0$, $d\tilde{\tau}/d\varrho = 2\varpi/(1-\varrho)^2 > 0$, $d\overline{\tau}/d\tau = 1 - (2\tau/\tilde{\tau}) > 0$, $d\overline{\tau}/d\varpi = (\tau/\tilde{\tau})^2 d\tilde{\tau}/d\varpi > 0$ and $d\overline{\tau}/d\varrho = (\tau/\tilde{\tau})^2 d\tilde{\tau}/d\varrho > 0$.

Before learning about the quality of bureaucrats, manufacturing firm $j$ chooses the price of manufactured goods that maximises the expected profit, as follows:

$$\max_{p_j} \mathbb{E}[\pi_j] \equiv (p_j - 1)q_j - \mathbb{E}\min[\tau d_j, h_o] - P^e(d_j - s), \tag{13.1}$$

and the first-order condition for profit maximisation yields the following:

$$\mathbb{E}[p_j] = \frac{\sigma}{\sigma-1}\left[1 - \frac{1}{\sigma}\left(\frac{p_i}{q_j}\right)\frac{\partial \mathbb{E}[\tau d_j, h_o]}{\partial p_i} + p^e\right],\ \mathbb{E}[p_i^*] = t\mathbb{E}[p_j], \tag{13.2a}$$

which is used with (13.1) to derive

$$\mathbb{E}[\pi_j] = \frac{q_j}{\sigma-1}\left[1 - \left(\frac{p_i}{q_j}\right)\frac{\partial \mathbb{E}[\tau d_j, h_o]}{\partial p_i} + p^e\right] - \mathbb{E}[\tau d_j, h_o] + p^e s. \tag{13.2b}$$

where $\mathbb{E}[p_i^*] = t\mathbb{E}[p_j]$ also holds for $\tau \neq \tau^*$.

After the manufacturing firm $j$ decides on its production, the quality of the bureaucrat $o$ is revealed. Hence, by substituting the efficient environmental tax rate in (12.16) into (12.18a) and (12.18b), we obtain the following manufactured goods prices and profits:

$$p = \tfrac{\sigma}{\sigma-1}(1 + \overline{\tau} + p^e), \tag{13.3}$$

and

$$\pi = \left(\tfrac{1+\overline{\tau}+p^e}{\sigma-1}\right)q + p^e s, \tag{13.4}$$

where, since environmental tax evasion weakens the pass-on of prices, keeping all other factors constant, manufactured goods prices fall due to tax evasion and profits fall due to a fall in sales.

### 13.2.6 R&D Sector

The production technology of an R&D firm in a perfectly competitive market is $\dot{A}_t = L_{A,t}/F_t$ in (3.10). From $F_t = F/A_t$ in global knowledge spillover and the free entry condition, $P_A = F/A$ is obtained. The share price is equal to the sum of the discounted present value of profits from period $t$ onwards as $P_{A,t} = \int_t^\infty e^{-[r(\iota)-r(t)]}\pi_\iota d\iota$. By taking the time derivative of this $P_{A,t}$, the non-arbitrage condition is obtained as $\pi + \dot{P}_A = rP_A$ in (3.9).

### 13.2.7 Market

In this economy, there are markets for manufactured goods, agricultural goods, labour, capital and emission allowances. The market clearing conditions for agricultural goods and capital are $D + D^* = L(1 - \nu)(E + E^*)$ and $\pi + \dot{P}_A = rP_A$, respectively. The market clearing condition for labour in (9.15) is $L_A + L_M + L_D = 2L$. From the demand function in (9.10), the market clearing condition for manufactured goods is expressed as follows:

$$x = \nu L(\tfrac{\sigma-1}{\sigma})\left(\tfrac{1}{1+\overline{\tau}+p^e}\right)\left(\tfrac{E}{a+\varphi a^*} + \tfrac{\varphi E^*}{a^*+\varphi a}\right), \tag{13.5a}$$

$$x^* = \nu L(\tfrac{\sigma-1}{\sigma})\left(\tfrac{1}{1+\tau^*+p^e}\right)\left(\tfrac{\varphi E}{a+\varphi a^*} + \tfrac{E^*}{a^*+\varphi a}\right), \tag{13.5b}$$

where price decline due to environmental tax evasion increases demand for manufactured goods in the North and South.

Under international double regulation, the government in the North imposes a higher environmental tax on its manufacturing firms than the government in the South, with $\tau > \tau^*$. Manufacturing firms located in the South can lower the price of manufactured goods due to the lower environmental tax. Keeping all other factors constant, as $x^* > x$, the increase in demand for manufactured goods in the South may allow manufacturing firms there to increase their profits. Since arbitrage opportunities regarding location arise, some manufacturing firms may choose to locate in the South. However, manufacturing firms located in the North can evade environmental taxes by bribing the bureaucrats. When this tax evasion causes $\overline{\tau} = \tau^*$, the arbitrage opportunity regarding the location disappears. From the non-arbitrage condition in (9.13) and $a + a^* = W + W^* = A$, $x = x^*$ holds via $\pi = \pi^*$. Hence, the tax rate difference between the North and South is defined as follows:

$$\overline{\overline{\tau}} \equiv \tau - \tau^*, \tag{13.6}$$

for $\overline{\tau}(\tau, \varrho, \varpi) = \tau^*$. Note that the difference in environmental tax rates between the North and South as $\overline{\overline{\tau}}$ implies the tax rate evasion of manufacturing firms in the North. This relationship is illustrated in Fig. 13.3.

The number of manufacturing firms located in the North is expressed as follows:

$$\gamma = \frac{a}{A} = \frac{E - \varphi E^*}{(1-\varphi)(E+E^*)}, \tag{9.16a}$$

which includes the home market effect in Krugman (1980). The market clearing condition for emission allowances is $a^* p^e (s - d^*) - ap^e (d - s) = 0$. Using (9.16a) and (9.16b) yields $as = (a/A)\overline{P} = \gamma \overline{P}$ and $a^* s = (a^*/A)\overline{P} = (1 - \gamma)\overline{P}$. From $as + a^* s = \overline{P}$, $P + P^* = ad + a^* d^* = \overline{P}$ is obtained in (10.28)

## 13.3 Equilibrium

### 13.3.1 Dynamic System

The BGP in the present model is an equilibrium path that satisfies three conditions. First, there is a constant, positive economic growth rate $g_{A,t} = \dot{A}_t / A_t > 0$. Second, the labour allocation of manufactured goods, R&D and agricultural firms is constant,

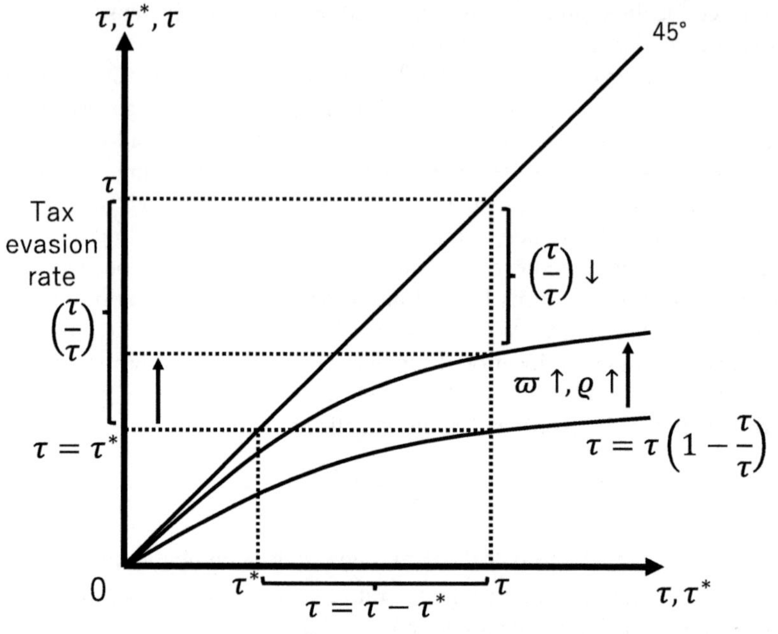


**Fig. 13.3** Tax evasion rate between the North and the South

as $L_{X,t} = L_X$, $L_{A,t} = L_A$ and $L_{D,t} = L_D$, respectively. Third, aggregate expenditure is constant, as $E_t + E_t^* = E + E^*$. We construct the law of motion for $E_t + E_t^*$.[1]

Using $a + a^* = W + W^* = A$ and $\pi = \pi^*$, (13.5a) and (13.5b) are rewritten as follows:

$$x = x^* = \nu L\left(\tfrac{\sigma-1}{\sigma}\right)\left(\tfrac{1}{1+\overline{\tau}+p^e}\right)\tfrac{E+E^*}{A}, \tag{13.7}$$

which is used with $D + D^* = L(1-\nu)(E + E^*)$ and $L_A = Fg_A$ to rewrite $L_A + L_M + L_D = 2L$ as follows:

$$Fg_A + L\left[1 - \nu + \nu\left(\tfrac{\sigma-1}{\sigma}\right)\left(\tfrac{1}{1+\overline{\tau}+p^e}\right)\right](E + E^*) = 2L, \tag{13.8}$$

[1] The method of deriving the steady-state value in this chapter adopts the method of deriving in Chap. 10. However, Hamaguchi (2022) derived the steady-state values by relying on the derivation method in Chap. 12. Therefore, the formula descriptions of expenditure, the number of firms located, permit allocation rent, emission allowance price and economic growth rate in Hamaguchi (2022) are similar to Chap. 12, yet different from this chapter. However, the economic implications remain the same.

where the decline in price pass-through due to tax evasion increases the demand for manufactured goods and labour.

Rewriting (13.4) by using $s = \overline{P}/A$ and (13.7) yields $\pi = [(\nu L)/\sigma][(E+E^*)/A] + p^e(\overline{P}/A)$ in (10.11). Substituting (10.11), $r = \rho$ and $g_A = -g_{PA}$ into $\pi + \dot{P}_A = rP_A$ in (10.11) yields $[(\nu L)/(\sigma F)](E+E^*) + p^e(\overline{P}/F) = \rho + g_A$ in (10.12). As Hamaguchi (2022) showed, the dynamic system consisting of (10.12) and (13.8) is deterministic and stable. In this steady state, $g = g_A = -g_{PA}$ holds.

### 13.3.2 Steady State

By using (13.7), $d = q/\theta$ and $a + a^* = A$, we can rewrite $ad + a^*d^* = \overline{P}$ as follows:

$$\overline{P} = \left(\tfrac{\sigma-1}{\sigma}\right)\left(\tfrac{\nu L}{1+\overline{\tau}+p^e}\right)(E+E^*), \tag{13.9}$$

where, when the total emission allowance caps the amount of pollution emissions, tax evasion weakens the pass-on of costs to manufactured goods, hence, demand for manufactured goods increases and pollution emissions expand. The price of emission allowances rises due to the increase in its demand. The pass-on of costs to manufactured goods reduces demand for manufactured goods and cuts pollution emissions, hence, the amount of pollution emissions falls within the total emission allowance.

Substituting (13.9) for (10.12) and rearranging gives the following claim about the rate of economic growth:

$$g = \tfrac{\sigma p^e+\overline{\tau}+1}{\sigma-1}\left(\tfrac{\overline{P}}{F}\right) - \rho, \tag{13.10}$$

where the profit per share depends on the allowance allocation rent. As the distribution effect in Hamaguchi (2020) stated, this rent expansion promotes economic growth.

We define $b \equiv \left[(\sigma p^e + \overline{\tau} + 1)/(\sigma - 1)\right]\left[\overline{P}/(2L)\right]$ as the allowance allocation rent per population. An increase in the environmental tax in the North increases this rent through price pass-through via an efficient environmental tax rate. However, if this environmental tax increase lowers the price of emission allowances, it reduces this rent. In addition, a reduction in the tax due to tax evasion further reduces the rent due to weakened price pass-through.

By substituting (13.8) into (13.10) and $g = g_A$, we obtain the following per capita expenditure worldwide:

$$E + E^* = \frac{2(1-b)+\frac{\rho F}{L}}{1-\nu+\nu\left(\frac{\sigma-1}{\sigma}\right)\left(\frac{1}{1+\overline{\tau}+p^e}\right)}, \tag{13.11}$$

where, keeping all the factors constant, the reduction in the environmental tax and the reduction in the tax rate due to tax evasion in the North increases expenditure through a decrease in the permit allocation rent. Furthermore, if the price of emission allowances increases due to this tax policy, as in $1 + \overline{\tau} + p^e$, household expenditure decreases. From (13.11), expenditure in the North and South can be expressed as follows:

$$E = \frac{1-b+\frac{\rho F}{L}k}{1-\nu+\nu\left(\frac{\sigma-1}{\sigma}\right)\left(\frac{1}{1+\overline{\tau}+p^e}\right)}, \tag{13.12a}$$

$$E^* = \frac{1-b+\frac{\rho F}{L}(1-k)}{1-\nu+\nu\left(\frac{\sigma-1}{\sigma}\right)\left(\frac{1}{1+\overline{\tau}+p^e}\right)}, \tag{13.12b}$$

where $k \equiv W/A > 1/2$ is the number of firms owned by the North household, which owns more than half of the world's firms.

By substituting (13.11) into (13.9), the equilibrium emissions price is derived as follows:

$$p^e = \nu L\left(\frac{\sigma-1}{\sigma}\right)\left(2 + \frac{\rho F}{L}\right)\left(\frac{1}{\overline{P}}\right) - \overline{\tau} - 1, \tag{13.13}$$

where from $dp^e/d\overline{\tau} = -1 < 0$, an increase in the efficient environmental tax rate through an environmental tax increase in the North causes the price of emission allowances to fall. This is because when the demand for manufactured goods falls and production shrinks, pollution emissions are reduced and the demand for emission allowance falls. However, a reduction in the tax rate due to tax evasion weakens the pass-on of prices and increases demand for manufactured goods, hence, the rise in demand for emission allowances due to increased pollution emissions causes the price of emission allowances to soar. Therefore, environmental tax evasion can strengthen the function of emission allowance trading by encouraging pollution reduction through the price of emission allowances.

Rewriting $b$ in this $p^e$ gives the following:

$$b = \frac{\overline{P}}{2L}\left(\frac{\sigma p^e+\overline{\tau}+1}{\sigma-1}\right) = \nu\left(1 + \frac{\rho F}{2L}\right) - (\overline{\tau} + 1)\left(\frac{\overline{P}}{2L}\right), \tag{13.14}$$

where an environmental tax increase in the North reduces the allowance allocation rent through a fall in the price of emission allowances in $db/d\overline{\tau} = -\overline{P}/(2L) < 0$. Therefore, a fall in the tax rate due to tax evasion increases the allowance allocation rent through a rise in the price of emission allowances. Substituting (13.14) into (13.10), we obtain the following equilibrium economic growth rate:

$$g = \frac{2L}{F}\left(\frac{\nu}{\sigma}\right) - (\overline{\tau} + 1)\left(\frac{\overline{P}}{F}\right) - (1 - \nu)\rho, \tag{13.15}$$

where an environmental tax increase in the North reduces the economic growth rate through a decrease in the allowance allocation rent in $dg/d\overline{\tau} = -\left(\overline{P}/F\right) < 0$. Therefore, a tax rate decrease due to tax evasion increases the economic growth rate through an increase in the allowance allocation rent.

By substituting (13.11), (13.12a) and (13.12b) into (9.16a), the number of firms located in the North at equilibrium is expressed as follows:

$$\gamma = \frac{(1-\varphi)(1-b)+\frac{\rho F}{L}[k-\varphi(1-k)]}{2(1-\varphi)\left(1-b+\frac{\rho F}{2L}\right)}, \quad (10.20)$$

where the concentration of firms in the North is influenced by the allowance allocation rent in $b$.

As explained in Chap. 10, the amount of FDI between the North and South is expressed as follows:

$$\dot{a} - \dot{W} = \frac{gA\left(k-\frac{1}{2}\right)[\varphi\rho F-L(1-\varphi)(1-b)]}{2L(1-\varphi)\left(1-b+\frac{\rho F}{2L}\right)}, \quad (10.21)$$

which implies the direction of FDI net flows that depend on the sign of $a - W$ and $\dot{a} - \dot{W} \gtreqless 0$ is affected by the following parameter conditions:

$$\overline{\varphi} \equiv \left(\frac{\varphi}{1-\varphi}\right)\frac{\rho F}{L} \gtrless 1 - b, \quad (10.22)$$

where if $\overline{\varphi} > 1 - b$, $\dot{a} - \dot{W} > 0$ holds and FDI from the South to the North occurs, while if $\overline{\varphi} \leq 1 - b$, $\dot{a} - \dot{W} \leq 0$ holds and FDI from the North to the South occurs. A decrease in the allowance allocation rent due to an increase in environmental taxes in the North induces FDI from the North to the South. However, an increase in the allowance allocation rent due to environmental tax evasion induces FDI from the South to the North.

By using $P_t = \int_0^{a_t} d_{j,t} dj$, $d = q/\theta$, $as = (a/A)\overline{P}$ and $a^* s = (a^*/A)\overline{P}$ in (9.16a), (9.16b) and (10.2), the total pollution emissions from the North, the South, and total pollution emissions from the North as a percentage of the South, respectively, are $P = \gamma\overline{P}$, $P^* = (1-\gamma)\overline{P}$ and $P/P^* = 1/\left[(1/\gamma) - 1\right]$ in (10.23). The total pollution emissions of the North and South are expressed as the pollution share obtained by multiplying the total emission allowance by the number of firms located there. Total pollution emissions from the North as a percentage of the South depend on the concentration of firms in the North.

By substituting (12.15) into $d = q/\theta$, (13.7) and (13.9), the bribe per bureaucrat at equilibrium is derived as follows:

$$h = \gamma\tau\overline{P}\left(\frac{1+\varrho}{2}\right), \quad (13.16)$$

where, the more firms in the North, the higher the tax evasion, increasing the amount of bribes per bureaucrat.

## 13.4 Comparative Statics

### *13.4.1 Effect of the North Environmental Tax*

The effects of the total emissions allowance and trade liberalisation on the economy and the environment are the same as those in the economic model in Chap. 10. However, trade liberalisation increases the total bribe amount in the North. In Appendix L, the effect of the total emissions allowance on the steady state is shown as follows:

$$\frac{dE+E^*}{d\overline{\tau}} \gtreqless 0,\ \frac{dE}{d\overline{\tau}} \gtreqless 0,\ \frac{dE^*}{d\overline{\tau}} \gtreqless 0,\ \frac{d\gamma}{d\overline{\tau}} < 0,\ \frac{d\dot{a}-\dot{W}}{d\overline{\tau}} < 0,$$

and

$$\frac{dP}{d\overline{\tau}} = \overline{P}\frac{\partial\gamma}{\partial\overline{\tau}} + \gamma,\ \frac{dP^*}{d\overline{\tau}} = -\overline{P}\frac{\partial\gamma}{\partial\overline{\tau}} + (1-\gamma) > 0,\ \frac{d}{d\overline{\tau}}\left(\frac{P}{P^*}\right) = \frac{1}{(1-\gamma)^2}\frac{\partial\gamma}{\partial\overline{\tau}} < 0,$$

and

$$\frac{dh}{d\tau} = \overline{P}\left(\frac{1+\varrho}{2}\right)\left(\gamma + \tau\frac{\partial\gamma}{\partial\overline{\tau}}\right),$$

where an increase in the environmental tax rate in the North increases the efficient environmental tax rate in $d\overline{\tau}/d\tau = 1 - (2\tau/\tilde{\tau}) > 0$.

Due to a fall in the price of emission allowances, the allowance allocation rent shrinks and the economic growth rate falls. Due to the pass-through of the price of emission allowances, manufactured goods prices fall and expenditure increases. However, due to the fall in the price of emission allowances, demand of manufactured goods as a proportion of expenditure increases in $[\cdot](E + E^*)$ in (10.10) and expenditure decreases. Regardless of the increase/decrease in expenditure, the relative market size of the North is large, hence, the home market effect leads to the concentration of firms from the North to the South and a decrease of the FDI amount. When the reduction in allowance allocation rent leads to $\overline{\varphi} < 1 - b$ in (10.22), the environmental tax increase induces FDI to move from the North to the South. As manufacturing firms that emit pollution are concentrated in the South, the total amount of pollution emitted in the South increases and the total amount of pollution emitted in the North as a proportion of the total in the South decreases. As the number of manufacturing firms located in the North decreases, $dh/d\overline{\tau} < 0$, the total amount of bribes in the North decrease as well. In Hamaguchi (2022), an increase in the efficient environmental tax rate improved welfare in the South. Although $\overline{\tau}(\tau, \varrho, \varpi) = \tau^*$ due to environmental tax evasion in the North, $\overline{\overline{\tau}} \equiv \tau - \tau^*$ in (13.6) expands due to environmental tax increases in the North. Therefore, under the double regulation that includes tax evasion, the pollution haven hypothesis occurs through the widening of the tax rate gap. Political and economic factors, such as tax evasion and corruption, may cause the pollution haven hypothesis. Therefore, Hamaguchi (2022) called this result the political pollution haven hypothesis.

### 13.4.2 Effect of Tax Evasion

In (13.6), $\overline{\overline{\tau}} \equiv \tau - \tau^*$ represents the tax rate gap between the North and South and implies the tax rate evasion of manufacturing firms in the North. As $d\overline{\tau}/d\tau = 1 - (2\tau/\tilde{\tau}) > 0$, an increase in the environmental tax rate in the North raises the efficient environmental tax rate and tax evasion. Due to this tax evasion, the environmental tax rate without tax evasion decreases by the amount of $\overline{\overline{\tau}}$. Therefore, we can interpret the effect of tax evasion as a fall in $\tau$ by the amount $\overline{\overline{\tau}}$. When $\tau/\tilde{\tau} = 0$ in $\overline{\tau}(\tau, \varrho, \varpi) = \tau[1 - (\tau/\tilde{\tau})]$, $\overline{\tau}(\tau, \varrho, \varpi) = \tau$ holds. This fall in the environmental tax rate implies the effect of environmental tax evasion.

Tax rate reductions due to environmental tax evasion increase the price of emission allowances. The rise in the price of emission allowances causes the allowance allocation rent to expand, boosting the economic growth rate. Regardless of changes in expenditure, the relative market size of the North remains large, the home market effect causes the concentration of firms from the South to the North and the amount of FDI expands. When the expansion of allowance allocation rent leads to $\overline{\varphi} < 1 - b$ in (10.22), the environmental tax increase induces FDI to move from the South to the North. As manufacturing firms that emit pollution are concentrated in the North, the total amount of pollution emitted in the South decreases and the total amount of pollution emitted in the North as a proportion of the South increases. Hence, the total amount of bribes in the North increases as the number of manufacturing firms increases.

In countries that impose relatively strict environmental regulations, environmental tax evasion is induced and polluting firms are concentrated. Therefore, there is a green haven effect in environmental tax evasion, as in Poelhekke and Van der Ploeg (2015). Furthermore, in the North, where the benefits of tax evasion through corruption are high, the accumulation of polluting firms is increasing the amount of bribes and pollution is escaping from the South to the North, which supports the corruption paradise of Candau and Dienesch (2017).

### 13.4.3 Effect of Penalty Rate and Southern Environmental Tax

As $d\overline{\tau}/d\varpi = (\tau/\tilde{\tau})^2 d\tilde{\tau}/d\varpi > 0$, a reduction in the fine lowers the efficient environmental tax rate. Furthermore, a reduction in the environmental tax in the South lowers the efficient tax rate because it encourages manufacturing firms in the North to evade taxes through location-related arbitrage. Through the same channels as in Sect. 4.1, the price of emission allowances, allowance allocation rent, economic growth rate, the number of firms located in the North, the amount of FDI, the total pollution emissions in the North, the total pollution emissions in the North as a proportion of the total in the South and the total bribe amount in the North increases. The tax rate gap of $\bar{\bar{\tau}} \equiv \tau - \tau^*$ increases due to environmental tax reduction in the South, however, environmental tax evasion in the North causes pollution to escape from the South to the North. Therefore, environmental tax evasion in developed countries prevents pollution haven caused by lax environmental regulations. This result is consistent with the dirty secret in Smarzynska and Wei (2003), in which corruption regarding environmental policy in the recipient country of FDI prevents pollution flight in the recipient country. In addition, as explained in Chap. 12, if the bureaucracy becomes more efficient through administrative reform, the government can lower the fine. In this case, too, the direction of pollution haven is from the South to the North. In both cases, pollution reduction in the South and economic growth bring about sustainable development. In the international community, tax evasion and corruption can lead to the pollution haven hypothesis, hence, by improving the quality of the political system, it is possible to avoid the political pollution haven hypothesis.

## References

Branger, F., & Quirion, P. (2014). Climate policy and the 'carbon haven' effect. Wiley Interdisciplinary Reviews: *Climate Change*, 5(1), 53–71. https://doi.org/10.1002/wcc.245

Candau, F., & Dienesch, E. (2017). Pollution haven and corruption paradise. *Journal of Environmental Economics and Management*, 85, 171–192. https://doi.org/10.1016/j.jeem.2017.05.005

Cole, M. A., Elliott, R. J., & Fredriksson, P. G. (2006). Endogenous pollution havens: Does FDI influence environmental regulations? *Scandinavian Journal of Economics*, 108(1), 157–178. https://doi.org/10.1111/j.1467-9442.2006.00439.x

Cole, M. A., & Fredriksson, P. G. (2009). Institutionalized pollution havens. *Ecological Economics*, 68(4), 1239–1256. https://doi.org/10.1016/j.ecolecon.2008.08.011

Fredriksson, P. G., List, J. A., & Millimet, D. L. (2003). Bureaucratic corruption, environmental policy and inbound US FDI: theory and evidence. *Journal of Public Economics*, 87(7–8), 1407–1430. https://doi.org/10.1016/S0047-2727(02)00016-6

Hamaguchi, Y. (2020). Dynamic analysis of bribery firms' environmental tax evasion in an emissions trading market. *Journal of Macroeconomics*, 63, 103169. https://doi.org/10.1016/j.jmacro.2019.103169

Hamaguchi, Y. (2021). Polluting firms' location choices and pollution havens in an R&D-based growth model for an international emissions trading market. *The Journal of International Trade & Economic Development*, 30(4), 625–642. https://doi.org/10.1080/09638199.2021.1889644

Hamaguchi, Y. (2022). Effect of environmental tax evasion on pollution havens within the EU's dual regulation system. *SN Business & Economics*, 2(12), 194. https://doi.org/10.1007/s43546-022-00368-2

Hamaguchi, Y. (2023). Pollution havens and agglomeration: The effect of globalization and technological spillover. *Applied Economics*, 56(19), 2223–2240. https://doi.org/10.1080/00036846.2023.2186361

IETA (2015) Overlapping policies with the EU ETS. 1–13. Available at https://www.ieta.org/resources/EU/IETA_overlapping_policies_with_the_EU_ETA.pdf.

Krugman, P. (1980). Scale economies, product differentiation, and the pattern of trade. *The American Economic Review*, *70*(5), 950–959. https://www.jstor.org/stable/1805774

Martin, R., Muûls, M., De Preux, L. B., & Wagner, U. J. (2014). Industry compensation under relocation risk: A firm-level analysis of the EU emissions trading scheme. *The American Economic Review*, 104(8), 2482–2508. https://doi.org/10.1257/aer.104.8.2482

Oestreich, A. M., & Tsiakas, I. (2015). Carbon emissions and stock returns: Evidence from the EU Emissions Trading Scheme. *Journal of Banking & Finance*, 58, 294–308. https://doi.org/10.1016/j.jbankfin.2015.05.005

Poelhekke, S., & Van der Ploeg, F. (2015). Green havens and pollution havens. *The World Economy*, *38*(7), 1159–1178. https://doi.org/10.1111/twec.12219

Smale, R., Hartley, M., Hepburn, C., Ward, J., & Grubb, M. (2006). The impact of CO2 emissions trading on firm profits and market prices. *Climate Policy*, 6, 29–46. https://doi.org/10.1080/14693062.2006.9685587

Smarzynska, B. K., & Wei, S. J. (2000). Corruption and composition of foreign direct investment: Firm-level evidence. *NBER working paper series*, 7969. https://doi.org/10.3386/w7969

Smarzynska, B. K., & Wei, S. J. (2003). Pollution havens and foreign direct investment: dirty secret or popular myth?. *Contributions in Economic Analysis & Policy*, 3(2). https://www.degruyter.com/journal/key/bejeap/html

Sorrell, S. (2002). The climate confusion: implications of the EU emissions trading directive for the UK climate change levy and climate change agreements. Science and Technology Policy Research. University of Sussex, Brighton. Available at http://www.sussex.ac.uk/spru/environment/research/ccrf.pdf

Wei, S. J. (2000). How taxing is corruption on international investors?. *Review of Economics and Statistics*, 82(1), 1–11. https://doi.org/10.1162/003465300558533

Wei, S. J., & Shleifer, A. (2000). Local corruption and global capital flows. *Brookings papers on economic activity*, 2000(2), 303–354. https://www.jstor.org/stable/2667361

Winkler, D. (2022). Pollution for Sale: Lobbying, Allowance Allocation and Firm Outcomes in the EU ETS. *Social Science Research Network*, https://doi.org/10.2139/ssrn.4114641

# Part V
# Industrial Structure Upgrading

# Chapter 14
# Endogenous Productivity Change

**Abstract** Gustafsson and Segerstrom (2010) extended the variety expansion model, considering households with preferences for varieties of goods, to an R&D-based heterogeneous firms' model. They introduced the difficulty of R&D, creating a semi-endogenous growth model in which the scale effect disappears. Under a symmetric two-country setting, firms are divided into export, local and non-production firms, depending on the degree of labour productivity. Entrepreneurs enter the market as one of the firms after subtracting their productivity, determined by a Pareto distribution. Trade liberalisation improves the productivity of the industry by encouraging the least productive local firms to exit and the most productive local firms to enter the export market. This is called the cleansing effect of trade liberalisation. This lowers the relative R&D difficulty and reduces the number of varieties because it increases the fixed R&D cost. Furthermore, due to the cleansing effect of trade liberalisation, the price index falls as the supply of goods increases and welfare improves through increased consumption. In a full endogenous growth model, trade liberalisation raises fixed R&D costs and lowers the economic growth rate.

## 14.1 Structure of R&D-Based Growth Model with Heterogenous Firms

The R&D-based growth model in Chap. 3 is extended following Gustafsson and Segerstrom (2010). Segerstrom (1998) developed a semi-endogenous growth model, in which the scale effect disappeared, by introducing the difficulty of R&D. This R&D difficulty is introduced into the economic model in Chap. 3. There are two symmetrical countries—the North and the South. Households in both places supply labour to the goods and the R&D sectors in their countries and obtain positive utility from goods consumption. Firms in the goods sector have different labour productivity and

 
Y. Hamaguchi, *Sustainable Development in Economic Growth Theory*,
https://doi.org/10.1007/978-981-96-7639-2_14

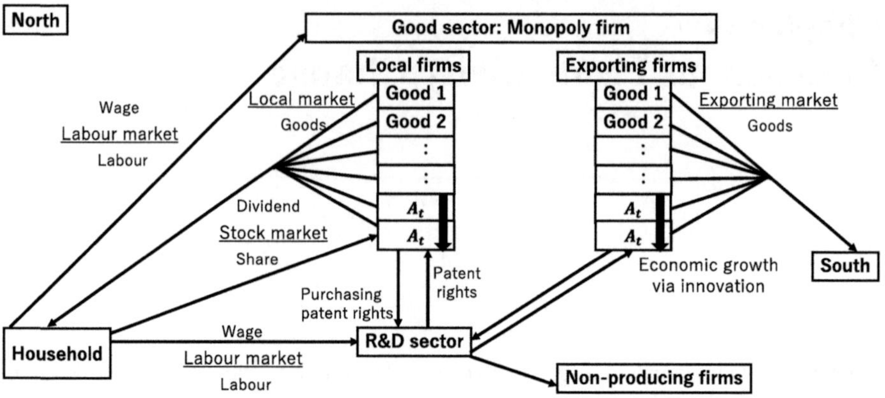


**Fig. 14.1** Structure of the R&D-based growth model with heterogenous firms

are classified into export and local firms according to the degree of their productivity. Entrepreneurs cannot know the productivity in advance and decide whether to enter the foreign or the domestic market according to anticipated productivity. When an export firm exports goods, it requires iceberg-type transportation costs. Unless necessary, we only describe the economy of the North. This economic structure is illustrated in Fig. 14.1.

## 14.2 The Model

### 14.2.1 Household

A fixed number of households live in each country. The size of each household is measured by the number of its members. The population size expands according to an exogenous population growth rate, with $n > 0$, hence, the population structure is $L_t = L_0 e^{nt}$. By making labour numeraire, the wage rate is $w_t = 1$.

The utility of the representative household between different periods is as follows:

$$U_t = \int_0^\infty \log Q_t e^{-(\rho - n)t} dt, \tag{14.1}$$

where the composition of a differentiated product is defined as follows:

$$Q_t = \left( \int_0^{A_t} x_{j,t}^{\frac{\sigma-1}{\sigma}} dj \right)^{\frac{\sigma}{\sigma-1}}, \tag{14.2}$$

where $A_t$ in the present model implies the total number of varieties that are produced domestically or exported internationally. The following demand function is derived from the static utility maximisation problem in Chap. 3:

$$x_{j,t} = \frac{p_{j,t}^{-\sigma}}{P_{M,t}^{1-\sigma}} \overline{E}_t, \quad (14.3)$$

where the price index for differentiated goods is defined as follows:

$$P_{M,t} \equiv \left( \int_0^{A_t} p_{j,t}^{1-\sigma} dj \right)^{\frac{1}{1-\sigma}}. \quad (14.4)$$

where $c_t \equiv \overline{E}_t / P_{M,t}$ is the consumption per capita. From the dynamic utility maximisation problem in Chap. 3, the Euler equation per capita is $\left(d\overline{E}_t/dt\right)/\overline{E}_t = r_t - \rho$. From $E_t = \overline{E}_t L_t$, the aggregate Euler equation is $\dot{E}_t / E_t = r_t - (\rho - n)$.

### *14.2.2 R&D Sector*

To develop blueprints for new varieties, R&D firms employ workers based on efficiency. As in Jones (1995), under the condition of $\varsigma < 1$ in the degree of knowledge and global spillovers, knowledge spillover in the R&D sector is defined as follows:

$$\frac{1}{\left(a_{L,t} + a_{E,t}\right)^{\varsigma}} = \frac{1}{(2A_t)^{\varsigma}}, \quad (14.5)$$

with symmetric equilibrium as $a_{L,t} = a_{E,t} = A_t$. In addition, $a_{L,t}$, $a_{E,t}$ and $A_t$ are the number of varieties in the local market, export market and world, respectively. Henceforth, the variables for local and export firms are labelled with the subscripts $L$ and $E$, respectively. Here, $\varsigma > 0$ is the standing-on-the-shoulder effect, which implies the positive knowledge spillover effect, while $\varsigma < 0$ is the fishing-out effect, which implies the negative knowledge spillover effect. This knowledge spillover effect is common to both the export and local markets. The fixed R&D costs for the variety of export and local firms are different. When developing a new variety for export firms, $F_E$ exogenous fixed costs are required and, for local firms, $F_L$ exogenous fixed costs are required.

After an R&D firm has successfully developed a new variety, an entrepreneur who purchases the design observes the unit input requirement $\psi$, which is the relevant cost for producing the variety. The entrepreneur subtracts $\psi$ from the probability density function $\tilde{g}(\psi)$ with support $\left[0, \overline{\psi}\right]$ and the corresponding cumulative distribution function $G(\psi)$. This $\psi$ does not change over time. The probability density function of $\psi$ is assumed to have the following Pareto distribution:

$$G(\psi) = \int_0^{\psi} \tilde{g}(\psi) d\psi = \left( \frac{\psi}{\overline{\psi}} \right)^{\Gamma},$$

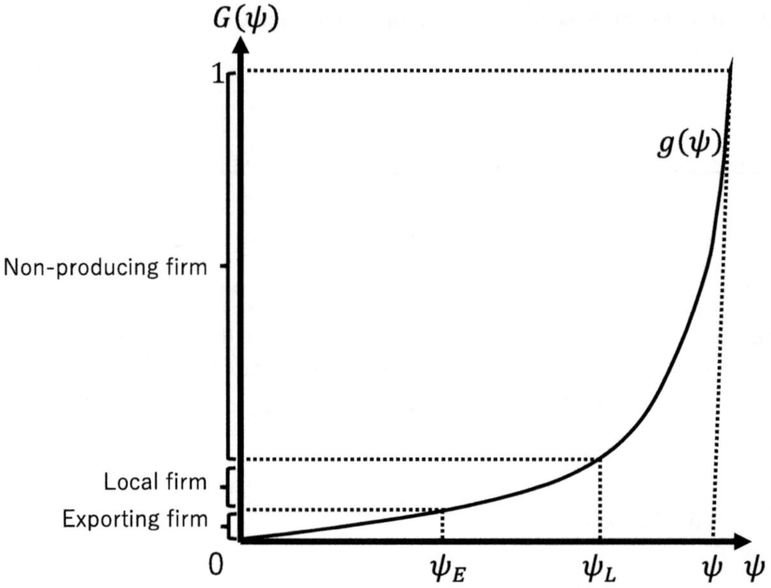


**Fig. 14.2** Distribution of productivity

where $\Gamma$ is the shape parameter and $\overline{\psi}$ is the scale parameter of the distribution (Fig. 14.2).

The heterogeneity of $\psi$ created through this distribution classifies firms into export, local and non-producing firms. Firms with $\psi_{L,t} < \psi < \overline{\psi}$ withdraw from the local market and become non-producing firms because the fixed R&D costs of entry exceed the value of the firm after entry. Firms with $\psi_{E,t} < \psi < \psi_{L,t}$ enter the local market and become a local firm because the value of the firm after entry exceeds the fixed R&D costs of entry. However, since the fixed R&D costs of entering the export market exceed the firm's value, it is unable to enter the export market. Firms that subtract $\psi$ in the range $0 < \psi < \psi_{E,t}$, enter the export market and become export firms because their firm value exceeds their fixed R&D costs. In summary, the threshold values for $\psi$ are $0 < \psi_{E,t} < \psi_{L,t} < \overline{\psi}$.

### 14.2.3 Goods Sector

The firms in this sector are in a monopolistic competition. When imitation is eliminated under an infinite patent period, each differentiated good is produced exclusively by its firm. Export and local firms produce differentiated goods, using labour as the only production factor. This production technology is symmetric across firms and the production function is $q_{j,t} = L^{X}_{j,t}$.

Firms that enter the local market by subtracting $\psi_{E,t} < \psi \leq \psi_{L,t}$ determine the price that maximises profit, given the demand for goods in (14.3), as follows:

$$\max_{p^L_{j,t}} \pi^L_{j,t} \equiv \left(p^L_{j,t} - \psi_j\right) q^L_{j,t}, \tag{14.6a}$$

and the first-order condition for profit maximisation asserts the following:

$$p^L_{j,t} = \frac{\sigma}{\sigma-1}\psi_j, \tag{14.7a}$$

where $\sigma/(\sigma - 1)$ is the mark-up. By substituting (14.7a) into (14.6a), the optimal profit for the local firm is as follows:

$$\pi^L_{j,t} = \frac{1}{\sigma}\left(\frac{\sigma-1}{\sigma}\right)^{\sigma-1}\left(\frac{P_{M,t}}{\psi_j}\right)^{\sigma-1} E_t, \tag{14.8a}$$

where, since the unit input requirement is passed on as higher prices, the profits of local firms decline.

Firms that enter the export market by subtracting $0 < \psi < \psi_{E,t}$ determine the price that maximises profits, given the demand for the good in (14.3), as follows:

$$\max_{p^E_{j,t}} \pi^E_{j,t} \equiv \left(p^E_{j,t} - t\psi_j\right) q^E_{j,t}, \tag{14.6b}$$

where export firms incur $t > 0$ iceberg-shaped transportation costs. The first-order condition for profit maximisation yields the following:

$$p^E_{j,t} = \frac{\sigma}{\sigma-1} t\psi_j, \tag{14.7b}$$

where the transportation costs are passed on to the price. By substituting (14.7b) for (14.6b), the optimal profit for the export firm is as follows:

$$\pi^E_{j,t} = \frac{\varphi}{\sigma}\left(\frac{\sigma-1}{\sigma}\right)^{\sigma-1}\left(\frac{P_{M,t}}{\psi_j}\right)^{\sigma-1} E_t, \tag{14.8b}$$

where $\varphi \equiv (1/t)^{\sigma-1}$ measures the degree of trade liberalisation.

### 14.2.4 Market Entry

The decision of whether an entrepreneur should enter the local or export market depends on the profit. Since the profits of local and export firms depend on $\psi_j$, the value of a firm in the stock market is related to the threshold values of $\psi = \psi_L$

and $\psi = \psi_E$. Firm value is the sum of the discounted present value of profits from the period $t$ onwards, $P^L_{A,t} = \int_t^\infty e^{-[r(\iota)-r(t)]}\pi_{\iota,L} d\iota$ and $P^E_{A,t} = \int_t^\infty e^{-[r(\iota)-r(t)]}\pi_{\iota,E} d\iota$. By time differentiating $P^L_{A,t}$ and $P^E_{A,t}$, respectively, we obtain the following non-arbitrage condition:

$$\pi_{L,t}(\psi_L) + \dot{P}^L_{A,t}(\psi_L) = r_t P^L_{A,t}(\psi_L), \ \ \pi_{E,t}(\psi_E) + \dot{P}^E_{A,t}(\psi_E) = r_t P^E_{A,t}(\psi_E),$$

which is rewritten as follows:

$$P^L_{A,t}(\psi_L) = \frac{\pi_{L,t}(\psi_L)}{r_t - \frac{\dot{P}^L_{A,t}(\psi_L)}{P^L_{A,t}(\psi_L)}}, \ \ P^E_{A,t}(\psi_E) = \frac{\pi_{E,t}(\psi_E)}{r_t - \frac{\dot{P}^E_{A,t}(\psi_E)}{P^E_{A,t}(\psi_E)}}, \tag{14.9}$$

where it is assumed that firms avoid the exogenous death rate, as in Gustafsson and Segerstrom (2010).

R&D firms develop blueprints for varieties in the local and export markets. Entrepreneurs who draw $\psi = \psi_L$, buy blueprints for varieties in the local market, while those who draw $\psi = \psi_E$, buy blueprints for varieties in the export market. From the free entry condition, we obtain the following stock prices for local and export firms, respectively:

$$P^L_{A,t} = \frac{F_L}{(2A_t)^\varsigma}, \ \ P^E_{A,t} = \frac{F_E}{(2A_t)^\varsigma}, \tag{14.10}$$

where $P^E_{A,t} > P^L_{A<t}$ for $F_E > F_L$ because the cost of entering the export market is higher than the cost of entering the local market. By substituting (14.9) into (14.8a) and (14.10), the conditions for free entry into the local market are derived as follows:

$$\frac{\frac{1}{\sigma}\left(\frac{\sigma-1}{\sigma}\right)^{\sigma-1}\left(\frac{p_{M,t}}{\psi_j}\right)^{\sigma-1} E_t}{r_t + \varsigma\frac{\dot{A}_t}{A_t}} = \frac{F_L}{(2A_t)^\varsigma}, \tag{14.11a}$$

which is derived from $\dot{P}^L_{A,t}(\psi_L)/P^L_{A,t}(\psi_L) = \varsigma\left(\dot{A}_t/A_t\right)$. By substituting (14.8b) and (14.10) into (14.9), the conditions for free entry into the export market are derived as follows:

$$\frac{\frac{1}{\sigma}\left(\frac{\sigma-1}{\sigma}\right)^{\sigma-1}\left(\frac{p_{M,t}}{\psi_j}\right)^{\sigma-1} E_t}{r_t + \varsigma\frac{\dot{A}_t}{A_t}} = \frac{1}{\varphi}\cdot\frac{F_E}{(2A_t)^\varsigma}. \tag{14.11b}$$

By using (14.11a), (14.11b) and $F_E > F_L$, the productivity gap between local and export firms can be expressed as follows:

$$\frac{\psi_{L,t}}{\psi_{E,t}} = \left(\frac{F_E}{\varphi F_L}\right)^{\frac{\sigma}{\sigma-1}} > 1, \tag{14.12}$$

for all $\varphi \in (0, 1)$. Note that trade liberalisation and fixed costs affect the entry of new entrepreneurs through the profits of export and local firms.

### 14.2.5 Incentives for Innovation

The conditions for free entry into local and export markets determine the incentive to develop new varieties. The expected benefits of developing new varieties are equal to the fixed R&D costs for new varieties:

$$\int_{\psi_{E,t}}^{\psi_{L,t}} \left[ \frac{\pi_{L,t}(\psi_L)}{r_t + \varsigma \frac{\dot{A}_t}{A_t}} - \frac{F_L}{(2A_t)^{\varsigma}} \right] dG(\psi) + \int_0^{\psi_{E,t}} \left[ \frac{\pi_{E,t}(\psi_E)}{r_t + \varsigma \frac{\dot{A}_t}{A_t}} - \frac{F_E}{(2A_t)^{\varsigma}} \right] dG(\psi) = \frac{F_I}{A_t},$$

which is rewritten by using (14.8a) and (14.8b) as follows:

$$\frac{\frac{1}{\sigma}\left(\frac{\sigma-1}{\sigma}\right)^{\sigma-1} P_{M,t}^{\sigma-1} \Delta_t E_t}{r_t + \varsigma \frac{\dot{A}_t}{A_t}} = \frac{\overline{F}_t}{A_t}, \tag{14.13}$$

where $\Delta_t$ is defined as follows:

$$\Delta_t \equiv \int_{\psi_{E,t}}^{\psi_{L,t}} \left(\frac{1}{\psi}\right)^{\sigma-1} \frac{\tilde{g}(\psi)}{G(\psi_{L,t})} d\psi + \varphi \int_0^{\psi_{E,t}} \left(\frac{1}{\psi}\right)^{\sigma-1} \frac{\tilde{g}(\psi)}{G(\psi_{L,t})} d\psi, \tag{14.14a}$$

which is the weighted average of the firms' productivity.

Furthermore, $\overline{F}_t$ is defined as the following ex-ante fixed expected cost of developing varieties:

$$\overline{F}_t \equiv F_I \frac{1}{G(\psi_{L,t})} + F_L + F_E \frac{G(\psi_{E,t})}{G(\psi_{L,t})},$$

which is rewritten with the properties of the Pareto distribution as:

$$\overline{F}_t \equiv F_I \left(\frac{\overline{\psi}}{\psi_{L,t}}\right)^{\Gamma} + F_L + F_E \left(\frac{\psi_{E,t}}{\psi_{L,t}}\right)^{\Gamma}. \tag{14.15}$$

Entrepreneurs who aim to enter the capital market need to pay fixed R&D costs. At this point, the entrepreneur has not yet observed his productivity. Therefore, they do not know whether the variety design purchased from the R&D firm generates sufficient profits to cover the fixed costs. Therefore, this is an ex-ante expected cost. The entrepreneur who subtracts $\psi$ from $\psi_{L,t} < \psi < \overline{\psi}$ abandons the new entry because they cannot cover the fixed cost required to enter the local market. In this case, $1/G(\psi_{L,t}) = \left(\overline{\psi}/\psi_{L,t}\right)^{\Gamma}$ implies the number of trial-and-error attempts to develop a variety that can generate enough profit to cover fixed R&D costs. Entrepreneurs who aim to enter a local market can acquire the necessary variety if they can cover the fixed costs of $F_L/(2A_t)^{\varsigma}$. Entrepreneurs who subtract $\psi_{E,t} < \psi < \psi_{L,t}$, pay the fixed costs and enter the local market. In this case, $F_L$ holds. Entrepreneurs who draw $\psi$ in the range $0 < \psi < \psi_{E,t}$ can acquire the variety necessary to enter the export market by paying the additional fixed R&D cost, $F_E/(2A_t)^{\varsigma}$. This entrepreneur can earn enough profit to cover the fixed costs of entering the export market. In this case, $\left(\psi_{E,t}/\psi_{L,t}\right)^{\Gamma} = G\left(\psi_{E,t}\right)/G\left(\psi_{L,t}\right)$ implies that the expected profit is sufficient to develop the variety that allows the firm to enter the export market.

R&D firms develop new varieties of blueprints by investing labour. The development mechanism is defined as follows:

$$\dot{A}_t = \frac{(2A_t)^{\varsigma}}{\overline{F}} L_{A,t}. \tag{14.16}$$

### 14.2.6 Market

This economy has goods, capital and labour markets. The clearing conditions for the goods market are as follows:

$$\frac{E_t}{P_{M,t}} = \int_{\psi_E}^{\psi_L} \psi_j q_{L,j} A_t \frac{\tilde{g}(\psi)}{G(\psi_L)} d\psi + \int_{0}^{\psi_E} t\psi_j q_{E,j} A_t \frac{\tilde{g}(\psi)}{G(\psi_L)} d\psi, \tag{14.17}$$

where the RHS is equal to the labour demand in the goods sector, as follows:

$$L_{X,t} = \int_{\psi_E}^{\psi_L} \psi_j q_{L,j} A_t \frac{\tilde{g}(\psi)}{G(\psi_L)} d\psi + \int_{0}^{\psi_E} t\psi_j q_{E,j} A_t \frac{\tilde{g}(\psi)}{G(\psi_L)} d\psi.$$

The market clearing condition for the labour market is $L_t = L_{X,t} + L_{A,t}$. The market clearing condition for the capital market is (14.9).

## 14.3 Equilibrium

### 14.3.1 Dynamic System

In the BGP equilibrium, $r_t = \rho$ from the Euler equation. When $\psi_{L,t} = \psi_L$ and $\psi_{E,t} = \psi_E$ are satisfied, (14.13) and (14.15) show that $\overline{F}$, $\psi_L$ and $\psi_{E,t}$ are constant in the BGP equilibrium. Hence, there is a unique and symmetric steady-state equilibrium.

Relative R&D difficulty is defined as follows:

$$\Lambda_t \equiv \frac{A_t^{\varsigma}}{\left(\frac{L_t}{A_t}\right)} = \frac{A_t^{1-\varsigma}}{L_t}, \tag{14.18}$$

which is measured by a proportion of the degree of absolute R&D difficulty $A_t^{\varsigma}$ to the market share corresponding to each variety $L_t/A_t$. The increase in relative R&D difficulty implies an increase in the number of varieties. Logarithmising (14.18) gives $\log \Lambda_t = (1 - \varsigma) \log A_t - \log L_t$. By differentiating this equation with respect to time, we obtain $\dot{\Lambda}_t/\Lambda_t = (1 - \varsigma)g - n = 0$. From (14.16) and $g = n/(1 - \varsigma)$, we can derive the following expression for the economic growth rate:

$$g = \frac{\dot{A}_t}{A_t} = 2^{\varsigma} L_{A,t}\left(\frac{A_t^{1-\varsigma}}{F}\right) = \frac{n}{1-\varsigma}, \tag{14.19}$$

where, to guarantee a positive economic growth rate, $0 \leq \varsigma < 1$ is assumed. In this case, the scale effect disappears and the economic growth rate is proportional to the population growth rate.

### 14.3.2 Steady State

We derive the stationary value of this economy. By using $\Delta_t = \Delta$ and $\tilde{g}(\psi)/G(\psi_L)$, we can summarise (14.4) as follows:

$$P_M^{1-\sigma} = \int_0^{A_t} p_j^{1-\sigma} dj = \int_{\psi_E}^{\psi_L} p_L(\psi)^{1-\sigma} a_L \frac{\tilde{g}(\psi)}{G(\psi_L)} d\psi + \int_0^{\psi_E} p_E(\psi)^{1-\sigma} a_E \frac{\tilde{g}(\psi)}{G(\psi_L)} d\psi,$$

which is rewritten by using (14.7a) and (14.7b) as follows:

$$P_M = \frac{\sigma}{\sigma-1}\left(\frac{1}{\Delta A}\right)^{\frac{1}{\sigma-1}}, \tag{14.20}$$

where the price index falls because the supply of goods increases due to an improvement in average productivity.

By taking the time derivative of (14.5), we can assert that $\dot{A}/A = -\varsigma g$. Using $r_t = \rho$, $\dot{A}/A = -\varsigma g$ and (14.20), (14.11a) and (14.11b) can be rewritten as follows:

$$\frac{\frac{1}{\sigma}\frac{E}{\Delta}}{\rho+\varsigma g} = \left(\frac{\Delta F_L}{2^{\varsigma}}\right)L, \tag{14.21a}$$

and

$$\frac{\frac{1}{\sigma}\frac{E}{\Delta}}{\rho+\varsigma g} = \left(\frac{1}{\varphi}\right)\left(\frac{\Delta F_E}{2^{\varsigma}}\right)L, \tag{14.21b}$$

which are used to rewrite (14.13) as follows:

$$\frac{\frac{E}{\sigma}}{\rho+\varsigma g} = \left(\frac{\Delta F}{2^{\varsigma}}\right)L. \tag{14.22}$$

Substituting (14.8a) and (14.8b) into (14.14a) yields:

$$\int_{\psi_E}^{\psi_L} A\pi_L \frac{\tilde{g}(\psi)}{G(\psi_L)} d\psi + \int_0^{\psi_E} A\pi_E \frac{\tilde{g}(\psi)}{G(\psi_L)} d\psi = \frac{E}{\sigma}.$$

which is the aggregate dividend income. Using (14.17) and (14.20) yields $L_X = [(\sigma - 1)/\sigma]E$, which is used with $L = L_X + L_A$ to derive the following:

$$E = L + \tfrac{E}{\sigma} - L_I, \tag{14.23}$$

which states that the aggregate expenditure consists of aggregate labour income $L$, aggregate dividend income $E/\sigma$ and wage payments to the R&D sector $L_I$. Using (14.5), (14.16) and (14.18), the labour demand in the R&D sector is expressed as follows:

$$L_I = \tfrac{\overline{F}}{2^{\varsigma}}(\Lambda L)g. \tag{14.24}$$

### 14.3.3 Productivity, Exit and Entry

By rewriting (14.14a), we obtain the following:

$$\Delta = \frac{\frac{1}{\psi_L^{\sigma-1}}}{1 - \frac{\sigma-1}{\Gamma}}\left[1 + \varphi\left(\frac{\psi_L}{\psi_E}\right)^{\sigma-1-\Gamma}\right],$$

which is further rewritten as

$$\Delta = \tfrac{\kappa}{\kappa-1}\left(\tfrac{1}{\psi_L^{\sigma-1}}\right)(1+\Omega), \tag{14.25}$$

which are derived from (14.12), $\kappa \equiv \Gamma/(\sigma - 1) > 1$, $F_{EL} \equiv F_E/F_L$ and $\Omega \equiv \varphi^{\kappa}/F_{EL}^{\kappa-1} \in [0, 1]$. Note that $\kappa > 1$ is defined to guarantee a finite $\Delta$. At $\Omega = 0$, with $\varphi$ falling and $F_{EL}$ increasing, there is a pure exchange economy with no trade. However, at $\Omega = 1$, with $t = 1$ and $F_E = F_L$, there is a perfectly free trade economy. Here, $d\Delta/d\Omega = [\kappa/(\kappa - 1)]\big(1/\psi_L^{\sigma-1}\big) > 0$ implies that trade liberalisation improves average productivity through the entry and exit of firms. This is the cleansing effect of trade liberalisation in Gustafsson and Segerstrom (2010).

By using (14.12) and (14.25), (14.15) can be expressed as follows:

$$\overline{F} = F_L\left(\tfrac{\kappa}{\kappa-1}\right)(1+\Omega), \tag{14.26}$$

where, due to the cleansing effect of $\Omega$, fixed R&D costs increase, increasing the cost of new entry. From (14.5), $\overline{F}/\big(a_{L,t} + a_{E,t}\big)^{\varsigma} = \overline{F}/(2A_t)^{\varsigma}$. By substituting $E/\sigma$ in (14.22) and (14.24) into (14.23) and using $g = n/(1 - \varsigma)$, the aggregate expenditure is composed of labour income and dividend income as follows:

$$E = L\left[1 + \Lambda\overline{F}\tfrac{(\rho-n)}{(2A)^{\varsigma}}\right]. \tag{14.27}$$

Using (14.12), (14.15) and (14.25), the cut-off unit input requirement for selling in the local market is as follows:

$$\psi_L = \overline{\psi}\left[\left(\frac{F_I}{F_L}\right)\left(\frac{\kappa-1}{1+\Omega}\right)\right]^{\frac{1}{\Gamma}}, \tag{14.28}$$

where, as in $d\psi_L/d\Omega = -\psi_L[\Gamma/(1+\Omega)] < 0$, trade liberalisation lowers $\psi_L$. Trade liberalisation raises the fixed R&D cost in (14.26). The least productive local firm is no longer able to earn enough profit to cover this cost and exits the local market to become a non-producing firm.

By substituting (14.28) for (14.12), the cut-off unit input requirement for selling in the export market is as follows:

$$\psi_E = \overline{\psi}\left[\left(\frac{F_I}{F_E}\right)\left(\frac{\kappa-1}{\frac{1}{\Omega}+1}\right)\right]^{\frac{1}{\Gamma}}, \tag{14.29}$$

where, as in $d\psi_E/d\Omega = \psi_E[\Gamma/(1+\Omega)] > 0$, trade liberalisation raises $\psi_E$. Trade liberalisation raises the fixed R&D cost in (14.24). The most productive firm in the local market can bear the fixed R&D cost necessary for developing varieties in the export market. This firm enters the export market and becomes an export firm.

By substituting (14.28) for (14.25), we can derive the average productivity of the firm as follows:

$$\Delta = \frac{\kappa}{\kappa-1}\left[\left(\frac{1}{\overline{\psi}}\right)\left(\frac{F_L}{F_I}\right)\left(\frac{1}{\kappa-1}\right)\right]^{\frac{1}{\Gamma}}(1+\Omega)^{1+\frac{1}{\kappa}}, \tag{14.30}$$

where, as in $d\Delta/d\Omega = [1+(1/\kappa)][\Delta/(1+\Omega)] > 0$, trade liberalisation improves the productivity of the industry by encouraging the least productive local firms to exit and the most productive local firms to enter the export market.

By substituting (14.26) and (14.27) for (14.22), the relative R&D difficulty is derived as follows:

$$\Lambda = \frac{2\varsigma}{\overline{\Lambda}F_L}\left(\frac{\kappa-1}{\kappa}\right)\left(\frac{1}{1+\Omega}\right), \tag{14.31}$$

for $\overline{\Lambda} \equiv (\sigma-1)\rho+\sigma\varsigma g+n$. As in $d\Lambda/d\Omega = -\Lambda/(1+\Omega) < 0$, trade liberalisation lowers relative R&D difficulty because the incentive for R&D activities decreases due to the increase in fixed costs. Hence, the number of varieties decreases.

### *14.3.4 Welfare*

Here, $Q = C = cL = E/P_M$ is the welfare measure. By substituting (14.20) and (14.27) into $c = E/(P_M L)$, we obtain the following per capita consumption:

$$c = \left[1 + \Lambda\overline{F}\left(\frac{\rho - n}{2\varsigma}\right)\right]\left(\frac{\sigma - 1}{\sigma}\right)(\Delta A)^{\frac{1}{\sigma-1}},$$

which is rewritten with (14.26) and (14.31) as follows:

$$c = \left(1 + \tfrac{\rho-n}{\overline{\Lambda}}\right)\left(\tfrac{\sigma-1}{\sigma}\right)\left(\tfrac{L}{F_L\overline{\Lambda}}\right)^{\frac{1}{\sigma-1}}\frac{1}{\psi_L}, \tag{14.32}$$

where $\varsigma = 0$ is assumed to make the comparative static cleaner in subsequent analysis.

By using (14.25) and (14.32), (14.1) can be expressed as a welfare level as follows:

$$U = \frac{1}{\rho-n}\log\left[\frac{\left(1+\frac{\rho-n}{\overline{\Lambda}}\right)\left(\frac{\sigma-1}{\sigma}\right)\left(\frac{L}{F_L\overline{\Lambda}}\right)^{\frac{1}{\sigma-1}}}{\overline{\psi}\left[\left(\frac{F_I}{F_L}\right)\left(\frac{\kappa-1}{1+\Omega}\right)\right]^{\frac{1}{\Gamma}}}\right], \tag{14.33}$$

where, as in $dU/d\Omega = (dU/d\psi_L)(d\psi_L/d\Omega) > 0$, trade liberalisation improves the average productivity of the industry by allowing the least productive local firms to exit to increase goods supply. This increase causes the price index to fall, hence, welfare improves due to increased consumption.

## 14.4 The Case of Full Endogenous Growth

In the semi-endogenous growth model, the scale effect disappears, hence, the economic policy cannot affect the economic growth rate. The economic model in the previous section is re-constructed as a full endogenous growth model.

The development rate of variety in (14.16) is redefined as follows:

$$\dot{A}_t = \left(\tfrac{A_t}{\overline{F}}\right)L_{A,t}, \tag{14.34}$$

where $g = \dot{A}_t/A_t = L_{A,t}/\overline{F}$ holds. (14.11a), (14.11b) and (14.13) are rewritten as follows:

$$\frac{\frac{1}{\sigma}\left(\frac{\sigma-1}{\sigma}\right)^{\sigma-1}\left(\frac{P_{M,t}}{\psi_j}\right)^{\sigma-1}E_t}{r_t+\frac{\dot{A}_t}{A_t}} = \frac{F_L}{A_t}, \quad \frac{\frac{1}{\sigma}\left(\frac{\sigma-1}{\sigma}\right)^{\sigma-1}\left(\frac{P_{M,t}}{\psi_j}\right)^{\sigma-1}E_t}{r_t+\frac{\dot{A}_t}{A_t}} = \frac{1}{\varphi}\frac{F_E}{A_t},$$

and

$$\frac{\frac{1}{\sigma}\left(\frac{\sigma-1}{\sigma}\right)^{\sigma-1}P_{M,t}^{\sigma-1}\Delta_t E_t}{r_t+\frac{\dot{A}_t}{A_t}} = \frac{\overline{F}_t}{A_t},$$

which is further rewritten as follows:

$$\frac{\frac{1}{\sigma}\left(\frac{\sigma-1}{\sigma}\right)^{\sigma-1}\frac{E_t}{\Delta_t}}{\rho+g_t} = F_L, \quad \frac{\frac{1}{\sigma}\left(\frac{\sigma-1}{\sigma}\right)^{\sigma-1}\frac{E_t}{\Delta_t}}{\rho+g_t} = \frac{F_E}{\varphi}, \tag{14.35a}$$

and

$$\frac{\frac{E_t}{\sigma}}{\rho+g_t} = \overline{F}. \tag{14.35b}$$

When we substitute $L_t = L_{X,t} + L_{A,t}$ and $L_{X,t} = [(\sigma - 1)/\sigma]E_t$ into (14.34), we obtain $g_t = [L_t - [(\sigma - 1)/\sigma]E_t]/\overline{F}_t$. Substituting (14.35b) into $g_t$ gives the following economic growth rate:

$$g = \frac{1}{\sigma\overline{F}} - \left(\frac{\sigma-1}{\sigma}\right)\rho, \tag{14.36}$$

where the economic growth rate increases as fixed R&D costs decrease. Using (14.35b) and (14.36), we obtain $E = L + \rho\overline{F}$ as expenditure, whereby, household expenditure depends on labour income and dividend income. Substituting (14.26) into (14.36), the economic growth rate at equilibrium is derived as follows:

$$g = \frac{1}{\sigma F_L}\left(\frac{\kappa-1}{\kappa}\right)\left(\frac{1}{1+\Omega}\right) - \left(\frac{\sigma-1}{\sigma}\right)\rho, \tag{14.37}$$

where, as in $dg/d\Omega = -[1/(\sigma F_L)][(\kappa - 1)/\kappa]\left[1/(1 + \Omega)^2\right] < 0$, trade liberalisation increases fixed R&D costs and lowers economic growth rates.

## References


Gustafsson, P., & Segerstrom, P. (2010). Trade liberalization and productivity growth. *Review of International Economics*, 18(2), 207–228. https://doi.org/10.1111/j.1467-9396.2010.00878.x

Jones, C. I. (1995). Time series tests of endogenous growth models. *The Quarterly Journal of Economics*, 110(2), 495–525. https://doi.org/10.2307/2118448

Segerstrom, P. S. (1998). Endogenous growth without scale effects. *The American Economic Review*, 1290–1310. https://www.jstor.org/stable/116872

# Chapter 15
# Discriminatory Environmental Taxes and the Porter Hypothesis

**Abstract** In R&D-based heterogeneous firms, pollution emissions and a discriminatory environmental tax are introduced. The environmental tax affects firms' entry and exit. Trade environment policies affect total pollution emissions through scale, composition and reallocation effects. Increasing taxes on local firms has a non-monotonic effect on average productivity and pollution emissions due to firms exiting the local market and entering the export market. Increasing taxes on export firms has a non-monotonic effect due to firms entering the local market and exiting the export market. In a border tax adjustment (BTA) effect, where the tax rate for local firms is higher than for export firms, welfare improves due to a tax increase for local firms and deteriorates due to a tax increase for export firms. Due to the cleaning effect of trade liberalisation, the average productivity improves. However, due to the positive composition effect, trade liberalisation increases pollution. In the pollution haven effect, due to the negative reallocation effect, trade liberalisation reduces pollution. Therefore, trade liberalisation has a non-monotonic welfare effect. Regarding a uniform environmental tax, trade liberalisation has no effect on pollution emissions and a positive welfare effect. Based on these results, the relationship with the Porter hypothesis is explained.

## 15.1 Introduction

The introduction of border tax adjustments (BTA) within the EU is a concern because the impact on the global South is ignored (Eicke et al., 2021), a GDP decline is predicted in China and Turkey (Acar et al., 2022; Chen, 2023) and the burden of climate policy is imposed on developing countries (Cosbey et al., 2019). This BTA increases the leakage rate in China (Jakob et al., 2013) and in countries with a trade and economic structure similar to the trade model proposed by Melitz (2003) (Balistreri and Rutherford, 2012). Since it is a discriminatory environmental tax between firms, it has the potential to affect the entry and exit of firms and change the industrial structure. To analyse this impact, the heterogeneous firm model developed by Melitz (2003) is necessary.

 
Y. Hamaguchi, *Sustainable Development in Economic Growth Theory*,
https://doi.org/10.1007/978-981-96-7639-2_15

Careful empirical analysis is ongoing on the impact of environmental policies on corporate productivity. Environmental policies worsen corporate productivity in the short term, however, its statistical significance is low (Dechezleprêtre and Sato, 2017). The negative effect of pollution on productivity (Tang et al., 2015), the non-monotonic relationship between environmental policy and productivity (Yang et al., 2021), the positive effect of environmental policy on productivity (Jiang et al., 2023) and the welfare cost of emission allowance allocation (Dardati and Sayagili, 2020) have been identified. In contrast, Shapiro and Walker (2018) acknowledged that environmental tax increases reduced pollution, yet argued that their effect on productivity was minimal. Even in Europe and the United States, there is no evidence of productivity improvements due to strict environmental policies (Rubashkina et al., 2015). Hong et al. (2024) argued that the lowering of trade barriers increased pollution emissions. Cherniwchan et al. (2017) concluded that the statistical significance of the pollution haven effect was high, while the statistical significance of the pollution haven hypothesis remained low.

By applying Melitz (2003) to environmental economics, the impact of environmental policies on entry and exit (Andersen, 2018; Anouliès, 2017; Cherniwchan and Najjar, 2022; Konishi and Tarui, 2015), the impact of trade policies on firm productivity (Kreickemeier and Richter, 2014; LaPlue, 2019) and the relationship between trade policy and technology (Coria and Kyriakopoulou, 2018; Cui, 2017) have been analysed. By taking into account the reallocation effect in Cherniwchan et al. (2017), trade liberalisation leads to improvements in productivity and environmental quality (Kreickemeier and Richter, 2014; Levy and Dinopoulos, 2016; LaPlue, 2019). When pollution abatement by firms is taken into account, the impact of trade liberalisation on pollution can vary across countries (Forslid et al., 2018). However, none of the model analyses are based on an R&D-based growth model. An R&D-based heterogeneous firm model analyses the impact of environmental policies on the entry and exit of export firms and the average productivity of firms through innovation under international economic conditions, considering the mechanism of the Porter hypothesis more rigorously.

In Andersen (2018) and Cherniwchan and Najjar (2022), environmental policies encourage firms to exit, while in Konishi and Tarui (2015) and Anouliès (2017), the policies do not affect exit. Hamaguchi (2024b) pointed out that a uniform environmental tax can be converted into a unilateral environmental tax, which impacts the entry and exit of environmental policies. This discriminatory environmental tax decreases domestic pollution and negative leakage (Richter et al., 2021). The case of emissions trading was analysed by Hamaguchi (2024a). Therefore, in the heterogeneous firm model of Melitz (2003), discriminatory environmental taxes, such as BTA, affect pollution emissions through changes in industrial structure. Yomogida and Tarui (2013) analysed the welfare effects of BTA in an imperfect competition model, however, there is no analysis in a heterogeneous firm model. Therefore, the economic model in this chapter fills these gaps.

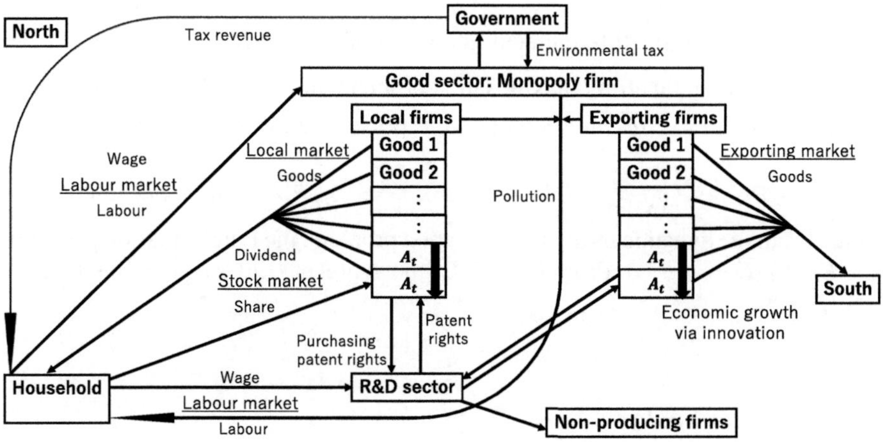


**Fig. 15.1** Structure of the R&D-based growth model with heterogenous polluting firms

## 15.2 The Model

### 15.2.1 Structure of R&D-Based Growth Model with Heterogenous Polluting Firms

In the economic model of Chap. 14, pollution emissions in the goods sector and a discriminatory environmental tax are introduced. Export and local firms in the goods sector emit pollution as a by-product. This pollution is reduced as the unit requirement of its production decreases. Households perceive a negative utility from this pollution emission. To internalise this negative externality, the government imposes a unilateral or uniform environmental tax on firms in the export and local sectors. This tax is distributed to households as lump-sum subsidies. Since this discriminatory environmental tax affects the entry and exit of firms, the environmental tax impacts the average productivity of firms. The other economic structure is the same as in Chap. 14. This economic structure is illustrated in Fig. 15.1.

### 15.2.2 Household

The utility function of a representative household at different times is as follows:

$$U_t = \int_0^{\infty} (\log Q_t - \eta_P \log P_t) e^{-(\rho - n)t} dt, \tag{15.1}$$

where the structure of differentiated goods is defined as $Q_t = \left(\int_0^{A_t} x_{j,t}^{\frac{\sigma-1}{\sigma}} dj\right)^{\frac{\sigma}{\sigma-1}}$ in (14.2). From the static utility maximisation problem, the demand function is derived as $x_{j,t} = \left(p_{j,t}^{-\sigma}/P_{M,t}^{1-\sigma}\right)\overline{E}_t$ in (14.3) and the price index of differentiated goods is defined as $P_{M,t} \equiv \left(\int_0^{A_t} p_{j,t}^{1-\sigma} dj\right)^{\frac{1}{1-\sigma}}$, where $c_t \equiv \overline{E}_t/P_{M,t}$ is the consumption per capita. From the dynamic utility maximisation problem, the Euler equation per capita is $\left(d\overline{E}_t/dt\right)/\overline{E}_t = r_t - \rho$. From $E_t = \overline{E}_t L_t$, the aggregate Euler equation is $\dot{E}_t/E_t = r_t - (\rho - n)$.

### 15.2.3 R&D Sector

R&D firms develop new varieties by hiring labour at an efficiency unit. Under the symmetric equilibrium, $a_{L,t} = a_{E,t} = A_t$, knowledge spillover in the R&D sector is defined as $1/\left(a_{L,t} + a_{E,t}\right)^{\varsigma} = 1/(2A_t)^{\varsigma}$ in (14.5). Henceforth, the variables for local and export firms are labelled $L$ and $E$, respectively. When developing a new variety for an export firm, there is an exogenous fixed cost of $F_E$ and, for a local firm, of $F_L$.

An entrepreneur who purchases blueprints from an R&D firm observes the unit input requirement $\psi$, which is the relevant cost of producing that variety. This entrepreneur subtracts $\psi$ from the probability density function $\tilde{g}(\psi)$ with support $\left[0, \overline{\psi}\right]$ and the corresponding cumulative distribution function $G(\psi)$. $\psi$ does not change over time. The probability density function of $\psi$ is assumed to have a Pareto distribution as follows:

$$G(\psi) = \int_0^{\psi} \tilde{g}(\psi) d\psi = \left(\frac{\psi}{\overline{\psi}}\right)^{\Gamma},$$

where $\Gamma$ is the shape parameter and $\overline{\psi}$ is the scale parameter of the distribution. Through this distribution, the types of firms are classified into non-producing firms in the range $\psi_{L,t} < \psi < \overline{\psi}$, local firms in the range $\psi_{E,t} < \psi < \psi_{L,t}$ and export firms in the range $0 < \psi < \psi_{E,t}$. The threshold value for $\psi$ is $0 < \psi_{E,t} < \psi_{L,t} < \overline{\psi}$.

### 15.2.4 Goods Sector

Local and export firms produce goods by inputting labour and pollution. The production technology is Cobb–Douglas technology. Here, $d_{L,t}$ and $d_{E,t}$ are the pollution input and $l_{L,j,t}^X$ and $l_{E,j,t}^X$ are the labour input of local and export firms, respectively. Hence, the production functions of the local and export firms are, respectively, $q_{j,t}^L = \left(d_{j,t}^L\right)^{\epsilon}\left(l_{L,j,t}^X\right)^{1-\epsilon}$ and $q_{j,t}^E = \left(d_{j,t}^E\right)^{\epsilon}\left(l_{E,j,t}^X\right)^{1-\epsilon}$, where $\epsilon \in (0, 1)$ and

$1 - \epsilon \in (0, 1)$ are the pollution and labour shares, respectively. The wage rate is numeraire, with w_t = 1. The variable cost functions of local and export firms are $C^L_{j,t} = l^X_{L,j,t} + \tau_L d^L_{j,t}$ and $C^E_{j,t} = l^X_{E,j,t} + \tau_E d^E_{j,t}$, where $\tau_L \in (0, 1)$ and $\tau_E \in (0, 1)$ are the environmental tax rates imposed on local and export firms, respectively.

For the cost minimisation problem, the variable production factor demands for pollution and labour in local and export firms are derived as follows:

$$d^L_{j,t} = \left[\frac{1}{\tau_L}\left(\frac{\epsilon}{1-\epsilon}\right)\right]^{1-\epsilon}\psi_j q^L_{j,t},\ l^X_{L,j,t} = \left[\frac{1}{\tau_L}\left(\frac{\epsilon}{1-\epsilon}\right)\right]^{-\epsilon}\psi_j q^L_{j,t}, \tag{15.2a}$$

and

$$d^E_{j,t} = \left[\frac{1}{\tau_E}\left(\frac{\epsilon}{1-\epsilon}\right)\right]^{1-\epsilon}\psi_j q^E_{j,t},\ l^X_{E,j,t} = \left[\frac{1}{\tau_E}\left(\frac{\epsilon}{1-\epsilon}\right)\right]^{-\epsilon}\psi_j q^E_{j,t}, \tag{15.2b}$$

which are used to derive $C^L_{j,t} = \left[\tau_L^\epsilon/\{\epsilon^\epsilon(1-\epsilon)^{1-\epsilon}\}\right]\psi_j q^L_{j,t}$ and $C^E_{j,t} = \left[\tau_E^\epsilon/\{\epsilon^\epsilon(1-\epsilon)^{1-\epsilon}\}\right]\psi_j q^E_{j,t}$. Note that $d^L_{j,t}/q^L_{j,t}$ in (15.a) and $d^E_{j,t}/q^E_{j,t}$ in (15.2b) are the pollution intensity specific to the firm. Keeping all factors constant, an increase in the environmental tax reduces pollution intensities through the effect of technology. Here, $\epsilon^\epsilon(1-\epsilon)^{1-\epsilon} \equiv \phi$ for $1/2 \le \phi < 1$ is assumed to derive $C^L_{j,t} = \left(\tau_L^\epsilon/\phi\right)\psi_j q^L_{j,t}$ and $C^E_{j,t} = \left(\tau_E^\epsilon/\phi\right)\psi_j q^E_{j,t}$.

Firms that enter the local market by subtracting $\psi_{E,t} < \psi \le \psi_{L,t}$, determine the price that maximises profit, given the demand for goods in (14.3), as follows:

$$\max_{p^L_{j,t}} \pi^L_{j,t} \equiv \left[p^L_{j,t} - \left(\frac{\tau_L^\epsilon}{\phi}\right)\psi_j\right]q^L_{j,t}, \tag{15.3a}$$

and the first-order condition for profit maximisation yields the following:

$$p^L_{j,t} = \frac{\sigma}{\sigma-1}\left(\frac{\tau_L^\epsilon}{\phi}\right)\psi_j, \tag{15.4a}$$

where the environmental tax is passed on in the price. By substituting (15.4a) for (15.3a), the optimal profit of the local firm is as follows:

$$\pi^L_{j,t} = \frac{1}{\sigma}\left(\frac{\sigma-1}{\sigma}\right)^{\sigma-1}\left(\frac{\phi}{\tau_L^\epsilon}\right)^{\sigma-1}\left(\frac{P_{M,t}}{\psi_j}\right)^{\sigma-1}E_t, \tag{15.5a}$$

where, since the unit requirement of its production is passed on in price, the profits of local firms decrease.

Firms that enter the export market by subtracting $0 < \psi < \psi_{E,t}$, determine the price that maximises profits, given the demand for the good in (14.3), as follows:

$$\max_{p^E_{j,t}} \pi^E_{j,t} \equiv \left[p^E_{j,t} - \left(\frac{t\tau_E^\epsilon}{\phi}\right)\psi_j\right]q^E_{j,t}, \tag{15.3b}$$

where export firms incur $t > 0$ iceberg-shaped transportation costs. The first-order condition for profit maximisation yields the following:

$$p_{j,t}^{E} = \frac{\sigma}{\sigma-1}\left(\frac{t\tau_{E}^{\epsilon}}{\phi}\right)\psi_{j}, \tag{15.4b}$$

where the transportation costs are passed on to the price. Substituting (15.4b) for (15.3b), the optimal profit for the export firm is as follows:

$$\pi_{j,t}^{E} = \frac{\varphi}{\sigma}\left(\frac{\sigma-1}{\sigma}\right)^{\sigma-1}\left(\frac{\phi}{\tau_{E}^{\epsilon}}\right)^{\sigma-1}\left(\frac{P_{M,t}}{\psi_{j}}\right)^{\sigma-1}E_{t}, \tag{15.5b}$$

where $\varphi \equiv (1/t)^{\sigma-1}$ measure the degree of trade liberalisation.

### 15.2.5 Market Entry

Firm profits determine whether to enter the local or export market. Since these profits depend on $\psi_j$, in the stock market, firm value is related to the threshold values of $\psi = \psi_L$ and $\psi = \psi_E$. Firm value is the sum of the discounted present value of profits from period $t$ onwards, $P_{A,t}^{L} = \int_{t}^{\infty} e^{-[r(\iota)-r(t)]}\pi_{\iota,L}d\iota$ and $P_{A,t}^{E} = \int_{t}^{\infty} e^{-[r(\iota)-r(t)]}\pi_{\iota,E}d\iota$. By time differentiating $P_{A,t}^{L}$ and $P_{A,t}^{E}$, respectively, we obtain the no arbitrage condition as $\pi_{L,t}(\psi_L) + \dot{P}_{A,t}^{L}(\psi_L) = r_t P_{A,t}^{L}(\psi_L)$ and $\pi_{E,t}(\psi_E) + \dot{P}_{A,t}^{E}(\psi_E) = r_t P_{A,t}^{E}(\psi_E)$, which is rewritten as $P_{A,t}^{L}(\psi_L) = \pi_{L,t}(\psi_L)/\left\{r_t - \left[\dot{P}_{A,t}^{L}(\psi_L)/P_{A,t}^{L}(\psi_L)\right]\right\}$ and $P_{A,t}^{E}(\psi_E) = \pi_{E,t}(\psi_E)/\left\{r_t - \left[\dot{P}_{A,t}^{L}(\psi_L)/P_{A,t}^{L}(\psi_L)\right]\right\}$ in (14.9).

The blueprints for varieties that cater to the local and the export markets are developed by R&D firms. Entrepreneurs who draw $\psi = \psi_L$, purchase the blueprints for the local market, while entrepreneurs who draw $\psi = \psi_E$, purchase the blueprints for the export market. From the free entry condition, the stock prices of local and export firms are, respectively, $P_{A,t}^{L} = F_L/(2A_t)^{\varsigma}$ and $P_{A,t}^{E} = F_E/(2A_t)^{\varsigma}$, where $P_{A,t}^{E} > P_{A,t}^{L}$ for $F_E > F_L$.

By substituting (15.5a) and (14.10) into (14.9), the conditions for free entry in the local market are derived as follows:

$$\frac{\frac{1}{\sigma}\left(\frac{\sigma-1}{\sigma}\right)^{\sigma-1}\left(\frac{\phi}{\tau_{L}^{\epsilon}}\right)^{\sigma-1}\left(\frac{P_{M,t}}{\psi_{j}}\right)^{\sigma-1}E_{t}}{r_{t}+\varsigma\frac{\dot{A}_{t}}{A_{t}}} = \frac{F_{L}}{(2A_{t})^{\varsigma}}, \tag{15.6a}$$

which is derived from $\dot{P}_{A,t}^{L}(\psi_L)/P_{A,t}^{L}(\psi_L) = \varsigma\left(\dot{A}_t/A_t\right)$. By substituting (14.9) into (15.5b) and (14.10), the conditions for free entry into the export market are derived as follows:

$$\frac{\frac{1}{\sigma}\left(\frac{\sigma-1}{\sigma}\right)^{\sigma-1}\left(\frac{\phi}{\tau_{E}^{\epsilon}}\right)^{\sigma-1}\left(\frac{P_{M,t}}{\psi_{j}}\right)^{\sigma-1}E_{t}}{r_{t}+\varsigma\frac{\dot{A}_{t}}{A_{t}}} = \frac{1}{\varphi}\cdot\frac{F_{E}}{(2A_{t})^{\varsigma}}. \tag{15.6b}$$

By using (15.6a), (15.6b) and $F_E > F_L$, the productivity gap between local and export firms can be expressed as follows:

$$\frac{\psi_{L,t}}{\psi_{E,t}} = \left(\frac{\tau_E}{\tau_L}\right)^{\epsilon}\left(\frac{F_E}{\varphi F_L}\right)^{\frac{\sigma}{\sigma-1}} > 1, \tag{15.7}$$

for all $\varphi \in (0, 1)$. Note that a uniform environmental tax of $\tau_L = \tau_E$ has no effect on productivity gap, as in Konishi and Tarui (2015). In contrast, a unilateral environmental tax of $\tau_L \neq \tau_E$ has effects on the gap and the discriminatory environmental tax plays a decisive role in the distribution of corporate productivity.

### *15.2.6 Incentives of Innovation*

The incentive to develop new varieties is determined by the conditions of free entry into local and export markets. The expected benefits of developing new varieties are equal to the fixed R&D costs for new varieties:

$$\int_{\psi_{E,t}}^{\psi_{L,t}}\left[\frac{\pi_{L,t}(\psi_L)}{r_t + \varsigma\frac{\dot{A}_t}{A_t}} - \frac{F_L}{(2A_t)^{\varsigma}}\right]dG(\psi) + \int_{0}^{\psi_{E,t}}\left[\frac{\pi_{E,t}(\psi_E)}{r_t + \varsigma\frac{\dot{A}_t}{A_t}} - \frac{F_E}{(2A_t)^{\varsigma}}\right]dG(\psi) = \frac{F_I}{A_t},$$

which is rewritten by using (15.5a) and (15.5b) as $\left[(1/\sigma)\{(\sigma-1)/\sigma\}P_{M,t}^{\sigma-1}\Delta_t E_t\right]/\left[r_t + \varsigma(\dot{A}_t/A_t)\right] = \overline{F}_t/A_t$ in (14.13), where $\Delta_t$ is defined as follows:

$$\Delta_t \equiv \int_{\psi_{E,t}}^{\psi_{L,t}}\left(\frac{1}{\psi}\right)^{\sigma-1}\frac{\tilde{g}(\psi)}{G(\psi_{L,t})}d\psi + \varphi\int_{0}^{\psi_{E,t}}\left(\frac{1}{\psi}\right)^{\sigma-1}\frac{\tilde{g}(\psi)}{G(\psi_{L,t})}d\psi, \tag{14.4a}$$

which is the weighted average of the firms' productivity. Furthermore, $\overline{F}_t$ is defined as the following ex-ante fixed expected cost of developing varieties:

$$\overline{F}_t \equiv F_I\frac{1}{G(\psi_{L,t})} + F_L + F_E\frac{G(\psi_{E,t})}{G(\psi_{L,t})},$$

which is further rewritten with the properties of the Pareto distribution as:

$$\overline{F}_t \equiv F_I\left(\frac{\overline{\psi}}{\psi_{L,t}}\right)^{\Gamma} + F_L + F_E\left(\frac{\psi_{E,t}}{\psi_{L,t}}\right)^{\Gamma}, \tag{14.15}$$

The blueprint for a new variety is developed by the labour input of R&D firms as $\dot{A}_t = \left[(2A_t)^{\varsigma}/\overline{F}\right]L_{A,t}$ in (14.16).

### 15.2.7 Market

This economy has goods, capital and labour market. The clearing conditions for the goods market are as follows:

$$\frac{E_t}{P_{M,t}} = \int_{\psi_E}^{\psi_L} \psi_j q_{L,j} A_t \frac{\tilde{g}(\psi)}{G(\psi_L)} d\psi + \int_0^{\psi_E} t\psi_j q_{E,j} A_t \frac{\tilde{g}(\psi)}{G(\psi_L)} d\psi = L_{X,t}, \tag{15.8}$$

where the RHS is equal to the labour demand in the goods sector. The market clearing condition for the labour market is $L_t = L_{X,t} + L_{A,t}$ and for the capital market is (14.9).

## 15.3 Equilibrium

### 15.3.1 Dynamic System

In the BGP equilibrium, $r_t = \rho$ holds from the Euler equation. When $\psi_{L,t} = \psi_L$ and $\psi_{E,t} = \psi_E$ are satisfied, (14.13) and (14.15) show that $\overline{F}$, $\psi_L$, and $\psi_{E,t}$ are constant in the BGP equilibrium. In this case, there is a unique and symmetric steady-state equilibrium. Relative R&D difficulty is defined as $\Lambda_t \equiv A_t^{\varsigma}/[L_t/A_t] = A_t^{1-\varsigma}/L_t$ in (14.18). As explained in the Chap. 14, the economic growth rate is $g = \dot{A}_t/A_t = n/(1-\varsigma) > 0$ for $0 \leq \varsigma < 1$.

### 15.3.2 Steady State

We derive the steady-state values in this economy. By using $\Delta_t = \Delta$ and $\tilde{g}(\psi)/G(\psi_L)$, (14.4) is aggregated as follows:

$$P_M^{1-\sigma} = \int_0^{A_t} p_j^{1-\sigma} dj = \int_{\psi_E}^{\psi_L} p_L(\psi)^{1-\sigma} a_L \frac{\tilde{g}(\psi)}{G(\psi_L)} d\psi + \int_0^{\psi_E} p_E(\psi)^{1-\sigma} a_E \frac{\tilde{g}(\psi)}{G(\psi_L)} d\psi,$$

which is rewritten by using (15.4a) and (15.4b) as $P_M = [\sigma/(\sigma-1)][1/(\Delta A)]^{1/\sigma-1}$ in (14.20). Using $r_t = \rho$, $\dot{A}/A = -\varsigma g$ and (14.20), (15.6a) and (15.6b) are rewritten as follows:

$$\frac{\frac{1}{\sigma}\left(\frac{\phi}{\tau_L^{\epsilon}}\right)^{\sigma-1}\left(\frac{E}{\Delta}\right)}{\rho+\varsigma g} = \left(\frac{\Lambda F_L}{2^{\varsigma}}\right)L, \tag{15.9a}$$

and

$$\frac{\frac{1}{\sigma}\left(\frac{\phi}{\tau_E^{\epsilon}}\right)^{\sigma-1}\left(\frac{E}{\Delta}\right)}{\rho+\varsigma g} = \left(\frac{1}{\varphi}\right)\left(\frac{\Lambda F_E}{2^{\varsigma}}\right)L, \tag{15.9b}$$

which are used to rewrite (14.13) as $(E/\sigma)/(\rho + \varsigma g) = \left[\left(\Lambda\overline{F}\right)/2^{\varsigma}\right]L$ in (14.22).

Substituting (14.8a) and (14.8b) into (14.14a) yields the following:

$$\int_{\psi_E}^{\psi_L} A\pi_L \frac{\tilde{g}(\psi)}{G(\psi_L)} d\psi + \int_0^{\psi_E} A\pi_E \frac{\tilde{g}(\psi)}{G(\psi_L)} d\psi = \frac{E}{\sigma}.$$

which is the aggregate dividend income. Using (15.8) and (14.20) yields $L_X = [(\sigma - 1)/\sigma]E$, which is used with $L = L_X + L_A$ to derive $E = L + (E/\sigma) - L_I$ in (14.23), where the aggregate expenditure consists of aggregate labour income $L$, aggregate dividend income $E/\sigma$ and wage payments to the R&D sector $L_I$. Using (14.5), (14.16) and (14.18), the labour demand in the R&D sector is expressed as $L_I = \left(\overline{F}/2^{\varsigma}\right)(\Lambda L)g$ in (14.24).

### 15.3.3 Productivity, Exit and Entry

By rewriting (14.14a), we obtain the following:

$$\Delta = \frac{\frac{1}{\psi_L^{\sigma-1}}}{1 - \frac{\sigma-1}{\Gamma}}\left[\left(\frac{\phi}{\tau_L^{\epsilon}}\right)^{\sigma-1} + \varphi\left(\frac{\phi}{\tau_E^{\epsilon}}\right)^{\sigma-1}\left(\frac{\psi_L}{\psi_E}\right)^{\sigma-1-\Gamma}\right],$$

which is further rewritten as:

$$\Delta = \frac{\kappa}{\kappa-1}\left(\frac{1}{\psi_L}\right)^{\sigma-1}\left(\frac{\phi}{\tau_L^{\epsilon}}\right)^{\sigma-1}\left(1 + \overline{\Omega}\right), \tag{15.10}$$

for $\overline{\Omega} \equiv (\tau_L/\tau_E)^{\epsilon\Gamma}\Omega$ and (15.7). $\kappa \equiv \Gamma/(\sigma - 1) > 1$, $F_{EL} \equiv F_E/F_L$, and $\Omega \equiv \varphi^{\kappa}/F_{EL}^{\kappa-1} \in [0, 1]$ are used to derive (15.10). There is a pure exchange economy with no trade in $\Omega = 0$ and a completely free trade economy in $\Omega = 1$. Here, $d\Delta/d\Omega = [\kappa/(\kappa - 1)]\left(1/\psi_L^{\sigma-1}\right)\left(\phi/\tau_L^{\epsilon}\right)^{\sigma-1}\partial\overline{\Omega}/\partial\Omega > 0$ implies that a cleansing effect of trade liberalisation is enhanced by a differentiated environmental tax policy of $(\tau_L/\tau_E)^{\epsilon\Gamma}$. In addition, environmental taxes on local firms and environmental tax cuts for export firms improve their average productivity. Hence, discriminatory environmental taxes affect the entry and exit of firms. In $\tau_L = \tau_E$, these effects disappear.

Using (15.7) and (15.10), (14.15) can be expressed as follows:

$$\overline{F} = F_L\left(\frac{\kappa}{\kappa-1}\right)\left(1 + \overline{\Omega}\right), \tag{15.11}$$

where the environmental tax increase for local firms and decrease for export firms increase the cost of new market entry due to the increase in fixed R&D costs caused by the cleansing effect of $\overline{\Omega}$. From (14.5), we obtain $\overline{F}/\left(a_{L,t}+a_{E,t}\right)^{\varsigma}=\overline{F}/(2A_t)^{\varsigma}$. By substituting $E/\sigma$ in (14.22), (14.24) into (14.23) and $g=n/(1-\varsigma)$ in (14.23), the aggregate expenditure becomes $E=L\left[1+\left\{\Lambda\overline{F}(\rho-n)\right\}/(2A)^{\varsigma}\right]$ in (14.27).

Using (15.7), (14.15) and (15.10), the cut-off unit input requirement of selling in the local market is as follows:

$$\psi_L=\overline{\psi}\left[\left(\tfrac{F_I}{F_L}\right)\left(\tfrac{\kappa-1}{1+\overline{\Omega}}\right)\right]^{\frac{1}{\Gamma}}, \tag{15.12}$$

where, as in $d\psi_L/d\tau_L=-\psi_L\left[1/\Gamma\left(1+\overline{\Omega}\right)\right]\left(\partial\overline{\Omega}/\partial\tau_L\right)<0$ and $d\psi_L/d\tau_E=-\psi_L\left[1/\Gamma\left(1+\overline{\Omega}\right)\right]\left(\partial\overline{\Omega}/\partial\tau_E\right)>0$, the environmental tax on local firms and the environmental tax cut on export firms lowers $\psi_L$. These raise the fixed R&D cost in (15.11). The least productive local firms are unable to earn enough profit to cover these costs and exit the local market and become unproductive firms.

By substituting (15.12) for (15.7), the cut-off unit input requirement of selling in the export market is as follows:

$$\psi_E=\overline{\psi}\left[\left(\tfrac{F_I}{F_E}\right)\left(\tfrac{\kappa-1}{\frac{1}{\overline{\Omega}}+1}\right)\right]^{\frac{1}{\Gamma}}, \tag{15.13}$$

where, as in $d\psi_E/d\tau_L=\psi_E[1/\Gamma(1+\Omega)]\left(\partial\overline{\Omega}/\partial\tau_L\right)>0$ and $d\psi_E/d\tau_E=\psi_E[1/\Gamma(1+\Omega)]\left(\partial\overline{\Omega}/\partial\tau_E\right)<0$, environmental tax increases for local firms and decreases for export firms raise $\psi_E$. These raise the fixed R&D costs in (15.11). The most productive local firm in the local market can bear the fixed costs necessary for developing varieties in the export market. It enters the export market and becomes an export firm.

By substituting (15.12) for (15.10), we can derive the following average productivity for the firm:

$$\Delta=\tfrac{\kappa}{\kappa-1}\left[\left(\tfrac{1}{\overline{\psi}}\right)\left(\tfrac{F_L}{F_I}\right)\left(\tfrac{1}{\kappa-1}\right)\right]^{\frac{1}{\Gamma}}\left(\tfrac{\phi}{\tau_L^{\epsilon}}\right)^{\sigma-1}\left(1+\overline{\Omega}\right)^{1+\frac{1}{\kappa}}, \tag{15.14}$$

where, as in $d\Delta/d\tau_L=[1+(1/\kappa)]\left[\Delta/\left(1+\overline{\Omega}\right)\right]\left(\partial\overline{\Omega}/\partial\tau_L\right)>0$ and $d\Delta/d\tau_E=[1+(1/\kappa)]\left[\Delta/\left(1+\overline{\Omega}\right)\right]\left(\partial\overline{\Omega}/\partial\tau_E\right)<0$, environmental tax increases on local firms and tax cuts on export firms improve the industry's productivity by encouraging the least productive local firms to exit and the most productive local firms to enter the export market. However, environmental tax increases on local firms worsen the productivity of the industry as a whole through the deterioration of the productivity of local firms.

By substituting (15.11) and (14.27) for (14.22), the relative R&D difficulty is derived as follows:

$$\Lambda = \frac{2\varsigma}{\overline{\Lambda} F_L}\left(\frac{\kappa-1}{\kappa}\right)\left(\frac{1}{1+\overline{\Omega}}\right), \tag{15.15}$$

for $\overline{\Lambda} \equiv (\sigma-1)\rho + \sigma\varsigma g + n$. As in $d\Lambda/d\tau_L = -[\Lambda/(1+\Omega)](\partial\overline{\Omega}/\partial\tau_L) < 0$ and $d\Lambda/d\tau_E = -[\Lambda/(1+\Omega)](\partial\overline{\Omega}/\partial\tau_E) > 0$, the environmental tax increase on local firms and decrease on export firms reduce the relative R&D difficulty and the number of varieties. This is because the incentive for R&D activities decreases due to the increase in fixed costs.

### *15.3.4 Pollution*

From (15.2a) and (15.2b), the pollution emitted by local firms producing variety $j$ and export firms can be expressed as follows:

$$\begin{aligned} d_{L,j} &= \frac{\phi^{\sigma-1}}{\tau_L^{\epsilon(\sigma-1)+1}}\left(\frac{\sigma-1}{\sigma}\right)\left(\frac{1}{\psi_j}\right)^{\sigma-1}\frac{E}{A\Delta}, \\ d_{E,j} &= \frac{\varphi}{t}\left(\frac{\phi^{\sigma-1}}{\tau_L^{\epsilon(\sigma-1)+1}}\right)\left(\frac{\sigma-1}{\sigma}\right)\left(\frac{1}{\psi_j}\right)^{\sigma-1}\frac{E}{A\Delta}, \end{aligned} \tag{15.16}$$

and the aggregation of these firm-level pollution emissions makes the following points:

$$P = \int_{\psi_E}^{\psi_L} A d_{L,j}\frac{\tilde{g}(\psi)}{G(\psi_L)}d\psi + \int_0^{\psi_E} A d_{E,j}\frac{\tilde{g}(\psi)}{G(\psi_L)}d\psi,$$

which is rewritten with (15.16) as follows:

$$P = E\left(\frac{\sigma-1}{\sigma}\right)\frac{\frac{1}{\tau_L}+\frac{\overline{\Omega}}{\tau_E}}{1+\overline{\Omega}}, \tag{15.17}$$

which is dependent on three effects. First, the term $E[(\sigma-1)/\sigma]$ is a scale effect, implying an increase in pollution associated with increased expenditure and production. Second, the term $(1/\tau_L)+(\overline{\Omega}/\tau_E)$ is a composition effect in Copeland and Taylor (2004) and Grossman and Kruger (1993), whereby, structural changes between industries with different pollution intensities affect pollution emissions. Third, the effect of $1+\overline{\Omega}$ is the reallocation effect in Cherniwchan et al. (2017) and Kreickemeier and Richter (2014) and the improvement in average productivity reduces pollution emissions by reallocating resources from low-productivity local firms to high-productivity export firms.

As can be seen from substituting (15.11) and (15.15) into $E = L\left[1+\left\{\Lambda\overline{F}(\rho-n)\right\}/(2A)^{\varsigma}\right]$ in (14.27), $\overline{\Omega}$ is not included in expenditure. Therefore, trade environment policies do not affect pollution emissions through the scale effect. However, composition and reallocation effects depend on the indirect effects of $\overline{\Omega}$ in addition to the direct effects of environmental taxes. Therefore, depending on which effect dominates, environmental taxes have a non-monotonic effect on total pollution emissions.

The following is obtained by dividing (15.16) into local and export firms and tabulating them:

$$P_L = \int_{\psi_E}^{\psi_L} Ad_{L,j}\frac{\tilde{g}(\psi)}{G(\psi_L)}d\psi,\ P_E = \int_{0}^{\psi_E} Ad_{E,j}\frac{\tilde{g}(\psi)}{G(\psi_L)}d\psi,$$

which is rewritten with (15.16) as follows:

$$P_L = E\left(\frac{\sigma-1}{\sigma}\right)\frac{\frac{1}{\tau_L}}{1+\overline{\Omega}},\ P_E = E\left(\frac{\sigma-1}{\sigma}\right)\frac{\frac{\overline{\Omega}}{\tau_E}}{1+\overline{\Omega}},$$

which is further used to derive the following amount of pollution emitted by export firms as a proportion of the total pollution emitted by local firms:

$$\tfrac{P_E}{P_L} = \left(\tfrac{\tau_L}{\tau_E}\right)^{1+\epsilon\Gamma}\overline{\Omega}, \tag{15.18}$$

which depends only on the reallocation effect.

### 15.3.5 Welfare

The per capita consumption obtained by substituting (14.20) and (14.27) into $c = E/(P_M L)$ can be rewritten as follows using (15.10), (15.11), and (15.15):

$$c = \left(1 + \tfrac{\rho-n}{\overline{\Lambda}}\right)\left(\tfrac{\sigma-1}{\sigma}\right)\left(\tfrac{L}{F_L\overline{\Lambda}}\right)^{\frac{1}{\sigma-1}}\tfrac{\phi}{\tau_L^{\epsilon}\psi_L}, \tag{15.19}$$

where $\varsigma = 0$ is assumed to make comparative static cleaner in subsequent analysis. Note that the positive cleansing effect of $\overline{\Omega}$ on $\overline{F}$ in (15.11) and the negative cleansing effect of $\overline{\Omega}$ on $\Lambda$ in (15.15) cancel each other out. Therefore, under $\varsigma = 0$, trade environment policies affect consumption only through the price effect of $\Delta$ average productivity on $P_M$.

Using (15.11), (15.17) and (15.19), we can express (14.1) in terms of the following welfare level:

$$U = \tfrac{1}{\rho-n}\left(\log\hat{c} - \eta_P\log\hat{P}\right) + \tfrac{\sigma-\eta_P(\sigma-1)}{(\sigma-1)(\rho-n)}L_0, \tag{15.20}$$

for

$$\hat{c} = \frac{\left(1+\frac{\rho-n}{\overline{\Lambda}}\right)\left(\frac{\sigma-1}{\sigma}\right)\left(\frac{L}{F_L\overline{\Lambda}}\right)^{\frac{1}{\sigma-1}}\left(\frac{\phi}{\tau_L^{\epsilon}}\right)}{\overline{\psi}\left[\left(\frac{F_I}{F_L}\right)\left(\frac{\kappa-1}{1+\overline{\Omega}}\right)\right]^{\frac{1}{\Gamma}}}, \quad \hat{P} = \left(1+\frac{\rho-n}{\overline{\Lambda}}\right)\frac{\frac{1}{\tau_L}+\frac{\overline{\Omega}}{\tau_E}}{1+\overline{\Omega}},$$

where trade environment policies have a non-monotonic effect on welfare through the improvement of utility due to increased consumption and the deterioration of utility due to pollution emissions.

## 15.4 Comparative Statics

### *15.4.1 Increasing of Environmental Tax on Local Firms*

Under a discriminatory environmental tax rate, the impact of the environmental tax on the economy and the environment varies depending on whether the environmental tax rate is greater for local or export firms. Henceforth, we call the case where $\tau_E > \tau_L$ the pollution haven effect and the case where $\tau_E < \tau_L$ the BTA effect. The reason for considering $\tau_E < \tau_L$as BTA is in accordance with Sanctuary (2018). The case where $\tau = \tau_E = \tau_L$ is a uniform environmental tax.

So far and in Appendix N, the effect of raising the environmental tax on local firms on the steady state is shown as follows:

$$\frac{d\psi_L}{d\tau_L} < 0, \quad \frac{d\psi_E}{d\tau_L} > 0, \quad \frac{d\Lambda}{d\tau_L} < 0, \quad \frac{dc}{d\tau_L} > 0, \quad \frac{dP}{d\tau_L} \gtreqless 0,$$

for $\tau_L \gtreqless \tau_E$ ands

$$\frac{d\Delta}{d\tau_L} \gtreqless 0,$$

for

$$\tau_L \gtreqless \left(\frac{1}{\kappa}\right)^{\frac{1}{\epsilon\Gamma}} \frac{\tau_E}{\Omega^{1/\epsilon\Gamma}} \equiv \tilde{\tau}_L,$$

where, although an environmental tax on local firms may have a non-monotonic effect on consumption, only a monotonic effect is shown due to analytical complexity.

In (15.4a), the environmental tax on local firms is passed on to prices. Keeping all factors constant, in (15.5a), profits decrease due to a decline in sales. In (15.6a), entrepreneurs aiming to enter the local market find it more difficult to purchase blueprints due to a decline in sales. In (15.11), a cleansing effect of $\overline{\Omega}$ increases the fixed R&D cost, therefore, the cost of new entry increases. Entrepreneurs who cannot bear the fixed cost give up on new entry and become non-productive firms. Hence, in (15.7), the productivity of local firms decreases. The profits of export firms are higher than local firms, therefore, they can bear the fixed R&D cost. Due to the decline in productivity of local firms, the productivity of export firms increases in (14.15). As a result, the relative R&D difficulty and the number of varieties decrease due to the increase in fixed costs.

In (15.14), this environmental policy improves the average productivity of the entire industry through a cleansing effect of $\overline{\Omega}$ under $\tau_L > \tilde{\tau}_L$ to encourage the exit of low-productivity local firms and the entry of high-productivity local firms into export markets. However, as the number of unproductive firms increases due to the deterioration of productivity among local firms, the average productivity of all firms may deteriorate. When the productivity improvement effect of the former dominates the productivity deterioration effect of the latter, the environmental policy deteriorates the average productivity of the industry when $\tau_L \leq \tilde{\tau}_L$. In this case, from $d\overline{\Omega}/d\tau_E > 0$ and $d\overline{\Omega}/d\Omega < 0$, the environmental tax on local firms has a greater effect on improving productivity, as the environmental tax on the export sector and trade liberalisation strengthen the cleansing effect of $\overline{\Omega}$.

Consumption depends on expenditure and the price index, however, the positive and negative effects of trade environment policy on consumption through expenditure cancel each other out. Therefore, the non-monotonic effect of environmental taxes on local firms' average productivity has a non-monotonic effect on consumption. In (15.19), an increase in environmental taxes on local firms improves average productivity through a cleansing effect of $\overline{\Omega}$. The price index falls in (14.20) due to an increase in the quantity of goods produced. This positive price effect increases household consumption and improves welfare.

The impact of environmental taxes on local firms' total pollution emissions depends on the positive composition effect and negative reallocation effect. The cleansing effect of $\tau_L$ on $\overline{\Omega}$ increases total pollution emissions due to the pollution intensity of export firms increasing as a result of the increase in production. The exit of local firms with low productivity reduces the total amount of pollution emitted, as local firms become less pollution-intensive. However, the improvement in average productivity due to the cleansing effect of $\tau_L$ on $\overline{\Omega}$ reduces pollution by reallocating resources from companies with low productivity to companies with high productivity.

In the BTA effect, when $\tau_E < \tau_L$, the positive composition effect dominates the negative reallocation effect, hence, total pollution emissions increase. In the pollution haven effect, when $\tau_E > \tau_L$, the negative reallocation effect dominates the positive composition effect, hence, total pollution emissions are reduced. Local firms' environmental taxes have a U-shaped effect on pollution. The environmental tax increase for export firms has a negative composition effect due to the deterioration of average productivity, therefore, complements the pollution reduction effect of the environmental tax on local firms. Here, $d\Delta/d\tau_L > 0$ in $\tau_L > \tilde{\tau}_L$ and $dP/d\tau_L < 0$ in $\tau_E > \tau_L$ are compatible. In this case, the environmental tax on local companies leads to a reduction in pollution through average productivity and the Porter hypothesis is implied. However, since the number of varieties decreases due to $d\Lambda/d\tau_L < 0$, it is not the Porter hypothesis through innovation.

Based on the above results, the environmental tax on local firms within the following tax rate range results in several relationships between average productivity and total pollution emissions. The trade-off between productivity deterioration and pollution reduction in $\tilde{\tau}_L > \tau_E > \tau_L$ and $\tau_E > \tilde{\tau}_L > \tau_L$, the trade-off relationship between productivity improvement and pollution expansion in $\tau_L > \tilde{\tau}_L > \tau_E$ and $\tau_L > \tau_E > \tilde{\tau}_L$, the lose-lose relationship between productivity deterioration and pollution expansion in $\tilde{\tau}_L > \tau_L > \tau_E$ and the win–win relationship between productivity improvement and pollution reduction in $\tau_E > \tau_L > \tilde{\tau}_L$.

In $\tilde{\tau}_L > \tau_E$, it is difficult to achieve productivity improvement and pollution reduction through environmental taxation on local firms. In this case, $\tilde{\tau}_L \gtreqless \tau_E$ is rewritten as $1/\kappa \gtreqless \Omega$. Trade liberalisation changes $1/\kappa \geq \Omega$ to $1/\kappa < \Omega$, thus, changes $\tilde{\tau}_L \geq \tau_E$ to $\tilde{\tau}_L < \tau_E$. In addition, an environmental tax increase on export firms changes $\tilde{\tau}_L \geq \tau_E$ to $\tilde{\tau}_L < \tau_E$. When the environmental tax rate for local firms is adjusted at $\tilde{\tau}_L < \tau_E$, a trade-off relationship between productivity and pollution can be realised or a win–win relationship can be achieved. Therefore, a policy mix of environmental and trade policies brings about sustainable development.

### 15.4.2 Increasing Environmental Tax on Export Firms

In the explanations so far and in Appendix N, the effect of raising environmental taxes on export firms on the steady-state value is shown as follows:

$$\frac{d\psi_L}{d\tau_E} > 0, \quad \frac{d\psi_E}{d\tau_E} < 0, \quad \frac{d\Delta}{d\tau_E} < 0, \quad \frac{d\Lambda}{d\tau_E} > 0, \quad \frac{dc}{d\tau_E} < 0, \quad \frac{dP}{d\tau_E} \gtreqless 0,$$

for $\tau_L \gtreqless \tau_E$.

In (15.4b), the environmental tax increase on export firms is passed on to prices. Ceteris paribus, in (15.5b), profits decline due to a fall in sales. In (15.6b), this fall in sales makes it difficult to purchase blueprints for varieties for the export market, so only highly productive entrepreneurs can enter the export market. On the other hand, in (15.11), fixed R&D costs are reduced due to the cleansing effect of $\overline{\Omega}$. The reduction in the cost of entry into the market makes it easier for unproductive non-enterprises to enter the local market. Entrepreneurs who cannot bear the fixed costs of the export market give up on entering the export market and aim to enter the local market, so ceteris paribus, in (15.7), the productivity of local firms declines. At this time, only entrepreneurs with high productivity enter the export market, so the productivity of export firms increases in (14.15). As a result, the relative R&D difficulty increases due to the decrease in fixed R&D costs, so the number of varieties increases.

In (15.14), this environmental policy worsens the average productivity of the entire industry through a cleansing effect of $\overline{\Omega}$, in order to encourage the entry of unproductive non-export firms and the entry of unproductive export firms into the local market. In (15.19), the environmental tax on export firms worsens average productivity through a cleansing effect of $\overline{\Omega}$. At this time, the price index rises in (14.20) due to a decrease in the quantity of goods produced. This negative price effect reduces household consumption and worsens welfare.

The impact of environmental taxes on total pollution emissions for export firms depends on the negative composition effect and the positive reallocation effect. The cleansing effect of $\tau_E$ on $\overline{\Omega}$ reduces the production of export firms due to a deterioration in average productivity, and increases total pollution emissions due to the non-polluting intensification of export firms. At this time, the entry of non-productive firms with low productivity leads to an increase in the pollution intensity of local firms, and the total amount of pollution emissions increases further. On the other hand, the deterioration of average productivity due to the cleansing effect of $\tau_E$ on $\overline{\Omega}$ expands pollution by reallocating resources from firms with high productivity to firms with low productivity.

In the case of the BTA effect at $\tau_E < \tau_L$, the negative composition effect dominates the positive reallocation effect, so total pollution emissions are reduced, while in the case of the pollution haven effect at $\tau_E > \tau_L$, the positive reallocation effect dominates the negative composition effect, so total pollution emissions increase. Environmental taxes on export firms have a U-shaped effect on pollution. Environmental taxes on local firms complement the pollution reduction effect of environmental taxes on export firms because the negative reallocation effect is mitigated by the improvement in average productivity. Here, since $d\Delta/d\tau_E < 0$ and $dP/d\tau_E < 0$ in $\tau_E > \tau_L$, in this case, the environmental tax increase for export firms does not improve average productivity, so it does not imply the Porter hypothesis. However, since $d\Lambda/d\tau_E > 0$, the number of varieties increases, so it can be said to be the Porter hypothesis through innovation.

### 15.4.3 Trade Liberalisation

In the explanations so far and in Appendix N, the effect of the reduction in transport costs due to trade liberalisation on the steady-state value is shown as follows:

$$\frac{d\psi_L}{d\Omega} < 0, \quad \frac{d\psi_E}{d\Omega} > 0, \quad \frac{d\Delta}{d\Omega} > 0, \quad \frac{d\Lambda}{d\Omega} < 0, \quad \frac{dc}{d\Omega} > 0, \quad \frac{dP}{d\Omega} \gtreqless 0,$$

for $\tau_L \gtreqless \tau_E$.

As explained in Chap. 14, a cleansing effect of trade liberalisation leads to an improvement in the productivity of local firms and a deterioration in the productivity of export firms, resulting in an improvement in average productivity and a decrease in relative R&D difficulty. At this time, the number of varieties decreases. In (15.7), with a uniform environmental tax where $\tau = \tau_E = \tau_L$, there is no difference in profit between firms due to the price pass-through of the environmental tax, so the environmental tax does not affect average productivity through the entry and exit of firms. However, since transport costs only apply to export firms, the price pass-through of transport costs by export firms leads to a difference in profit between firms. Therefore, trade policy affects average productivity through the entry and exit of firms. Improving average productivity reduces the price index, and this increases consumption.

In (15.17), with a uniform environmental tax where $\tau = \tau_E = \tau_L$, the positive composition effect and negative reallocation effect cancel each other out, so trade liberalisation has no effect on total pollution emissions. In this case, the composition effect depends on the environmental tax for local and export firms, so the effect of trade liberalisation on total pollution emissions depends on the environmental tax rate. In the case of the BTA effect where $\tau_E < \tau_L$ the positive composition effect dominates the negative reallocation effect, so total pollution emissions increase, while in the case of the pollution haven effect where $\tau_E > \tau_L$, the negative reallocation effect dominates the positive composition effect, so total pollution emissions are reduced. An increase in environmental taxes for export firms reinforces the negative composition effect and mitigates the positive composition effect, so it complements the pollution reduction effect of trade liberalisation.

## 15.5 Welfare Effect

### *15.5.1 Increasing of Environmental Tax on Local and Export Firms*

Differentiating (20) with respect to $\tau_E$ asserts the following:

$$\frac{dU}{d\tau_E} = \frac{1}{(\rho - n)\big(1 + \overline{\Omega}\big)}\left[\frac{1}{\Gamma} + \eta_P\left(1 - \frac{1 + \overline{\Omega}}{1 + \frac{\tau_L}{\tau_E}\overline{\Omega}}\right)\right]\frac{\partial \overline{\Omega}}{\partial \tau_E} < 0,$$

for $1 > \big(1 + \overline{\Omega}\big)/\big[1 + \overline{\Omega}(\tau_L/\tau_E)\big]$ on $\tau_L \geq \tau_E$. In the case of the BTA effect at $\tau_E < \tau_L$, the negative composition effect of the environmental tax on export firms dominates the positive reallocation effect, so total pollution emissions are reduced and welfare is improved. However, the deterioration in average productivity caused by this environmental tax reduces consumption, so utility deteriorates. The negative welfare effect of the latter dominates the positive welfare effect of the former, so the environmental tax on export firms has a negative welfare effect.

Differentiating (15.20) with respect to $\tau_L$ asserts the following:

$$\frac{dU}{d\tau_L} = \frac{1}{\rho - n} \cdot \frac{\partial \hat{c}}{\partial \tau_L} - \frac{\eta_P}{\rho - n} \cdot \frac{\partial \hat{P}}{\partial \tau_L} > 0,$$

for $\tau_L > \tau_E$ because $d\hat{c}/d\tau_L > 0$ and $d\hat{P}/d\tau_L \leq 0$ hold. In the case of the BTA effect with $\tau_L > \tau_E$, an environmental tax on local firms improves welfare through increased consumption and reduced pollution. Therefore, the adoption of a BTA policy through an environmental tax cut for export firms complements the welfare effect of an environmental tax on local firms. In contrast, in the case of the pollution haven effect with $\tau_E > \tau_L$, $dU/d\tau_L \gtreqless 0$ for $\tau_L \leq \tau_E$ because $d\hat{c}/d\tau_L > 0$ and $d\hat{P}/d\tau_L \geq 0$ hold. An environmental tax increase for local firms may have a non-monotonic welfare effect due to increased consumption and pollution. However, since a complete analytical proof is difficult, it is necessary to verify it by numerical analysis.[1] In the case of a uniform environmental tax where $\tau = \tau_E = \tau_L$, the environmental tax no longer affects the entry and exit behaviour of firms, and average productivity also does not change. Since consumption and pollution also do not change through this productivity, the welfare effect of the environmental tax disappears.

### *15.5.2 Trade Liberalisation*

Under $\tau = \tau_L = \tau_E$, differentiating (20) concerning $\tau$ and $\Omega$ yields the following:

$$\frac{dU}{d\Omega} = \frac{1}{\Gamma(\rho - n)\left(1 + \overline{\Omega}\right)} \frac{\partial \overline{\Omega}}{\partial \Omega} > 0, \quad \frac{dU}{d\tau} = \frac{1}{\tau}\left(\frac{\eta_P - \varepsilon}{\rho - n}\right) \gtreqless 0,$$

for $\eta_P \gtreqless \epsilon$. Trade liberalisation improves welfare monotonically because it increases consumption and reduces pollution. Whether an environmental tax improves or worsens welfare depends on whether households value consumption or pollution more. However, under a discriminatory environmental tax rate, trade liberalisation may worsen welfare.

Differentiating (15.20) by $\Omega$ yileds the following:

$$\frac{dU}{d\Omega} = \frac{1}{(\rho - n)\left(1 + \overline{\Omega}\right)} \left[\left(\frac{1}{\Gamma} + \eta_P\right) - \eta_P\left(\frac{1 + \overline{\Omega}}{1 + \frac{\tau_L}{\tau_E}\overline{\Omega}}\right)\right] \frac{\partial \overline{\Omega}}{\partial \Omega} \gtreqless 0,$$

for

$$\hat{\Omega} \equiv \left(\frac{\tau_E}{\tau_L}\right)^{\varepsilon\Gamma} \left(\frac{\frac{1}{\eta_P \Gamma} - 1}{1 - \frac{\tau_L}{\tau_E} \cdot \frac{1}{\eta_P \Gamma}}\right) \gtreqless \Omega,$$

[1] In Hamaguchi (2024b, p16), the $\tau_E$ in formula (36) is a typo and should be $\tau_L$. Therefore, only the effect of $dc/d\tau_L > 0$ exists. As a result, the inverse U-shaped relationship between $\tau_L$ and $c$ in Proposition 4.2 becomes a positive relationship and the $dc/d\tau_L < 0$ at $\tau_E < \tau_L$ in Proposition 4.5 does not exist. However, this does not change the main results of the paper.

where $\hat{\Omega} > 0$ holds on $\tau_L/\tau_E < \eta_P\Gamma < 1$ and $\tau_L < \tau_E$ or $1 < \eta_P\Gamma < \tau_L/\tau_E$ and $\tau_E < \tau_L$. A cleansing effect of trade liberalisation improves welfare by increasing consumption. However, depending on the environmental tax rate, that trade policy may increase or decrease pollution. When the improvement in welfare due to increased consumption through trade liberalisation dominates the deterioration in welfare due to increased pollution in $\hat{\Omega} > \Omega$, the trade policy has a positive welfare effect. On the other hand, when the deterioration in welfare due to increased pollution through trade liberalisation dominates the improvement in welfare due to increased consumption in $\hat{\Omega} \leq \Omega$, the trade policy has a negative welfare effect. Here, from $d\hat{\Omega}/d\eta_P < 0$ when households place more importance on their preference for pollution than on consumption, trade liberalisation is more likely to improve welfare. Regardless of whether there is international trade or a discriminatory environmental tax, the more households improve their environmental preferences, the more trade and environmental policies can demonstrate their welfare effects.

## References


Acar, S., Aşıcı, A. A., & Yeldan, A. E. (2022). Potential effects of the EU's carbon border adjustment mechanism on the Turkish economy. *Environment, Development and Sustainability*, 24(6), 8162–8194. https://doi.org/10.1007/s10668-021-01779-1

Andersen, D. C. (2018). Accounting for loss of variety and factor reallocations in the welfare cost of regulations. *Journal of Environmental Economics and Management*, 88, 69–94. https://doi.org/10.1016/j.jeem.2017.10.005

Anouliès, L. (2017). Heterogeneous firms and the environment: A cap-and-trade program. *Journal of Environmental Economics & Management*, 84, 84–101. https://doi.org/10.1016/j.jeem.2017.02.004

Balistreri, E. J., & Rutherford, T. F. (2012). Subglobal carbon policy and the competitive selection of heterogeneous firms. *Energy Economics*, 34, S190–S197. https://doi.org/10.1016/j.eneco.2012.08.002

Chen, G. (2023). Impact of carbon border adjustment mechanism on China's manufacturing sector: A dynamic recursive CGE model based on an evolutionary game. *Journal of Environmental Management*, 347, 119029. https://doi.org/10.1016/j.jenvman.2023.119029

Cherniwchan, J., Copeland, B. R., & Taylor, M. S. (2017). Trade and the environment: New methods, measurements, and results. *Annual Review of Economics*, 9(1), 59–85. https://doi.org/10.1146/annurev-economics-063016-103756

Cherniwchan, J., & Najjar, N. (2022). Do environmental regulations affect the decision to export?. *American Economic Journal, Economic Policy*, 14(2), 125–160. https://doi.org/10.1257/pol.20200290

Copeland, B., & Taylor, M. S. (2004). Trade, growth, and the environment. *Journal of Economic Literature*, 42(1), 7–71. https://doi.org/10.1257/.42.1.7

Coria, J., & Kyriakopoulou, E. (2018). Environmental policy, technology adoption and the size distribution of firms. *Energy Economics*, 72, 470–485. https://doi.org/10.1016/j.eneco.2018.04.025

Cosbey, A., Droege, S., Fischer, C., & Munnings, C. (2019). Developing guidance for implementing border carbon adjustments: Lessons, cautions, and research needs from the literature. *Review of Environmental Economics and Policy*, 13(1), 3–22. https://doi.org/10.1093/reep/rey020

Cui, J. (2017). Induced clean technology adoption and international trade with heterogeneous firms. *The Journal of International Trade & Economic Development*, 26(8), 924–954. https://doi.org/10.1080/09638199.2017.1320579

Eicke, L., Weko, S., Apergi, M., & Marian, A. (2021). Pulling up the carbon ladder? Decarbonization, dependence, and third-country risks from the European carbon border adjustment mechanism. *Energy Research & Social Science*, 80, 102240. https://doi.org/10.1016/j.erss.2021.102240Forslid et al. (2018)

Grossman, G., & Krueger, A. B. (1993). Environmental impacts of a North American free trade agreement. In P. M. Garber (Ed.), The U.S.-Mexico free trade agreement (pp. 13–56). MIT Press.

Hamaguchi, Y. (2024a). Whether to Abolish or Introduce Dual Regulation as Trade and Environmental Policy?. *China & World Economy*, 32(1), 57–95. https://doi.org/10.1111/cwe.12516

Hamaguchi, Y. (2024b). Effects of a policy mix of uniform or unilateral environmental tax and trade liberalization on economic welfare. *Journal of Applied Economics*, 27(1), 2375913. https://doi.org/10.1080/15140326.2024.2375913

Hong, L., Liu, X., Liu, B., Cao, K., & Xia, Q. (2024). The impact of reducing trade barriers on enterprises' pollution emissions: Evidence from China, managerial and decision economics. *Managerial and Decision Economics*. https://doi.org/10.1002/mde.4087

Jakob, M., Marschinski, R., & Hübler, M. (2013). Between a rock and a hard place: A trade-theory analysis of leakage under production- and consumption-based policies. *Environmental & Resource Economics*, 56(1), 47–72. https://doi.org/10.1007/s10640-013-9638-y

Konishi, Y., & Tarui, N. (2015). Emissions trading, firm heterogeneity, and intra-industry reallocations in the long run. *Journal of the Association of Environmental and Resource Economists*, 2(1), 1–42. https://doi.org/10.1086/679905

Kreickemeier, U., & Richter, P. M. (2014). Trade and the environment: The role of firm heterogeneity. *Review of International Economics*, 22(2), 209–225. https://doi.org/10.1111/roie.12092

LaPlue, L. D. (2019). The environmental effects of trade and environmental policy within and across sectors. *Journal of Environmental Economics & Management*, 94, 118–139. https://doi.org/10.1016/j.jeem.2019.01.007

Levy, T., & Dinopoulos, E. (2016). Global environmental standards with heterogeneous polluters. *International Review of Economics & Finance*, 43, 482–498. https://doi.org/10.1016/j.iref.2016.01.009Melitz (2003)

Melitz, M. J. (2003). The impact of trade on intra-industry reallocation and aggregate industry productivity. *Econometrica*, 71(6), 1695–1725. https://doi.org/10.1111/1468-0262.00467

Richter, U., Kreickemeier, P. M., & Richter, P. M. (2021). Environmental policy and firm selection in the open economy. *Journal of the Association of Environmental Economics and Resource Economists*, 8(4), 655–690. https://doi.org/10.1086/713040

Rubashkina, Y., Galeotti, M., & Verdolini, E. (2015). Environmental regulation and competitiveness: Empirical evidence on the porter hypothesis from European manufacturing sectors. *Energy Policy*, 83, 288–300. https://doi.org/10.1016/j.enpol.2015.02.014

Sanctuary, M. (2018). Border carbon adjustments and unilateral incentives to regulate the climate. *Review of International Economics*, 26(4), 826–851. https://doi.org/10.1111/roie.12344

Shapiro, J. S., & Walker, R. (2018). Why is pollution from US manufacturing declining? The roles of environmental regulation, productivity, and trade. *The American Economic Review*, 108(12), 3814–3854. https://doi.org/10.1257/aer.20151272

Yomogida, M., & Tarui, N. (2013). Emission taxes and border tax adjustments or oligopolistic industries. *Pacific Economic Review*, 18(5), 644–673. https://doi.org/10.1111/1468-0106.12045

# Chapter 16
# Porter and Pollution Haven Hypotheses

**Abstract** The R&D-based heterogeneous firms model, with a discriminatory environmental tax, is extended to a full endogenous growth model. Environmental tax evasion is applied to export firms. Trade liberalisation improves average productivity through the cleansing effect of entering the export market. However, it leads to a decrease in the economic growth rate due to an increase in fixed costs, pollution and bribes due to the composition effect. This implies the pollution haven hypothesis. An increase in the uniform environmental tax lowers the economic growth rate and has a non-monotonic effect on average productivity and total pollution emissions. An increase in the unilateral environmental tax on export firms encourages low-productivity export firms to exit the market, leading to economic growth and pollution reduction, implying a weak Porter hypothesis. When the total bribe increases, it implies the sanding-the-wheels-of-trade hypothesis. Although environmental tax evasion improves firms' productivity, it decreases economic growth and increases pollution emissions, impeding sustainable development through the pollution haven hypothesis. The improvement in the quality of the political system due to a decrease in the fine rate increases the tax rate, which decreases economic growth and increases pollution. Therefore, the improvement in the quality of the political system impedes sustainable development.

## 16.1 Introduction

According to Porter (1991) and Porter and van der Linde (1995), strict environmental policies encourage firms to innovate concerning pollution, which in turn increases international competitiveness and contributes to the reduction of global pollution emissions. This is known as the Porter hypothesis. However, Palmer et al. (1995) argue that strict environmental policies reduce international competitiveness. According to a survey by Cohen and Tubb (2018), the statistical significance of this hypothesis is low or non-existent, and this is particularly true in empirical analyses of developing countries. The presentation of new mechanisms through theoretical analysis will provide useful suggestions for empirical analysis through hypothesis

 
Y. Hamaguchi, *Sustainable Development in Economic Growth Theory*,
https://doi.org/10.1007/978-981-96-7639-2_16

construction and variable selection. Many studies interpret the Porter hypothesis as meaning that environmental policies lead to pollution reduction through innovation, but strictly speaking, it is necessary to relate it to international economics. Therefore, analysis that utilises the R&D-based heterogeneous firms model in Chap. 15 and this chapter is effective.

A thought-provoking empirical study is Fu and Jian (2021), which shows that the statistical significance of the Porter hypothesis in China disappears when controlling for corruption. It has been empirically confirmed that corruption lowers the level of environmental policy regulation and consequently increases pollution emissions (Welsch 2004; Pellegrini and Gerlagh 2006; Aidt 2011; Aklin et al. 2014). When analysing the Porter hypothesis with an eye to international economics, it is also relevant to the pollution haven hypothesis. This point is analysed in Chap. 13, which considers environmental tax evasion by firms in developed countries. The reason for the markedly low statistical significance of the Porter hypothesis in developing countries is thought to be due to corruption in environmental policy. Firms in developing countries may even bribe government officials to overlook environmental tax evasion. In developing countries with low-quality political systems, the ability to collect taxes declines, leading to a deterioration in environmental quality (Blackman 2000; Baksi and Bose 2010; Biswas and Thum 2017).

In addition to environmental tax evasion, firms sometimes bribe government officials to advance their trade transactions more favourably. Thanh et al. (2021) empirically examine whether or not bribing government officials promotes or inhibits firms' decisions to start exporting. About bribery and trade, Aidt (2003, 2009, 2011) proposes the greasing-the-wheel-of-trade hypothesis and the sanding-the-wheel-of-trade hypothesis. According to the former hypothesis, bribery of bureaucrats facilitates administrative procedures and promotes exports. According to the latter hypothesis, unproductive costs and activities related to corruption inhibit exports. Bribery of bureaucrats reduces the entry costs of polluting firms (Biswas and Thum 2017). Therefore, corruption in environmental policy encourages the entry of polluting firms and leads to the expansion of pollution. At this time, trade liberalisation increases pollution emissions due to the lowering of regulatory standards caused by corruption and lobbying (Damania et al. 2003; Fredriksson 1999). When the level of environmental regulations is lowered due to corruption in a country that accepts FDI, the polluting haven hypothesis arises because polluting firms are attracted to the country through FDI (Fredriksson and Sevensson 2003; Fredriksson et al. 2005; Wilson and Damania 2005). There is a risk that political and economic factors will encourage environmental degradation due to trade liberalisation.

Barbier et al. (2005) and Ranjan and Bakshi (2006) analyse the impact of corruption on the relationship between free trade regimes and resource sustainability in an endogenous growth model but assume that productivity between firms is homogeneous. Environmental tax evasion in Chap. 12 is applied to the analysis of the political pollution haven hypothesis in Chap. 13, but Chap. 15 takes into account heterogeneous productivity between firms. In the introductions to these chapters, the author refers to previous studies on the environmental tax evasion model and the pollutive heterogenous firms model, but there has been no analysis that takes into account corruption, tax evasion and growth in the R&D-based heterogenous firms model. The economic model in this chapter presents the mechanisms of the greasing-the-wheel-of-trade hypothesis and the sanding-the-wheel-of-trade hypothesis, in addition to the Porter hypothesis and the pollution haven hypothesis.

## 16.2 The Model

### *16.2.1 Structure of R&D-Based Growth Model with Heterogenous Polluting Firms and Tax Evasion*

The economic model based on the semi-endogenous growth model in Chap. 15 is extended to the full endogenous growth model explained in Chap. 14. In addition, because the environmental tax rate for export firms is higher than that for local firms, export firms engage in environmental tax evasion by paying bribes to bureaucrats. This tax evasion negotiation is based on the economic model in Chap. 12. Based on these settings, we will explain how corruption in relation to environmental policy affects the Porter hypothesis and pollution haven hypothesis. This economic structure is illustrated in Fig. 16.1. As the explanation of the model settings overlaps with the previous chapters, we will only explain the main changes and focus on explaining the economic mechanisms. For the basic model settings, please refer to Chaps. 12 and 15.

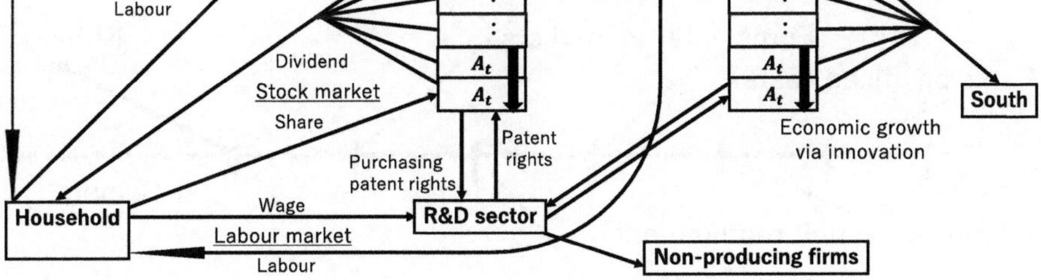


**Fig. 16.1** Structure of the R&D-based growth model with heterogenous polluting firms and tax evasion

### 16.2.2 Timing

To internalise the negative externalities of pollution emissions, the government imposes an environmental tax on local and export firms. In doing so, the government dispatches a bureaucrat to each firm. The bureaucrat observes the amount of pollution emissions by the firm to which he is dispatched, and then demands and collects the environmental tax from the firm. As $\tau_E > \tau_L$, the government imposes a higher environmental tax rate on export firms than on local firms, because the government wants to prevent export firms from exporting pollution-intensive goods to foreign markets. At this time, export firms bear a heavier tax burden than local firms. Therefore, export firms have an incentive to commit environmental tax evasion by paying bribes to government officials. On the other hand, local firms, which have a relatively low environmental tax rate, do not have this tax evasion incentive. Therefore, local firms pay the environmental tax without negotiating tax evasion with government officials.

The timing of the game between the export firm and the bureaucrat is as follows. The entrepreneur purchases a new variety of designs from the R&D firm, bearing the fixed R&D cost. The entrepreneur draws the unit labour with pollution requirements and finds that he/she can enter the market as an export firm. Therefore, he enters the export market, conducts production activities, and emits pollution. The government dispatches a bureaucrat to the export firm. The export firm observes the quality of the dispatched bureaucrat. Depending on the quality of the bureaucrat, the export firm decides whether to pay the environmental tax or to evade the tax by bribing the bureaucrat. When the tax evasion negotiation breaks down, the export firm must pay the full amount of the environmental tax. On the other hand, when the tax evasion negotiation is successful, the export firm evades part of the tax amount and pays part of the evaded amount to the bureaucrat as a bribe. This sequence is repeated every period. This is because the government sends new bureaucrats to the export firms and local firms each term (Fig. 16.2).

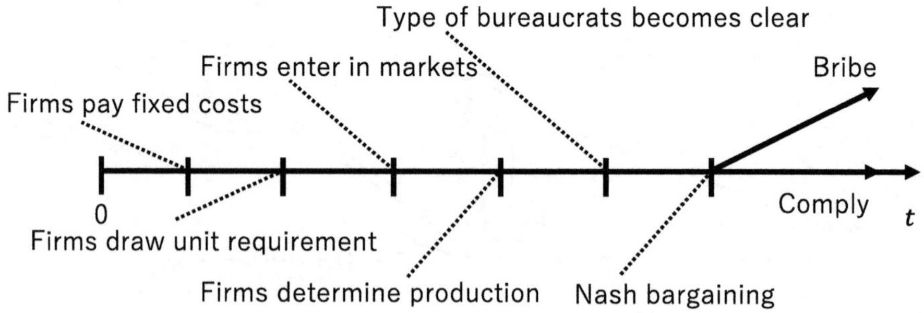


**Fig. 16.2** Timing

### 16.2.3 Tax Evasion

As explained in Chap. 12, by considering negotiations with the export firm $j$, the bureaucrat $o$ maximises his bribe through the following:

$$\max_{h_{o,t}} \left(h_{o,t} - \xi_{o,t}\varpi_{o,t} d_{j,t}^{E}\right)^{\varrho} \left(\tau_E d_{j,t}^{E} - h_{o,t}\right)^{\varrho - 1},$$

and this first-order condition yields the following:

$$h_{o,t} = \varrho \tau_E d_{j,t}^{E} + (1 - \varrho)\xi_{o,t}\varpi_{o,t} d_{j,t}^{E}. \tag{16.1}$$

The expected bribe costs for the export firm $j$ are as follows:

$$\mathbb{E}\left[\tau_E d_{j,t}^{E}, h_{o,t}\right] \equiv \left(1 - \frac{\tau_E}{\varpi_{o,t}}\right)\tau_E d_{j,t}^{E} + \left(\frac{\tau_E}{\varpi_{o,t}}\right)h_{o,t},$$

where this implies the ratio of firms that pay tax and those that evade tax.

By using (12.15), this cost can be rewritten as follows:

$$\mathbb{E}\left[\tau_E d_{j,t}^{E}, h_{o,t}\right] = \overline{\tau}_E\left(\tau_E, \varrho, \xi_{o,t}, \varpi_{o,t}\right) d_{j,t}^{E},$$

for

$$\overline{\tau}_E\left(\tau_E, \varrho, \xi_{o,t}, \varpi_{o,t}\right) \equiv \tau_E\left[1 - (1 - \varrho)\left(\frac{\tau_E}{\varpi_{o,t}} - \xi_{o,t}\right)\right],$$

where $\overline{\tau}_E\left(\tau_E, \varrho, \xi_{o,t}, \varpi_{o,t}\right)$ is an efficient environmental tax rate, and the second term on the right-hand side implies a tax rate. Here, $0 < \tau_E < \varpi_{o,t}$ and $0 < \varpi_{o,t} < 1$ hold. Using $\xi_{o,t} = \xi = \tau/(2\varpi)$, $\mathbb{E}\left[\tau_E d_{j,t}^{E}, h_{o,t}\right]$ is rewritten as follows:

$$\mathbb{E}\left[\tau_E d_{j,t}^{E}, h_t\right] = \overline{\tau}_E(\tau_E, \varrho, \varpi) d_{j,t}^{E},$$

for

$$\overline{\tau}_E(\tau_E, \varrho, \varpi) = \tau_E\left[1 - \tfrac{\tau_E(1-\varrho)}{2\varpi}\right] = \tau_E\left(1 - \tfrac{\tau_E}{\tilde{\tau}_E}\right), \tag{16.2}$$

where $\tilde{\tau}_E \equiv (2\varpi)/(1 - \varrho) > \tau_E$. Note that $\tau_E/\tilde{\tau}_E$ is the tax evasion rate, and the higher the environmental tax rate, the higher the tax evasion rate is by $1/\tilde{\tau}_E$.

### 16.2.4 Export Firms

By replacing $\tau_E$ with $\overline{\tau}_E$ in Chap. 15, the tax evasion behaviour of export firms is taken into account. Firms that enter the export market by subtracting $0 < \psi < \psi_{E,t}$ determine the price that maximises profits, given the demand for the good in (14.3), as follows:

$$\max_{p^E_{j,t}} \pi^E_{j,t} \equiv \left[p^E_{j,t} - \left(\frac{t\overline{\tau}^{\epsilon}_E}{\phi}\right)\psi_j\right]q^E_{j,t}, \tag{16.3}$$

and the first-order condition for profit maximisation asserts the following:

$$p^E_{j,t} = \frac{\sigma}{\sigma-1}\left(\frac{t\overline{\tau}^{\epsilon}_E}{\phi}\right)\psi_j, \tag{16.4}$$

where the transportation costs are passed on to the price. By substituting (4) for (3), the optimal profit for the export firm is as follows:

$$\pi^E_{j,t} = \frac{\varphi}{\sigma}\left(\frac{\sigma-1}{\sigma}\right)^{\sigma-1}\left(\frac{\phi}{\overline{\tau}^{\epsilon}_E}\right)^{\sigma-1}\left(\frac{P_{M,t}}{\psi_j}\right)^{\sigma-1}E_t, \tag{16.5}$$

where $\varphi \equiv (1/t)^{\sigma-1}$ measures the degree of trade liberalisation. As shown in Chap. 15, firms that draw $\psi_{E,t} < \psi \leq \psi_{L,t}$ enter the local market.

Firm profits determine entry into the local and export markets. From the free entry condition, the stock prices of local and export firms are, respectively, $P^L_{A,t} = F_L/(2A_t)^{\varsigma}$ and $P^E_{A,t} = F_E/(2A_t)^{\varsigma}$ in (14.10). By substituting (5) and (14.10) into the non-arbitrage condition in (14.9), the free entry condition in the export market is derived as follows:

$$\frac{\frac{1}{\sigma}\left(\frac{\sigma-1}{\sigma}\right)^{\sigma-1}\left(\frac{\phi}{\overline{\tau}^{\epsilon}_E}\right)^{\sigma-1}\left(\frac{P_{M,t}}{\psi_j}\right)^{\sigma-1}E_t}{r_t+\frac{\dot{A}_t}{A_t}} = \frac{1}{\varphi}\cdot\frac{F_E}{A_t}. \tag{16.6}$$

By using (15.6a), (16.6), and $F_E > F_L$, the productivity gap between local and exporting firms can be expressed as follows:

$$\frac{\psi_{L,t}}{\psi_{E,t}} = \left(\frac{\overline{\tau}_E}{\tau_L}\right)^{\epsilon}\left(\frac{F_E}{\varphi F_L}\right)^{\frac{\sigma}{\sigma-1}} > 1, \tag{16.7}$$

for all $\varphi \in (0, 1)$. From $\tau_E > \overline{\tau}_E$, environmental tax evasion reduces the productivity gap, because it increases the profits of export firms through a fall in the price of goods. Using a uniform environmental tax of $\tau = \tau_L = \tau_E$, (16.7) can be rewritten as:

$$\frac{\psi_{L,t}}{\psi_{E,t}} = \left(1-\frac{\tau}{\tilde{\tau}}\right)^{\epsilon}\left(\frac{F_E}{\varphi F_L}\right)^{\frac{\sigma}{\sigma-1}} > 1, \tag{16.8}$$

where, even with a uniform environmental tax, there is a disparity in tax rates between export firms and local firms due to environmental tax evasion by export firms. Therefore, environmental tax evasion plays a decisive role in the distribution of firms' productivity. From now on, a uniform environmental tax of $\tau = \tau_L = \tau_E$ is assumed.

## 16.3 Equilibrium

### *16.3.1 Steady State*

In the BGP equilibrium, $r_t = \rho$ holds from the Euler equation. When $\psi_{L,t} = \psi_L$ and $\psi_{E,t} = \psi_E$ are satisfied, (14.13) and (14.15) show that $\overline{F}$, $\psi_L$, and $\psi_{E,t}$ are constant in the BGP equilibrium. At this time, there is a unique and symmetric steady-state equilibrium.

From the definition of $\overline{F}_t$, we can obtain the fixed R&D cost in (14.15). R&D firms develop new varieties of blueprints by inputting labour. The development mechanism is $\dot{A}_t = \left(A_t/\overline{F}\right)L_{A,t}$. in (14.34). Aggregate price indexes and dividend income are as in Chap. 15. Then, (15.6a) and (16.6) can be rewritten as

$$\frac{\frac{1}{\sigma}\left(\frac{\phi}{\tau^{\epsilon}}\right)^{\sigma-1}\left(\frac{E}{\Delta}\right)}{\rho+g} = F_L, \quad \frac{\frac{1}{\sigma}\left(\frac{\phi}{\tilde{\tau}^{\epsilon}}\right)^{\sigma-1}\left(\frac{E}{\Delta}\right)}{\rho+g} = \frac{F_E}{\varphi}, \tag{16.9}$$

which are used to rewrite (14.13) as $(E/\sigma)/(\rho+g) = \overline{F}$ in (14.35b).

By rewriting (14.14a), we obtain the following:

$$\Delta = \frac{\frac{1}{\psi_L^{\sigma-1}}}{1-\frac{\sigma-1}{\Gamma}}\left[\left(\frac{\phi}{\tau^{\epsilon}}\right)^{\sigma-1} + \varphi\left(\frac{\phi}{\tilde{\tau}^{\epsilon}}\right)^{\sigma-1}\left(\frac{\psi_L}{\psi_E}\right)^{\sigma-1-\Gamma}\right],$$

which is further rewritten as

$$\Delta = \frac{\kappa}{\kappa-1}\left(\frac{1}{\psi_L}\right)^{\sigma-1}\left(\frac{\phi}{\tau^{\epsilon}}\right)^{\sigma-1}\left(1+\overline{\overline{\Omega}}\right), \tag{16.10}$$

for

$$\overline{\overline{\Omega}} \equiv \left(\frac{1}{1-\frac{\tau}{\tilde{\tau}}}\right)^{\epsilon\Gamma}\Omega,$$

where $d\Delta/d\Omega = [\kappa/(\kappa-1)]\left(1/\psi_L^{\sigma-1}\right)(\phi/\tau^{\epsilon})^{\sigma-1}\partial\overline{\overline{\Omega}}/\partial\Omega > 0$ implies that a cleansing effect of trade liberalisation is further enhanced by tax evasion of $\tau/\tilde{\tau}$. While the environmental tax increase improves the average productivity of firms through the tax rate, it also worsens the average productivity of firms due to the increase in the cost of entry caused by the price decrease.

### 16.3.2 Economic Growth

By using (16.8) and (16.10), (14.15) can be expressed as follows:

$$\overline{F} = F_L\left(\tfrac{\kappa}{\kappa-1}\right)\left(1+\overline{\overline{\Omega}}\right), \tag{16.11}$$

where tax evasion of $\tau/\tilde{\tau}$ increases its fixed R&D costs due to the cleansing effect of $\overline{\overline{\Omega}}$, and therefore its new entry costs increase. Substituting $L_t = L_{X,t} + L_{A,t}$ and $L_{X,t} = [(\sigma-1)/\sigma]E_t$ into $\dot{A}_t = \left(A_t/\overline{F}\right)L_{A,t}$ in (14.34), we obtain $g_t = [L_t - [(\sigma-1)/\sigma]E_t]/\overline{F}_t$ Substituting this $g_t$ into $(E/\sigma)/(\rho+g) = \overline{F}$ in (14.35b) gives the following economic growth rate:

$$g = \tfrac{1}{\sigma\overline{F}} - \left(\tfrac{\sigma-1}{\sigma}\right)\rho, \tag{16.12}$$

where tax evasion of $\tau/\tilde{\tau}$ increases fixed R&D costs due to the cleansing effect of $\overline{\overline{\Omega}}$, and the economic growth rate declines. By using (14.35b) and (16.12), we obtain $E = L + \rho\overline{F}$ as expenditure and household expenditure depend on labour income and dividend income.

### 16.3.3 Firms' Productivity

Using (16.8), (14.15), and (16.10), the cut-off unit input requirement for selling in the local market is as follows:

$$\psi_L = \overline{\psi}\left[\left(\tfrac{F_I}{F_L}\right)\left(\tfrac{\kappa-1}{1+\overline{\Omega}}\right)\right]^{\frac{1}{\Gamma}}, \tag{16.13}$$

where, as in $d\psi_L/d(\tau/\tilde{\tau}) = -\psi_L\left[1/\Gamma\left(1+\overline{\Omega}\right)\right]\left[\partial\overline{\Omega}/\partial(\tau/\tilde{\tau})\right] < 0$, tax evasion of $\tau/\tilde{\tau}$ decrease $\psi_L$. Due to the rise in fixed R&D costs through environmental tax evasion, the least productive local firm no longer earns enough profit to cover these costs. This firm exits the local market and becomes a non-productive firm.

By substituting (16.13) into (16.78), the cut-off unit input requirement for selling in the export market is as follows:

$$\psi_E = \overline{\psi}\left[\left(\tfrac{F_I}{F_E}\right)\left(\tfrac{\kappa-1}{\frac{1}{\overline{\Omega}}+1}\right)\right]^{\frac{1}{\Gamma}}, \tag{16.14}$$

where, as in $d\psi_E/d(\tau/\tilde{\tau}) = \psi_E[1/\Gamma(1+\Omega)]\left[\partial\overline{\Omega}/\partial(\tau/\tilde{\tau})\right] > 0$, tax evasion of $\tau/\tilde{\tau}$ increases $\psi_E$. Even if fixed R&D costs rise due to environmental tax evasion, the most productive local firms in the local market can bear the fixed R&D costs necessary for developing varieties for export markets, so they enter export markets and become export firms.

By substituting (16.13) for (16.10), the following average productivity of companies can be derived:

$$\Delta = \tfrac{\kappa}{\kappa-1}\left[\left(\tfrac{1}{\overline{\overline{\psi}}}\right)\left(\tfrac{F_L}{F_I}\right)\left(\tfrac{1}{\kappa-1}\right)\right]^{\frac{1}{\Gamma}}\left(\tfrac{\phi}{\tau^{\epsilon}}\right)^{\sigma-1}\left(1+\overline{\overline{\Omega}}\right)^{1+\frac{1}{\kappa}}, \tag{16.15}$$

where, as in $d\Delta/d(\tau/\tilde{\tau}) = [1+(1/\kappa)]\big[\Delta/\big(1+\overline{\Omega}\big)\big]\big[\partial\overline{\Omega}/\partial(\tau/\tilde{\tau})\big] > 0$, tax evasion of $\tau/\tilde{\tau}$ improves the productivity of the industry as a whole by encouraging the least productive local firms to exit and the most productive local firms to enter the export market.

### 16.3.4 Pollution and Corruption

The total amount of pollution discharged is as follows:

$$P = \int_{\psi_E}^{\psi_L} Ad_{L,j}\frac{\tilde{g}(\psi)}{G(\psi_L)}d\psi + \int_{0}^{\psi_E} Ad_{E,j}\frac{\tilde{g}(\psi)}{G(\psi_L)}d\psi,$$

which is rewritten with (15.16) as follows:

$$\tfrac{P}{E} = \left(\tfrac{\sigma-1}{\sigma}\right)\frac{\frac{1}{\tau}+\frac{\overline{\overline{\Omega}}}{\overline{\tau}}}{1+\overline{\overline{\Omega}}}, \tag{16.16}$$

where $P/E$ in (16.16) is the total pollution emission per expenditure. Tax evasion of $\tau/\tilde{\tau}$ increases expenditure in $E = L + \rho\overline{F}$ through fixed R&D costs. Therefore, environmental tax evasion increases total pollution emission through the scale effect in $E[(\sigma-1)/\sigma]$. However, this scale effect complicates the analysis of the effect of environmental taxes on pollution. Hamaguchi (2023) omits the scale effect by analysing the effect of environmental taxes and trade liberalisation on $P/E$ in (16.16). In addition, to simplify the reallocation effect, Hamaguchi (2023) assumes the total pollution emissions of efficient units as follows:

$$\frac{\tilde{P}}{E} = \left(\frac{\sigma-1}{\sigma}\right)\left(\frac{1}{\tau}\right)^{\epsilon(\sigma-1)}\left(\frac{1}{\tau}+\frac{\overline{\overline{\Omega}}}{\overline{\tau}}\right),$$

where Hamaguchi (2023) explains the impact of trade environment policies on pollution by interpreting $(1/\tau)^{\epsilon(\sigma-1)}$ as a composition effect rather than a reallocation effect, and $\left[(1/\tau)+\left(\overline{\overline{\Omega}}/\overline{\tau}\right)\right]$ as a reallocation effect rather than a composition effect. For analysis and explanation in this case, please refer to Hamaguchi (2023).

Here, $P/E$ in (16.16) is further rewritten with (16.2), (16.11), and $E = L + \rho\overline{F}$ as follows:

$$P = \left(\tfrac{\sigma-1}{\sigma}\right)\left[\tfrac{L}{1+\overline{\overline{\Omega}}} + \rho F_L\left(\tfrac{\kappa}{\kappa-1}\right)\right]^{\frac{1+\frac{\overline{\overline{\Omega}}}{1-(\tau/\tilde{\tau})}}{\tau}}, \tag{16.17}$$

where $\left(1+\overline{\overline{\Omega}}\right)$, in the scale effect, is dominated by $1/\left(1+\overline{\overline{\Omega}}\right)$ in the reallocation effect and so, the scale effect disappears. While tax evasion of $\tau/\tilde{\tau}$ reduces total pollution emissions through the reallocation effect, environmental tax evasion increases total pollution emissions through the composition effect.

Aggregating (15.16) for local and export firms yields the following:

$$P_L = \frac{1}{\tau}\left(\frac{\sigma-1}{\sigma}\right)\left[\frac{L}{1+\overline{\overline{\Omega}}} + \rho F_L\left(\frac{\kappa}{\kappa-1}\right)\right],$$

$$P_E = \frac{\overline{\overline{\Omega}}}{\tilde{\tau}}\left(\frac{\sigma-1}{\sigma}\right)\left[\frac{L}{1+\overline{\overline{\Omega}}} + \rho F_L\left(\frac{\kappa}{\kappa-1}\right)\right],$$

which is further used to derive the following amount of pollution emitted by export firms as a proportion of the total pollution emitted by local firms:

$$\frac{P_E}{P_L} = \frac{\Omega}{\left(1-\frac{\tau}{\tilde{\tau}}\right)^{1+\varepsilon\Gamma}}, \tag{16.18}$$

where tax evasion of $\tau/\tilde{\tau}$ increases the proportion of total pollution emissions from export firms to the total pollution emissions of local firms.

The total bribe amount aggregated is expressed as follows:

$$\hat{h}_E = \int_0^{\psi_E} A h_{E,j}\frac{\tilde{g}(\psi)}{G(\psi_L)}d\psi,$$

where by substituting $\xi_{o,t} = \xi = \tau/(2\varpi)$ into (16.1), we obtain $h_E = \left[(1+\varrho)/2\right](\tau/A)d_E$. Using $h_E$ and $P_E$ in $\hat{h}_E$, the aggregate bribe is rewritten as follows:

$$\hat{h}_E = \left(\tfrac{\tau}{\tilde{\tau}}\right)\left(\tfrac{1+\varrho}{2}\right)\left(\tfrac{\sigma-1}{\sigma}\right)\left[\tfrac{L}{\left(1/\overline{\overline{\Omega}}\right)+1} + \rho F_L\overline{\overline{\Omega}}\left(\tfrac{\kappa}{\kappa-1}\right)\right], \tag{16.19}$$

where the positive composition effect dominates the negative reallocation effect. Thus, tax evasion of $\tau/\tilde{\tau}$ increases aggregate bribes to increase the benefits of tax evasion through the expansion of pollution by export firms.

## 16.4 Comparative Statics

### 16.4.1 Effect of Trade Liberalisation

As explained so far and in Appendix O, the effect of the decrease in transport costs due to trade liberalisation on the steady-state value is shown as follows:

$$\frac{d\psi_L}{d\Omega} < 0, \ \frac{d\psi_E}{d\Omega} > 0, \ \frac{d\Delta}{d\Omega} > 0, \ \frac{d\overline{F}}{d\Omega} > 0, \ \frac{dg}{d\Omega} < 0,$$

and

$$\frac{d}{d\Omega}\left(\frac{P_E}{P_L}\right) > 0, \ \frac{dP}{d\Omega} > 0, \ \frac{d\hat{h}_E}{d\Omega} > 0,$$

where even in cases where there is environmental tax evasion by export firms, the impact of trade liberalisation on the entry and exit of firms and average productivity is the same as in cases where there is no environmental tax evasion. However, in the full endogenous growth model, trade liberalisation increases fixed R&D costs. The increase in the cost of new entry stalls the development of new varieties, and so the economic growth rate falls. Even with a uniform environmental tax of $\tau = \tau_L = \tau_E$, due to tax evasion of $\tau/\tilde{\tau}$, the environmental tax rate for local firms is higher than that for export firms. Therefore, as in Chap. 15, where $dP/d\Omega > 0$ for $\tau_L > \tau_E$, the composition effect dominates the reallocation effect, and trade liberalisation increases total pollution emissions. Because the benefits of tax evasion increase due to the expansion of pollution, trade liberalisation increases total bribes. This result implies the pollution haven hypothesis because the expansion of the export sector due to trade liberalisation increases pollution emissions. At this time, the economic growth rate also decreases. Furthermore, because total bribes are also increasing, it suggests the corruption paradise in Candau and Dienesch (2017).

### 16.4.2 Effect of Environmental Tax

As explained so far and in Appendix O, the effect of the environmental tax on the steady-state value is shown as follows:

$$\frac{d\psi_L}{d\tau} < 0, \ \frac{d\psi_E}{d\tau} > 0, \ \frac{d\Delta}{d\tau} \gtreqless 0, \ \frac{d\overline{F}}{d\tau} > 0, \ \frac{dg}{d\tau} < 0,$$

and

$$\frac{d}{d\tau}\left(\frac{P_E}{P_L}\right) > 0, \ \frac{dP}{d\tau} \gtreqless 0, \ \frac{d\hat{h}_E}{d\tau} > 0,$$

where in the case of environmental tax evasion by export firms, the impact of environmental tax increases on firm entry and exit and average productivity is the same as that of environmental tax increases on local firms in the case of no environmental tax evasion. However, it is not possible to derive the threshold for the non-monotonic effect of environmental tax evasion on average productivity analytically. In a full endogenous growth model, environmental tax increases fixed R&D costs. The increase in the cost of new entry stalls the development of new varieties, and the economic growth rate declines. Environmental tax increases the pollution emissions of export firms through the composition effect, and the ratio of the total pollution emissions of export firms to the total pollution emissions of local firms increases. While the total pollution emissions decrease due to the reallocation effect, they increase due to the composition effect, so it depends on which effect dominates. In addition to the environmental tax increase, the pollution expansion of export firms increases the benefits of tax evasion, so the environmental tax increase expands the total bribe. This result implies the greasing-the-wheels-of-trade hypothesis in Thanh et al. (2021).

In the case of a uniform environmental tax of $\tau = \tau_L = \tau_E$, an increase in the environmental tax rate reduces the economic growth rate. However, in the case of a unilateral environmental tax of $\tau_L \neq \tau_E$, the cleansing effect can be rewritten as follows:

$$\overline{\overline{\Omega}} \equiv \left(\frac{\tau_L}{\tau_E}\right)^{\epsilon\Gamma} \left(\frac{1}{1 - \frac{\tau_E}{\tilde{\tau}_E}}\right)^{\epsilon\Gamma} \Omega,$$

which is used to derive the following:

$$\frac{d\psi_E}{d\tau_E} < 0, \ \frac{d\overline{F}}{d\tau_E} < 0, \ \frac{dg}{d\tau_E} > 0,$$

where an environmental tax on export firms encourages them to exit the market, while also stimulating economic growth through a reduction in fixed R&D costs. Furthermore, using a unilateral environmental tax of $\tau_L \neq \tau_E$, (16.17) is rewritten as follows:

$$P = \left(\frac{\sigma - 1}{\sigma}\right)\left[\frac{L}{1 + \overline{\overline{\Omega}}} + \rho F_L\left(\frac{\kappa}{\kappa - 1}\right)\right]\left[\frac{1}{\tau_L} + \frac{\overline{\overline{\Omega}}}{\tau_E[1 - (\tau_E/\tilde{\tau}_E)]}\right],$$

where $dP/d\tau_E < 0$ holds because the composition effect dominates the reallocation effect. Therefore, environmental tax increases on export firms lead to sustainable development through economic growth and pollution reduction. This result implies the weak Porter hypothesis and is consistent with the empirical results of Zhou et al. (2022) and Wu et al. (2022).

Differentiating (16.19) with respect to $\tau_E$ yields the following:

$$\frac{d\hat{h}_E}{d\tau_E} = \frac{\hat{h}_E}{\tau_E} + \left(\frac{\tau}{\tilde{\tau}}\right)\left(\frac{1+\varrho}{2}\right)\left(\frac{\sigma-1}{\sigma}\right)\left[\frac{L}{\left[\left(1/\overline{\overline{\Omega}}\right)+1\right]^2} + \rho F_L\left(\frac{\kappa}{\kappa-1}\right)\right]\underbrace{\frac{\partial\overline{\overline{\Omega}}}{\partial\tau_E}}_{(-)} \gtreqless 0,$$

where although tax evasion of $\tau_E/\tilde{\tau}_E$ increases the total amount of bribes, it reduces the total amount of bribes due to the reduction of pollution caused by the cleansing effect of $\overline{\overline{\Omega}}$. When $d\hat{h}_E/d\tau_E > 0$, an environmental tax increase on export firms increases the total amount of bribes and also encourages the exit of export firms from the market. This result implies the sanding-the-wheels-of-trade hypothesis in Thanh et al. (2021).

### 16.4.3 Effect of Tax Evasion

In Chap. 12, the impact of environmental tax evasion on the economy and the environment was interpreted as the effect of environmental tax reduction. Here, we interpret the increase in the tax evasion rate of $\tau/\tilde{\tau}$ due to environmental tax increases as the effect of tax evasion. As explained so far and in Appendix O, the effect of environmental tax increase on the steady state is shown as follows:

$$\frac{d\psi_L}{d(\tau/\tilde{\tau})} < 0, \quad \frac{d\psi_E}{d(\tau/\tilde{\tau})} > 0, \quad \frac{d\Delta}{d(\tau/\tilde{\tau})} > 0, \quad \frac{d\overline{F}}{d(\tau/\tilde{\tau})} > 0, \quad \frac{dg}{d(\tau/\tilde{\tau})} < 0,$$

and

$$\frac{d}{d(\tau/\tilde{\tau})}\left(\frac{P_E}{P_L}\right) > 0, \quad \frac{dP}{d(\tau/\tilde{\tau})} > 0, \quad \frac{d\hat{h}_E}{d(\tau/\tilde{\tau})} > 0,$$

where environmental tax evasion causes the least productive local firms to exit the market and become unproductive firms. Furthermore, it causes the most productive local firms to enter the export market and become export firms. As a result, average productivity improves. However, environmental tax evasion also raises fixed R&D costs. Therefore, the increase in the cost of new entry stalls the development of new varieties and lowers the economic growth rate. Environmental tax evasion increases the pollution emissions of export firms through the composition effect, so the proportion of total pollution emissions accounted for by export firms increases in the total pollution emissions of local firms. Because the composition effect dominates the reallocation effect, environmental tax evasion increases total pollution emissions. Because the benefits of tax evasion increase with pollution expansion, environmental tax evasion increases total bribes. The expansion of the export sector associated with environmental tax evasion is increasing pollution emissions, and this result implies the political pollution haven hypothesis. At the same time, economic growth is also declining.

Environmental tax evasion improves the productivity of firms, but it also leads to a decline in economic growth and an increase in pollution emissions, which in turn impedes sustainable development. As explained in Chap. 12, the decline in the rate of fines and the bargaining power of bureaucrats can be interpreted as an improvement in the quality of the political system. From $d(\tau/\tilde{\tau})/d\varpi = -(\tau/\tilde{\tau}^2)d\tilde{\tau}/d\varpi < 0$ and $d(\tau/\tilde{\tau})/d\varrho = -(\tau/\tilde{\tau}^2)d\tilde{\tau}/d\varrho < 0$, the reduction in the fine rate and the bureaucrat's bargaining power further increases the tax rate of $\tau/\tilde{\tau}$. Therefore, improving the quality of the political system does not promote sustainable development, but rather impedes it. This result is in contrast to Chaps. 12 and 13. Furthermore, in the R&D-based heterogeneous firms model, the pollution haven hypothesis is accompanied by a decrease in the economic growth rate. When considering heterogeneous firms, the impact of the quality of the political system on sustainable development remains an issue that needs to be clarified.

## References

Aidt, T. S. (2003). Economic analysis of corruption: a survey. *The Economic Journal*, 113(491), F632–F652. https://doi.org/10.1046/j.0013-0133.2003.00171.x

Aidt, T. S. (2009). Corruption, institutions, and economic development. *Oxford Review of Economic Policy*, 25(2), 271–291. https://doi.org/10.1093/oxrep/grp012

Aidt, T. S. (2011). "Chapter 1: Corruption and Sustainable Development". In International Handbook on the Economics of Corruption, Volume Two. Cheltenham, UK: Edward Elgar Publishing. https://doi.org/10.4337/9780857936523.00007

Aklin, M., Bayer, P., Harish, S. P., & Urpelainen, J. (2014). Who blames corruption for the poor enforcement of environmental laws? Survey evidence from Brazil. *Environmental Economics and Policy Studies*, 16(3), 241–262. https://doi.org/10.1007/s10018-014-0076-z

Baksi, S., & Bose, P. (2010). Environmental regulation in the presence of an informal sector. *University of Winnipeg Department of Economics Working Paper*, 3, 1–28. http://ideas.repec.org/s/win/winwop.html

Barbier, E. B., Damania, R., & Léonard, D. (2005). Corruption, trade and resource conversion. *Journal of Environmental Economics and Management*, 50(2), 276–299. https://doi.org/10.1016/j.jeem.2004.12.004

Biswas, A. K., & Thum, M. (2017). Corruption, environmental regulation and market entry. *Environment and Development Economics*, 22(1), 66–83. https://doi.org/10.1017/S1355770X16000218

Blackman, A. (2000). Informal sector pollution control: what policy options do we have?. *World Development*, 28(12), 2067–2082. https://doi.org/10.1016/S0305-750X(00)00072-3

Candau, F., & Dienesch, E. (2017). Pollution haven and corruption paradise. *Journal of Environmental Economics and Management*, 85, 171–192. https://doi.org/10.1016/j.jeem.2017.05.005

Cohen, M. A., & Tubb, A. (2018). The impact of environmental regulation on firm and country competitiveness: A meta-analysis of the porter hypothesis. *Journal of the Association of Environmental and Resource Economists*, 5(2), 371–399. https://doi.org/10.1086/695613

Damania, R., Fredriksson, P. G., & List, J. A. (2003). Trade liberalization, corruption, and environmental policy formation: theory and evidence. *Journal of Environmental Economics and Management*, 46(3), 490–512. https://doi.org/10.1016/S0095-0696(03)00025-1

Fredriksson, P. G. (1999). The political economy of trade liberalization and environmental policy. *Southern Economic Journal*, 65(3), 513–525. https://doi.org/10.1002/j.2325-8012.1999.tb00173.x

Fredriksson, P. G., Neumayer, E., Damania, R., & Gates, S. (2005). Environmentalism, democracy, and pollution control. *Journal of Environmental Economics and Management*, 49(2), 343–365. https://doi.org/10.1016/j.jeem.2004.04.004

Fredriksson, P. G., & Svensson, J. (2003). Political instability, corruption and policy formation: the case of environmental policy. *Journal of Public Economics*, 87(7–8), 1383–1405. https://doi.org/10.1016/S0047-2727(02)00036-1

Fu, T., & Jian, Z. (2021). Corruption pays off: How environmental regulations promote corporate innovation in a developing country. *Ecological Economics*, 183, 106969. https://doi.org/10.1016/j.ecolecon.2021.106969

Hamaguchi, Y. (2023). Environmental tax evasion as a determinant of the Porter and pollution haven hypotheses in a corrupt political system. *Economic Analysis and Policy*, 79, 610–633. https://doi.org/10.1016/j.eap.2023.06.032

Palmer, K., Oates, W. E., & Portney, P. R. (1995). Tightening environmental standards: the benefit-cost or the no-cost paradigm?. *Journal of Economic Perspectives*, 9(4), 119–132. https://doi.org/10.1257/jep.9.4.119

Pellegrini, L., & Gerlagh, R. (2006). Corruption, Democracy, and Environmental Policy: An Empirical Contribution to the Debate. *The Journal of Environment & Development*, 15(3), 332–354. https://doi.org/10.1177/1070496506290960

Porter, M. (1991). American's Green Strategy. Scientific America, 168.

Porter, M. E., & van der Linde, C. (1995). Toward a new conception of the environment-competitiveness relationship. *Journal of Economic Perspectives*, 9 (4), 97–118. https://doi.org/10.1257/jep.9.4.97

Ranjan, P., & Bakshi, B. (2006). Corruption, Environmental Resources, and International Trade. *Topics in Economic Analysis & Policy*, 6(1). https://doi.org/10.2202/1538-0653.1515

Thanh, T. T., Thang, D. N., & Anh, P. T. H. (2021). Bribery, export decisions, and institutional constraints: Evidence from cross-country firm-level data. *Economic Analysis and Policy*, 69, 585–612. https://doi.org/10.1016/j.eap.2021.01.010

Welsch, H. (2004). Corruption, growth, and the environment: a cross-country analysis. *Environment and Development Economics*, 9(5), 663–693. https://doi.org/10.1017/S1355770X04001500

Wilson, J. K., & Damania, R. (2005). Corruption, political competition and environmental policy. *Journal of Environmental Economics and Management*, 49(3), 516–535. https://doi.org/10.1016/j.jeem.2004.06.004

Wu, J., Chen, Z., & Guo, C. (2022). How does anti-corruption affect green innovation? Evidence from China. *Economic Analysis and Policy*, 73, 405–424. https://doi.org/10.1016/j.eap.2021.12.004

Zhou, D., Zhong, Z., Chen, L., Gao, W., & Wang, M. (2022). Can the joint regional air pollution control policy achieve a win-win outcome for the environment and economy? Evidence from China. *Economic Analysis and Policy*, 74, 13–33. https://doi.org/10.1016/j.eap.2022.01.011

# Chapter 17
# Conclusion

**Abstract** This book clarifies the following mechanism of sustainable development. In Chaps. 4 and 5, environmental and financial policies bring about sustainable development via innovation. This effect is the distribution effect. However, this effect is greatly influenced by the degree of elasticity of substitution in Chap. 8. In Chaps. 6 and 7, households' preferences for leisure and social status influence the growth effect by the marginal rate of substitution between them and consumption. In Chaps. 10 and 11, the emission allowance rent affects the firms' location, leading to the pollution haven hypothesis, tourism-led growth hypothesis, and sustainable tourism. In Chap. 12, environmental tax evasion with corruption under overlapped regulation promotes economic growth. In Chap. 13, the pollution haven hypothesis through tax evasion is presented. In Chap. 15, environmental policy brings about the Porter hypothesis through industrial structure. In Chap. 16, the impact of tax evasion on the Porter hypothesis is discussed. The results of this book are all dependent on scale effect, but robustness is confirmed for some of the results. The significance of this book for numerical analysis and empirical analysis is then discussed, and the construction of a theory of sustainable economic growth is left as a further issue.

## 17.1 Aim of This Book

After the concept of sustainable development was proposed, coupled with the development of endogenous growth theory in the 1990s, the basic mechanisms of sustainable development, such as the compatibility of pollution reduction and economic growth and the feasibility of achieving this through environmental policy, were vigorously researched. As a result, the theoretical assumptions and various conditions that affect sustainable development were clarified, and quantitative verification through empirical analysis was also promoted. However, since 2000, as the global warming problem has worsened to the point of threatening to boil the Earth, sustainable development has been integrated with the Millennium Development Goals and elevated to the SDGs, and the resolution of environmental issues through cooperation and collaboration between governments, businesses and citizens is being sought within

 
Y. Hamaguchi, *Sustainable Development in Economic Growth Theory*,
https://doi.org/10.1007/978-981-96-7639-2_17

global society. At this time, it has become necessary to not only strike a balance between pollution reduction and economic growth, but also to coexist with various socioeconomic factors, such as the importance of innovation, economic globalisation and environmental justice. However, it was not until after 2000 that the R&D-based growth model, which had developed dramatically in the 1990s, began to be applied to areas such as firm location, international trade, international tourism, and political economy. As a result, it was not until after 2010 that these endogenous growth models began to be applied to environmental issues in earnest. Opportunities to widely share the theoretical achievements made during this period were limited.

The aim of this book is to explain the mechanisms of sustainable development in the R&D-based growth model based on the author's research achievements, and to explain the theoretical mechanisms of major topics in environmental economics, such as the pollution haven hypothesis, sustainable tourism, environmental tax evasion, and Porter's hypothesis. After explaining the typical R&D-based models, the applied models for natural environmental problems are introduced. In the main text and appendices, the derivation process of the economic models and the methods of proving the main propositions are all described, making this a self-contained specialist book. While conveying basic analytical methods to theoretical researchers interested in sustainable development, it also provides theoretical results that are useful for empirical researchers in making decisions such as hypothesis construction and variable selection. Furthermore, it provides specific policy implications for policymakers and global citizens, such as environmental policies and institutional points to note that promote sustainable development.

## 17.2 Main Results

### *17.2.1 Parts I and II*

In Chap. 1, the research trends up to recent years are briefly described, and in Chaps. 2 and 3, the basic structure of the variety expansion model is explained, and in Chaps. 9 and 14, the application models to endogenous firm location and industrial structure are explained.

In Chap. 4, the basic mechanism by which innovation through environmental policy leads to sustainable development through pollution reduction and economic growth is introduced. Environmental taxes are passed on to prices, so demand for goods falls. Goods firms reduce production, so pollution is also reduced. There is a shift in labour from the goods sector to the R&D sector, so variety is developed and the economy grows. Environmental taxes have a U-shaped welfare effect due to reduced consumption from reduced production, increased consumption from economic growth, and reduced pollution. Reducing the number of emission allowances also has a U-shaped welfare effect, as the price of emission allowances is passed on to the price of goods, resulting in economic growth due to the transfer of labour from the goods sector to the R&D sector. Furthermore, as the emission allowances allocated for free are potential rents, the increase in profits due to the rents stimulates the incentive to develop varieties, and the effect of this on economic growth is called the distribution effect. The simple model structure makes it possible to analyse applications to the location of firms and industrial structure.

In Chap. 5, the variety expansion model is extended to include a monetary policy based on endogenous money supply and interest rate manipulation. Households under the cash-in-advance (CIA) constraint lend their money to R&D firms. R&D firms under the CIA constraint use the borrowed funds to pay researchers. In the case of an environmental tax, a reduction in the nominal interest rate leads to deflation due to the Fisher effect, so the real money supply increases. Therefore, because lending to R&D firms increase labour demand, there is a shift of labour from the goods sector to R&D sectors. As economic growth increases, pollution is reduced due to a decrease in production in the goods sector, and there is an inverted U-shaped effect on welfare. Emission allowances cap the production of goods firms, so the growth-enhancing effect of the nominal interest rate disappears. Depending on the level of emission allowances and interest rates, there is a trade-off, win–win, or lose-lose relationship between sustainable development and financial market development.

However, the growth-enhancing effect of environmental policies in a variety expansion model with a certain elasticity of substitution depends on the non-homothetic preferences of households. In the case where the mark-up rate declines as a result of the production of goods, an environmental tax increase leads to an increase in pollution emissions and a decrease in economic growth through the perfect pass-through effect. Depending on the demand composition, competition between firms in the goods sector is created, and the growth-enhancing effect of environmental policies changes. Furthermore, in the growth model based on Chap. 4, the growth-enhancing effect of environmental policy disappears when the elasticity of substitution is 1. At this time, by taking into account the preferences of households in addition to the introduction of physical capital, it is possible to bring out the growth effect.

In the case of considering leisure time, the reduction of emission allowances lead to economic growth and improve welfare through the substitution effect. Due to the demand for pollution-reducing goods, final-goods firms increase production of final goods by investing in intermediate goods. The rise in the price of intermediate goods encourages the development of new varieties in order to increase monopoly profits. The opportunity cost of leisure increases, and leisure is substituted for work, as the demand for labour in the R&D sector increases the wage rate. As a result, the economy grows due to the development of varieties. When the pollution preference parameter is high, welfare improves.

Next, when households have more assets than the average in society, the social status preference, which perceives utility from social status, is taken into account. A reduction in the total emission allowance not only reduces the amount of pollution emitted through pollution abatement goods, but also affects the economic growth rate through the marginal rate of substitution (MRS) for assets and consumption. This effect is the substitution effect, and it depends on the crowding-out effect and the resource reallocation effect. Under certain parameter conditions, the resource reallocation effect dominates the crowding-out effect, so reducing the emission allowance improves welfare by stimulating economic growth through the substitution effect. In all growth models, the growth-enhancing effect of environmental policy depends on household preferences and the production technology of R&D firms, because the growth-enhancing effect of emission allowances disappears in the case of no leisure or social status preference and in the lab-equipment model.

### *17.2.2 Parts III and IV*

By utilising the R&D-based location model, it is possible to analyse the pollution haven hypothesis and the mechanisms of sustainable tourism. In Chap. 10, the same level of emission allowances allocated to manufacturing firms in the North and South generates an allowance allocation rent, so a reduction in the total emission allowance brings economic growth due to the distribution effect. In addition, this rent affects the home market effect. In terms of global spillovers, a reduction in the total emissions allowance and trade liberalisation leads to a green haven effect, with pollution reduction in the South and pollution increase in the North, through the location of firms from the South to the North. Improvements in pollution abatement productivity lead to a pollution haven effect, with pollution increase in the South and pollution reduction in the North, through the location of firms from the North to the South, and a decrease in economic growth rates. The interaction between local spillovers and allowance allocation rent leads to a poverty trap in terms of the location of firms. In the steady state of over-accumulation in the North, trade liberalisation leads to the pollution haven hypothesis and economic growth through the location of firms from the North to the South, resulting in increased pollution in the South and reduced pollution in the North.

In Chap. 11, in addition to pollution emissions, the crowding effect in tourist destinations worsens the quality of the environment, and through its external effects, it worsens the productivity of the tourism sector. Reducing the total emissions allowance is likely to increase tourism consumption, as it brings economic growth and tourism mobility through pollution haven from the South to the North and the improvement of the global environmental quality. This environmental policy achieves tourism-led growth and sustainable tourism. In the case of low airfares, their reduction leads to a decrease in tourism consumption due to the rise in the price of tourism goods caused by tourism pollution and externalities. Therefore, while it promotes industrialisation and economic growth in the North, it also causes environmental degradation and a decline in tourism, which may hinder sustainable tourism. In the case of high airfares, their reduction leads to industrialisation and an improvement in environmental quality in the South due to a decline in tourism, in exchange for low growth.

Furthermore, in Chap. 11, it is pointed out that the external effects of the tourism sector can lead to the malfunctioning of environmental policy, as the high price of emission allowances can undermine the incentive for manufacturing firms to reduce pollution. Even if strict environmental policies are introduced, if their growth-enhancing effects are undermined by political and economic factors such as corruption and tax evasion, it is difficult to achieve sustainable development by raising the level of regulation. At this time, it is necessary to identify the factors that undermine the growth-enhancing effects and to improve the system.

In Chap. 12, it is pointed out that overlapped double regulation is a factor that inhibits the growth-enhancing effect. While the reduction of emission allowances decreases pollution and also grows the economy through the distribution effect, the increase in the environmental tax rate inhibits this distribution effect through the fall in the price of emission allowances, resulting in a fall in the economic growth rate. Furthermore, because emission allowances cap production volume, the environmental tax does not affect the amount of pollution. This additional regulatory cost provides an incentive for manufacturing firms to evade taxes. The level of corruption and tax evasion is determined through negotiations between bureaucrats and manufacturing firms. The reduction in the environmental tax rate due to tax evasion increases the allowance allocation rent through a rise in the price of emission allowances, and so the economic growth rate rises. The reduction in the tax rate due to environmental tax increases the bribe rate, and so the economic growth rate falls through a fall in the price of emission allowances. Therefore, a reduction in tax rates due to tax evasion, rather than environmental tax increases, promotes sustainable development. However, improving the quality of the political system by reducing the rate of fines and the negotiating power of bureaucrats enhances the sustainability of society through an increase in economic growth.

In Chap. 13, the pollution haven hypothesis due to corruption and tax evasion is analysed. Manufacturing firms in the North pay bribes to government officials to evade environmental taxes, as they are subject to higher environmental tax rates than those in the South. The decline in the price of emission allowances due to higher environmental taxes in the North lowers economic growth rates through the distribution effect. The change in expenditure associated with the passing on of the price leads to a reduction in pollution in the North and an increase in pollution in the South, through a decline in the location of firms and FDI from the North to the South. As the tax rate gap between the North and South widens, the total bribes in the North decrease due to a decline in the number of manufacturing firms located there, but due to political and economic factors, the pollution haven hypothesis occurs. A reduction in the fine rate changes the direction of pollution haven from the South to the North, leading to sustainable development through a reduction in pollution and economic growth in the South. The political pollution haven hypothesis can be avoided by improving the quality of the political system.

### 17.2.3 Part V

Finally, the Porter hypothesis is analysed by considering the entry and exit of firms through environmental policy. In Chap. 15, environmental taxes can affect the entry and exit behaviour of firms due to differences in tax rates between firms. Trade environmental policies affect total pollution emissions through scale effects, composition effects, and reallocation effects. Increasing taxes on local firms has a non-monotonic effect on average productivity and pollution emissions, reducing the number of varieties, due to firms exiting the local market and entering the export market. Increasing taxes on export firms has a non-monotonic effect on average productivity and pollution emissions, increasing the number of varieties, due to firms entering the local market and exiting the export market. In the case of a border tax adjustment (BTA) effect where the tax rate for local firms is higher than that for export firms, there is an improvement in welfare due to the tax increase for local firms and a deterioration in welfare due to the tax increase for export firms. Due to the cleaning effect of trade liberalisation, average productivity improves. In the case of a BTA effect, due to the positive composition effect, trade liberalisation increases pollution. In the case of a pollution haven effect where the tax rate for local firms is lower than that for export firms, due to the negative reallocation effect, trade liberalisation reduces pollution. Therefore, trade liberalisation has a non-monotonic welfare effect. In the case of a uniform environmental tax, the two effects cancel each other out, so trade liberalisation has no effect on pollution emissions and only has a positive welfare effect.

In Chap. 16, the relationship between corruption, tax evasion and growth is analysed concerning the Porter hypothesis. In doing so, the environmental tax evasion in Chap. 12 is applied to export firms. Trade liberalisation improves average productivity through the cleansing effect of trade liberalisation and by entering export markets, but it also leads to a decrease in economic growth due to an increase in fixed costs and an increase in pollution and bribery due to the composition effect. This result implies the pollution haven hypothesis. A tax increase under a uniform environmental tax lowers the economic growth rate and has a non-monotonic effect on average productivity and total pollution emissions. A tax increase on export firms under a unilateral environmental tax promotes the exit of low-productivity export firms from the market, leading to economic growth and pollution reduction, and thus implies the weak Porter hypothesis. When the total bribe increases, this implies the sanding-the-wheels-of-trade hypothesis. Although environmental tax evasion improves corporate productivity, it also leads to a decrease in economic growth and an increase in pollution emissions, and therefore impedes sustainable development through the pollution haven hypothesis. The improvement in the quality of the political system due to a decrease in the fine rate increases the tax rate, which in turn leads to a decrease in economic growth and an increase in pollution. Therefore, the improvement in the quality of the political system impedes sustainable development.

The impact of improvements in the quality of political institutions on sustainable development is contrasted in Chaps. 12 and 13. Furthermore, in the R&D-based

heterogeneous firms model, the pollution haven hypothesis is accompanied by a decrease in economic growth. When heterogeneous firms are taken into account, the impact of the quality of political institutions on sustainable development remains an issue that needs to be clarified.

## 17.3 Limitations and Future Tasks of This Book

### *17.3.1 Scale Effect*

This book has analysed the mechanisms of sustainable development through environmental policies from a variety of perspectives by utilising the R&D-based growth model. However, there are still issues that need to be improved. The first is the scale effect. The variety expansion model in this book relies on economies of scale in all but Chaps. 14 and 15, and population expansion brings about economic growth by increasing the number of workers in the R&D sector. Jones (1995) used OECD data from after World War II to find that, despite the increase in the number of scientists and engineers in the United States, France, West Germany, and Japan, total factor productivity, which implies the rate of technological progress, remained at a certain level. As explained in footnote 5 in Chap. 2, this empirical finding led to rapid progress in the development of endogenous growth models in which economic growth rates are endogenously determined within an economic model, while at the same time not including scale effects.

However, when analysing sustainable development through environmental policy in an R&D-based model, this research direction poses a major challenge. This is because environmental policy, through the various effects explained in this book, ultimately promotes the transfer of labour from the goods sector to the R&D sector, resulting in pollution reduction and economic growth. In an R&D-based growth model without scale effects, environmental policy is unable to manifest this growth-enhancing effect. In an R&D-based model without scale effects, as we saw in Chaps. 14 and 15, the rate of population growth influences economic growth. Therefore, if environmental policy affects endogenous population growth, it is theoretically possible to maintain its growth-enhancing effect. However, in general, endogenous population growth complicates economic models, making it difficult to derive rigorous intuitions based on complete analytical solutions. Furthermore, the empirical relationship between population growth and economic growth is still being debated, and it is difficult to say that a definitive conclusion has been reached. The same is true for the empirical relationship between population and the environment.

Here, Futagami (2012) makes a point that is worth listening to. Based on the above discussion on the scale effect, he argues that we should place importance on the robustness of the effect of economic policy not changing depending on whether or not there is a scale effect. In Kremer (1993), there is a positive relationship between the world population and economic growth rate from 1 million years before the Common

Era. This result is in contrast to Jones (1995). Therefore, the empirical existence or non-existence of scale effects may depend on how the span of the analysis period is set. Furthermore, the existence or non-existence of scale effects may also depend on whether the analysis is conducted on a single country, a region or the world. It is difficult to say that there is clear agreement on what kind of empirical analysis method is preferable. Here, Futagami (2012) draws attention to Temple's (2003) argument. As long as we cannot observe long-term data that would allow us to make any judgements about economic growth, we lack the evidence needed to judge the relative merits of growth models, so we should adopt as the basis for policy decisions the policy conclusions that can be drawn from as many economic growth models as possible (Temple, 2003). In light of this discussion, Futagami and Iwaisako (2007) show that the optimal patent policy is finite in both cases with and without scale effects, proving its robustness.

In Chap. 16, it is assumed that $\tau = \tau_L = \tau_E$, but due to the tax rate of $\tau_E/\widetilde{\tau}_E$, the environmental tax rate for export firms is lower than for local firms. Therefore, the economic model in Chap. 16, which includes scale effects, is the same as the case of $\tau_E < \tau_L$ in the economic model in Chap. 15, which does not include scale effects. In both cases, trade liberalisation leads to an improvement in the productivity of local firms and a deterioration in the productivity of export firms due to the cleansing effect of trade liberalisation, and as a result, it improves average productivity and increases total pollution emissions. Therefore, the effect of trade liberalisation is robust. In the case of the existence of scale effects, the environmental tax rate for export firms is lowered through an increase in the tax rate for local firms. This reduction in tax rate is an environmental tax cut for export firms in the case where there is no scale effect. In both cases, this leads to an improvement in productivity for local firms and a deterioration in productivity for export firms. However, in the case where there is a scale effect, it has a non-monotonic effect on average productivity and total pollution emissions, while in the case where there is no scale effect, it leads to an improvement in average productivity and a reduction in total pollution emissions. Therefore, the robustness of the environmental policy is somewhat undermined with regard to average productivity and total pollution emissions. In light of the above, a future challenge will be to conduct a robustness analysis to see whether the main results of this book, which were derived on the assumption of scale effects, also hold in the R&D-based model without scale effects.

### 17.3.2 Numerical Analysis

The analysis in this book not only derives analytically complete closed solutions, but also provides analytical proofs for many of the comparative static analyses. Therefore, it is possible to intuitively and rigorously grasp the effects of environmental policies. However, if scale effects are to be eliminated, it is necessary to clarify the impact of environmental policies on population growth after endogenizing the population growth rate, otherwise it will not be possible to show the effect of promoting economic growth. As the model becomes more complex, it becomes more difficult to derive analytically complete closed solutions. Furthermore, as a result of the refinement and application of R&D-based growth models, there is a possibility that economic models based on numerical analysis will become the standard in the future. Under these circumstances, will analytical and qualitative model analysis continue to survive as a powerful analytical tool?

What is suggestive here is Klein (2020), in which the impact of patent protection by secrecy and patent protection by intellectual property rights on growth and welfare is analysed. What is characteristic is that, in a simple R&D-based growth model, after deriving an analytically complete closed solution and clarifying the policy implications through analytical comparative static analysis, the policy effects are quantitatively analysed through numerical analysis. When the derivation of the steady state is completely dependent on numerical analysis, it may become difficult to accurately grasp the theoretical mechanisms of environmental policy. As an approach to quantitatively confirming the results of qualitative model analysis using numerical analysis, and as a hybrid approach in Klein (2020), the analytical approach will continue to play an important role in the future.

### *17.3.3 Empirical Analysis*

This book analyses sustainable development using a theoretical approach. Until the 1990s, theoretical analysis was more common than empirical analysis due to limitations in statistical software and statistical data. However, since 2000, improvements in statistical software and the development of statistical data have progressed. Furthermore, as environmental issues have become increasingly internationalised, a succession of environmental journals have been published, and the number of empirical papers on the environment has increased, dramatically. Rather than the traditional approach of verifying qualitative results in theoretical analysis through empirical analysis and then reconstructing an economic model consistent with the empirical results, it is now also possible to use empirical analysis alone to self-consistently clarify the mechanisms related to sustainable development. The theoretical results in Chap. 6 have since been empirically confirmed by Xu et al. (2024) for similar mechanisms.

Even in these circumstances, theoretical analysis is probably an important analytical approach that can be compared to empirical analysis. One reason for this is the lack of data. Certainly, various types of data are being developed, but in some cases, it may be difficult to collect data in the first place. One example of this is data related to illegal activities such as corruption and tax evasion, and the informal economy. As analysed in Chaps. 12, 13 and 16, it is possible to derive qualitative mechanisms through theoretical analysis even in the absence of data. In preparation for future data development, clarifying as many mechanisms related to sustainable development as possible will lead to expanding the possibilities for empirical analysis. Following the traditional approach, it will also continue to be effective to verify the mechanisms of theoretical analysis through empirical analysis and to construct economic models that explain empirical facts.

## 17.4 Towards Sustainable Economic Growth Theory

This book clarifies the basic mechanisms of sustainable development through innovation. However, the analysis is not sufficient, because new environmental problems and environmental policies are emerging one after another. In addition, socioeconomic factors that have been considered to be unrelated to environmental problems are coming into the spotlight. Sustainable finance in Chap. 5 is one example. Instead of focusing on pollution reduction and economic growth through innovation in environmental policy, important topics such as renewable resources and energy are not covered. The dynamic integrated model of climate and economy developed by Prof. Nordhaus has been refined to date (Nordhaus, 2018). This advanced model is also omitted in this book. By applying the analytical framework in this book to these topics, we can build a more comprehensive theory of sustainable economic growth.

Furthermore, the author herself is continuing to research mechanisms related to sustainable development. The book could not include ongoing research on the relationship between income inequality and sustainable development, sustainable finance and sustainable tourism in R&D-based heterogeneous firms and location models, and the pollution haven hypothesis through imitation. Furthermore, with the discovery of marine mineral resources and blue carbon, the blue economy, which focuses on marine ecosystems and economic zones, is attracting attention as a new concept. At present, the planetary boundaries of the ocean economy have not been exceeded, but if the lessons of the past are not applied, we will fall into the danger of depletion. Applying the approach of this book to the blue economy will reveal useful policy implications. The construction of a theory of sustainable economic growth is still incomplete and further development is awaited.

## References

Futagami, K. (2012). Dynamic macroeconomic theory (Dougaku Makuro Keizaigaku : Seichou Riron No Haxtuten). Nihon Hyouron Sya, *In Japanese.*

Futagami, K., & Iwaisako, T. (2007). Dynamic analysis of patent policy in an endogenous growth model. *Journal of Economic Theory*, 132(1), 306–334. https://doi.org/10.1016/j.jet.2005.07.009

Jones, C. I. (1995). R & D-based models of economic growth. *Journal of Political Economy*, 103(4), 759–784. https://doi.org/10.1086/262002

Klein, M. A. (2020). Secrecy, the patent puzzle and endogenous growth. *European Economic Review*, 126, 103445. https://doi.org/10.1016/j.euroecorev.2020.103445

Kremer, M. (1993). Population growth and technological change: One million BC to 1990. *The Quarterly Journal of Economics*, 108(3), 681–716. https://doi.org/10.2307/2118405

Nordhaus, W. (2018). Evolution of modeling of the economics of global warming: changes in the DICE model, 1992–2017. *Climatic change*, 148(4), 623–640. https://doi.org/10.1007/s10584-018-2218-y

Temple, J. (2003). The long-run implications of growth theories. *Journal of Economic Surveys*, 17(3), 497–510. https://doi.org/10.1111/1467-6419.00202

Xu, S., Huang, J., & Zheng, K. (2024). Create or squeeze out? The effect of environmental protection tax on labor demand and labor demand transfer: evidence from China. *Clean Technologies and Environmental Policy*, 1–16. https://doi.org/10.1007/s10098-024-03059-8

# Appendix

The and derivation of equations and proofs of results in the main text are provided in the appendix.

## A Chapter 2

### *Derivation of (2.3)*

Differentiating $W_t = K_t + P_{A,t}A_t$ with time, we obtain $\dot{W}_t = \dot{K}_t + P_{A,t}\dot{A}_t + \dot{P}_{A,t}A_t$. Substituting this expression into (2.2), we assert the following:

$$\dot{W} = r_t K_t + A_t \pi_t + w_t L + \dot{P}_{A,t} A_t - C_t,$$

which is substituted for $K_t$ in $W_t = K_t + P_{A,t}A_t$ to obtain the following:

$$\dot{W} = r_t \left( W_t - P_{A,t} A_t \right) + A_t \pi_t + w_t L + \dot{P}_{A,t} A_t - C_t,$$

which is further rewritten as follows:

$$\dot{W} = r_t W_t + A_t \left( \pi_t + \dot{P}_{A,t} - r_t P_{A,t} \right) + w_t L - C_t. \tag{A.1}$$

Here, when the non-arbitrage condition (2.4) holds in (A.1), (2.3) is derived.



Y. Hamaguchi, *Sustainable Development in Economic Growth Theory*,
https://doi.org/10.1007/978-981-96-7639-2

## Derivation of Inverse Price Elasticity of Demand

Define $p_{j,t}$ in (2.12) as the inverse demand function of $p_{j,t} = p_{j,t}(x_{j,t})$. Substituting this inverse demand function into the profit function in (2.13) and differentiating it yields

$$p'_{j,t}(x_{j,t})x_{j,t} + p_{j,t}(x_{j,t}) - r_t = 0, \tag{A.2}$$

for $j = 1,2, \cdots, A_t$. (A.2) is rewritten as follows:

$$p_{j,t}(x_{j,t}) = \frac{1}{1-\left(\frac{p'_{j,t}(x_{j,t})x_{j,t}}{p_{j,t}(x_{j,t})}\right)} \cdot r_t, \tag{A.3}$$

where the denominator in the right-hand side of (A.3), $-p'_{j,t}(x_{j,t})x_{j,t}/p_{j,t}(x_{j,t})$, is the reciprocal price elasticity of demand. This $-p'_{j,t}(x_{j,t})x_{j,t}/p_{j,t}(x_{j,t})$ is added to $p'_{j,t}(x_{j,t}) = \alpha(1-\alpha)L_{Y,t}^{1-\alpha}x_{j,t}^{\alpha-2}$ and $p_{j,t} = \alpha L_{Y,t}^{1-\alpha}x_{j,t}^{1-2}$, then $-p'_{j,t}(x_{j,t})x_{j,t}/p_{j,t}(x_{j,t}) = 1-\alpha$. Using this result, (2.14) can be derived.

## Derivation of (2.19)

From the household's budget constraint in (2.2), the market clearing condition for the goods market in (2.19) is derived. Substituting (2.11), (2.17) and (2.18) into (2. 2) yields the following:

$$\begin{aligned} \dot{K}_t + P_{A,t}\dot{A}_t &= r_tK_t + A_t\pi_t \\ &\quad + (1-\alpha)\left(\frac{\int_0^{A_t} x_{j,t}dj}{L_{Y,t}}\right)^{\alpha} L_{Y,t} + P_{A,t}\delta A_tL_{A,t} - C_t, \end{aligned}$$

which is rewritten by using (2.9) and (2.16) as follows:

$$\dot{K}_t + P_{A,t}\dot{A}_t = r_tK_t + A_t\pi_t + (1-\alpha)Y_t + P_{A,t}\dot{A}_t - C_t,$$

which is further rewritten as follows:

$$\dot{K}_t = r_tK_t + A_t\pi_t + (1-\alpha)Y_t - C_t. \tag{A.4}$$

Here, substituting (2.14) into (2.12) and rearranging, we obtain $r_t = \alpha^2(Y_t/K_t)$. Substituting this $r_t = \alpha^2(Y_t/K_t)$ into (2.15), we obtain $\pi_t = \alpha(1-\alpha)(Y_t/A_t)$. Substituting these $r_t$ and $\pi_t$ into (A.4) yields the following:

$$\dot{K}_t = \alpha^2 Y_t + \alpha(1-\alpha)Y_t + (1-\alpha)Y_t - C_t,$$

which is organised to obtain (2.19).

## Derivation of (2.20)–(2.22)

Substituting (2.14) into (2.12) and rearranging gives $r_t = \alpha^2 y_t$. Substituting this interest rate into (2.15) yields $\pi_t = \alpha(1-\alpha)y_t\omega_t$. Rewriting $Y_t = K_t^\alpha (A_t L_{Y,t})^{1-\alpha}$ yields the following:

$$y_t = \left(\frac{A_t L_{Y,t}}{K_t}\right)^{1-\alpha}$$
$$\Leftrightarrow \frac{y_t^{\frac{1}{1-\alpha}}}{A_t} = \frac{L_{Y,t}}{K_t} \Leftrightarrow \frac{K_t}{L_{Y,t}} = y_t^{-\frac{1}{1-\alpha}} A_t. \tag{A.5}$$

Substituting (2.11) into (2.17) and rearranging (2.11), we obtain $P_{A,t}\delta A_t = (1-\alpha)(K_t/L_{Y,t})y_t$. Combining this equation with (A.5) argues that $y_t = [(1-\alpha)/(\delta P_{A,t})]^{\frac{1-\alpha}{\alpha}}$, as stock prices rise implies that the final good per capital decreases. Substituting $r_t = \alpha^2 y_t$ and $\pi_t = \alpha(1-\alpha)y_t\omega_t$ into (2.4) and rearranging, we claim the following stock price growth rate:

$$\frac{\dot{P}_{A,t}}{P_{A,t}} = \alpha^2 y_t - \frac{\alpha(1-\alpha)y_t\omega_t}{P_{A,t}} = \alpha^2 y_t - \alpha\delta y_t^{\frac{1}{1-\alpha}}\omega_t, \tag{A.6}$$

which $y_t = [(1-\alpha)/(\delta P_{A,t})]^{\frac{1-\alpha}{\alpha}}$ is used to derive. The first term on the right-hand side in (A.6) is the real interest rate and its second term is the dividend per share price. Here, the time derivative of $y_t = [(1-\alpha)/(\delta P_{A,t})]^{\frac{1-\alpha}{\alpha}}$, we obtain $(\alpha/1-\alpha)(\dot{y}_t/y_t) = -\dot{P}_{A,t}/P_{A,t}$. Substituting (A.6) into this equation, we obtain (2.20).

Dividing both sides of (2.19) by $K_t$, we obtain the following:

$$\frac{\dot{K}_t}{K_t} = y_t - z_t, \tag{A.7}$$

and, substituting $r_t = \alpha^2 y_t$ into (2.8), we obtain

$$\frac{\dot{C}_t}{C_t} = \alpha^2 y_t - \rho. \tag{A.8}$$

Therefore, substituting (A.7) and (A.8) for $\dot{z}_t/z_t = \dot{C}_t/C_t - \dot{K}_t/K_t$, we obtain (2.21).

Here, we rewrite $Y_t = K_t^{\alpha}\left(A_t L_{Y,t}\right)^{1-\alpha}$ in $\omega_t \equiv K_t/A_t$ to obtain $L_{Y,t} = y_t^{\frac{1}{1-\alpha}}\omega_t$. Substituting $L_{Y,t} = y_t^{\frac{1}{1-\alpha}}\omega_t$ into (2.18), we obtain $L_{A,t} = L - y_t^{\frac{1}{1-\alpha}}\omega_t$. Substituting this $L_{A,t}$ into (2.16), we obtain

$$\frac{\dot{A}_t}{A_t} = \delta\left(1 - y_t^{\frac{1}{1-\alpha}}\omega_t\right). \tag{A.9}$$

Therefore, substituting (A.7) and (A.9) into $\dot{\omega}_t/\omega_t = \dot{K}_t/K_t - \dot{A}_t/A_t$, we obtain (2.22). A three-dimensional dynamic system has thus been constructed.

## Derivation of $g_C$ and $g_A$

Now, (2.24) in steady state is $P_A^* = \pi^*/r^*$. Substituting (2.11) into (2.17) and rearranging, we obtain $P_A^*\delta A^* = (1-\alpha)\left(Y^*/L_Y^*\right)$. From these two equations, the following can be derived:

$$(1-\alpha)\frac{Y^*}{L_Y^*} = \frac{\delta\pi^*}{r^*}A^*. \tag{A.10}$$

Here, $r_t = \alpha^2 y_t$ is substituted into (2.15), the resulting $\pi_t = \alpha(1-\alpha)y_t\omega_t$ is rewritten as $\pi^* = \alpha(1-\alpha)(Y^*/A^*)$. Substituting this profit function into (A.10), we obtain the quantity of labour in the final goods sector with the real interest rate as variable as $L_Y^* = r^*/\alpha\delta$. By further substituting $L_Y^* = r^*/\alpha\delta$ into (2.16) with (2.18) substituted, the growth rate of the variety is derived as $g_A^* = \delta L - (r^*/\alpha)$. The growth rate of consumption is obtained from (2.8). By solving for these two growth rates, the steady state growth rate and the interest rate can be obtained.

# B Chapter 3

## Derivations of (3.4)

The problem of utility maximisation is solved in two stages. First, as the first stage, the problem of expenditure minimisation is solved. That problem is formulated as follows:

$$\min_{x_{j,t}} \int_0^{A_t} p_{j,t}x_{j,t}dj, \text{ s.t. } Q_t = \left(\int_0^{A_t} x_{j,t}^{\frac{\sigma-1}{\sigma}} dj\right)^{\frac{\sigma}{\sigma-1}},$$

and the first-order condition for the expenditure minimisation problem asserts the following:

$$\frac{x_{j,t}^{-1/\sigma}}{x_{i,t}^{-1/\sigma}} = \frac{p_{j,t}}{p_{i,t}},$$

which is substitution for (3.2) to derive the following:

$$x_{i,t} = \frac{p_{j,t}^{-\sigma}}{\left(\int_0^{A_t} p_{i,t}^{1-\sigma} dj\right)^{\frac{\sigma}{\sigma-1}}} Q_t. \tag{B.1}$$

By integrating the expression obtained by multiplying both sides of this $x_{i,t}$ by $p_{j,t}$, the following is obtained:

$$\int_0^{A_t} p_{j,t} x_{j,t} dj = \left(\int_0^{A_t} p_{i,t}^{1-\sigma} di\right)^{\frac{1}{1-\sigma}} Q_t,$$

where the price index for differentiated goods is defined as (3.5). Then, $P_{M,t} = \int_0^{A_t} p_{i,t} x_{i,t} di / Q_t$ holds. Then, (B.1) is rewritten as follows:

$$x_{i,t} = \left(\frac{p_{i,t}}{P_{M,t}}\right)^{-\sigma} Q_t. \tag{B.2}$$

Next, as the second step, the following static utility maximisation problem is formulated:

$$\max_{Q_t} \log Q_t, \text{ s.t. } E_t = \int_0^{A_t} p_{j,t} x_{j,t} dj = P_{M,t} Q_t,$$

and the following can be derived from the first-order condition for utility maximisation:

$$Q_t = \frac{E_t}{P_{M,t}},$$

which is substitution for (B.2) to derive (3.4).

## Derivations of (3.6)

By integrating $\dot{W}_t + E_t = r_t W_t + w_t L$ from $t = 0$ to $t = \infty$, we obtain the following budget constraint:

$$\int_0^{\infty} E_t e^{-rt} dt = W_0 + \int_0^{\infty} w_t L e^{-rt} dt,$$

where the TVC condition is $\lim_{t\to\infty} W_t e^{-rt} \geq 0$. By using (3.2) and $E_t = p_t x_t A_t$, the utility function of the household in (3.1) can be rewritten as follows:

$$U_t = \int_0^\infty \log A_t^{\frac{\sigma}{\sigma-1}} x_t e^{-\rho t} dt = \int_0^\infty \log A_t^{\frac{1}{\sigma-1}} p_t E_t e^{-\rho t} dt.$$

Therefore, the dynamic utility maximisation problem is formulated as follows:

$$\max_{E_t} U_t = \int_0^\infty \log A_t^{\frac{1}{\sigma-1}} p_t E_t e^{-\rho t} dt,$$

$$\text{s.t.} \int_0^\infty E_t e^{-rt} dt = W_0 + \int_0^\infty w_t L e^{-rt} dt,$$

which is used to construct the following Lagrange function:

$$\mathcal{L} = \int_0^\infty \log A_t^{\frac{1}{\sigma-1}} p_t E_t e^{-\rho t} dt + \lambda_t \left[ \int_0^\infty E_t e^{-rt} dt - W_0 - \int_0^\infty w_t L e^{-rt} dt \right],$$

and the first-order condition for the dynamic utility maximisation problem yields the following:

$$\frac{1}{E_t} e^{-\rho t} = \lambda_0 e^{-rt},$$

which is log-differentiated with respect to $t$ to derive the Euler Eq. (3.6).

# C Chapter 4

## Derivations of (4.13)

By organising (4.7), we obtain $L_X^*$ in (4.13). Substituting this $L_X^*$ for $L_X^* + L_R^* = L$ in (3.11), we obtain $L_A^*$ in (4.13). Substituting $L_{R,t} = F_t \dot{A}_t = F g_t$ into $L_X^* + L_R^* = L$ in (3.11) and rearranging, we obtain $g^*$ in (4.13); substituting $L_X^*$ in (4.13) into $P_t = L_{X,t}/\theta$ and obtain $P^*$ in (4.13).

## Proof of Comparative Statics for Tax

Differentiating (4.12) with respect to the environmental tax yields the following:

$$\frac{d\varepsilon^*}{d\tau} = -(L+\rho F)\left[\frac{1}{\sigma} - \frac{1-(1/\sigma)}{1+\tau/\theta}\right]^{-2}\left[\frac{1-(1/\sigma)}{1+(\tau/\theta)}\right]\frac{1}{\theta} < 0.$$

Differentiating $L_X^*$ in (4.12) with respect to the environmental tax yields the following:

$$\frac{dL_X^*}{d\tau} = -\frac{\varepsilon^*}{\theta[1+(\tau/\theta)]^2} + \frac{1}{1+(\tau/\theta)}\frac{\partial\varepsilon^*}{\partial\tau} < 0,$$

where this result is used to derive effects of environmental tax on other economic variables. Differentiating $L_R^*$, $D^*$, and $g^*$ in (4.12) from the environmental tax yields

$$\frac{dL_R^*}{d\tau} = -\frac{\partial L_X^*}{\partial\tau} > 0, \quad \frac{dg^*}{d\tau} = -\frac{1}{F}\frac{\partial L_X^*}{\partial\tau} > 0, \quad \frac{dD^*}{d\tau} = \frac{1}{\theta}\frac{\partial L_X^*}{\partial\tau} < 0.$$

## Proof of Comparative Statics for Permit

Differentiating $L_X^*$ with respect to the permit yields $dL_x^*/d\overline{P} = \theta > 0$. Differentiating $L_R^*$ in (4.12) and $g^*$ in (4.22) from the permit yields

$$\frac{dL_R^*}{d\overline{P}} = -\frac{\partial L_X^*}{\partial\overline{P}} < 0, \quad \frac{dg^*}{d\overline{P}} = -\frac{1}{F}\frac{\partial L_X^*}{\partial\overline{P}} < 0.$$

# D Chapter 5

## Proof of Comparative Statics for Nominal Interest Rate

Differentiating (5.11) with respect to the nominal interest yields the following:

$$\frac{d\varepsilon^*}{di} = \frac{\sigma(L+\rho F)}{\left(\frac{1}{1+io_A} - \frac{\sigma-1}{1+(\tau/\theta)}\right)^2}\cdot\frac{o_A}{(1+io_A)^2} > 0.$$

Differentiating $L_X^*$ in (4.13) with respect to the nominal interest rate yields the following:

$$\frac{dL_X^*}{di} = \frac{1}{1+(\tau/\theta)}\frac{\partial\varepsilon^*}{\partial i} > 0,$$

where this result is used to derive effects of nominal interest rate on other economic variables. Differentiating $L_R^*$, $D^*$, and $g^*$ in (4.13) from the nominal interest rate yields

$$\frac{dL_R^*}{di} = -\frac{\partial L_X^*}{\partial i} < 0, \quad \frac{dg^*}{di} = -\frac{1}{F}\frac{\partial L_X^*}{\partial i} < 0, \quad \frac{dD^*}{di} = \frac{1}{\theta}\frac{\partial L_X^*}{\partial i} > 0.$$

Differentiating $\Pi^*$ in (5.8), $m^*$ in (5.9), and $B^*$ in (5.10) from the nominal interest rate yields

$$\frac{d\Pi^*}{di} = \frac{1}{F(\sigma-1)}\frac{\partial L_X^*}{\partial i} > 0,$$
$$\frac{dm^*}{di} = -\frac{tm^*}{F(\sigma-1)}\frac{\partial L_X^*}{\partial i} < 0,$$
$$\frac{dB^*}{di} = \frac{\partial m^*}{\partial i} - o_H\frac{\partial \varepsilon^*}{\partial i} < 0.$$

## Proof of Level Effect of Environmental Tax in Monetary Economy

Differentiating (5.11) with respect to the environmental tax yields the following:

$$\frac{d\varepsilon^*}{d\tau} = -\frac{\sigma(L+\rho F)}{\left(\frac{1}{1+io_A} - \frac{\sigma-1}{1+(\tau/\theta)}\right)^2} \cdot \frac{\sigma-1}{\left(1+\frac{\tau}{\theta}\right)^2} \cdot \frac{1}{\theta} < 0,$$

which is further differentiated with respect of nominal interest rare as follows:

$$\left|\frac{d\varepsilon^{*2}}{d\tau di}\right| = \frac{2}{\frac{1}{1+io_A} - \frac{\sigma-1}{1+(\tau/\theta)}} \cdot \frac{o_A}{(1+io_A)^2} \cdot \frac{\partial \varepsilon^*}{\partial \tau} > 0.$$

# E Chapter 6

## Derivation of (6.14)–(6.16)

Substituting $P_t = \overline{P}$ into (6.9), we obtain $p_t^e/Z_t = 1/\overline{P}$. Substituting this expression (6.8) into (6.11) yields the followings:

$$r_t = \alpha^2 y_t - \left(1/\overline{P}\right), \tag{E.1}$$

which is substituted for (6.12) to derive $\pi_t = \alpha(1-\alpha)y_t\omega_t$. Substituting (E.1) and $\pi_t = \alpha(1-\alpha)y_t\omega_t$ into (2.4) and rearranging, we claim the following stock price growth rates:

$$\begin{aligned}\frac{\dot{P}_{A,t}}{P_{A,t}} &= \alpha^2 y_t - \left(\frac{1}{\overline{\overline{P}}}\right) - \frac{\alpha(1-\alpha)y_t\omega_t}{P_{A,t}} \\ &= \alpha^2 y_t - \left(\frac{1}{\overline{\overline{P}}}\right) - \alpha\delta y_t^{\frac{1}{1-\alpha}}\omega_t, \end{aligned} \tag{E.2}$$

which $y_t = \left[(1-\alpha)/\left(\delta P_{A,t}\right)\right]^{\frac{1-\alpha}{\alpha}}$ is used to derive. Differentiating $y_t = \left[(1-\alpha)/\left(\delta P_{A,t}\right)\right]^{\frac{1-\alpha}{\alpha}}$ with time, we obtain $(\alpha/1-\alpha)(\dot{y}_t/y_t) = -\dot{P}_{A,t}/P_{A,t}$. Substituting (6.14) into this equation, we obtain (2.20).

Dividing both sides of (6.13) by $K_t$ and using (6.6) and $P_t = \overline{P}$ to organise, we obtain

$$\frac{\dot{K}_t}{K_t} = y_t - z_t - \left(\frac{1}{\overline{\overline{P}}}\right), \tag{E.3}$$

and, substituting (E.1) into (2.8), we obtain

$$\frac{\dot{C}_t}{C_t} = \alpha^2 y_t - \left(\frac{1}{\overline{\overline{P}}}\right) - \rho. \tag{E.4}$$

Therefore, substituting (E.3) and (E.4) for $\dot{z}_t/z_t = \dot{C}_t/C_t - \dot{K}_t/K_t$, we obtain (6.15).

Substituting (6.5) into (2.17) yields:

$$\begin{aligned}\delta P_{A,t}A_t &= \frac{1-\beta}{\beta}\frac{C_t}{l_t} \\ \Leftrightarrow l_t &= \frac{1-\beta}{\beta\delta}\frac{C_t}{K_t}\frac{K_t}{A_t}\frac{1}{P_{A,t}} \\ \Leftrightarrow l_t &= \frac{1-\beta}{\beta(1-\alpha)}y_t^{\frac{\alpha}{1-\alpha}}\omega_t z_t, \end{aligned} \tag{E.5}$$

where, by rearranging this equation, we obtain (6.20). Then, substituting $L_{Y,t}+L_{A,t}+l_t = 1$, $L_{Y,t} = y_t^{\frac{1}{1-\alpha}}\omega_t$, and (E.5) into (2.16) yields the following:

$$\frac{\dot{A}_t}{A_t} = \delta\left(1 - y_t^{\frac{1}{1-\alpha}}\omega_t - \frac{1-\beta}{\beta(1-\alpha)}y_t^{\frac{\alpha}{1-\alpha}}\omega_t z_t\right). \tag{E.6}$$

Therefore, substituting (E.3) and (E.6) into $\dot{\omega}_t/\omega_t = \dot{K}_t/K_t - \dot{A}_t/A_t$, we obtain (6.16). A three-dimensional dynamic system has thus been constructed.

# F Chapter 7

The same derivation process in Appendix E can be used to obtain $\dot{y}_t/y_t$. In addition, by setting $l_t = 0$ in the derivation process for $\dot{\omega}_t/\omega_t$ in Appendix E, we obtain $\dot{\omega}_t/\omega_t$ in (7.9). Using (7.7) and (E.3), into which (7.6) and (E.1) are substituted, we obtain $\dot{z}_t/z_t$ in (7.8).

From $\dot{y}_t = 0$ in (6.14), we obtain the stationary value of $\omega_t$ in (7.11). By substituting this stationary value into $\dot{\omega}_t = 0$ in (7.9), we obtain the stationary value of $z_t$ in (7.12). Substituting these two stationary values into $\dot{z}_t = 0$ in (7.8) gives the following quadratic equation for the stationary value of $y_t, f(y^*) = f_1 y^{*2} - f_2 y^* + f_3$, where

$$f_1 \equiv \alpha(1+\alpha)(1+\theta_W),$$

$$f_2 \equiv \delta + \rho + \alpha\delta\theta_W + \frac{(1+\alpha)^2(1+\theta_W)}{\alpha\overline{P}},$$

$$f_3 \equiv \frac{(1+\alpha)(1+\theta_W) + \alpha\overline{P}(\delta+\rho+\alpha\delta\theta_W)}{\alpha\overline{P}}.$$

By solving this quadratic equation for $f(y^*) = 0$ under the parameter conditions in $(2+\delta+\rho+\alpha\delta\theta_W)/[4\alpha(1+\alpha)] \geq 1+\theta_W$, and defining $B_3$ and $B_4$, a positive, distinct real solution is derived as (7.10).

# G Chapter 8

There is no proof in the appendix for this chapter.

# H Chapter 9

## Derivations of (9.4) and (9.7)

As in Chap. 3, the problem of utility maximisation is solved in two stages. First, the expenditure minimisation problem is solved. That problem is formulated as follows:

$$\min_{x_{j,t}} \int_0^{a_t} p_{j,t} x_{j,t} dj + \int_0^{a_t^*} t p_{i,t}^* x_{i,t} di + P_{D,t} D_t,$$

$$\text{s.t. } Q_t = \left( \int_0^{A_t} x_{j,t}^{\frac{\sigma-1}{\sigma}} dj \right)^{\frac{\sigma}{\sigma-1}},$$

and the first-order condition for the expenditure minimisation problem yields the following:

$$\frac{x_{j,t}^{-1/\sigma}}{x_{i,t}^{-1/\sigma}} = \frac{p_{j,t}}{p_{i,t}},$$

which is substitution for (9.2) to derive the following:

$$x_{i,t} = \frac{p_{j,t}^{-\sigma}}{\left(\int_0^{A_t} p_{i,t}^{1-\sigma} dj\right)^{\frac{\sigma}{\sigma-1}}} Q_t. \tag{H.1}$$

By integrating the expression obtained by multiplying both sides of this $x_{i,t}$ by $p_{j,t}$, the following is obtained:

$$\int_0^{A_t} p_{j,t} x_{j,t} dj = \left(\int_0^{A_t} p_{i,t}^{1-\sigma} di\right)^{\frac{1}{1-\sigma}} Q_t,$$

where the price index for differentiated goods is defined as (9.5). Then, $P_{M,t} = \int_0^{A_t} p_{i,t} x_{i,t} di / Q_t$ holds. (H.1) is rewritten as follows:

$$x_{i,t} = \left(\frac{p_{i,t}}{P_{M,t}}\right)^{-\sigma} Q_t. \tag{H.2}$$

Next, as the second step, the following static utility maximisation problem is formulated:

$$\max_{Q_t, D_t} \log\left(Q_t^{\nu} D_t^{1-\nu}\right), \text{ s.t. } E_t = P_{M,t} Q_t + P_{D,t} D_t,$$

and the following can be derived from the first-order condition for utility maximisation:

$$Q_t = \frac{\nu E_t}{P_{M,t}},\ D_t = \frac{(1-\nu) E_t}{P_{D,t}}$$

which is substituted for (H.2) to derive $x_{j,t} = p_{j,t}^{-\sigma} P_{M,t}^{\sigma-1} \nu E_t$ in (9.6). Here, $p_i^* = tp_j$ is rewritten as $p_j = tp_i^*$, which is substituted for $x_{j,t} = p_{j,t}^{-\sigma} P_{M,t}^{\sigma-1} \nu E_t$ to derive $x_{i,t} = t^{-\sigma} p_{i,t}^{*-\sigma} P_{M,t}^{\sigma-} \nu E_t$ in (9.6).

Next, the dynamic utility maximisation problem is formulated as follows:

$$\max_{Q_t, D_t} U_t = \int_0^{\infty} \log\left(Q_t^{\nu} D_t^{1-\nu}\right) e^{-\rho t} dt,$$

$$\text{s.t.} \int_0^{\infty} \mathcal{H}_t e^{-rt} dt = \int_0^{\infty} \left(\int_0^{a_t} p_{j,t} x_{j,t} dj + \int_0^{a_t^*} tp_{i,t}^* x_{i,t} di + P_{D,t} D_t\right) e^{-rt} dt,$$

which is used to construct the following Lagrange function:

$$\mathcal{L} = \int_0^{\infty} \log\left(Q_t^{\nu} D_t^{1-\nu}\right) e^{-\rho t} dt$$

$$+\lambda_t \left[\int_0^{\infty} \mathcal{H}_t e^{-rt} dt - \int_0^{\infty} \left(\int_0^{a_t} p_{j,t} x_{j,t} dj + \int_0^{a_t^*} t p_{i,t}^* x_{i,t} di + P_{D,t} D_t\right) e^{-rt} dt\right],$$

and the first-order condition for the dynamic utility maximisation problem asserts the following:

$$\frac{d\mathcal{L}}{dD_t} = \frac{1-\nu}{D_t} e^{-\rho t} - \lambda_t e^{-rt} = 0,$$

$$\frac{d\mathcal{L}}{dQ_t} = \frac{\nu}{Q_t} e^{-\rho t} - P_{M,t} \lambda_t e^{-rt} = 0,$$

where $P_{D,t} = 1$ holds. By combining these first order conditions, we obtain the following expenditure:

$$E_t = \frac{e^{(r-\rho)t}}{\lambda_t},$$

which $E_t = D_t + P_{M,t} Q_t$ is used to derive. Log-differentiating $E_t = e^{(r-\rho)t}/\lambda_t$ with respect to $t$ yields the Euler equation in (9.7)

## Derivations of (9.16a)

From $\pi = \pi^*$ in (9.14), $x = x^*$. Substituting (9.12a) and (9.12b) into $x = x^*$, we obtain the following:

$$\frac{E}{a + \varphi a^*} + \frac{\varphi E^*}{a^* + \varphi a} = \frac{\varphi E}{a + \varphi a^*} + \frac{E^*}{a^* + \varphi a},$$

which is rewritten as follows:

$$\frac{1}{a + \varphi a^*} E = \frac{1}{a^* + \varphi a} E^*,$$

which is further rewritten as $(a^* + \varphi a)E = (a + \varphi a^*)E^*$. Adding $aE$ to both sides of this relationship yields the following:

$$AE + \varphi\left(aE - a^* E^*\right) = a\left(E + E^*\right),$$

which $a+a^* = A$ in (9.13) is used to derive. By dividing both sides of this relationship by $A$, we obtain the following:

$$E + \varphi\left(\frac{a}{A}E - \frac{a^*}{A}E^*\right) = \frac{a}{A}(E + E^*),$$

which is divided by $E + E^*$ and $a^* = A - a$ in (9.13) is used to derive the following:

$$\frac{E}{E + E^*} + \varphi\left[\frac{a}{A}\frac{E}{E + E^*} - \left(1 - \frac{a}{A}\right)\frac{E^*}{E + E^*}\right] = \frac{a}{A},$$

which is rearranged as follows:

$$\frac{E}{E + E^*} - \frac{\varphi E^*}{E + E^*} = \frac{a}{A},$$

which derive $\gamma = a/A$ in (9.16a).

## Derivations of (9.25)

Now, $\dot{a} - \dot{W}$ is rewritten as follows:

$$\begin{aligned}\dot{a} - \dot{W} =& A\left(\frac{a}{A}\cdot\frac{\dot{a}}{a} - \frac{W}{A}\cdot\frac{\dot{W}}{W}\right)\\ =& A\left(\frac{a}{A}\cdot\frac{\dot{A}}{A} - \frac{W}{A}\cdot\frac{\dot{W}}{W}\right)\\ =& gA(\gamma - k),\end{aligned} \tag{H.3}$$

which $\gamma = a/A$, $k = W/A$, $\dot{A} = \dot{a}$, and $g = \dot{A}/A = \dot{W}/W$ are used to derive. Substituting $\gamma$ in (9.23) into (H.3) yields the following:

$$\dot{a} - \dot{W} = gA\left[\frac{(1-\varphi) + \left(\frac{\rho F}{L}\right)[k - \varphi(1-k)]}{(1-\varphi)\left(2 + \frac{\rho F}{L}\right)} - k\right],$$

which is rewritten as follows:

$$\dot{a} - \dot{W} = gA\left[\frac{L(1-\varphi) + \rho F[k - \varphi(1-k)] - k(1-\varphi)(2L + \rho F)}{(1-\varphi)(2L + \rho F)}\right],$$

which is further rewritten as follows:

$$\dot{a} - \dot{W} = gA\left[\frac{\varphi\rho F(2k-1) - L(1-\varphi)(2k-1)}{2L(1-\varphi)\left(1+\frac{\rho F}{2L}\right)}\right],$$

which is rearranged to derive (10.21).

# I Chapter 10

## Comparative Statics of Emission Allowance

Differentiating (10.15), (10.16a), and (10.16b) with respect to $\overline{P}$ yields

$$\frac{dE+E^*}{d\overline{P}} = -\frac{\left[2\frac{\partial b}{\partial \overline{P}} - \frac{E+E^*}{1-\nu+\nu\left(\frac{\sigma-1}{\sigma}\right)\left[\frac{1}{1+(p^e/\theta)}\right]}\left[\frac{1}{1+(p^e/\theta)}\right]^2\left(\frac{1}{\theta}\right)\frac{\partial p^e}{\partial \overline{P}}\right]}{1-\nu+\nu\left(\frac{\sigma-1}{\sigma}\right)\left[\frac{1}{1+(p^e/\theta)}\right]} \gtreqless 0,$$

$$\frac{dE}{d\overline{P}} = -\frac{\left[\frac{\partial b}{\partial \overline{P}} - \frac{E}{1-\nu+\nu\left(\frac{\sigma-1}{\sigma}\right)\left[\frac{1}{1+(p^e/\theta)}\right]}\left[\frac{1}{1+(p^e/\theta)}\right]^2\left(\frac{1}{\theta}\right)\frac{\partial p^e}{\partial \overline{P}}\right]}{1-\nu+\nu\left(\frac{\sigma-1}{\sigma}\right)\left[\frac{1}{1+(p^e/\theta)}\right]} \gtreqless 0,$$

$$\frac{dE^*}{d\overline{P}} = -\frac{\left[\frac{\partial b}{\partial \overline{P}} - \frac{E^*}{1-\nu+\nu\left(\frac{\sigma-1}{\sigma}\right)\left[\frac{1}{1+(p^e/\theta)}\right]}\left[\frac{1}{1+(p^e/\theta)}\right]^2\left(\frac{1}{\theta}\right)\frac{\partial p^e}{\partial \overline{P}}\right]}{1-\nu+\nu\left(\frac{\sigma-1}{\sigma}\right)\left[\frac{1}{1+(p^e/\theta)}\right]} \gtreqless 0.$$

Differentiating (10.20) and (10.21) with respect to $\overline{P}$ yields

$$\frac{d\gamma}{d\overline{P}} = \frac{(1+\varphi)\left(k-\frac{1}{2}\right)}{2(1-\varphi)\left(1-b+\frac{\rho F}{2L}\right)^2}\left(\frac{\rho F}{L}\right)\underbrace{\frac{\partial b}{\partial \overline{P}}}_{(-)} < 0,$$

$$\frac{d\gamma}{d\overline{P}} = \frac{(1+\varphi)\left(k-\frac{1}{2}\right)}{2(1-\varphi)\left(1-b+\frac{\rho F}{2L}\right)^2}\left(\frac{\rho F}{L}\right)\underbrace{\frac{\partial b}{\partial \overline{P}}}_{(-)} < 0,$$

## Comparative Statics of Pollution Abatement Productivity

Differentiating (10.15), (10.16a), and (10.16b) with respect to $\theta$ yields

$$\frac{dE + E^*}{d\theta} = -\frac{2\frac{\partial b}{\partial \theta} + \theta_1 (E + E^*)\left(p^e - \theta \frac{\partial p^e}{\partial \theta}\right)}{1 - \nu + \nu\left(\frac{\sigma - 1}{\sigma}\right)\left[\frac{1}{1 + (p^e/\theta)}\right]} > 0,$$

$$\frac{dE}{d\theta} = -\frac{\frac{\partial b}{\partial \theta} + \theta_1 E\left(p^e - \theta \frac{\partial p^e}{\partial \theta}\right)}{1 - \nu + \nu\left(\frac{\sigma - 1}{\sigma}\right)\left[\frac{1}{1 + (p^e/\theta)}\right]} > 0,$$

$$\frac{dE^*}{d\theta} = -\frac{\frac{\partial b}{\partial \theta} + \theta_1 E^*\left(p^e - \theta \frac{\partial p^e}{\partial \theta}\right)}{1 - \nu + \nu\left(\frac{\sigma - 1}{\sigma}\right)\left[\frac{1}{1 + (p^e/\theta)}\right]} > 0,$$

for

$$\theta_1 \equiv \frac{\left[\frac{1}{1 + (p^e/\theta)}\right]^2 \left(\frac{1}{\theta}\right)^2}{1 - \nu + \nu\left(\frac{\sigma - 1}{\sigma}\right)\left[\frac{1}{1 + (p^e/\theta)}\right]}.$$

Differentiating (10.20) and (10.21) with respect to $\varphi$ yields

$$\frac{d\gamma}{d\theta} = \frac{(1 + \varphi)\left(k - \frac{1}{2}\right)}{2(1 - \varphi)\left(1 - b + \frac{\rho F}{2L}\right)^2}\left(\frac{\rho F}{L}\right)\underbrace{\frac{\partial b}{\partial \theta}}_{(-)} < 0,$$

$$\frac{d\dot{a} - \dot{W}}{d\theta} = \left(\frac{\dot{a} - \dot{W}}{g}\right)\underbrace{\frac{\partial g}{\partial \theta}}_{(-)}$$
$$+ \left[\frac{gAL(1 - \varphi)\left(k - \frac{1}{2}\right)}{2(1 - \varphi)\left(1 - b + \frac{\rho F}{2L}\right)} + \frac{\dot{a} - \dot{W}}{\left(1 - b + \frac{\rho F}{2L}\right)}\right]\underbrace{\frac{\partial b}{\partial \theta}}_{(-)} < 0.$$

Differentiating (10.15), (10.16a), and (10.16b) with respect to $\varphi$ yields

$$\frac{dE + E^*}{d\varphi} = 0, \quad \frac{dE}{d\varphi} = 0, \quad \frac{dE^*}{d\varphi} = 0.$$

Differentiating (10.20) and (10.21) with respect to $\varphi$ yields

$$\frac{d\gamma}{d\varphi}=\frac{2}{2(1-\varphi)^2\left(1-b+\frac{\rho F}{2L}\right)}\left(k-\frac{1}{2}\right)\left(\frac{\rho F}{L}\right)>0,$$

$$\frac{d\dot{a}-\dot{W}}{d\varphi}=\frac{gA\left(k-\frac{1}{2}\right)[\rho F+L(1-b)]}{2(1-\varphi)\left(1-b+\frac{\rho F}{2L}\right)}+\frac{\dot{a}-\dot{W}}{\varphi}>0.$$

## Comparative Statics of Trade Liberalisation

Differentiating (10.24) and (10.25) with respect to $\varphi$ yields $d(E+E^*)/d\varphi=0$, $dE/d\varphi=0$, $dE^*/d\varphi=0$. Differentiating (10.26) with respect to $\varphi$ yields

$$\frac{dp_l^e}{d\varphi}=-\frac{\nu L}{\overline{P}}\left(\frac{\sigma-1}{\sigma}\right)\left(\frac{\rho F}{\gamma_l^2 L}\right)\frac{\partial\gamma_l}{\partial\varphi}<0,$$
$$\frac{dp_h^e}{d\varphi}=-\frac{\nu L}{\overline{P}}\left(\frac{\sigma-1}{\sigma}\right)\left(\frac{\rho F}{\gamma_h^2 L}\right)\frac{\partial\gamma_h}{\partial\varphi}>0,$$

which (10.30) is used to derive. Differentiating (10.23) with respect to $\varphi$ yields

$$\frac{dP_l}{d\varphi}=\overline{P}\frac{\partial\gamma_l}{\partial\varphi}>0,\quad \frac{dP_l^*}{d\varphi}=-\overline{P}\frac{\partial\gamma_l}{\partial\varphi}<0,$$
$$\frac{d}{d\varphi}\left(\frac{P_l}{P_l^*}\right)=\frac{1}{(1-\gamma_l)^2}\frac{\partial\gamma_l}{\partial\varphi}>0,$$

and

$$\frac{dP_h}{d\varphi}=\overline{P}\frac{\partial\gamma_h}{\partial\varphi}<0,\quad \frac{dP_h^*}{d\varphi}=-\overline{P}\frac{\partial\gamma_h}{\partial\varphi}>0,$$
$$\frac{d}{d\varphi}\left(\frac{P_h}{P_h^*}\right)=\frac{1}{(1-\gamma_h)^2}\frac{\partial\gamma_h}{\partial\varphi}<0.$$

Differentiating (10.27) and (9.32) with respect to $\varphi$ yields

$$\frac{dg_l}{d\varphi}=\frac{\left(2\nu L-\overline{P}\right)}{F}\frac{\partial\gamma_l}{\partial\varphi}>0,\ \frac{dg_h}{d\varphi}=\frac{\left(2\nu L-\overline{P}\right)}{F}\frac{\partial\gamma_h}{\partial\varphi}<0,$$

and

$$\frac{d\left(\dot{a}-\dot{W}\right)\big|_{\gamma=\gamma_l}}{d\varphi}=A(1-\gamma_l)\frac{\partial g_l}{\partial\varphi}-gA\frac{\partial\gamma_l}{\partial\varphi},$$

$$\frac{d\left(\dot{a}-\dot{W}\right)\big|_{\gamma=\gamma_h}}{d\varphi}=A(1-\gamma_h)\frac{\partial g_h}{\partial \varphi}-gA\frac{\partial \gamma_h}{\partial \varphi}.$$

# J Chapter 11

## Comparative Statics of Emission Allowance

Differentiating (11.12) with respect to $\overline{P}$ yields

$$b=\frac{\nu(\sigma-1)\left(2+\frac{\rho F}{L}\right)-\frac{\nu\theta\overline{P}}{L}\left[\sigma-1+2L\left(\frac{1+\theta}{\theta}\right)\right]-\frac{\theta\overline{P}}{L}(\sigma-1)\left(\overline{\chi}+\overline{N}\right)}{2(\sigma-1)\left[\left(\overline{\chi}+\overline{N}\right)+2\nu L\right]},$$

$$\frac{db}{d\overline{P}}=-\frac{\nu\theta\left[\sigma-1+2L\left(\frac{1+\theta}{\theta}\right)\right]+\theta(\sigma-1)\left(\overline{\chi}+\overline{N}\right)+(\sigma-1)\left(2bL^2+\theta\overline{P}\right)\overbrace{\frac{\partial\overline{N}}{\partial\overline{P}}}^{(-)}}{2L(\sigma-1)\left[\left(\overline{\chi}+\overline{N}\right)+2\nu L\right]},$$

where $db/d\overline{P}<0$ under $d\overline{N}/d\overline{P}=0$.

Differentiating (11.9), (11.10a), and (11.10b) with respect to $\overline{P}$ yields

$$\frac{dE+E^*}{d\overline{P}}=-\frac{\frac{\partial b}{\partial\overline{P}}-\theta_2(E+E^*)\frac{\partial p^e}{\partial\overline{P}}}{\overline{\chi}+\overline{N}+\nu\left(\frac{\sigma-1}{\sigma}\right)\left[\frac{1}{1+(p^e/\theta)}\right]}\gtreqless 0,$$

$$\frac{dE}{d\overline{P}}=-\frac{\frac{\partial b}{\partial\overline{P}}-\theta_2E\frac{\partial p^e}{\partial\overline{P}}}{\overline{\chi}+\overline{N}+\nu\left(\frac{\sigma-1}{\sigma}\right)\left[\frac{1}{1+(p^e/\theta)}\right]}\gtreqless 0,$$

$$\frac{dE^*}{d\overline{P}}=-\frac{\frac{\partial b}{\partial\overline{P}}-\theta_2E^*\frac{\partial p^e}{\partial\overline{P}}}{\overline{\chi}+\overline{N}+\nu\left(\frac{\sigma-1}{\sigma}\right)\left[\frac{1}{1+(p^e/\theta)}\right]}\gtreqless 0.$$

for

$$\theta_2\equiv\frac{1}{\overline{\chi}+\overline{N}+\nu\left(\frac{\sigma-1}{\sigma}\right)\left[\frac{1}{1+(p^e/\theta)}\right]}\left[\frac{1}{1+(p^e/\theta)}\right]^2\left(\frac{1}{\theta}\right).$$

Differentiating (10.20) and (10.21) with respect to $\overline{P}$ yields

$$\frac{d\gamma}{d\overline{P}} = \frac{(1+\varphi)\left(k-\frac{1}{2}\right)}{2(1-\varphi)\left(1-b+\frac{\rho F}{2L}\right)^2}\left(\frac{\rho F}{L}\right)\underbrace{\frac{\partial b}{\partial \overline{P}}}_{(-)} < 0,$$

$$\frac{d\dot{a}-\dot{W}}{d\overline{P}} = \left(\frac{\dot{a}-\dot{W}}{g}\right)\underbrace{\frac{\partial g}{\partial \overline{P}}}_{(-)} + \left[\frac{gAL(1-\varphi)\left(k-\frac{1}{2}\right)}{2(1-\varphi)\left(1-b+\frac{\rho F}{2L}\right)} + \frac{\dot{a}-\dot{W}}{\left(1-b+\frac{\rho F}{2L}\right)}\right]\underbrace{\frac{\partial b}{\partial \overline{P}}}_{(-)} < 0,$$

where $\partial b/\partial \overline{P} < 0$ is assumed.

Differentiating (10.23) and (11.8) with respect to $\overline{P}$ yields

$$\frac{dP}{d\overline{P}} = \overline{P}\frac{\partial \gamma}{\partial \overline{P}} + \gamma, \quad \frac{dP^*}{d\overline{P}} = -\overline{P}\frac{\partial \gamma}{\partial \overline{P}} + (1-\gamma),$$

$$\frac{d}{d\overline{P}}\left(\frac{P}{P^*}\right) = \frac{1}{(1-\gamma)^2}\frac{\partial \gamma}{\partial \overline{P}} > 0,$$

$$\frac{dY}{d\overline{P}} = \frac{Y}{E+E^*}\frac{\partial E+E^*}{\partial \overline{P}} - \frac{2\chi_N L}{\hat{t}}(E+E^*),$$

$$\frac{dY}{d\overline{P}} = \frac{Y}{E+E^*}\frac{\partial E+E^*}{\partial \overline{P}} - \frac{2\chi_S L}{\hat{t}}(E+E^*).$$

## Comparative Statics of Airfare

Differentiating (11.12) with respect to $\hat{t}$ yields

$$\frac{db}{d\hat{t}} = -\frac{\theta\overline{P}+2bL}{2L\left[\left(\overline{\chi}+\overline{N}\right)+2\nu L\right]}\frac{\partial \overline{N}}{\partial \hat{t}} \gtreqless 0,$$

$d\overline{N}/d\hat{t} \gtreqless 0$ for $\overline{t} \gtreqless \hat{t}$ and $\left(\chi_S\widehat{N}\right)/(2\chi_N) > \overline{P}$.

Differentiating (11.9), (11.10a), and (11.10b) with respect to $\overline{P}$ yields

$$\frac{dE+E^*}{d\hat{t}} = -\frac{\frac{\partial b}{\partial \hat{t}} - \theta_2(E+E^*)\frac{\partial p^e}{\partial \hat{t}} + (E+E^*)\frac{\partial \overline{N}}{\partial \hat{t}}}{\overline{\chi}+\overline{N}+\nu\left(\frac{\sigma-1}{\sigma}\right)\left[\frac{1}{1+(p^e/\theta)}\right]} \gtreqless 0,$$

$$\frac{dE}{d\overline{P}} = -\frac{\frac{\partial b}{\partial \hat{t}} - \theta_2 E \frac{\partial p^e}{\partial \hat{t}} + E^* \frac{\partial \overline{N}}{\partial \hat{t}}}{\overline{\chi} + \overline{N} + \nu\left(\frac{\sigma-1}{\sigma}\right)\left[\frac{1}{1+(p^e/\theta)}\right]} \gtreqless 0,$$

$$\frac{dE^*}{d\overline{P}} = -\frac{\frac{\partial b}{\partial \hat{t}} - \theta_2 E^* \frac{\partial p^e}{\partial \hat{t}} + E^* \frac{\partial \overline{N}}{\partial \hat{t}}}{\overline{\chi} + \overline{N} + \nu\left(\frac{\sigma-1}{\sigma}\right)\left[\frac{1}{1+(p^e/\theta)}\right]} \gtreqless 0,$$

for

$$\theta_2 \equiv \frac{1}{\overline{\chi} + \overline{N} + \nu\left(\frac{\sigma-1}{\sigma}\right)\left[\frac{1}{1+(p^e/\theta)}\right]}\left[\frac{1}{1+(p^e/\theta)}\right]^2\left(\frac{1}{\theta}\right).$$

Differentiating (10.20) and (10.21) with respect to $\hat{t}$ yields

$$\frac{d\gamma}{d\hat{t}} = \frac{(1+\varphi)\left(k-\frac{1}{2}\right)}{2(1-\varphi)\left(1-b+\frac{\rho F}{2L}\right)^2}\left(\frac{\rho F}{L}\right)\frac{\partial b}{\partial \hat{t}} \gtreqless 0,$$

$$\frac{d\dot{a}-\dot{W}}{d\hat{t}} = \left(\frac{\dot{a}-\dot{W}}{g}\right)\frac{\partial g}{\partial \hat{t}} + \left[\frac{gAL(1-\varphi)\left(k-\frac{1}{2}\right)}{2(1-\varphi)\left(1-b+\frac{\rho F}{2L}\right)} + \frac{\dot{a}-\dot{W}}{\left(1-b+\frac{\rho F}{2L}\right)}\right]\frac{\partial b}{\partial \hat{t}} \lesseqgtr 0,$$

for $db/d\hat{t} \gtreqless 0$ in $\overline{t} \gtreqless \hat{t}$ and $\left(\chi_S \widehat{N}\right)/(2\chi_N) > \overline{P}$.

Differentiating (10.23) and (11.8) with respect to $\overline{P}$ yields

$$\frac{dP}{d\hat{t}} = \bar{P}\frac{\partial \gamma'}{\partial \hat{t}} < 0, \quad \frac{dP^*}{d\hat{t}} = -\bar{P}\frac{\partial \gamma'}{\partial \hat{t}} > 0,$$

$$\frac{d}{d\hat{t}}\left(\frac{P}{P^*}\right) = \frac{1}{(1-\gamma)^2}\frac{\partial \gamma}{\partial \hat{t}} < 0,$$

$$\frac{dY}{d\hat{t}} = \frac{Y}{E+E^*}\frac{\partial E+E^*}{\partial \hat{t}} + \frac{2\chi_N L}{\hat{t}^2}(E+E^*),$$

$$\frac{dY^*}{d\hat{t}} = \frac{Y^*}{E+E^*}\frac{\partial E+E^*}{\partial \widehat{T}} + \frac{2\chi_S L}{\hat{t}^2}(E+E^*) - \frac{Y^*}{\hat{t}}.$$

# K Chapter 12

There is no proof in the appendix for this chapter.

# L Chapter 13

Differentiating (13.11), (13.12a), and (13.12b) with respect to $\overline{\tau}$ yields

$$\frac{dE+E^*}{d\overline{\tau}} = -\frac{\left[2\frac{\partial b}{\partial \overline{\tau}} - \frac{E+E^*}{1-\nu+\nu\left(\frac{\sigma-1}{\sigma}\right)\left(\frac{1}{1+\overline{\tau}+p^e}\right)}\left(\frac{1}{1+\overline{\tau}+p^e}\right)^2\frac{\partial p^e}{\partial \overline{\tau}}\right]}{1-\nu+\nu\left(\frac{\sigma-1}{\sigma}\right)\left(\frac{1}{1+\overline{\tau}+p^e}\right)} \gtreqless 0,$$

$$\frac{dE}{d\overline{\tau}} = -\frac{\left[\frac{\partial b}{\partial \overline{\tau}} - \frac{E}{1-\nu+\nu\left(\frac{\sigma-1}{\sigma}\right)\left(\frac{1}{1+\overline{\tau}+p^e}\right)}\left(\frac{1}{1+\overline{\tau}+p^e}\right)^2\left(\frac{1}{\theta}\right)\frac{\partial p^e}{\partial \overline{\tau}}\right]}{1-\nu+\nu\left(\frac{\sigma-1}{\sigma}\right)\left(\frac{1}{1+\overline{\tau}+p^e}\right)} \gtreqless 0,$$

$$\frac{dE^*}{d\overline{\tau}} = -\frac{\left[\frac{\partial b}{\partial \overline{P}} - \frac{E^*}{1-\nu+\nu\left(\frac{\sigma-1}{\sigma}\right)\left(\frac{1}{1+\overline{\tau}+p^e}\right)}\left(\frac{1}{1+\overline{\tau}+p^e}\right)^2\left(\frac{1}{\theta}\right)\frac{\partial p^e}{\partial \overline{\tau}}\right]}{1-\nu+\nu\left(\frac{\sigma-1}{\sigma}\right)\left(\frac{1}{1+\overline{\tau}+p^e}\right)} \gtreqless 0.$$

Differentiating (10.20), (10.21), and (13.16) with respect to $\overline{\tau}$ yields

$$\frac{d\gamma}{d\overline{\tau}} = \frac{(1+\varphi)\left(k-\frac{1}{2}\right)}{2(1-\varphi)\left(1-b+\frac{\rho F}{2L}\right)^2}\left(\frac{\rho F}{L}\right)\underbrace{\frac{\partial b}{\partial \overline{\tau}}}_{(-)} < 0,$$

$$\begin{aligned}\frac{d\dot{a}-\dot{W}}{d\overline{\tau}} =& \left(\frac{\dot{a}-\dot{W}}{g}\right)\underbrace{\frac{\partial g}{\partial \overline{\tau}}}_{(-)} \\ &+ \left[\frac{gAL(1-\varphi)\left(k-\frac{1}{2}\right)}{2(1-\varphi)\left(1-b+\frac{\rho F}{2L}\right)} + \frac{\dot{a}-\dot{W}}{\left(1-b+\frac{\rho F}{2L}\right)}\right]\underbrace{\frac{\partial b}{\partial \overline{\tau}}}_{(-)} < 0,\end{aligned}$$

$$\frac{dh}{d\tau} = \overline{P}\left(\frac{1+\varrho}{2}\right)\left(\gamma+\tau\frac{\partial\gamma}{\partial\overline{\tau}}\right) \gtreqless 0,$$

where $dh/d\varpi = (h/\gamma)(\partial\gamma/\partial\varpi) < 0$ is derived.

# M Chapter 14

There is no proof in the appendix for this chapter.

# N Chapter 15

Differentiating $\overline{\Omega} \equiv (\tau_L/\tau_E)^{\epsilon\Gamma}\Omega$ in (15.10) with respect to $\tau_L$, $\tau_E$, and $\Omega$ yields

$$\frac{d\overline{\Omega}}{d\tau_L} = \epsilon\Gamma\left(\frac{\overline{\Omega}}{\tau_L}\right) > 0, \quad \frac{d\overline{\Omega}}{d\tau_E} = -\epsilon\Gamma\left(\frac{\overline{\Omega}}{\tau_E}\right) < 0,$$
$$\frac{d\overline{\Omega}}{d\Omega} = \epsilon\Gamma\left(\frac{\overline{\Omega}}{\Omega}\right) > 0,$$

where these results are used in various places in the subsequent proofs.

Differentiating (15.11) and (15.15) with respect to $\tau_L$, $\tau_E$, and $\Omega$ yields

$$\frac{d\overline{F}}{d\tau_L} = \frac{\overline{F}}{1+\overline{\Omega}} \cdot \frac{\partial\overline{\Omega}}{\partial\tau_L} > 0, \quad \frac{d\overline{F}}{d\tau_E} = \frac{\overline{F}}{1+\overline{\Omega}} \cdot \frac{\partial\overline{\Omega}}{\partial\tau_E} < 0,$$
$$\frac{d\overline{F}}{d\Omega} = \frac{\overline{F}}{1+\overline{\Omega}} \cdot \frac{\partial\overline{\Omega}}{\partial\Omega} > 0,$$

and

$$\frac{d\Lambda}{d\tau_L} = \frac{\Lambda}{1+\overline{\Omega}} \cdot \frac{\partial\overline{\Omega}}{\partial\tau_L} < 0, \quad \frac{d\Lambda}{d\tau_E} = \frac{\Lambda}{1+\overline{\Omega}} \cdot \frac{\partial\overline{\Omega}}{\partial\tau_E} > 0,$$
$$\frac{d\Lambda}{d\Omega} = \frac{\Lambda}{1+\overline{\Omega}} \cdot \frac{\partial\overline{\Omega}}{\partial\Omega} < 0.$$

Differentiating (15.14) with respect to $\tau_L$, $\tau_E$, and $\Omega$ yields

$$\frac{d\Delta}{dt_E} = \left(1+\frac{1}{\kappa}\right)\left(\frac{\Delta}{1+\overline{\Omega}}\right)\frac{\partial\overline{\Omega}}{\partial\tau_E} < 0,$$
$$\frac{d\Delta}{d\Omega} = \left(1+\frac{1}{\kappa}\right)\left(\frac{\Delta}{1+\overline{\Omega}}\right)\frac{\partial\overline{\Omega}}{\partial\Omega} > 0,$$

and

$$\frac{d\Delta}{d\tau_L} = -\frac{\epsilon\Delta(\sigma-1)}{\tau_L} + \left(1+\frac{1}{\kappa}\right)\left(\frac{\Delta}{1+\overline{\Omega}}\right)\frac{\partial\overline{\Omega}}{\partial\tau_L} \gtreqless 0,$$

which is rewritten as follows:

$$\left(1+\frac{1}{\kappa}\right)\left(\frac{\Delta}{1+\overline{\Omega}}\right)\left(\frac{\epsilon\Gamma\overline{\Omega}}{\tau_L}\right) \gtreqless \frac{\epsilon\Delta(\sigma-1)}{\tau_L},$$

which is further rewritten as follows:

$$\tau_L \gtreqless \left(\frac{1}{\kappa}\right)^{\frac{1}{\epsilon\Gamma}} \frac{\tau_E}{\Omega^{1/\epsilon\Gamma}} \equiv \tilde{\tau}_L.$$

Differentiating (15.17) with respect to $\tau_L$, $\tau_E$, and $\Omega$ yields

$$P = E\left(\frac{\sigma-1}{\sigma}\right)\frac{\frac{1}{\tau_L}+\frac{\overline{\Omega}}{\tau_E}}{1+\overline{\Omega}}$$

$$\frac{dP}{d\Omega} = \frac{E}{\tau_L}\left(\frac{\sigma-1}{\sigma}\right)\left(\frac{1}{1+\overline{\Omega}}\right)^2\left(\frac{\tau_L}{\tau_E}-1\right)\frac{\partial\overline{\Omega}}{\partial\Omega} \gtreqless 0,$$

and

$$\frac{dP}{d\tau_L} = \frac{E}{\tau_L}\left(\frac{\sigma-1}{\sigma}\right)\left(\frac{1}{1+\overline{\Omega}}\right)^2\left(\frac{\tau_L}{\tau_E}-1\right)\frac{\partial\overline{\Omega}}{\partial\tau_L} \gtreqless 0,$$

for $\tau_L \gtreqless \tau_E$ and

$$\frac{dP}{d\tau_E} = \frac{E}{\tau_L}\left(\frac{\sigma-1}{\sigma}\right)\left(\frac{1}{1+\overline{\Omega}}\right)^2\left(\frac{\tau_L}{\tau_E}-1\right)\frac{\partial\overline{\Omega}}{\partial\tau_E} \lesseqgtr 0,$$

for $\tau_L \gtreqless \tau_E$.

Differentiating (15.19) with respect to $\tau_L$, $\tau_E$, and $\Omega$ yields

$$\frac{dc}{d\Omega} = -\frac{c}{\psi_L}\cdot\frac{\partial\psi_L}{\partial\Omega} > 0,\quad \frac{dc}{d\tau_E} = -\frac{c}{\psi_L}\cdot\frac{\partial\psi_L}{\partial\tau_E} < 0,$$

and

$$\begin{aligned}\frac{dc}{d\tau_L} &= -c\frac{\epsilon}{\tau_L} + c\frac{\overline{\Omega}}{1+\overline{\Omega}}\left(\frac{\epsilon}{\tau_L}\right)\\ &= c\frac{\overline{\Omega}}{1+\overline{\Omega}}\left(\frac{\epsilon}{\tau_L}\right)(1+\overline{\Omega}-\overline{\Omega}) > 0.\end{aligned}$$

# O Chapter 16

Differentiating (16.17) and (16.19) with respect to $\Omega$ yields

$$\frac{dP}{d\Omega}=\frac{1}{\tau}\left(\frac{\sigma-1}{\sigma}\right)\left(\frac{L}{1-\left(\tau/\widetilde{\tau}\right)}\right)\left[\frac{\tau}{\widetilde{\tau}}\frac{1}{\left(1+\bar{\bar{\Omega}}\right)^{2}}+\frac{\rho F_{L}}{L}\left(\frac{\kappa}{\kappa-1}\right)\right]\frac{\partial\bar{\bar{\Omega}}}{\partial\Omega}>0,$$

$$\frac{d\widehat{h}_E}{d\Omega}=\left(\frac{\tau}{\bar{\tau}}\right)\left(\frac{1+\varrho}{2}\right)\left(\frac{\sigma-1}{\sigma}\right)\left[\frac{L}{\left(1+\bar{\bar{\Omega}}\right)^{2}}+\rho F_{L}\left(\frac{\kappa}{\kappa-1}\right)\right]\frac{\partial\bar{\bar{\Omega}}}{\partial\Omega}>0.$$

Differentiating (16.15) with respect to $\Omega$ yields

$$\frac{d\Delta}{d\tau}=\Delta\left[\left(1+\frac{1}{\kappa}\right)\frac{1}{1+\bar{\bar{\Omega}}}\frac{\partial\bar{\bar{\Omega}}}{\partial\tau}-\frac{\epsilon(\sigma-1)}{\tau}\right]\gtreqless 0,$$

which is rewritten as follows:

$$\frac{\Gamma}{\sigma-1}\left(1+\frac{1}{\kappa}\right)\gtreqless\frac{\widetilde{\tau}}{\tau}\left(1-\frac{\tau}{\widetilde{\tau}}\right)^{\epsilon\Gamma}\left[\left(1-\frac{\tau}{\widetilde{\tau}}\right)+\Omega\right].$$

Differentiating (16.19) with respect to $\tau$ yields

$$\frac{d\widehat{h}_E}{d\tau}=\frac{\widehat{h}_E}{\tau}+\left(\frac{\tau}{\bar{\tau}}\right)\left(\frac{1+\varrho}{2}\right)\left(\frac{\sigma-1}{\sigma}\right)\left[\frac{L}{\left(1+\bar{\bar{\Omega}}\right)^{2}}+\rho F_{L}\left(\frac{\kappa}{\kappa-1}\right)\right]\frac{\partial\bar{\bar{\Omega}}}{\partial\tau}>0.$$

Differentiating (16.17) and (16.19) with respect to $\tau/\widetilde{\tau}$ yields

$$\frac{dP}{d(\tau/\tilde{\tau})}=\frac{1}{\tau}\left(\frac{\sigma-1}{\sigma}\right)\left(\frac{L}{1-(\tau/\tilde{\tau})}\right)\left[\frac{\tau}{\tilde{\tau}}\frac{1}{\left(1+\bar{\bar{\Omega}}\right)^{2}}+\frac{\rho F_{L}}{L}\left(\frac{\kappa}{\kappa-1}\right)\right]\frac{\partial\bar{\bar{\Omega}}}{\partial\tau/\tilde{\tau}}$$
$$+\frac{1}{\tau}\left(\frac{\sigma-1}{\sigma}\right)\left[\frac{L}{1+\bar{\bar{\Omega}}}+\rho F_{L}\left(\frac{\kappa}{\kappa-1}\right)\right]\frac{\bar{\bar{\Omega}}}{[1-(\tau/\tilde{\tau})]^{2}}>0,$$

$$\frac{d\hat{h}_E}{d\tau}=\hat{h}_E\left(\frac{\bar{\tau}}{\tau}\right)+\left(\frac{\tau}{\bar{\tau}}\right)\left(\frac{1+\varrho}{2}\right)\left(\frac{\sigma-1}{\sigma}\right)$$
$$\times\left[\frac{L}{\left(1+\overline{\overline{\Omega}}\right)^{2}}+\rho F_{L}\left(\frac{\kappa}{\kappa-1}\right)\right]\frac{\partial\overline{\overline{\Omega}}}{\partial\tau}>0.$$

# Index




Y. Hamaguchi, *Sustainable Development in Economic Growth Theory*,
https://doi.org/10.1007/978-981-96-7639-2